JOHN LIND OF MINNESOTA

JOHN LIND

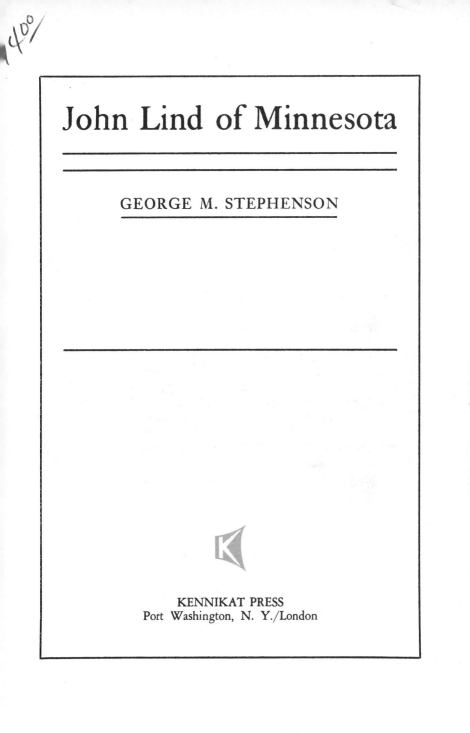

John Lind of Minnesota

GEORGE M. STEPHENSON

KENNIKAT PRESS
Port Washington, N. Y./London

42260

KENNIKAT PRESS SCHOLARLY REPRINTS

Dr. Ralph Adams Brown, Senior Editor

Series in
LATIN-AMERICAN HISTORY AND CULTURE
Under The General Editorial Supervision of
Dr. Harold F. Peterson
University Professor of History, State University of New York

JOHN LIND OF MINNESOTA

First published in 1935
Reissued in 1971 by Kennikat Press
Library of Congress Catalog Card No: 73-130335
ISBN 0-8046-1389-3

Manufactured in the United States of America

ACKNOWLEDGMENTS

IT IS the fortune of few biographers to find ready at hand such a bulk of material as that pertaining to the life and public services of John Lind. The author thought himself very fortunate when at the advice of mutual friends this material was placed at his disposal, without any reservation whatsoever, by Mrs. Lind, through whose foresight and industry much of it was preserved. Her kindly interest and generosity permitted the author to utilize Governor Lind's study as a workshop for the preparation of the manuscript, a task made even more congenial by interesting and profitable conversations.

Over a period of years the author has also had the privilege of consulting formally and informally with a host of friends and acquaintances of Governor Lind. Although it has not been possible to cite every instance of such assistance, the sum total of their counsel has been woven into the texture of the book.

For encouragement and kind words and deeds at a time when sympathy counted more than anything else, the author is under everlasting obligation to his colleagues in the department of history in the University of Minnesota. Dean Guy Stanton Ford, Professor Lester B. Shippee, and Professor Theodore C. Blegen have read portions of the manuscript. Needless to add, the author assumes sole responsibility for such errors of judgment or fact as the book may contain.

GEORGE M. STEPHENSON

University of Minnesota
June, 1935

CONTENTS

ILLUSTRATIONS

JOHN LIND OF MINNESOTA

I

THE EMIGRANT BOY

IN THE sixty-seventh year of his life John Lind of Minnesota wrote a miniature autobiographical sketch in the form of a letter to his son, John Lind, Jr., congratulating him upon having reached his majority. The reminiscent letter was written in a Washington hotel on the occasion of one of his frequent trips to the nation's capital:

I hardly know what to write you except to congratulate and wish you well. I have no advice to offer. My conduct and life have not always been wise. They might have been better but they could also have been worse. So far as I have had any success it has been because I tried to think out clearly what I wanted to do and then I have stuck to my resolution and "done it.". . .

As I look back at this record there are only a few things that come to my mind clearly and they are: The people have used me pretty well on the whole. They trusted me and I trusted them. There were lots of men in public life and among my opponents who were brighter and cleverer than I, but who have not fared so well at the hands of the masses. I do not know just why. There is only one thing I can think of and that is that it has always given me pleasure to be of help to my fellow man who needed help, as best I could.

I am not at all sure that any of this stuff will interest you; there is nothing particularly interesting in it unless it be the point that I made up my mind to certain things early in life. I stuck to my plans with constant work and determination and won out. This may be of value for you to think about. I cannot say that my life has been a success on the whole, but it might have been worse.

You have reached a point where it is well for you to make up your mind clearly what shall be your first goal. Keep your eye on it with steadiness and determination and you will make it. No one can stop you. In your intercourse with men remember that they are human beings very much like you however they may differ in age or appearance. Treat them just as you would like to have men treat you and they will be your friends.[1]

John Lind was one of the hundreds of thousands of Swedish immigrants who had reason to be grateful to America for the opportunities it gave them. The "America letters" written by immigrants to friends and relatives in the Old Country bear witness to the magic that America exercised in transforming men and women into prosperous and optimistic citizens. They relate in detail how the doors of opportunity opened to them and to their countrymen. The student of history who has perused a mass of such letters would hardly object to the assumption that John Lind furnished the text for hundreds, if not thousands, of the letters that crossed the Atlantic.

John Lind was born on March 25, 1854, on a farm known as Persgård in Kånna parish, near Ljungby, in the province of Småland, Sweden.[2] "My ancestors," he wrote on one occasion, "occupied a farm in the province of Småland known as Lindbacken (the Lind hill). When my father arrived in America, he dropped the 'backen' part of the name and that is how my name is Lind."[3] Like the great majority of the rural population of Sweden, Lind's forbears did not enjoy the distinction of having surnames.

His ancestors in both lines had lived in the Ljungby region for several generations, and some of them were prominent in the community and well-to-do. His mother's grandfather was a soldier under Charles XII. His mother was the daughter of Jonas Persson, and was known in Sweden as Catherina Jonasdotter.

[1] Lind to John Lind, Jr., September 15, 1921, in the Lind Papers.

[2] During the last year of his life Lind inquired of a cousin in Kånna how long the farm that was claimed to be the birthplace of his father had remained in the family. His correspondent properly consulted the rector of the parish, but he was unable to settle the matter definitely.

[3] Ralph Stockman to Lind, April 1, 1929, and draft of Lind's reply in the Lind Papers. The Swedish spelling is "Linnebacken."

She married Gustaf Jonasson, the son of Jonas Gabrielsson. If John Lind had remained in Sweden, he would have been known as Johan Gustafsson. When John was about six months old, his father moved from Persgård to Lindbacken in Södra Ljunga.[4]

The province of Småland is reputed to have the poorest soil and the most versatile and energetic people in the whole kingdom of Sweden. It has been said that if a Smålander were marooned with a goat on a rock in the Atlantic Ocean, he would make a living. The industry, resourcefulness, and ambition of the Smålander, combined with his ready tongue, his superstitious nature, and his delight in the mystical and the wonderful is proverbial. Even in the best of times the table set by the thrifty housewife was bare of everything but mere necessities. Lind's parents were land-owning farmers and were more fortunate than many of their neighbors, but crop failures caused by early and late frosts spared neither renter nor freeholder. By hard work, frugal living, and good management the Smålander could rise in the economic scale and become a freeholder, as the history of the Lind family shows.

During the earlier years of the emigration movement from Sweden, Småland furnished more than its share of the horde that crowded the emigrant ships. Glowing "America letters" expounding the wonders and riches of the Western World fired the imagination of this ambitious and energetic people, schooled in thrift by the stony soil and small farms. But for the letters from friends and relatives who had struck it rich in the "Land of Canaan" it would have been unbelievable that there was a Minnesota where a large farm might be had for the asking and where farmers counted their chickens by the hundreds, and cattle, horses, and hogs by the scores. Even better evidence was furnished in the person of a returned emigrant whose ready-made clothing was far more elegant than the homespun gar-

[4] This information is taken from a letter from J. A. Arvidsson to Lind, dated May 8, 1930, and from the genealogical tree of his own family compiled by Professor Alexander P. Anderson of Red Wing, Minnesota, who kindly lent it to the author.

ments of the Smålander and whose gold watch and watch chain shone on a Sunday morning at the parish church. This explains why Sibley, Nicollet, and Brown counties in Minnesota attracted hundreds of emigrants from the region surrounding Ljungby.

If the emigration from this region at the close of the Civil War seemed like an exodus, in 1868 it was a stampede. In the recollection of its oldest inhabitant Småland had never been visited by a scourge such as that precipitated by successive crop failures in 1867, 1868, and 1869. For weeks and months fervent prayers for rain were unanswered. From April to September, 1868, rain fell only two or three times and then for only two or three hours in all. Everything was scorched by the sizzling heat; trees were burned black and died. The lean cows roamed at large. Houses and farms were deserted. The unripe rye was chopped up, dried in ovens, ground into flour, and made into bread. When even this scanty fare was denied, the people ate grass.

It was in this fateful year 1868 that Gustaf and Catherina Lind made the greatest decision of their lives. They resolved to sell their farm and seek a better existence in the New World. A cousin of John Lind's mother, Solomon Anderson, who had emigrated before the Civil War, had returned to visit his native parish after his adventure in pioneering in Goodhue County, Minnesota, had proved successful. If Solomon Anderson was true to the type of returned emigrant, it may be assumed that he waxed eloquent in portraying the wonders and opportunities of his adopted country and assured his relatives that they would be cared for on their arrival there. In the presence of his father the returned emigrant said to the youthful John Lind that if he wanted to go to America, he would furnish the necessary money. Lind's mother, who was in the kitchen, overheard the remark and projected herself into the conversation by saying, "If John goes, we all go."

In the spring of 1868 the farm was sold, and shortly the Lind family, consisting of the parents, two sons, and three daughters, was to experience the tragedies and hardships that became a lifelong memory and collectively constitute a long and eventful chapter in the history of American immigration.[5]

The details of the transatlantic voyage of the Lind family are unknown, except for the death of a daughter at Liverpool; but the reader familiar with the history of immigration will visualize the unspeakable emigrant hotels, overcrowded with sick, tired, and discouraged men, women, and children and infested with disreputable agents who sought to fatten on the gullibility and inexperience of people to whom everything outside their native parishes was strange. Conditions in the steerage were worse, if that was possible. When they landed at Castle Garden, they had to run the gauntlet of sharks and runners whose business it was to cheat the arrivals at exchange, overcharge them for excess baggage, and perhaps sell them railway tickets to wrong destinations, or at least to earn a commission by selling them transportation on the line they represented, regardless of the shortest and most comfortable route.

The Lind family went directly to a Swedish settlement in Spring Creek Valley, Featherstone Township, Goodhue County, Minnesota, not far from Vasa, known far and wide as "Mattson's settlement" from the name of the founder, Colonel Hans Mattson, who for many years played an important part in the history of the state. For a time the Lind family enjoyed the hospitality of the home of John Anderson, a brother of Solomon, until they moved into a temporary house, a crude and unplastered structure, built for them by neighbors. In the spring they moved into a log house, about a half mile from the Anderson place. Within a few months a farm was purchased near Cannon Falls, where they resided for four years. During these years the Lind family drained the cup of poverty and hardship. At one time when they were near despair the young John trapped an

---

[5] This information was given to the author in a letter from Professor Alexander P. Anderson, dated May 9, 1933, and in a conversation with Mrs. Mary Scherer of Winthrop, Minnesota, on May 31, 1931. Professor Anderson is a son of John Anderson, a brother of Solomon. Mrs. Scherer was a sister of John Lind. She died in June, 1931, as a result of injuries sustained in an automobile accident.

otter and sold the pelt for fifteen dollars to purchase provisions for the family.[6]

In 1872 a homestead claim was taken in Cornish Township, Sibley County, about four miles west and four miles south of Winthrop. More land was purchased in the course of years and eventually the farm was increased to 480 acres. The homestead claim remained the residence of Lind's parents until old age brought the comforts of a home in the village of Winthrop. Gustaf Lind lived to see his son elected to three successive terms in Congress, and Mrs. Lind lived to rejoice over her son's triumphant election to the office of governor of Minnesota. In the Swedish Methodist cemetery, not far from the Lind homestead, is the family burial lot, with markers bearing the following inscriptions: "Gustaf Lind, April 11, 1826 – June 9, 1895" and "Catherina Lind, April 6, 1832 – April 9, 1912."

Unlike many Americans of Swedish birth who have taken little interest in their family history, Lind never forgot his Swedish heritage, although he did not identify himself with the Swedish-Americans as a group; and with advancing age he interested himself more and more in the study of the origin of the population of Sweden and the history of his family. It seems strange that, fond as he was of travel, Lind made only one visit to his native land – and that not until 1912, on the occasion of the Olympic games at Stockholm when he and his family visited the scenes of his boyhood and revived and made new acquaintances with relatives and friends. At Lindbacken he visited an uncle and at Persgård he spent many pleasant hours with his cousin, J. A. Arvidsson, with whom he remained in correspondence to the year of his death. Every Christmas he sent presents to his relatives, who considered it a great honor to be the object of attention from so distinguished a man. He wrote excellent Swedish letters and was of service to many immigrants in handling their business correspondence for them. Nothing was more appreciated by his parents than a Swedish letter from the pen of Congressman Lind. He even liked to write Swedish to his sister,

[6] Conversation with Professor Alexander P. Anderson, May 28, 1933.

THE LIND HOME IN SMALAND, SWEDEN,
BIRTHPLACE OF JOHN LIND

who understood English as well as her brother.[7] In 1928 he wrote a letter to a Stockholm bookseller in the provincial dialect of Småland, to the surprise of the correspondent, who marveled that the dialect could live so long in the United States.[8] Throughout his life Lind remained a reader of Swedish papers published in the United States, and for a time after his re-election to Congress in 1888 subscribed to a weekly published in Sweden. After reading a biographical sketch of himself in a Swedish monthly published in New York in January, 1897, he surprised the author of the article by complimenting him on the excellence of his Swedish, though he described the contents as "blarney." The author especially appreciated the compliment because Lind had detected his effort to eliminate the Low German prefixes in his style.[9]

The fortunes of the "Swede boy" during his first years in the adopted country will be recorded in later chapters, but it is convenient here to set down some observations about his heritage. From his parents Lind inherited sterling qualities. Unlike many immigrants who came to America in middle age, his parents learned to speak English. During the Spanish-American War, his mother, craving news about Lieutenant John Lind and fearing that her friends and relatives might not tell her all the war news, even learned to read English. She was a woman of unusual abilities, with a keen and active mind. Lind was fond of quoting her sayings to illustrate quaint and homely truths. His father was a practical, though unsystematic, man who knew how to get on in the world. During his visit to Sweden Lind observed that his uncle at Lindbacken, Anders Jonasson, resembled his father but had more fun and humor in his make-up.[10] Gustaf Lind fol-

[7] Lind to Mrs. Jacob Scherer, August 14, 24, 1924; J. A. Arvidsson to Lind, February 8, 1913, January 23, 1915; Lind to F. L. Anderson, April 26, 1924 (?), a letter kindly sent to the author by Professor Alexander P. Anderson. When the present writer visited Kånna on August 2, 1928, he met persons who had spoken to Lind at the time of his visit in 1912.

[8] Björck and Börjesson to Lind, January 11, 1929.

[9] Conversation with Dr. Victor Nilsson of Minneapolis, December 30, 1932. The article was published in *Valkyrian*, January, 1897.

[10] Lind to Mrs. Jacob Scherer, August 14, 1924.

lowed the example of his countrymen and soon after his arrival took out citizenship papers, by virtue of which his son became naturalized.[11]

The first years in America were a severe schooling for the immigrants; they were engaged in a ceaseless struggle with poverty in a strange land with a strange tongue. John Lind shared the poverty of the pioneer home. Fortunately nature provided an abundance of game and endowed him with a love of hunting that never forsook him. The fourteen-year-old lad already cherished the ambition to "be something" and visualized the day when he would be known as a civil engineer. But the immigrant boy was not to have a part in the development of his adopted state by making blue prints and carrying a rod and chain. Instead he was to advance the progress of civilization in the schoolhouse, before the bar, in the halls of Congress, and in the office of the chief executive of the state.

His youthful dream was shattered by an event that not only shunted his life into an entirely different channel but was destined to linger in his memory to his dying day. On the day after Christmas, 1868, the year of his arrival in America, while he was out hunting, John Lind poked the barrel of his shotgun in the mud, causing it to explode and to mutilate his left hand. The thumb was almost severed, more than half of the first finger was blown off, and the remainder was "peeled." The artery was also cut. The middle finger was but slightly injured, and the third and fourth fingers altogether uninjured. They could be opened and shut and the middle finger could be moved. The boy wrapped his lacerated hand in a handkerchief and returned to the home of Solomon Anderson, where he was staying at the time. Anderson hitched his oxen to a sled and took him to a surgeon in Red Wing. The frightened boy implored the surgeon not to amputate his hand, but when he came out of the anesthesia he learned that his request had not been granted.

[11] *Investigation of Mexican Affairs* (Report of the Subcommittee on Foreign Relations of the United States Senate, Senate Document no. 285, 66th Congress, 2d Session, serial nos. 7665, 7666, Washington, 1920), p. 2317.

That winter, during which John attended school in Red Wing, he saw the surgeon on the street a number of times, but he could never muster the courage to speak to him; in fact he shuddered every time he saw the man whose knife had deprived him of his hand. In the spring he had a talk with a physician who, after learning the particulars of the accident, told him that amputation had been unnecessary. In the fall of that year (1869) Lind was in St. Paul and decided to consult a surgeon on Third Street. By that time he could speak English pretty well and had no difficulty in making himself understood. At the conclusion of an extended conversation the doctor expressed the opinion that three fingers might have been saved. About a year and a half after the accident Lind decided to call on the Red Wing surgeon to ask him why he had amputated his hand in view of the fact that many persons, including members of the medical profession, had expressed the opinion that the operation was unnecessary. What happened in the office of the Red Wing surgeon can best be related in Lind's own words, as written to his attorney, S. L. Pierce, on January 27, 1874.

When I got into the office I first asked him whether he remembered me. He said he did not. I then told him that he had amputated my hand, etc. He denied having done it but I assured him that he had and that I remembered him well. He then looked in his Memorandum and read it to me something like this. December 26 Boy brought in by Anderson with hand blown to pieces (or shattered, do not remember which) and amputated. I then told him that my hand was not blown to pieces, that three fingers were not hurt, that I could use them, and that I could also use the thumb. He told me that it was not so. I of course told him that I remembered it, etc., but he got mad and told me to get out of the office. Then I thought I had reason to believe that I had been wronged and I resolved that I should find out what I could do about it. I came to the conclusion, however, that I should not try to do anything before I became of age.[12]

[12] This statement is undated, but judging from internal evidence it seems likely that it was written in 1874. The first part of the statement has been lost.

Almost exactly seven years after the accident, on December 23, 1875, the case came to trial in the district court at Red Wing. Again we shall allow Lind to relate in his own words what took place. On August 26, 1886, more than ten years after the event, when the "Swede boy" was in the public eye as a candidate for Congress, he wrote the following letter to the defendant, in reply to a communication from the surgeon protesting the publication of an item about the trial in the *St. Paul Pioneer Press*:

Referring to your letter of the 24th inst. I beg leave to inform you that the item referred to which appeared in the P. P. was published without my knowledge or consent. I presume it was traceable to a communication sent to the *Winona Republican* by S. L. Pierce Esq. which was also written without my procurement, knowledge or consent. . . .

I would further state frankly that I disclaim any title to the ideal and romantic coloring given to my character you refer to and I deprecate its publication as much as you do. . . .

On the trial — after your testimony and after the testimony of the experts — especially that of Dr. Staples (whose conduct and statements impressed me very strongly and favorably) I felt somewhat in doubt and asked Mr. Pierce, my counsel, whether there was any reasonable chance to recover or sustain a verdict on the evidence. He said: "John I think the case is very doubtful and if you are willing I think it would be as well to drop the case right here, but I will talk to Judge Wilder first." He then spoke to the Judge (Wilder) (I did not hear the conversation) and came back and told me that Judge Wilder told him "that if I dropped it there would never be a word said about costs or witness fees." I told Mr. Pierce that that was satisfactory and he immediately announced my determination to Judge Crosby. The only thing done further was that Judge Wilder requested Judge Crosby to instruct the jury to bring in a verdict for the defendant, which was done.

My reason for making the suggestion stated, and for dropping the case was largely because I believed its continuance useless under the evidence. I claim no different motive. I could not help thinking, and I still believe that you could and ought to have made an effort to save my hand. But the case was undoubtedly such upon the evidence,

that the law justified you in making short work of a "county job."
Since the trial I have rarely mentioned the matter and have not
spoken your name a dozen times.

Your suggestion about my paying your expenses was probably
made in jest and as such requires no answer.

Allow me to assure you again that no one regrets more than I do
the sad experience resulting from the misfortune that sent me to
your office in Dec. 68. Any reference to it is as unpleasant to me as
it is to you. And I shall spare no effort to prevent the publication
of anything on the subject.[13]

Serious as the misfortune was for the "Swede boy," with
characteristic determination and fortitude he set out to make a
career; and he never alluded to it to gain sympathy, either among

[13] This letter is found on page 328 of Lind's letterpress copy, which begins
with September 17, 1884. An item in the *Red Wing Argus* of December 30,
1875, states that the case was "continued on trial during the day, and was
finally dismissed at plaintiff's cost." A communication published in the *St. Paul
Pioneer Press* of December 25, 1875, headed "Malpractice. Happy Termination
of a Suit at Red Wing — Honorable and Magnanimous Conduct of the Plaintiff's Attorney," is a complete vindication of the defendant. The following
statement gives the keynote of the communication: "It is well to be a good,
but not *too* good a surgeon in Red Wing, it seems." Five surgeons were on
hand to testify that the surgery was exactly what it should have been and
what they would have done in like circumstances. A communication from S. L.
Pierce in the *Winona Daily Republican*, July 17, 1886, gives a somewhat different version of what took place at the trial. "At the trial John made out a
strong case, but when Dr. —— was examined on his own behalf he had a full
and careful statement of the condition of the hand and the effort he made to
save it. John watched him with intense interest, and when he had concluded
his testimony, told me he was satisfied with the explanation. He regretted the
doctor had failed to tell him all about it when he called on him at his office.
He told me that as he was now satisfied that the doctor had been careful in
doing the best he could for him, he wanted me, as his attorney, to publicly
acknowledge the fact for him. This I did then and there, to the astonishment
and gratification of the doctor, his friends and the great crowd in the court
room. It was by no means certain that the jury would not have given him the
verdict, for the case and the deportment of the plaintiff was well calculated to
win the sympathy of the jury. I mention this incident as a good illustration of
the character of Mr. Lind. So straightforward and impressive was the young
litigant on this occasion, and so different from that of ordinary parties to a
law suit, that Judge Crosby, the presiding Judge, wrote me a letter commending his conduct and manliness in the highest terms, and expressing the belief
that the young law student would be heard from." A letter from Alexander P.
Anderson to the author, dated May 9, 1933, relates some of the details of the
accident and trial.

friends or on the platform. His good right hand wrote a clear, bold, steel-cut script. He could harness and drive a team of horses, but he never drove an automobile. In his office and study his associates had occasion to see the dexterity with which he filled and lighted his faithful pipe. In earnest conversation and on the platform he had a characteristic habit of tapping his left wrist. His neighbors in New Ulm and in Minneapolis could bear out Lind's own statement made before a Senate committee in 1920: "I am well marked to start with." [14]

[14] Senate Document no. 285, 66th Congress, 2d Session, p. 2340.

II

FRONTIER TEACHER, LAWYER, AND RISING POLITICIAN

IN THE midst of sorrow and despair John Lind was among friends. The pioneers of Goodhue County were not strangers to grief and hardship, and they understood the seriousness of the misfortune that had overtaken the fourteen-year-old immigrant boy. The frontier could be inexorable, but it could also be kindly.

The door of opportunity opened for John Lind when he was admitted to the Central Schoolhouse in Red Wing in the early weeks of 1869. The "motherly" teacher, Mrs. Sterns, who consented to take the boy into her room, lived to congratulate him on his nomination for Congress in 1886. In reply to her letter she received the following acknowledgment of his debt of gratitude:

But your letter and the kindly — I might say motherly — interest you have taken in my success since the first day you saw me, is dearer to me than all. . . .

Your assistance came, and your kindness encouraged me at a time when it did me the most service and was the most needed. Hope and despair were contending for the mastery with about an even chance for success when I first went up to the Central School House and asked to be examined for admission. You consented to take me into your room — encouraged me, and made room for me at your desk.[1]

The brief period of schooling at Red Wing was followed by matriculation at St. Ansgar's Academy in East Union, Carver County, an institution supported and controlled by the Swedish Lutheran Minnesota Conference of the Augustana Synod, under

[1] Lind to Mrs. Sterns, July 23, 1886.

the presidency of the Reverend Andrew Jackson. At this institution all the instruction, except in United States history, was in Swedish. For two and half months in the spring of 1869 Lind studied reading, spelling, grammar, geography, arithmetic, United States history, and penmanship.[2] He did not thrive in the puritanical atmosphere of this community, however, and in the fall he was back in Red Wing. Here one of his schoolmates was Tams Bixby, who ultimately became a master of political strategy, as Lind learned to his sorrow thirty years later. While they were attending school Lind and Bixby, in their spare moments, were partners in a business enterprise which consisted of excursions into the country to pick strawberries to sell to the residents of Red Wing.

Lind's progress in school was rewarded with a third-grade teacher's certificate, dated November 14, 1870, and signed by J. F. Pingrey, superintendent of schools in Goodhue County. His grades on a scale of 10 were as follows: orthography, 6; reading, 8; writing, 8; grammar, 8; arithmetic, 10; geography, 8; history, 3. His first term as a school teacher was probably in District No. 18, after which he taught a term or two in West Vasa, known as "Klarka Dalen," near Spring Garden. Here he lived in the home of Solomon Anderson.

When Lind essayed the rôle of schoolmaster he was only sixteen years old. Alexander P. Anderson, who was a scholar in Lind's first school, recalls that the teacher spoke broken English and used Swedish as much as English, which was probably just as well, since the children were bilingual. The qualifications for a country school teacher in those days were not high; and Lind's neighbors were probably happy that the youth had the opportunity to support himself. One of the directors, a Mr. Rosby, was of the opinion that anybody who had a book could teach school.[3]

[2] This information is in the records of Gustavus Adolphus College, St. Peter, Minnesota, by which name St. Ansgar's Academy became known after its removal to St. Peter. Professor Conrad Peterson of Gustavus Adolphus College kindly furnished the author with a transcript of the record.

[3] Conversation with Professor Anderson, May 28, 1933.

In 1872 the Lind family moved to Cornish Township in Sibley County, and the following year John taught school at Clear Lake in Severance Township, part of the time in the home of J. D. Jackson and part of the time in the home of Swan Lindstrom, the first settler in the township. There were no schoolhouses in the township, and the terms were only three or four months long.[4]

In 1874 Lind entered the employ of J. Newhart, a lawyer in New Ulm. "Mr. Newhart was not much of a lawyer," according to Lind. "He did not have many cases in court, most of his work was collecting notes and loaning money on mortgages, but he had some law books and he needed help." Lind slept in a little room in the rear of the office and boarded with the family. For the first two years his remuneration was fifteen dollars a month and twenty-five dollars thereafter. Newhart worked in the office until ten o'clock every night, and Lind worked with him. After Newhart left, Lind read law until one o'clock. During the winter he taught school in the Klossner District, near New Ulm, for which he received fifty dollars a month and board. Saturdays and Sundays he worked in Newhart's office. This extra work paid him four dollars a week.[5]

By 1874 the ambitious young man had saved enough money to enable him to attend the University of Minnesota. But when he learned that the grasshopper plague of that year had placed his parents in financial straits, he changed his plans. One evening there was a knock at the door of the Lind home. It was the young law student, who had come to tell them that he had decided to postpone his university study for a year in order to furnish them with money to buy seed.[6] He seems also to have considered attending the St. Paul Business College and Telegraphic Institute, located on the corner of Third and Jackson streets.

[4] Reminiscences of A. A. Gulbranson in the *Gibbon Gazette*, April 2, 1926. Gulbranson attended Lind's school for only one day, when he gave it up to cut cordwood.
[5] Lind to John Lind, Jr., September 15, 1921.
[6] Conversation with Mrs. Mary Scherer, May 31, 1931.

The next year his plans for study at the University of Minnesota were realized. He also taught night school in a building near the old Union Station. During his residence in Minneapolis he roomed with Albert W. Rankin, who was destined to have a long career as an educator and as professor of education at the University of Minnesota. He also formed a lifelong friendship with Andrew Holt of Carver, who became a justice of the Supreme Court of Minnesota. Holt was a native-born son of Swedish parents, and he and Lind discussed their plans for the future and the obstacles and problems that appeared to lie before them. Among the studies Lind pursued was German composition, a subject that appealed to him because of the large German population at New Ulm, where he had already learned enough of the language to be of value to him in Newhart's office. He learned to speak and write the language, an accomplishment he must have valued on more than one occasion, not least while he was President Wilson's personal representative in Mexico.

While he was attending the University Lind was casting about for a place to hang out his shingle; he probably wrote several letters to lawyers with the view of forming connections that would enable him to make an auspicious beginning. A reply to one such letter has been preserved. E. V. Price, an attorney at Willmar, replied that he wanted a Scandinavian partner and gave Lind his promise that if he proved to be what he represented himself, he would receive an equal share of the profits on condition that he would stand half the expense and furnish an equal amount of books.[7]

Events determined otherwise, however. In the late winter of 1876 Lind left the University to resume work in the office of Newhart, whose failing health had caused him to request Lind's return. Lind remained in Newhart's employ until the late summer of the following year. In the meantime he was admitted to the bar.[8]

[7] E. V. Price to Lind, November 22, 1875.
[8] Lind's affidavit before the clerk of the district court of Brown County applying for permission to take the bar examination is dated November 24,

The young lawyer soon won the respect of the members of the legal profession and the confidence of the public. In the course of years he became known as "Honest John" — no mean recommendation for an aspirant to political preferment. The key to his conduct may be found in a letter from Andrew Holt: "If, as you say, we cannot yet exercise any influence to raise our nation we certainly can by adherence to justice and diligence search for wisdom and knowledge and raise ourselves above suspicion and contempt in the eyes of those with whom we come in contact."[9] The successful lawyer was pointed out by parents as an example for their children to emulate.[10] He took an active part in the affairs of the community and did many favors for young men in order to encourage and assist them in their work. A newspaper editor who for two years occupied an adjoining office and was associated with him in many ways stated that Lind was an inveterate worker; that after burning the midnight oil over unfinished briefs, he had been known to work all night preparing a case for trial the next day, simply for charity. He said Lind's head was large, but his heart was larger; and some of his hardest professional work was performed gratuitously for someone with whom he sympathized.[11] His letters reveal him to have been a man of sound judgment, intelligence, and system, with a kindly interest in people. He developed an English style that might well be envied by persons who do not labor under the handicap of foreign birth and ignorance of the English language until their fifteenth year. It is remarkable that although he lived in Swedish and German communities until he was past middle age, there was scarcely a suggestion of a "brogue" in his speech.

To be admitted to the bar and to become a reasonably suc-

1876. On the reverse side of the application is a statement of B. F. Webber addressed to M. G. Hanscome, judge of the district court, certifying to the character of Lind and giving his opinion as to his qualifications.

[9] Andrew Holt to Lind, March 5, 1876.

[10] F. W. Hauenstein to Knute Nelson, New Ulm, August 2, 1898, in the Nelson Papers.

[11] *Redwood Reveille* (Redwood Falls), July 10, 1886.

cessful lawyer at the time Lind embarked on his career required
no great amount of legal knowledge. With a smattering of law,
the qualities of a "good mixer," and a gift of speech, a young
man was fairly sure of making a living. Lind possessed these
qualifications. He liked to study and to investigate; he had a
bent for controversy characteristic of the sons of Småland; his
speeches were logical and seasoned with a pinch of irony that
sometimes became exceedingly caustic. He was a very effective
jury lawyer and he could usually convince the doubtful, if not
by logic, then by irony or appeal to the emotions, though he
sometimes made a poor fist of a case in which he was not convinced of the righteousness of his client's cause. In other words,
he was a poor devil's advocate. The letters he wrote during the
earlier years of his legal practice indicate a growing clientele
and a high sense of duty and justice. "I never advise lawing if
I can get substantial justice without," was his statement to an
opposing attorney.[12] With reference to another case he wrote:
"Charley . . . is and always has been a friend of mine. Hence
I do not feel like waging war on him personally — any more than
I should be disposed to take a case against you. I am ready to
defend a friend against the world. But I can see no propriety in
attacking one friend in behalf of another."[13] He could also use
vigorous language, as is indicated by a letter to a Canadian correspondent: "The attorney you went to see must be a damned
fool. . . . Those Canucks don't know anything anyway."[14]

From his account book, which begins with the date August
17, 1877, we learn that at about this time he began boarding at
the Dacotah House, run by Adolph Seiter. This remained his
home for two years, when he became a householder. On September 17, 1877, he rented an office from Herman Winkler for
three dollars a month. At the first of the next year he drew up a
contract with Winkler stipulating that he was to pay four dollars a month for the ensuing year, and the following year five

LIND AS A STUDENT AT THE
UNIVERSITY OF MINNESOTA

dollars a month, provided Winkler did not desire the room for his own use.[15]

The business that came to the frontier lawyer included drawing up contracts and mortgages, instituting mortgage sales, and handling collections, divorce cases, and personal damage suits. During his first years his fees ranged from a dollar and a half to seventy-five dollars. One lucrative source of income was the business of making collections for Cyrus H. McCormick and Leander J. McCormick, co-partners as C. H. McCormick and Bro., manufacturers of harvesting machinery. Many of his cases necessitated traveling, often by "livery rigs."

In addition to his activity as a lawyer, from 1877 to 1879 Lind served as superintendent of schools in Brown County. The tall, wiry, sandy-haired, blue-eyed Scandinavian, driving a single horse hitched to a buggy on his visits to district schools and courthouses, became a familiar figure within a wide radius of New Ulm.

Rumor soon had it that the superintendent was showing unusual interest in a school presided over by Miss Alice A. Shepard, an attractive young woman who had attended the Mankato Normal School and had begun teaching at the age of fifteen, a year earlier even than the superintendent. She was the daughter of Richard and Rowena Charity (Stratton) Shepard, who resided on a farm near Mankato. Richard Shepard was the son of Peletiah Shepard of Ashtabula County, Ohio, who had served as a private in Captain John R. Reaves's company of the Third Regiment Ohio Militia, commanded by Lieutenant Colonel Nathan King. Richard Shepard carried on the migratory tradition of this Connecticut family by moving to Wisconsin and later settling in Minnesota.[16]

Miss Shepard introduced herself to the county superintendent by applying for a teacher's certificate. Not many months elapsed before the superintendent visited her school and so prolonged

[15]Account book, p. 11.

[16] William C. Mills to Mrs. John Lind, October 12, 1903; John Lind to Western Reserve Historical Society, December 3, 1903; F. Ainsworth to John Lind, November 25, 1903; information furnished by Mrs. Lind.

his stay that courtesy no less than professional expediency demanded that she share her lunch with him. The following summer she received a letter from the superintendent suggesting that she apply for a school not far from New Ulm. In the course of time John Lind wrote a letter to Richard and Rowena Shepard, then in San Francisco, to which he received this reply:

We will have to ask your pardon and forgiveness for neglecting so long to answer your letter, but you ought to know and of course you do know that we ought to take time to consider a case in which we are to decide in our own minds for the happiness or misery of a dear and loved child. And so we have looked the case well over and so we have come to the following conclusion and that is We wave all objections to your and our dear child's union providing you will use all efforts reasonable to come with her to this country and make a home. That is our only objection: leaving her in that cold and disagreeable country, and I am fearful that if she gets married there, she will always remain there, but we have to part with her some time and I suppose there is no other way but to submit to fate. . . . John, for I expect we will soon have to adress you as our son John, take her if you want to; she is a good child and will always be true to you and I know it; and my parting wish is that no dark cloud shall ever come between you and blight what might otherwise be a happy home. . . . Hoping and trusting that all will be well in the unknown and misterious future . . .

The sequel to the letter was published in the *Mankato Review* of September 2, 1879.

A very quiet and enjoyable affair took place at the residence of A. R. Shepard in West Mankato, on the morning of September 1st, it being the marriage of John Lind, attorney at Law, and county superintendent, of New Ulm, Brown County, to Miss Alice A. Shepard, youngest daughter of A. R. Shepard. The happy couple were kindly remembered with a number of substantial presents. They left by yesterday's train for a visit to St. Paul and Minneapolis.[17]

The honeymoon included attendance at what eventually became the "largest state fair in the country" and an outing at

[17] Shepard's letter was dated May 4, 1879. Mrs. Lind's father was Richard, not A. R., Shepard.

Lake Calhoun. To meet these extraordinary expenses the groom borrowed the sum of sixty dollars.

For the next year and a half Mr. and Mrs. John Lind resided in New Ulm. It was high time for the strenuous lawyer and educator to have the comforts of a home and the watchful care of a wife, for his health had begun to show the effects of overwork and exposure.

Lind's election to the position of superintendent of schools testifies to his early interest in public affairs. He was a staunch Republican, as anyone familiar with the political tendencies of the Swedish-Americans would feel safe in assuming. In 1880 he rejoiced over the "glorious" Republican victory that assured the succession of James A. Garfield to "Old Eight to Seven" Hayes. He had already begun to "play politics" by recommending his friends to the leaders of the party. Among his papers is a draft of a letter written on brown wrapping paper, shortly after he had set up his own office, to a politician in Nicollet County bringing to his attention the name of his fellow student at the University, Albert W. Rankin, for the Republican nomination for superintendent of schools. "I do this on my own motion," he wrote, "actuated by a desire to benefit the schools of our vicinity as well as to assist my friend if in my power to do so. And I hope you will not set me down as a 'bull-dozer' or bore on account of it."

Lind's second step up the ladder of political advancement was taken in May, 1881, when he became receiver of public moneys and disbursing agent in the land office at Tracy, in Lyon County. He was appointed by President Garfield on the recommendation of ex-Senator A. J. Edgerton of Dodge County. Knowing the uncertainties of politics, Lind continued active in the legal profession and retained his office at New Ulm. Shortly after taking up his residence at Tracy he wrote a letter to an attorney at Washington, D. C., soliciting business.

I am confident that though I may not be able to give you many cases myself hereafter I shall have plenty of opportunities to recommend you to paying clients and of course I shall take pleasure in doing so every opportunity I have. I think I shall like the office first rate and pecuniarily it will certainly be preferable to my law practice, though I have been doing very well in New Ulm. I have taken in a partner Mr. Frank L. Randall who in connection with my former clerk will continue my law practice at New Ulm. Firm name Lind and Randall.[18]

While it can hardly be said that the remuneration at the Tracy land office was high, judged by the standards of the twentieth century, yet the position was something in the nature of a political plum. C. B. Tyler continued to serve as register, and W. O. Musser was employed as clerk, Lind and Tyler paying the latter something in addition to the salary allowed by the government. In addition to the fixed salary of $1,000, Lind received commissions and fees, which fluctuated and sometimes were pitifully small. In a report to the commissioner of the General Land Office Lind wrote as follows: "For the quarter ending Mch. 31st 1883, you will note that our sal's, fees and com's amounted to only $340.05 for each and only a little more the preceding *qr*. . . . It is necessary for us to employ a clerk, whom we pay $75.00 per mo. Adding to this the expense of rent and fuel, there is a trifle more than the salary left us."

The position was no sinecure. The Tracy office had all the old records and correspondence of the Winona, Henderson, and St. Peter offices and the entire records and correspondence relating to the lands of the Redwoods District prior to its establishment in 1872, as well as all lists and certifications of lands granted to railroads—all of which entailed a large correspondence. When Lind took over the office, emigration from Europe, especially from Germany, Norway, and Sweden, was at high tide. He assisted thousands of settlers, native and foreign born, to take homestead claims; and his ability to speak and write Ger-

[18] Lind to C. A. Vedder, June 9, 1881. Lind kept copies of his correspondence from June 7, 1881, to July 7, 1887, in two books which are in his papers. There are letters pertaining to the business of the land office and to his work as attorney. The firm of Lind and Randall was dissolved on January 1, 1884, to be succeeded by that of Lind and Hagberg (C. A. Hagberg).

man and Swedish was of great advantage, not only from the standpoint of efficiency but in gaining good will and confidence. Settlers knew that in the person of John Lind they were dealing with a public official who would always support them against the railroad corporations. He refused every application of the railroad companies to have lands certified and his action was sustained — a fact that was not concealed in political campaigns and perhaps explains in part why he was known as "Honest John."[19]

At Tracy Lind added to his income by acting as agent for A. E. Johnson and Company, a St. Paul firm engaged in selling steamship and railway tickets. In company with H. H. Molin and David H. Evans, who later became a prominent political figure, he also made a contract with the government for carrying mail from Tracy to Watertown and other points. There was considerable complaint about the mail service at Tracy, and Lind addressed a letter of protest to the general superintendent of mail service at Washington.

During the winter season when we had snow blockades, we went without mail for several weeks at a time, except when by private arrangements or by subscriptions from the citizens, we were occasionally enabled to procure teams to carry and receive our mail at Sleepy Eye. We bore this "without a murmur." And when the gov't, later, established temporary service we had regular daily mails. Since the R. R. Co. resumed to carry, we have not had one mail on time. They have been late on an average from 10 to 18 hours per day, and have arrived at a time making it impossible to attend to correspondence the same day, but now we receive no mail at all. Last Friday we had none and at this writing we have had only one mail . . . in five days. When we will receive another we don't know. This is owing to no accidents or unusual condition of the elements. The road

[19] Lind to E. Eccleston, September 7, 1886. On March 23, 1887, while he was a member of Congress, Lind wrote to Governor A. R. McGill: "In case the Winona & St. Peter R. R. Co. makes application for deeds for any land in our county (Brown) will you please advise me of the fact and allow me a reasonable time to show cause in behalf of settlers why such lands should not be deeded."

is open, trains arrive and depart, but carry no mails and have no mail cars.[20]

Lind also served as clerk of the district school, a position his experience as county superintendent amply qualified him for. Although Lind seems never to have cherished the ambition to become wealthy — in money matters some of his business associates thought him naïve — he showed, from the time he embarked on an independent career, an aptitude for taking advantage of opportunities to profit by the progress and development of the country. Even before moving to Tracy he had, in April, 1881, made a homestead entry. He went on the land in person, paid for improvements, and had the ground broken and sown to a crop. His appointment to the land office the following month, however, gave him no time to build a house or to prove up. He therefore petitioned the commissioner of the General Land Office to permit him to pay for the tract, about four months before he relinquished the position in the land office. Shortly after arriving at Tracy he purchased for eight hundred dollars a farm in Cornish Township, Sibley County, and he and his brother Solomon engaged in farming under the name of John Lind and Bro. He also built a residence at Tracy.[21]

Lind's tenure of office at Tracy was not determined by his popularity nor his usefulness to the community. The election of Grover Cleveland in 1884, the first Democrat to break the succession of Republican presidents since Abraham Lincoln, was a notification that his days in the land office were numbered; and on June 10, 1885, he notified the commissioner of the General Land Office that his successor had taken office and that thereafter his letters should be addressed to New Ulm.

The next twelve months brought great events for the New Ulm lawyer. In the summer, winter, and early spring the local papers presented his name before the public in connection with

[20] Letter dated April 3, 1883.
[21] Lind to Burchard, June 8, 1881. Lind figured in several land deals and always took great pride in his farms. In 1903 he said, "What little property I own in the world is invested in farms." *Congressional Record*, 58th Congress, 2d Session, p. 212.

the Republican nomination for Congress. Lind carefully refrained from making any statement and serenely took his family
on a trip to California to visit Mrs. Lind's parents. When he returned at the end of March, 1886, he learned that during his
absence the papers had been more solicitous than ever; and on
November 2, 1886, John Lind, at the age of thirty-two, was
accorded the distinction of being the first Swedish-born American to be elected to Congress.

III

THE FIRST CAMPAIGN FOR CONGRESS

WHEN Lind threw his hat into the political ring, the rumblings of a political revolution in the state had already been heard. From 1886 to 1896 politics were topsy turvy; a discontented West and a restless labor world expressed themselves in third party movements, which culminated in the organization of the Populist party. The election of Grover Cleveland in 1884 was a harbinger of disasters that were to overtake the Republican party and later the Democratic party also. The organization of the Farmers' Alliance and Industrial Union and the People's party was symptomatic of the widespread dissatisfaction with the old parties, fighting sham battles over issues that had ceased to be vital.

This western insurgency was a factor to be reckoned with. The famous Haymarket riot in Chicago in 1886 had aroused conservatives to what they believed to be the menace of radicalism; for weeks the press featured the details of the trial which resulted in the execution of some of the anarchists and the imprisonment of others. Anarchism and socialism were identical in the public mind. Terence Powderly was the apostle of organized labor, and men like Henry George the single-taxer and Edward Bellamy the socialist were writing books that laid bare the injustices of the social order and suggested remedies. The public lands were rapidly nearing exhaustion; Uncle Sam was no longer rich enough to give every man a hundred and sixty acres of land. It was a period of farm mortgages and rapid increase of urban wealth at the expense of the rural sections. Declining prices were believed by many to be caused by the shrinkage of gold and the cornering of that commodity by the "gold bugs."

The unpopularity of the railroad magnates registered itself in the enactment, in 1887, of the Interstate Commerce Act. The influence of wealth and big business in government caused the Senate to be referred to as the "House of Lords."

The inception of Lind's congressional career may be related in his own words, as written to his son thirty-five years after the event:

> While I was with Mr. Newhart I used to try a good many cases in Justice Court and there was an old Justice in West Newton by the name of Ballinger before whom I had many cases. He was a great friend of mine. I stayed at his house over night once and we sat up and talked until midnight and he said to me — I think I was 22 then — "John I want to live long enough to see you go to Congress. I know you can go when you are older." I laughed and said I thought he was fooling. He said no "You will see." I thought he was fooling, but after I went to bed I commenced to think about it and made up my mind that night to go to Congress but I never said a word about it to anybody for 9 years. In the meantime I became well acquainted in that part of the state. Was in the Tracy land office for 4 years and helped thousands of settlers to get their homesteads. The time was ripe as I viewed it. I made a hard fight for the nomination and was elected by 10,000 majority.[1]

Lind "saw" a number of men to "feel out" his chances for the nomination, and addressed a letter to James B. Wakefield, who was serving his second term as representative from the second congressional district, to learn the latter's attitude. On the fourth of April he received a cordial letter from the congressman stating that he was not a candidate to succeed himself, advising Lind to "go in," and promising to assist him "by letters or otherwise in any place or to any person where his good offices might be of avail." Lind was authorized to show the letter to friends, but Wakefield did not want his withdrawal from the race made public until he saw fit to give it to the press. The two men were warm friends, and Lind would not have "gone in" if Wakefield had decided to make the race. On the eighth of April Lind an-

[1] Lind to John Lind, Jr., September 15, 1921.

nounced his candidacy and immediately wrote a number of letters to "key men" stating his reasons and soliciting support.[2]
He also wrote to two competitors for the honor he was seeking. To O. B. Turrell of Redwood Falls he wrote on April 9
as follows:

As I have come to the conclusion to "enter the field" as a candidate for Congress, I hasten to inform you of the fact according to
my promise. I regret exceedingly that our interests should clash in
this matter, but I feel almost certain that from the fact that our acquaintance, though limited, has always been pleasant, as well as from
the further fact that I have always sincerely supported and assisted
you in the past, as your friends are aware, you will feel convinced
that my course with reference to yourself and your candidacy
though necessarily opposed to you, will be such as one gentleman
and Republican has the right to look for at the hands of another. . . .

With sincere wishes for your success in everything except your
Congressional aspirations, I remain as ever, Very truly yours,

JOHN LIND

To E. P. Freeman of Blue Earth he wrote in the same vein,
adding: "for with the natural exception of No. 1, I know of no
man in the Dist. whom I would rather see succeed Mr. Wakefield than yourself."

How the campaign had "shaped up" by the beginning of
June is revealed in a letter to John Hannor of Redwood Falls.

While at Redwood Falls I called on Mr. Turrell and had quite a
talk with him. I asked him candidly how he felt as to supporting me
for second choice and he explicitly declared that he was not in position to give me any assurance or encouragement on that score and
declared that the first duty of the opposing candidates would be to
unite to dispose of me. . . . But I have come to the conclusion that
as far as Turrell is concerned I have nothing to lose by his ill-
will. . . . Mr. Turrell has been very defiant since he returned from
Worthington. I believe that he has made arrangements with C. H.
Smith of that place and as the latter is the general land agent of the

---

[2] Copies of these letters are in the book beginning with the date September
17, 1884.

Sioux City and St. Paul R. R. Co. and has the whole power of that concern to back him — the combination would be quite formidable if Turrell succeeds in roping in this upper country as the "farmer's" and alliance candidate. Turrell may be a true reformer, but if he is, he has kept mighty sly about it in the past. While in the legislature I fail to think of or find a single reformatory measure that he introduced or supported. On the contrary he voted against the Illinois R. R. and grain law which was the only measure introduced that was calculated to be of any benefit. He opposed the reduction of the rate of interest and while on the board in your county he did not raise his voice in behalf of the Barney and Co.'s lands in your county.[3]

That Lind was out for the support of the "reform element" is evident from this letter, as well as from the following letter to S. J. Abbott of Winnebago City, dated May 18.

. . . I have learned of matters within the last few weeks that lead me to think that money may be used in behalf of candidates, or at least one, who is known to be less hostile to the R. R. Co.'s than I am. I have fought them in court and out of court — in the land office and before the Interior Deprmt. I don't fear their money either if I can have a "fair shake at them." The only thing I fear is that they may "bamboozle" the farmers in localities where I am not acquainted by the cry of "lawyer" etc.

When the Republican convention was called to order at Mankato on the morning of July 7, Lind was confident of his nomination. As early as April he had written: "I have many warm friends East of here. Nicollet and Sibley I am certain of. In the tier of counties South of this Judicial Dist. I have many friends and in some of the counties have had ⅓ of the voters on juries at different times."[4] By May 1 he felt certain of the support of delegates from Sibley, Brown, Nicollet, Murray, Lincoln, Lyon, Lac qui Parle, and probably Yellow Medicine.[5] As it turned out, he was backed by nine counties.

The Lind men came to the convention with a splendid organi-

---

[3] Turrell was eliminated from the list of candidates when he failed to carry his own county.

[4] Letter to Davidson, April 9, 1886; to Stockenström, April 30, 1886.

[5] Lind to A. Söderström and M. Lunnow, May 1, 1886.

zation, led by Colonel Joseph Bobleter of New Ulm, who, after
the usual preliminaries of a political convention, moved that an
informal ballot be taken. Lind received sixty-six votes, three
more than necessary for the nomination. The Lind men howled
with joy, and immediately anti-Lind delegates moved that the
nomination be made unanimous, whereupon the nominee was
escorted to the hall. He suggested that the platform be read before he addressed the convention.[6]

This document was undoubtedly the production of Lind. It
was decidedly Populistic in spirit or, in more modern termi-
nology, progressive. The preamble recited the radical changes
in industrial and social relations that had been effected by the
inventions of the preceding decades, particularly by the substi-
tution of machinery and mechanical appliances for manual labor
and by the invention of new agencies for transportation. "These
inventions could be utilized and the changes brought about only
by the aid of large amounts of organized capital in the form of
corporations, many of which exercise governmental functions
and franchises; and . . . history and our own experience teach
us that capital so aggregated and empowered becomes aggressive, grasping, and dangerous to public and individual welfare
and inimical to the permanency of our institutions unless properly regulated and restrained by law."

In order to emphasize the radical character of the platform,
we shall look at it through the eyes of a leading Republican
organ of the state, the *Minneapolis Tribune*, which accurately
summarized its provisions and sensed the "insurgency" of the
author of it.

Mr. John Lind, nominated yesterday, is said to be thirty-two years
old. He has had no legislative experience, and is not generally known
in the state. He has had the position of land office receiver at Tracy.
The platform adopted at yesterday's convention is said to have been
written by Mr. Lind. It is extremely crude. Without any intention of

[6] The proceedings of the convention are reported in the *St. Paul Pioneer
Press*, July 8, 1886, and in the *Mankato Review*, July 13, 1886. The result of
the informal ballot was as follows: John Lind, 66; E. P. Freeman, 21; M. D. L.
Collester, 12; C. H. Smith, 15; L. Quackenbush, 10.

reflecting upon the committee on resolutions, we must in all candor pronounce their platform the crudest, most impractical, and altogether unsophisticated ever adopted by a body of Republicans. The first resolution makes it "the imperative duty of our candidate to enact such laws as will secure equal rights to life, liberty, and property to every one." The second demands "that Congress create a commission to ascertain and adjust all differences between employer and employed which shall have power to enforce its decrees," a thing which Congress has no power or authority to do, and which nobody advocates or desires or would endure, excepting yesterday's convention at Mankato. The third is a plank on the interstate railroad question which far transcends Mr. Reagan's wildest proposition. The fourth is a plank on land-grant forfeitures which advocates a sweeping policy never before proposed by Republicans anywhere, and far more severe than that pursued by the Democrats of the present House committee. The fifth declares that "it is the duty of Congress by proper legislation to prevent the manufacture of any substance for food that is unwholesome," etc., etc. It is not within the range of congressional jurisdiction to do anything of the sort. The sixth demands a "thorough revision of the tariff" on a plan which, to say the least, does not indicate familiarity with the subject.

The *Tribune* is a Republican paper, and it is not disposed to criticize a Republican convention, its nominee, or its platform in any ungracious spirit. But it would not be faithful to Republicanism if it had abstained from comment upon this extraordinary pronunciamento at Mankato. Party platforms ought to be more than a tissue of meaningless sentences. They ought to be carefully scrutinized. They ought to be intelligent, well-considered, and truly representative. The Mankato resolutions are not creditable to the intelligence of the second district, and do not, as a whole, reflect the views of a dozen thoughtful Republicans in that part of the state.

Mr. Lind is undoubtedly a man of force, character, and native ability. . . . But if he is the author of the platform on which he runs, he will go to Congress with very much to learn about public questions, and very poorly qualified to represent and serve Minnesota. If he has the right stuff in him — and we are informed that he has — he will learn rapidly.[7]

[7] *Minneapolis Tribune,* July 8, 1886.

This editorial is representative of the "copy" that emanated from the editorial sanctums of certain Twin City papers during the twenty years Lind was a candidate or potential candidate for public office. The editorial writer was a better interpreter of old-line Republicanism than he was a prophet. John Lind did not "learn rapidly." In fact, he never learned to sing a *Te Deum* in honor of party regularity; and the older he grew the more discordant became his voice in the political chorus, whether sung by a Republican or Democratic choir. He was in reality a political orphan all his life, as he later publicly acknowledged.

Except for the compliments he paid to traditional Republicanism, Lind's speech to the Mankato convention was no more palatable to the "stand-pat" Republican organs than was his platform. He began by saying that he knew some objections had been made to him because of his youth. Though young in years, he had had years of hardy training on the frontier. When his parents settled in Sibley County, he said, the country was new, with hardly a sod shanty. He had shared the hardship and suffering incident to the grasshopper scourge. He had regretted that he was not old enough to vote for General Grant, but he had the satisfaction of knowing that he had distributed tickets for him at the polls. In reply to the statement of the Democrats that "the rascals had been turned out," it might be said that "the rascals and some ex-rebels are in." Such a reply, he thought, might not redound to his party's credit more than this: There was more satisfaction in belonging to the Grand Old Party, under which every reform in the past quarter of a century had been brought about, than in belonging to a party held together simply by the spoils of office. The Republican party had stood by the country in the hour of its greatest danger.

After this prologue, which conformed to the Republican dogmas of the eighties, the speaker went on to praise the planks of the platform. In referring to the legislation of Congress, he said it "almost made him swear" to read about the Democratic opposition to the oleomargarine bill for the protection of the dairy interests and to the creation of an Interstate Commerce

Commission on constitutional grounds. He avowed that Congress had the right to legislate upon all matters of national interest. Referring to the tariff, he asserted that certain articles should be placed on the free list — tea, coffee, sugar, manila for the manufacture of binding twine, possibly lumber, and other articles of daily consumption. He denied that he was a free trader, but he also denied that the interest of industries required the present high tariff.[8]

Lind's personal assets in the political campaign were summarized as follows by a reporter in the *St. Paul Pioneer Press:*

The unanimity with which John Lind received the congressional nomination in the second district over such old Republican wheelhorses as Freeman, Turrell, Collester, and Smith is an honor of which he may well be proud. A young man who had just completed the study of law and attained his majority when Hayes was elected president, he has now a larger personal following than any other politician in that part of the state. He has practiced law in the entire western end of the district, and where he has made acquaintances they can invariably be counted upon as his political friends. He has a remarkable faculty for remembering faces and incidents, and is seldom mistaken in the name of a person he has once met. He has always a pleasant word for the rustic and can tell to a certainty whether he has met the granger at a term of court in Yellow Medicine, a Lac qui Parle picnic, or at a Fourth of July celebration, or county fair at Madelia.[9]

His foreign nationality was a more dubious advantage. Today Scandinavian birth has come to be regarded as distinctly a political asset in Minnesota. Since the turn of the century the state has had a succession of Scandinavian governors, and the saying has become current that Minnesota does not care what the nationality of her governor is so long as he is a Scandinavian. But it was not always so. Not until 1892, with the election of a Norwegian, Knute Nelson, was the office first filled by a Scandinavian. This political strategist had been elected to Congress in

[8] A digest of the speech was printed in the *Mankato Review* of July 13, 1886.
[9] Printed in the *Martin County Sentinel*, July 16, 1886.

1882, after a contest that attracted the attention of the entire state. The fact of the matter is that when John Lind and Knute Nelson first appeared on the political stage, their foreign birth was more a liability than an asset.[10]

It was natural, of course, for Lind's supporters to take advantage of the clannishness and racial pride of the Scandinavians. The Democratic *Winnebago City Press* even went so far as to declare that "there was not a Lind delegation in the convention that was not kicked into it with Scandinavian buskins." Lind himself wrote to the editors of the *Svenska Folkets Tidning* of Minneapolis and to the St. Paul correspondent of *Hemlandet* of Chicago, both Swedish papers, thanking them for their kindly mention of his candidacy for the nomination.[11]

But while nationality is a string that can be skillfully played upon in a political contest, it works both ways, and Lind was convinced that in some localities it would be advertised to his prejudice that he was a Swede. The Democratic *St. Paul Globe* evidently thought that the prospect of having a Swedish congressman would not appeal to the majority of voters, or it would scarcely have seasoned its stories about Lind with innuendo and sarcasm. After his nomination Lind wrote to a supporter as follows:

The fact of my foreign birth will lose me no votes for my American friends are as warm and sincere in their support as any I have. Thus far they have done more for me than any other class. They know full well that I have used no argument of that kind to further my interests — nor have I ever in any respect drawn any nationality lines. But just as you say, I am aware that it will be talked to my prejudice in localities and for that reason it is highly important that I go into the counties you name to get acquainted.[12]

To another aspirant to political honors he wrote:

We are both young men and have acquired what we have in the

[10] William Bickel to Knute Nelson, August 18, 1892, in the Nelson Papers.
[11] Lind to Söderström and Lunnow, May 1, 1886; to Herman Stockenström, April 30, 1886.
[12] Lind to W. R. Estes, July 23, 1886.

way of knowledge and recognition by our own efforts. We have had the same obstacles of language and foreign birth to overcome. . . . You undoubtedly appreciate the fact that though a person of foreign birth may be ever so competent, still people are inclined to doubt it, or at least they have suspicions until they can actually see him and ascertain for themselves.[13]

It is safe to conclude, however, that the question of nationality did not affect the outcome of the election one way or the other. Neither the Swedish nor the Norwegian vote was strong in southwestern Minnesota. The densest Norwegian population was in the southeastern part of the state, which was not in Lind's district, and there were relatively few Swedish settlements in his district.[14] Lind's majority was too large to make necessary a minute examination of the election returns, even if the documents were available.

The most serious problem that faced Lind in the campaign was how to satisfy the members of the Farmers' Alliance. The Farmers' Alliance congressional convention was held at Mankato on September 22 and placed in nomination A. H. Bullis, one of the largest breeders of Hereford cattle in the state. For years he had been active in farmers' movements and was a member of the Alliance. He was also nominated by the Democratic convention at Mankato on the same day, after a conference between delegates to both conventions. There were several hundred alliances in the district, and most of the members were Republicans.[15] The Democratic platform was more detailed and radical than the Republican.[16] Lind was well acquainted with many members of the Alliance and took pains to assure them that he

[13] Lind to Joseph Rachie, October 18, 1886. To Joseph Farmer he wrote on July 29, 1886, that the only serious argument that had been used against him up to that time was his nationality.
[14] See the map showing the distribution of the Norwegian element in Carlton C. Qualey, "Pioneer Norwegian Settlement in Minnesota," *Minnesota History*, September, 1931, p. 267.
[15] *Mankato Review*, September 28, November 9, 1886.
[16] Broadside "To the Farmers' Alliances of Second Congressional District," signed by John Diamond and George W. Haigh, treasurer and secretary, respectively, of the State Farmers' Alliance.

would support certain measures and advocate the appointment of certain men indorsed by the Alliance.[17]

But he was not the type of politician who promises everything. His correspondence was frank and straightforward, and he ventured to take issue with men who sought to enlist his support in behalf of pet measures. The Prohibition party ran a candidate against him, but in a district with a considerable German population there was little to fear from such a competitor. To a minister who had pledged him his support, Lind wrote as follows:

I note what you say about the prohibition movement and I appreciate the truth of a great deal of what you say in regard to the Republican party. . . . The prohibitionists are agitators and reformers and as such are extremists. Every reform has been inaugurated by that class of men. A true reformer is a sort of a crank on the subject he devotes his attention to. It is necessary that he should be such — if he were not, he would not have the zeal to brave the opposition he meets. Even Luther was an extremist. Men so thoroughly wrapped up in any one thing are apt, and do overlook everything that does not bear on the subject of their endeavors. A reformer is rarely practical or prudent. If he were, he would not be worth much as a reformer. That class of men alone could hardly govern a country like ours with so many varied interests, material as well as social. The Republican party feels that there are other questions as well that demand our thought and attention and that it cannot afford to make this question, or any other one, the sole object of its care and effort. I should regret nothing more than to see the Republican party torn to pieces by this question. Temperance reformers and the Republicans can quarrel and find fault with each other as much as they like. The two, however, are practically working together hand in hand for the improvement of humanity. The temperance reformer being the "forerunner" paving the way. The Republican following in his wake — in sympathy with him but more cool and considerate and better prepared to serve, establish and perpetuate such reforms as the former has prepared the way for.[18]

[17] Lind to Nels M. Pearson, June 21, 1886; to H. G. Stordock, November 22, 1886; to C. C. Hutchard, July 23, 1886.
[18] Lind to J. W. Powell, July 16, 1886.

Although the tariff in 1886 had not assumed the national importance it came to have in the presidential campaign of 1888 and later, Lind's district had already been infected with the tariff-for-revenue idea that some years later was to bring defeat to a veteran Republican congressman by a Democrat pledged to a low tariff. The incumbent, James B. Wakefield, had branded himself an "insurgent" by voting for the consideration of the Democratic Morrison bill; and in the Lyon County convention of 1884 Lind had introduced a resolution approving his action, which, however, was voted down. In 1886 the Democrats praised Wakefield and attacked Lind's more conservative position. In two letters that show Lind had given the tariff and currency considerable thought he expounded his views at length.

In the first place the rumor that has gained currency that I am a believer in a high protective tariff is unfounded and false. . . . Some of the opposition candidates or their friends who knew nothing else except that I am a Swede to say against me started the "yarn" that I am a "high protective tariff man" and the P. P. [*Pioneer Press*] took it up. . . .

I believe that a tariff on imports affords the most convenient method of raising a revenue for defraying the expenses of the government. I further believe that in exercising this right of taxation, Congress under the Constitution and in pursuance of the practices of other nations has the right to levy such revenue in such manner as to encourage and protect domestic industries and commerce. . . . Free traders and many of our big mouthed politicians deny this right — but I believe in the *right* and to this extent believe in a protective tariff.

The right to exercise this power depends upon the situation and condition of the country and its industries and reduces itself with *me* to a question of expediency and national economy. That a protective tariff has served a good purpose in this country and on some industries is serving such purpose today, I firmly believe. History proves it. . . . That some features of our tariff law are antiquated and directly detrimental . . . I appreciate as fully as any one. . . .

The most dangerous feature of a protective system is its tendency to create monopolies. But on examination it will be seen that these monopolies are limited to a great extent to the productions of the *mines* and the *forests*. . . . These sources of industry are usually owned by a few individuals or syndicates. Hence I would be in favor of, and believe in the reduction to a *tariff for revenue,* at least, on all productions of this class. . . . If these things cannot be profitably produced, and those industries carried on without protection, let nature's riches remain in store until they can be extracted with profit. . . .

You overlook one matter that in my opinion is as serious a grievance as the tariff and that is the transportation question. The *cost of transportation to market is always paid by the farmer* or producer. This is a maxim — one of the few maxims of political economy. To an impartial mind are not the grievances of transportation greater than those of the tariff? . . . We cannot afford to lose sight of it by any "free trade" stampede. I believe that the railroad problem demands as patient, honest and thorough consideration as any of the questions of the day. Upon its solution depends our future prosperity and I might say liberty. A railroad is a natural monopoly and nothing but state control or assumption will make it the servant of the public, that it ought to be and that the law says it is. . . . If the cost of transportation comes out of the farmer, then it follows that proximity to market enhances the value of the farmer's productions. Now which will bring our farmer the better return to have his market in our own East or to compete with 8 cts. a day labor of India in the English market? [19]

This letter from the pen of the thirty-two-year-old candidate for Congress is the prototype of Lind's tariff speeches from the Mills bill of 1888 to the proposal for Canadian reciprocity in his last term of Congress, 1903–05, when he professed allegiance to the Democratic party. His views were "western," and this may explain in part why he held the Farmers' Alliance vote.

On the other leading issue of the day, namely, silver, Lind's views were likewise "western." This was the rock that split both parties and eventually drove Lind from the Republican fold and made him a political orphan until he found shelter in the Democratic household.

[19] Lind to E. J. Hodgson, July 19, 1886. The other letter, dated September 7, 1886, was addressed to E. Eccleston.

I believe in the "coin" of the Constitution, viz.: Silver and gold as advocated by Alex Hamilton and in the ratio of values adopted under his advice. I have no dread of the silver dollar, like the Pioneer Press. The only difficulty I expect to experience with it, is "in the gittin' of it." Our past experience in national finances teaches us that inflation causes a rise in values and previously existing credits are contracted. The reverse of this is equally true, contracting the medium of exchange — money, contracts values, enhances all existing credits and injures the debtor class. The duty of a good government is to maintain a stable, reliable currency, or medium of exchange, sufficient in quantity to meet the demands of the business of the country and to avoid both contraction and inflation. It must, however, in a country like ours, constantly increasing in commerce, development and actual wealth, increase in volume, from year to year, to keep pace with such advancement, for otherwise it would simply be contraction. Gold as a sole standard is not found in sufficient quantities to maintain the present, or the proper, ratio between the amount of the money and the wealth of the country. Hence the necessity of resorting to silver "to help out." This might be done by the issuance of greenbacks as has been done in the past, but when we consider the danger of inflation when you once open the gate, as well as the greater adaptability of coin for foreign commerce, it seems to me that no one can deny the propriety of silver coinage.[20]

In the eighties and nineties no candidate for Congress could escape interrogation by the G. A. R. on the matter of pensions. In reply to a communication emanating from this powerful organization, Lind had no hesitation in "cheerfully" indorsing their resolutions with the possible exception of the one pertaining to the widow of a marriage entered into subsequent to the war. "I might have some hesitancy in voting for it should I have the opportunity," he said.[21]

The results of the election were as startling to the people of the state as they were gratifying to Lind. In an election that revealed the growing strength of the Farmers' Alliance, the election of three Democratic congressmen out of five, and a plurality

[20] Lind to E. Eccleston, September 7, 1886.
[21] Lind to E. M. Pope, October 6, 1886.

of only 2,600 for A. R. McGill, the Republican candidate for governor, Lind towered above the other successful candidates by polling a majority of almost 10,000 votes over his Democratic opponent and a plurality of some 7,500 over Bullis and George J. Day, the Prohibition candidate. The only other Republican congressman elected was Knute Nelson in the fifth district, and he had no Democratic opponent.

Especially gratifying was the indorsement given Lind by his own Brown County. In this county the Democratic candidate for governor, A. A. Ames of Minneapolis, received over fourteen hundred votes against some nine hundred for McGill, whereas Lind's vote was over fifteen hundred against less than eight hundred for Bullis. An attack on a Republican parade and an outrage on the flag by hoodlums in Minneapolis the night before the election, alleged to have been instigated by Democrats, are said to have cost Ames the election.

The landslide for Lind in an "off year" is easy to explain. "Honest John" had a large number of friends to start with, and during the campaign the number increased. His straightforward discussion of the issues, his reputation for integrity, his fundamental understanding of the people with whom he mingled, his plain common sense, instilled confidence. Lest it be supposed that these are the words of an admiring biographer, the following news item from the *St. Paul Globe*, a Democratic organ, written somewhat over a year after the election, may be given in corroboration.

The most casual observer of politics in the second congressional district of Minnesota cannot but reach the conclusion that John Lind has become a fearful and monstrous bugaboo to both of the political parties. His ability as a politician, his hold upon the people, have been magnified in extent until the obscure country lawyer, through no particular effort of his own, has grown to the proportions of a mammoth. Make the inquiry of any Republican in the district, "In what lies Mr. Lind's remarkable strength?" He will almost invariably say, "He is a Norwegian." Ask a Democrat the same question and his answer will be, "The district is overwhelmingly Republican."

Both replies are more or less false. Neither of them account for Lind's nomination, election, nor majority. If you choose to define a phenomenon as the result of an unexpected series of occurrences, then Lind is one. When Jim Wakefield retired the people said, "Adieu, Mediocrity!" Just as truthfully they might have exclaimed on Lind's appearance, "Oh, thou accident!" The blind, stumbling, senseless Goddess of Chance made Lind an M. C. . . . It was not sagacity on the part of Lind that nominated him, but a lack of concentrated opposition. . . .

Let it be understood that this district is not Norwegian, nor that any man could be elected in it solely on his nationality. The pivotal counties of this district are Blue Earth, Brown, Faribault, Lac qui Parle, Le Sueur, Lyon, Nicollet, Sibley, Waseca, and Yellow Medicine. Of the congressional vote they cast nearly two-thirds — say 21,000 odd votes — of which not 2,500 are Scandinavian. The other ten counties, casting some 11,000 votes, are said to have, on a careful estimate, 1,500 Scandinavian votes, making a total in the district of about 4,000. Clearly his own countrymen did not elect Mr. Lind.[22]

Lind's personal popularity is attested by the fact that in a region strongly infected with Populistic doctrines he was elected to Congress for three successive terms as a Republican. His popularity was still running high when he retired, voluntarily, in 1892. The second congressional district, which comprised the entire southwestern part of the state, twenty-two counties in all, was almost exclusively rural and its population was made up of native Americans, Irish, Germans, Norwegians, and Swedes. Lind was regarded as a "good" Republican — and he would have resented any suggestion that he was not — but his course is suggestive of that of the elder Robert M. La Follette in Wisconsin up to the time he bolted in 1924 and accepted the presidential nomination by a "fusion" of many elements that did not approve of the old parties. Lind also adhered to the Republican label — and he was proud of it — until a combination of circumstances and events drove him out of the party. On roll calls he was usually recorded as voting "regular," but he espoused bills that were too radical to meet the approval of old-line party men.

[22] *St. Paul Globe*, December 31, 1887.

IV

CONGRESS, 1887–1889

THE FIRST session of the Fiftieth Congress, which convened on December 5, 1887, to continue until October 10, 1888, was up to that time the longest in congressional history. In the Senate there were 39 Republicans and 37 Democrats, but in the House the Democrats were in undisputed control. Among the prominent members of the House were William McKinley, Henry Cabot Lodge, Nelson Dingley, Joseph Gurney Cannon, John D. Long, Richard P. Bland, Roger Q. Mills, Samuel J. Randall, James B. Weaver, William Bourke Cockran, Charles F. Crisp, Samuel S. Cox, Robert M. La Follette, and Jacob H. Gallinger. Lind found himself in the Republican minority. He cast one of the 147 votes for Thomas Brackett Reed of Maine for speaker against 163 for John G. Carlisle of Kentucky. He was appointed to the Committee on the Post Office and Post Roads.

On February 7, 1887, shortly after Lind's election to Congress, the Interstate Commerce Act had become a law. The act, which was a very conservative beginning in the direction of federal regulation of interstate commerce, was defective in machinery and authority for enforcing the decisions and orders of the commission created by it.

In June Lind was present at a business men's convention in Faribault, at which Knute Nelson presented the history of the Interstate Commerce Act and showed how the railways had tried to thwart its purposes and to misrepresent it to the people. Lind took part in the discussion and put in a word for equitable rates.[1]

Lind's chief interest during his first term was in perfecting

[1] *Mankato Review,* June 14, 1887.

the machinery and extending the scope of this act in order to eliminate the abuses and undesirable practices of the railways that had been brought to the attention of the public and that had been complained of by the Farmers' Alliance.

It will be recalled that in the capacity of receiver in the Tracy land office Lind had watched the railway companies like a hawk. He acquired an insight into the chicanery of these corporations that stood him in good stead as a legislator. As was characteristic of him throughout his entire public career, his course was shaped with reference to the interests of the common man.

The case of the Winona and St. Peter Railroad Company is typical of the machinations of the railways at that time and illustrates Lind's attitude toward public service companies. In a letter to the *St. Paul Globe* in March, 1887, he gave the history of this corporation.[2]

In your issue of Monday last, you suggest that my friends should come forward and "explain away certain rumors floating about," from which you say my reputation is liable to suffer. Last Fall the "Globe" came out one day and published me as a defaulter in the land office to the extent of some thousand and the following day it took it all back. . . . But as there may possibly be some few among your many patrons who are not in tears over the "rumored" iniquities that I am trying to perpetrate against that most deserving institution, the Winona & St. Peter Land Company, I will trespass on your space to give a little history of the tax proceedings which lately caused that company's friends to cry "scheme" and "jobbery" in the legislature and who are now so solicitous of my good name that they would be willing to have me drop this tax business to "save my reputation."

"Barney and others," the proprietors of the Winona and St. Peter Railroad Company and franchises as reorganized after the public and "state foreclosure proceedings," held a grant of lands equal to a solid belt of lands ten miles in width extending across

[2] A copy of the communication in the Lind Papers is undated, but it was probably written in the middle of March.

the state from Winona on the east to the Big Sioux River in Dakota on the west. On the strength of this security they built the road to Waseca — about one hundred miles — and then on October 31, 1867, transferred the road and its franchises to the Chicago and Northwestern, the latter company agreeing to assume the debts of the former, complete the road, acquire the title from the government to the lands embraced in the grant, and deed to "Barney and others" the amount of lands owing the road for the portion built by them. Thus about half a million acres of the best lands in the state were given to "Barney and others" as a premium. To facilitate the holding and disposal of these lands, "Barney and others" incorporated as the Winona and St. Peter Land Company. Since the lands in the eastern counties had been largely sold and settled before the road was located, the railroad was permitted to select lands in lieu in the western counties. Not being a railroad company, the land company's holdings were not exempt from taxation, but it succeeded adroitly in getting them exempted for many years in most of the counties. In 1886 W. W. Braden, state auditor, ordered the lands in Brown County to be placed on the tax lists for the collection of back taxes for the omitted years. The land company refused to pay, and the county commissioners employed the firm of Lind and Hagberg to assist the county attorney in prosecuting the company.

For the purpose of providing a mode of "back assessments" a bill was drafted, which received the approval of the state auditor and the attorney-general. Lind explained its provisions to the joint committee on taxation. It passed the Senate, but was killed in the House. Its defeat Lind attributed to the railroad lobby. "It would seem that a bill that is not backed by the railroad lobby stands no show in our Legislature," he wrote.[3]

The county commissioners employed Lind to handle the tax cases for a contingent fee which, under the terms stated by Lind, was far from remunerative. In the latter part of 1888 Lind argued before the Minnesota Supreme Court the case of Brown,

[3] Lind to W. W. Braden, March 14, 1887.

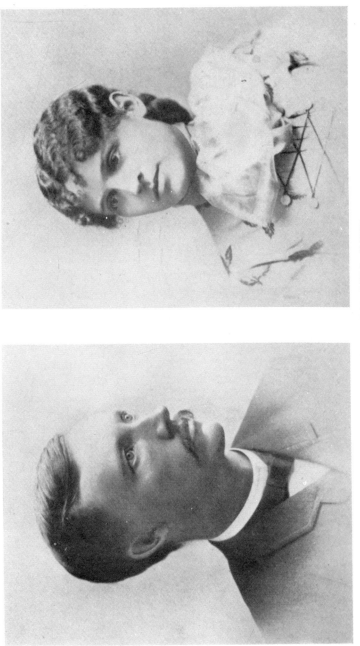

CONGRESSMAN AND MRS. LIND

Redwood, and other counties against the Winona and St. Peter Railway Company for back taxes. The railway company had appealed from the decision of the district court, which had rendered a decision unfavorable to it. Eventually Brown County recovered somewhat more than $50,000, which was used to defray the expenses of erecting a courthouse.

In Congress Lind offered an amendment by which land grants to railways would be forfeited if, when sold, they "were not at the time of such sale in the actual possession of or had improvements made thereon by a person other than such purchasers." He also introduced a resolution for the forfeiture of the grant of lands made to the Hastings and Dakota Railroad Company under an act approved July 4, 1866, which provided that if the railway was not built within ten years of its acceptance of the lands, they were to revert to the United States.[4] Lind's efforts to obtain the forfeiture of lands held by corporations received the hearty commendation of the Knights of Labor in resolutions adopted by delegates to the assembly of the order in Minnesota.[5]

In the first session Lind also introduced an amendment to the Interstate Commerce Act making it unlawful, except in special cases, to charge more for a short than for a long haul on the same line, under satisfactory and similar circumstances and conditions.[6]

Shortly after his election Lind addressed letters to the American ministers in Berlin, Copenhagen, London, Stockholm, Berne, and Vienna requesting them to send him compilations of laws, rules, and regulations pertaining to the railways in those countries. He also wrote to Governor McGill suggesting the appoint-

[4] *Congressional Record*, 50th Congress, 1st Session, January 9, 1888, p. 321; July 5, p. 5912. On February 20, 1892, Lind secured the passage of a resolution asking the secretary of the interior to furnish the House with information with reference to the action taken by the State of Minnesota to annul the charter and forfeit the franchises of the Hastings and Dakota Railroad. *Congressional Record*, 52d Congress, 2d Session, p. 241.

[5] *Labor Echo*, January 28, 1888.

[6] *Congressional Record*, 50th Congress, 1st Session, September 12, 1888, pp. 8554, 8581-83.

ment to the Railroad Commission of a man satisfactory to the farmer element "in order to justify the expectations of that class and to redeem the pledges that some of us made on the stump." He suggested either Eric Olson of Martin County, editor of the *Labor Echo*, published in St. Paul as the organ of the Knights of Labor and of the Farmers' Alliance, or H. G. Stordock of Rothsay. One element of Stordock's strength, according to Lind, was the fact that "Jim Hill hates him so intensely and has done all he could to defeat him."

It is not an individual but our pledges and the best interests of the party that I plead for. Nothing is more evident to me in the political revolution of today, than the fact that the people are not only restive and watchful of political matters. But party obligations are below par and they are particularly hostile to such as may properly be called "the old wheel horses."[7]

That Lind was aware of the fact that his record was not satisfactory to the railways is evident from a letter he wrote to H. B. Strait, a candidate for United States senator.

I hope to be able to start for Washington by Feby. 10th. How is it, are the R. R. Co.'s from Chicago east in the habit of furnishing passes to members, or rather members elect? I have mileage to Chicago. I do not propose to ask any of the North Western Co.'s for passes, though I shall probably accept them if offered as long as it is not illegal. With regard to the eastern roads I feel differently. They are not likely to ask any legislation at the hands of Congress and if I can get a pass from Chicago to Washington by doing only what is proper and customary, I should be glad to have it.[8]

Immediately after Congress convened, bills were introduced in the Senate with reference to the control, ownership, and operation of telegraph lines by the government. The General Assembly of the Knights of Labor of Minnesota adopted resolutions favoring the establishment of a system of postal telegraphy, and letters were addressed to the Minnesota senators and congressmen to ascertain their views. Lind responded by expressing his belief in government ownership and control, but stated further that in his opinion Congress was not ready for this step.

The arguments against it are, that it would increase patronage to such an extent that the party in power would become invincible; also, that the secrecy of the service might be violated when the interests of the party in power demanded. The same objections may be urged against the post office department, and with more force. Its employes outnumber those engaged in telegraphy five to one. It has been, and is, prostituted to party politics. But still, who would favor a transfer of our mail service from the United States to Jay Gould. More than half of the telegraph operators are women, who have no vote. The entire argument rests on the assumption that the vicious "spoils system" will always continue, and that the employes of the government will always regard themselves as servants of the party and not of the public.[9]

Notwithstanding his belief that the only possible immediate step was merely to place telegraph lines under government supervision and control, he argued on the floor of the House that since the telegraph business was a natural monopoly, the only ultimate solution was government ownership and operation.[10]

Legislation designed to benefit actual settlers on the public lands had a strong advocate in John Lind. He opposed discrimination in the matter of homestead entries between citizens and persons who had declared their intention of becoming citizens. He had never known an instance, he said, in which a man who had declared his intention had proved disloyal to the country. "Disloyalty," he said, "does not come from men who have had the enterprise and grit to cross the Atlantic in order to help make this country what it is."[11]

[9] Lind to J. E. Cronin, December 31, 1887, in the *Labor Echo*, January 28, 1888.

[10] *Congressional Record*, 50th Congress, 1st Session, February 16, 1888, pp. 1298–99.

[11] *Congressional Record*, 50th Congress, 1st Session, March 27, 1888, pp. 2460–62.

Lind's independent vote on the question of the Canadian fisheries was unusual for a new member and laid him open to the charge of unpatriotic conduct, since it meant opposing President Cleveland's request for enlarged powers in dealing with a foreign government. In a special message dated February 20, 1888, Cleveland submitted to the Senate a treaty with Great Britain providing for a settlement of disputes growing out of the rights claimed by American fishermen in British North American waters. The New England senators opposed the treaty, however, and it failed of ratification. This aroused the indignation of the president, and on August 23, 1888, he sent his famous "retaliation message" to Congress, in which he recommended immediate legislative action conferring upon him the power to suspend by proclamation the operation of all laws and regulations permitting the transit of goods, wares, and merchandise in bond across or over the territory of the United States to or from Canada. He reiterated his belief that the treaty satisfactorily met the situation, that it did not sacrifice national pride or dignity, but in view of its rejection by the Senate he recommended legislation that would "subserve the interests of our people and maintain the high standard and becoming pride of American citizenship."

Lind opposed the bill to carry out the proposed retaliatory measures of the president on the ground that it would injure Minnesota. He said that with one stroke of the pen the president could reduce by at least seven cents a bushel the value of the sixty million bushels of Minnesota and Dakota wheat that would be sent to the markets of the East and the Seaboard; that he could enhance the exactions of the railways by at least twenty-five per cent; and that he could rob Duluth of nearly half her shipping and ruin the trade of the Twin Cities. He concluded his speech as follows:

I plead not for Canada, nor for England — I hate England, or rather I hate and despise her policy of dealing with other nations and peoples weaker than herself. Her sense of right is measured by her power to defy it; her love of justice by the gold it will fetch. . . .

If we have grievances, let us demand their redress in a spirit and manner becoming our dignity. If such demands are unheeded, let us enforce our rights in the spirit of American patriotism and valor.[12]

The bill passed the House on September 8, 1888, by a vote of 176 to 4, Lind casting one of the few negative votes. The *St. Paul Globe* was prompted to comment that "of all the Northwestern congressmen, John Lind was the only one so unpatriotic as to put himself on record as an enemy to his country." The *St. Paul Dispatch*, however, reacted quite differently, asserting that Lind had the courage of his convictions and did not behave as did the other "scared patriots of the House."

With a Democratic president and House of Representatives and a Republican Senate, it was inevitable that the proceedings of the Fiftieth Congress should take the form of skirmishes preparatory to the presidential campaign of 1888. As it proved, Cleveland's epochal annual message of 1887, which was devoted altogether to tariff revision, joined the issue and made the tariff the paramount issue of the campaign. The Democrats wrote their ideas of tariff revision in the Mills bill; and the Republican majority in the Senate formulated its own measure. The words "free trade" and "protection" were bandied about freely all during the session.

Although Lind was a tariff reformer and wrote into his platform a plank declaring for a thorough revision of the existing law, including the extension of the free list, he voted against the Mills bill. When he began to study economic questions, he was strongly impressed with the arguments of the free traders, but at the time of his election to Congress he was a firm believer in protection. He made a distinction between a tariff for revenue and a tariff for protection. He admitted the necessity of reducing the surplus in the treasury by reducing the revenue, but he was not in favor of accomplishing this by subordinating the

---

[12] *Congressional Record*, 50th Congress, 1st Session, pp. 8422–26, 8439–40. The bill was defeated in the Senate, at which it was aimed instead of at Canada.

principle of protection of American industries to the principle of tariff for revenue only. Sugar, which was largely imported, he favored placing on the free list if the revenue was not needed for the expenses of the government. On the other hand, he believed in the protection of cotton fabrics. On these imports not only was the duty added to the price of the commodity but because of the skill of American workingmen and the steady demand of a protected market, American manufacturers sold their products more cheaply than similar commodities were made and sold in Europe. His explanation was that American manufacturers had an immense home market with a regular and known demand. If the bars were let down, "English temporary overproductions would find an outlet here at ruinous prices to our manufacturers and we cannot estimate how much injury might result."

To the argument that the American farmer was compelled to sell his wheat in England; that the English market fixed the prices of his products; that he was compelled to meet "pauper" competition and should therefore be permitted to buy where he could buy cheapest, he replied that the export of wheat was falling off at a remarkable rate and that there were indications that within a few years no wheat would be exported. The wheat-producing area in the United States was, he thought, diminishing from year to year.

Dakota is settled and Minnesota is fast getting out of exclusive wheat culture. Wheat raising is preeminently the industry of the frontier — the homesteader's crop. It requires the least capital in the start, returns the quickest money, and pays the best while the soil is new. But exclusive wheat raising is and must of necessity be a temporary industry. The conditions which caused our large wheat export have ceased to exist . . . and increase of population is growing faster than the annual wheat crop. . . . With increased home consumption and smaller surplus for export our farmers will get better prices. And in this connection farmers forget that England buys our wheat for bread — not for love. She would not buy a bushel more tomorrow if we had free trade. . . . And what would we gain by admitting her to our markets? Probably cheaper goods temporarily. But the results to many industries in the East would be disastrous. . . .

The statement that the price of our agricultural machinery is affected by the tariff is simply ridiculous. . . . We make the best and cheapest farm machinery in the world. The best evidence of this is the fact that we export millions of dollars' worth annually. . . . The tears shed over the decline of our shipping don't alarm me much. Our domestic commerce, which is greater and more valuable than the foreign commerce of all the world, concerns me more. . . . Our citizens can invest their money in railroad building and other enterprises and receive twice or three times the returns that the same capital would yield if invested in the "free ships" of England.[13]

Lind's contribution to the proposed tariff legislation consisted in the introduction of a bill to place on the free list all books and pamphlets printed in foreign languages and an amendment to the Mills bill to add to the free list machinery used in the manufacture of binding twine. He did not think the removal of the tariff on lumber would have the effect of lowering the price to an appreciable extent, but if it did have that effect, so much the better. What appealed to him more than anything else was that it would decrease the consumption of American timber and thus save the forests. This attitude was wholly in keeping with his love of wild life and his solicitude for the preservation of the beauties of nature, a trait that never deserted him.

He favored a duty on flaxseed, and stated that perhaps more flaxseed was raised and more linseed oil manufactured in his district than in any other district in the country. He maintained that a tariff on this commodity had stimulated and developed an industry that enabled the consumer to purchase cheaper oil. Under no circumstances was he in favor of removing the excise on whiskey, but he thought the removal of the tax on tobacco might redound to the benefit of his constituents by enabling them to obtain the reduction of other taxes.

[13] Lind to O. N. Bronson, August 26, 1888; interview in the *St. Paul Globe*, December 30, 1888.

On the whole, Lind's dissatisfaction with the Mills bill grew out of his conviction that it was framed largely in the interest of the East. On the final passage of the bill the vote was 162 to 149. Lind voted with the Republicans in the negative. Knute Nelson, his Republican colleague, voted for the bill. La Follette voted with the Republican minority.[14]

The vote on the Mills bill was probably Lind's greatest test during his first term in Congress, and he seems to have sensed the sentiment of the people of his district, although the Democratic *St. Paul Globe*, which for some reason had a special animus toward him, took occasion to contrast his course with that of Knute Nelson.[15] The low-tariff Republican *Chicago Tribune* was very complimentary of Lind's course, as were a number of Democratic organs — which prompted the conservative Republican Chicago Swedish weekly, *Hemlandet*, to say that his Democratic tendencies were not becoming. "The true Republican garb would suit him so much better," it said. "If the Scandinavians are anything, they are Republicans and protectionists, and it is indeed a freak of fortune that the only two Scandinavians in Congress should not be likewise."[16] As a supporter of the Republican party through thick and thin it was natural for the Chicago weekly to criticize Lind for his departure from Republican orthodoxy, but the editor was hardly accurate in his statement about the Scandinavians. If the Swedish press accurately reflected the tendencies of its readers, there was not a little dissatisfaction among them with the Republican party. *Svenska Folkets Tidning* of Minneapolis deserted the Republican fold and supported Cleveland in 1888, and *Svenska*

[14] *Congressional Record*, 50th Congress, 1st Session, pp. 220, 4777, 5065–67, 5225, 6660; interview in the *St. Paul Globe*, December 30, 1888.

[15] *St. Paul Globe*, March 21, 1888. The *Redwood Reveille* of April 21 stated that the *Globe's* hostility to Lind could be easily explained. Several years before, it stated, it had charged that his accounts in the Tracy land office were not in proper shape and that he was indebted to the government for a large sum of money. Lind immediately notified the *Globe* editor that unless a correction were made he would commence an action for libel. "The *Globe* crawfished and withdrew its charges, but since that time it has never lost an opportunity to show its animosity toward our representative in Congress."

[16] *Hemlandet*, 1888, nos. 16 and 18.

Amerikanaren of Chicago was a warm advocate of tariff revision.[17]

Naturally Lind's refusal to accept the principle of free trade brought criticism upon him. The Nobles County Farmers' Alliance adopted resolutions condemning his course, to which Lind replied in a long letter that was published in full in the *St. Paul Globe* on April 9, 1888. He stated that the Mills bill was sectional and unfair, because it repealed the small protection the northern farmer had hitherto enjoyed. If the interests of the public demanded the removal of the tariff on the farm products of the North, why, he asked, did not the same rule apply to the South?

Lind's renomination was a foregone conclusion. In spite of divided opinion on the Mills bill, there was little doubt that he had been very efficient in securing pensions for veterans and other "good things" for his district.[18] The Republican convention held at Mankato on May 15, 1888, renominated him by acclamation and the platform "especially" indorsed his views on the tariff and land grants.[19] His Democratic opponent was Morton S. Wilkinson of New Richland, an elderly man and former United States senator and congressman, who featured tariff reform in his speeches.

Lind took little part in the campaign. The extended session of Congress kept him in Washington until the first week of October, when he was granted an indefinite leave of absence. It was a Republican year, but the success of the national Republican ticket had little effect on Lind's fortunes. His plurality was 9,219, slightly less than in the previous campaign. The total vote showed an increase of almost seven thousand votes over 1886, an indication that the vote was divided in almost exactly the old proportion. Lind carried every county except Brown and Sibley. Both candidates lost their home counties. Lind ran ahead of Harrison and Governor Merriam in every county, and of the

---

[17] See the *St. Paul Globe* and the *Chicago Herald* of August 12, 1888.
[18] See the *Congressional Record*, 50th Congress, 1st Session, pp. 220, 4545–46.
[19] *Mankato Register*, May 17, 1888.

five Republican congressmen elected, only one, S. P. Snider in the fourth district, had a slightly larger plurality. Lind's phenomenal success as a vote getter caused his name to be mentioned in connection with the governorship in the next campaign. His popularity and influence are seen also in the solicitude of the rival senatorial candidates for his support.[20]

[20] See letters to Lind from Washburn, November 23, 1888; D. M. Sabin, December 21, 1888; F. S. Brown, December 24, 1888; H. B. Strait, December 28, 1888; and W. C. Corbett, January 3, 1889.

V

CONGRESS, 1889–1891

DURING his second term in Congress John Lind for the only time in his legislative career had the experience of being a member of the majority party. The Fifty-first Congress enacted legislation that was fraught with disaster for the Republican party and destined to have a far-reaching effect, culminating in one of the most exciting periods of American politics. Lind had a part in the passage of the McKinley Tariff Act and the Sherman Silver Purchase Act. The House was presided over by "Czar" Thomas Brackett Reed, whose famous parliamentary ruling has caused his name to be remembered as one of its notable speakers. The Republicans were in control of both branches of Congress, with 51 Republicans and 37 Democrats in the Senate and 176 Republicans and 155 Democrats in the House. Lind was appointed a member of the Committee on Mileage, the Committee on Commerce, and the Select Committee on Reform in the Civil Service.

At the time of his re-election Lind was in the good graces of the Republican leaders. Even the *Minneapolis Tribune*, which had seriously questioned the orthodoxy of his platform in 1886, published a dispatch from its Washington correspondent stating that it was not too much to say that no new member of the Fiftieth Congress stood higher in the estimation of both parties. He quoted a member of Congress as saying, "You always know where to find him. He is a Republican and advocates the principles of his party on all proper occasions." [1]

In an interview with a reporter for the *St. Paul Dispatch* the young congressman said:

[1] *Minneapolis Tribune*, December 23, 1887.

With a Republican president, a Republican Senate, a Republican House, with a Republican speaker, we will rule America as America should be ruled. The rights of Dakota and other territories will be recognized promptly and speedy justice will be meted out. The government is now in a condition to begin where it was forced to halt four years ago and resume its progressive march in the direction of national advancement and prosperity.[2]

The biggest political battles raged around the tariff and the currency, but before discussing Lind's part in these issues, we may consider for a moment his activity in behalf of his constituents and in matters of less importance.

During the campaign of 1888 the Republicans had sung songs about Cleveland's vetoes of pension bills. Lind joined with the Republican majority in passing the Dependent Pensions Bill, a measure similar to that vetoed by Cleveland.[3]

Speaking on the bill to grant copyright protection to foreign authors, which had passed the Senate, Lind said:

I deem it proper to say that so far as my observation goes the sentiments that have left a permanent impression on the human mind, the truths that have appealed to mankind and made succeeding generations wiser and better have not been called forth by the prospective gains under copyright legislation. On the contrary, they have come from the heart and brain of the struggling and poverty-stricken laborers in the world's great workshop, whose experience and trials have taught them to see, feel, and sympathize with the wants and woes of mankind. But the object of this bill is not to protect our American authors, for they are already protected, but under the guise of protecting our authors it seeks to confer an absolute monopoly on the American publisher of every foreign literary production written in our language which is copyrighted here. . . . The textbook trust is strong enough now. This bill will make it stronger. Free schools and cheap books made it possible for me to occupy a seat on this floor.[4]

[2] Clipping in the Lind Papers.
[3] *Congressional Record*, 51st Congress, 1st Session, pp. 4062–63.
[4] *Congressional Record*, 51st Congress, 1st Session, p. 4151. The International Copyright Bill became a law at the next session of Congress.

Lind objected to a bill providing for the compulsory attend-ance of witnesses before registers and receivers of land offices, which permitted a contestant to a claim to go before the register and receiver and make an affidavit of poverty, thereby compel-ling that official to subpoena witnesses without payment of fees. Lind argued that this legislation would enable speculators to harass settlers still further. In every community in which public lands were located, he said, there were hordes of men who made a living by instituting suits against settlers and compromising them for a consideration. In the past the inability to compel attendance of witnesses had been a restraint on such actions.[5]

Lind received the gratitude of his constituents, as well as of voters in other parts of the state, by obtaining the passage and approval, in May, 1890, of the so-called Lind Judicial Bill by which the federal district courts in Minnesota were reorganized. The act, which provided for semiannual terms of courts in Min-neapolis, St. Paul, Duluth, Winona, Mankato, and Fergus Falls, made it unnecessary for litigants any longer to incur the expense and inconvenience of having their cases tried in St. Paul. It had the united opposition of the attorneys representing that city.[6]

His effort to obtain the enactment of a law to establish Indian schools in various parts of the country, including the institution at Pipestone in his own district, was only the beginning of his benevolent interest in these wards of the government. He called the attention of Congress to the fact that there were in Minne-sota over eight hundred Indians, scattered in small reservations, who had no educational advantages and hence were in danger of growing up to be worthless and shiftless and a curse to them-selves and to the communities in which they resided. He pleaded that they be given the opportunity to educate their hands as well

[5] *Congressional Record*, 51st Congress, 1st Session, pp. 1963-66.
[6] For comments see the *Winona Herald* of April 22, 1890, and the *Mankato Register* of May 1, 1890. The *Herald* stated that Lind deserved the hearty thanks of the state at large. "In fact his comprehensive grasp of the wants of the entire state, and his fidelity to the people in this and other measures, com-pels us to enquire whether there is not some first class senatorial material in the make up of the honest and industrious member from the third [sic] dis-trict."

as their minds in industrial schools. He was convinced that to teach an Indian to read and nothing more was to throw away both time and money.[7] From the Committee on Naval Affairs William G. McAdoo reported a bill prohibiting enlistment in the navy of persons who were not citizens of the United States, with the exception of those who had declared their intention to become naturalized. McAdoo presented statistics showing that there were in the navy 3,668 natives as against 4,278 of foreign birth, only a small percentage of whom had been naturalized. Lind offered an amendment, which was accepted by McAdoo and passed, providing that enlistment and service in the navy for a period of five years should be considered as residence in the United States for the purpose of acquiring citizenship. When a man enlisted and swore to support the flag, he felt, it should be considered a declaration of intention. Lind was, of course, in favor of encouraging foreigners to become citizens, but he saw no danger in the enlistment of aliens in the navy and called attention to an article by Admiral Porter in the *North American Review* praising the conduct of the crew of the "Trenton" in the harbor of Apia, Samoa, during the terrible hurricane. Of the four hundred sailors in the crew, all but forty were foreigners, mostly Scandinavians. "In the whole course of my naval experience I have never known a case of more perfect discipline than was exhibited on board the 'Trenton,'" wrote the admiral.[8]

On the two major items of legislation passed by the Fifty-

[7] Lind to Freeman Talbot, January 1, 1887; *Congressional Record*, 51st Congress, 1st Session, pp. 10704–05. The *St. Paul Globe* of March 13, 1890, commented as follows: "Among the few things in Mr. Lind's congressional career that we find occasion to commend there is nothing that meets our more sincere approbation than his proposition to have the government establish an Indian school at Pipestone. The bill provides for an appropriation of $30,000, an insignificant sum in comparison with what ought to be expended for this purpose; yet if he succeeds in getting this modest appropriation he will have scored a good point and we will cheerfully award him the full measure of praise for his achievement."

[8] *Congressional Record*, 51st Congress, 1st Session, pp. 3156–60. Admiral Porter's article on "Discipline in the Navy" appeared in the *North American Review* for April, 1890.

first Congress – the Sherman Silver Purchase Act and the Mc-Kinley Tariff – Lind voted with the Republican majority, but he was not entirely satisfied with either act. The rising tide of Populism and the admission of North and South Dakota, Washington, Montana, Idaho, and Wyoming in 1889 and 1890 greatly complicated the problem of framing financial and tariff legislation satisfactory to a majority in both houses, to say nothing of the country as a whole. There was no doubt about the willingness of the Republicans in both houses to enact a high protective tariff; but in the Senate there was a majority in favor of the free coinage of silver which held up consideration of the McKinley bill until the House, opposed to free coinage, gave evidence of its willingness to repeal the Bland-Allison Act of 1878 and to substitute for it a measure that yielded more to the Silverites, who were most numerous in the West. The Silver Purchase Bill and the McKinley Tariff, therefore, were sent on their way to the White House after weeks of logrolling at the other end of Pennsylvania Avenue.

In the House the Free Silverites tried to defeat less radical bills by filibustering tactics. When Lind projected himself into the debate there were three bills before the House: (1) the committee or "Windom" bill; (2) the Republican or House Caucus Bill; and (3) the Bland Free Coinage Bill. Of the three Lind thought the "Windom" bill the most objectionable because it proposed to repeal the Bland-Allison Act, which to a limited extent recognized silver as a money metal. The "Windom" bill reduced silver to the level of other commodities to be left with the government for security. It proposed that the government should buy at the market price as much silver as the mine owners chose to offer, paying for it in treasury notes redeemable in such quantities of silver bullion as were equal in value to the face value of the notes, or in gold at the option of the government. The caucus bill, which was framed by the Republican majority, limited the issue of notes to $4,500,000 monthly. Lind favored this measure.

He began his speech on "Silver Bullion Certificates" by referring to the hard times and by citing the fact that the prices of agricultural products had declined, with but few interruptions, since 1873. He denied that overproduction and labor-saving devices were the causes; the trouble was rather under-consumption, since the farmers were unable to buy because of the low prices they were receiving for their products. He presented tables of statistics purporting to show that prices were greatly affected by the quantity of money.

As to the free coinage proposition, I am free to say that personally I believe it not only the best, but the quickest way of settling the whole question. We produce half of the world's silver. We are the richest and greatest nation on earth. France, by keeping her mints open to both metals at a fixed ratio, maintained their parity for over a century. We could do the same. The talk about our mint being flooded with the silver of Europe is absurd. . . . But there are some objections to the unlimited free coinage at this time. Silver is now worth less than gold. If we should pass Mr. Bland's bill we would give every bullion owner a bonus of nearly 30 per cent. I prefer to give this to the government. Besides, it would be unfair to deny that many conservative citizens of good judgment, and who are not prejudiced by their interests, sincerely fear that a free-coinage law would be disastrous. I feel confident to the contrary. At the same time I believe it better prudence to yield something even to prejudice, when you can serve the people as well and effect your object as speedily by adopting a measure equally efficacious, but less objectionable to all classes. Public confidence and approval are the mainstay of all legislation, especially of a financial character. Such a measure is the Republican House Caucus Bill.[9]

Lind believed that the bill would raise the price of silver to par within two years after its passage, and further that there was an advantage in issuing silver certificates, for thereby the expense of coinage would be saved and the danger of exporting the silver in the dollars would be averted. He did not regret the loss of the dollars as bullion but as money.

On Bland's motion to recommit the "Silver Bullion Certifi-

[9] *Congressional Record*, 51st Congress, 1st Session, June 6, 1890, pp. 5692-97.

cates Bill" to the Committee on Coinage, Weights, and Measures, with instructions to report back a free coinage bill, Lind voted *nay* with La Follette, McKinley, and Lodge.[10]

When the House bill came to the Senate, that body promptly substituted for it a free coinage bill and also turned down the McKinley Tariff Bill on the calendar as a notification to the protectionists that they would have to yield something more substantial to the silver cause. The silver bill was eventually sent to a conference committee, from which it emerged greatly modified. It required the treasury to purchase not more than 4,500,000 ounces of silver per month, instead of $4,500,000 worth, to be paid for in legal tender bills and to be redeemed in gold or silver at the discretion of the secretary of the treasury. The bill reported by the conference committee also contained a provision, suggested by Senator John Sherman, pledging the government to maintain the two metals on a parity.

On the final passage of the Sherman Silver Purchase Bill, Lind was recorded as "not voting," but it may be assumed that it was satisfactory to him, since on a test vote to repeal the act on February 9, 1893, sponsored by Republicans and opposed by Democrats and Free Silverites, he voted with Bryan, Bland, Dolliver, and Tillman, all Free Silverites, against Dingley, Lodge, and other conservatives.[11]

Lind's vote on the silver bill was not a test of party loyalty, for in the campaign of 1888 neither party had placed itself on record with reference to silver coinage. There were Silver Republicans as well as Silver Democrats, the West being their favorite stamping ground. In view of Lind's later political affiliations, it is important to get his record straight on the currency.

After the victory of 1888 the Republicans were in a position to pass a tariff bill that embodied their principles. However, in view of the dissatisfaction in the Northwest with Republican protection as expressed by such men as John Lind and Knute

[10] *Congressional Record*, 51st Congress, 1st Session, June 7, 1890, pp. 5813–14. The vote was 116 yeas and 140 nays.
[11] *Congressional Record*, 52d Congress, 2d Session, February 9, 1893, p. 1382.

Nelson and by the Minnesota Republican convention in September, 1888, there was method in the madness of the Republican leaders in Congress in calling the McKinley bill a "bill to reduce the revenue and equalize duties on imports." It greatly extended the protective principle and materially increased the rates on competing products. It was framed chiefly in the interests of the manufacturing East. The temper of Minnesota may be indicated somewhat by the comment of the *Albert Lea Standard* on May 9, 1890, while the bill was under consideration: "Among the three hundred and fifty papers of the state, not half a dozen support the McKinley bill. Do you hear this, Messrs. Davis, Washburn, Dunnell, Lind, Hall, Snider, and Comstock, or don't you want to hear it?"

Although Lind voted for the bill on its final passage, as did such Westerners as La Follette and Dolliver, he endeavored to have certain features modified and voted with the Democrats in defeating the efforts of McKinley to shut off debate. He made a fight for free sugar and a reduction in the duty on binding twine. In a letter to the secretary of the Farmers' Alliance he stated that he had argued the necessity of placing binding twine on the free list before the Committee on Ways and Means. He asserted that by the placing of raw material on the free list, the duty on manufactured twine had increased nearly 700 per cent.

With an eye on the uneasy West the Republican leaders in the Senate inserted reciprocity provisions; and the bill retained them when it came from the conference committee. Lind avowed that it was a better bill than when it left the House and stated that he was almost tempted to vote to send it back once more to the Senate — a remark that evoked loud applause on the Democratic side.

And I want to say here, Mr. Speaker, that I voted for this bill, not because I think it is just to my people, not because it was what they demanded and needed, but simply and solely to discharge a constitutional duty that rested upon the House to originate tariff legislation. I wanted to send it to that body where the glorious West can be heard, where selfishness does not rule supreme as it does in certain quarters here. . . . It went there and came back a better bill.[12]

The extended debates and parliamentary maneuvers over the tariff bill made it impossible for Lind to return to Minnesota until the beginning of October. When he arrived he faced angry blasts of public opinion against the McKinley Act. He was greeted with statements in the Republican press in his district that he was the ablest and most industrious member of the Minnesota delegation. On the day of his arrival in St. Paul from Washington he was interviewed by the *St. Paul Dispatch*, which reported him as saying that the recent session had done more real work than any session for a decade, in spite of the filibustering tactics of the Democrats. Lind thought the silver legislation would be of incalculable benefit to the farmers of the Northwest. He admitted that the McKinley bill was not exactly such a measure as he himself would have drawn up, but thought it far better than the law it superseded. Although the Minnesota delegation did all in their power to obtain a proper adjustment of the tariff, they were not inclined to cry, "I won't play because I cannot have things my own way."[13]

Lind's nomination at the Mankato convention on July 23, 1890, was a perfunctory procedure. There was no contest. The nominee was ushered into the hall, where he thanked his friends and explained the various measures before Congress.[14] A few days before election he issued an appeal to the voters in which he reviewed the record of the preceding Congress and praised the Silver Purchase Act, the Sherman Anti-Trust Law, the Original Package Law, and the Dependent Pensions Act. In answer to the charge that the McKinley Act had raised prices, he asserted that the rise was because the country was enjoying better times. The tariff, he said, did not affect the prices of com-

---

[12] *Congressional Record*, 51st Congress, 1st Session, pp. 5033, 5053–54, 6262, 10630, 10640–41. Lind's letter to John Lathrop, secretary of the Farmers' Alliance, is printed in the *Redwood Reveille* of May 10, 1890.

[13] Printed in the *New Ulm Review* of October 8, 1890.

[14] *New Ulm Review*, July 30, 1890.

modities produced in quantities sufficient to supply our own people.[15]

Lind's opponent was General James H. Baker of Blue Earth County, a man with an excellent war record, a long political experience, and considerably more ability than his opponents in previous campaigns. He ran as the Farmers' Alliance candidate, with the indorsement of the Democrats. He featured tariff revision and condemned the McKinley Act unequivocally.

Lind survived the unpopularity of the McKinley bill and the surge of the Farmers' Alliance and was re-elected by a small margin. He received 20,788 votes; Baker, 20,306; Ira B. Reynolds, the Prohibition candidate, 1,146. The victory was a great triumph. Lind was the only Republican elected to Congress; the Democrats and the Alliance people each supplied two of the other four members of the Minnesota delegation. "John Lind, the only Minnesota Republican in the Fifty-second Congress, looms up like Mount Ararat after the deluge," was the comment of the *Duluth Tribune*.[16] The vote for governor gave Merriam, Republican, 88,111; Thomas Wilson, Democrat, 85,844; Sidney M. Owen, Alliance, 58,513.

Though it is perhaps impossible to explain with certainty the remarkable circumstance that Lind survived the political tornado of 1890, one fact is clear: It was not by a surrender of Republican principles or an apology for his party's record. He voted against the Mills bill and for the McKinley bill and justified his action both on the stump and in Congress. It was probably his personal popularity, his reputation for integrity, the friendliness of the war veterans, and the popularity in his district of the Silver Purchase Act, together with his effective speech in favor of it. Lind was also able to handle the patronage without damage to himself, though in the case of the Mankato post office it appeared for a time that there was a serious fac-

---

[15] Printed in the *Martin County Sentinel* of October 31, 1890.

[16] Quoted in the *Martin County Sentinel* of November 14, 1890. There was talk of General Baker contesting the election. *St. Paul Dispatch* and *Mankato Register*, quoted in the *New Ulm Review*, December 3, 1890, November 27, 1891.

tional fight in the making. The editor of the *Mankato Free Press*, L. P. Hunt, was anxious to get the appointment, but the selection of W. W. P. McConnell, a man who stood high in G. A. R. circles and carried the esteem of his fellow citizens, together with the erection of a new post office made possible by an appropriation through Lind's efforts, dispelled the brewing storm.[17]

In a memorandum dated November 11, 1890, Lind made a diagnosis of the political situation which is interesting not only as a document coming from one who was almost swept away by the torrent but as a contribution worthy of consideration by students of history.

He did not question that the McKinley bill was a factor that contributed to the downfall of the Republicans, but he did not believe it was a principal cause of the disaster in the West and Northwest. In Minnesota the Alliance movement was the immediate cause of the change of the political complexion of the congressional delegation. If free trade, or a purely revenue tariff, was what the majority of the voters of the state desired, he argued that the election would have shown an increase in the Democratic vote; but no such increase occurred in the vote of any candidate for a state or federal office. On the contrary, the falling off of the Democratic vote was more marked than that of the Republican, in spite of the fact that three-fourths of the Alliance membership was made up of Republicans. "Democratic success is therefore not due to any accession to the Democratic vote but to defection from the Republican ranks by the Alliance movement." There was no connection, he believed, between the Alliance movement and the McKinley bill. He saw the proof of this in the fact that some of the ablest advocates of free trade doctrines in the House of Representatives were the first to suffer defeat at the hands of the Alliance. The nucleus of

[17] *Mankato Free Press*, April 28, May 9, 12, 1890; *Redwood Reveille*, May 10, 1890; *Mankato Review*, April 29, May 13, 1890; *Waseca Radical*, May 7, 1890. Lind received a thousand dollars from the Republican Congressional Committee to aid him in the campaign for re-election. The committee regretted that the sum was not larger and stated that it was impossible to "raise much means this year." Letter dated October 20, 1890.

the Alliance movement, in his opinion, was the demand for better transportation rates and greater saving in the warehousing and handling of staple crops.

In the North the present Alliance movement had its birth in Dakota. The hardships and disappointments incident to the opening and settlement of a new country; failure of crops, distance from markets and high rates of transportation furnished the cause. The agitation and discussion incident to the adoption of the state constitutions afforded the opportunity. . . . [The farmer] did not stop to consider that, while good times give prosperity, they are like "good" growing weather as conducive to tares and thistles as to corn; that many of the grievances of which he complained so justly were the result of the times and our economic development rather than of the neglect of officers or parties.

An extensive personal acquaintance and familiarity with the condition of the farmers and recent travels through the counties of his district convinced Lind that there was not a more prosperous farming community in the world. The gist of the farmer's complaint was not that he was poor or suffering but that others who labored and deserved less received the greater share of the profit on his products. This was also the complaint of organized labor. He had no faith in the future of the Alliance as a political party because there was no unanimity of opinion about remedies for the situation. It would be wanting if put to the test of administration.

As a negative party — one of protest and agitation — it is and probably will be a success for some years to come. The traditional conservatism of the farmer, in the West at least, is a myth. . . . Parties rest very lightly on his shoulders. Change of administrations and of representatives for experimental purposes alone will be the rule rather than the exception during the continuance of the tentative period which we are in. This to the writer's mind accounts for the result of the recent elections rather than the passage of the McKinley bill.

VI

CONGRESS, 1891–1893

IN THE Fifty-second Congress the Republicans were in a hopeless minority in the House of Representatives. There were 235 Democrats, 88 Republicans, and 9 Alliance men. In the Senate were 47 Republicans, 39 Democrats, and 2 Independents. Notwithstanding the fact that Lind was the only Republican member from Minnesota, he fared better in committee assignments than did his colleagues. He was placed on the Committees on Interstate and Foreign Commerce, Private Land Claims, and Pacific Railroads, and on the select committee authorized under a resolution of February 10, 1892, to investigate the methods, management, and practices of the Bureau of Pensions. It was a stormy Congress, especially during the second session. There was difficulty in maintaining a quorum, because members absented themselves to prevent the transaction of business. In the debates on the rules and their enforcement Lind played politics and embarrassed the Democrats by quoting from their platform.[1]

Lind's interest in shipping was sharpened during his service in the House; for four years he was a member of the Committee on Interstate and Foreign Commerce, and he was instrumental in securing the passage of several amendments to the Interstate Commerce Act. He was convinced that transportation was the problem that cried most loudly for solution, even more than the tariff. In 1890 he withheld from publication his speech on the Sherman Anti-Trust Bill because, after looking over his notes, he concluded that the act did not solve the problems that faced the American people. " 'Competition' as we then used and

[1] *Congressional Record*, 52d Congress, 2d Session, pp. 1964–66.

understood the term would not and could not solve many of the problems then and now confronting society," he said many years later.[2]

From the Committee on Interstate and Foreign Commerce Lind introduced a bill relating to contracts of common carriers, which upon its passage and approval in 1893 became known as the Harter Act. It marked a new era in ocean transportation and became the Magna Charta of shippers the world over. It became the model for similar legislation in many foreign countries, including Canada, Australia, and New Zealand. It became the "accepted code of law governing ocean freight transportation of almost the entire world."[3]

A Millers' League had been organized in 1891 by the *Northwestern Miller* of Minneapolis for the purpose of expediting flour shipments. Through the instrumentality of this organization a bill was introduced by M. D. Harter of Ohio, a miller. Lind reported it out from the committee and ably supported it on the floor of the House in opposition to the combined steamship interests, who employed the best legal talent and fought it from first to last.

The purpose of the Harter bill, as explained by Lind, was to protect the shippers of flour and other western commodities. Nearly all the carrying of these commodities was done by foreign steamship companies, which exacted most unreasonable bills of lading, not only exempting themselves from every kind of risk incident to transportation but stipulating that the American shipper should have his rights or claims adjudicated according to the laws of Great Britain and only in the courts of that country. The bill provided that the shipowner could not exact bills of lading that exempted him from liability properly to receive, stow, carry, or deliver, according to mark or description, any lawful cargo intrusted to him for carriage. It also gave the shipowner certain immunities from loss or damage incurred dur-

[2] Lind to C. W. Bunn. This letter is undated, but it was written some time after 1925. See Lind to Guy D. Goff of the Shipping Board, January 21, 1921.
[3] William C. Edgar, *The Medal of Gold* (Minneapolis, 1925), pp. 177–80.

ing the voyage. As passed with Senate amendments—the purpose of which was to eliminate possible legal technicalities—the bill was satisfactory, Lind stated, to American shippers, to legitimate and honest steamboat interests, and to the underwriters.[4] For this service, as well as others, Lind was tendered a complimentary dinner on March 20, 1894, at the Minneapolis Club by the millers of the Northwest.

On a proposed amendment to the Interstate Commerce Act Lind read a minority report, signed by himself and S. R. Mallory, protesting the effort to legalize contracts for the division of traffic. The amendment, according to the report, proposed to legalize "railroad wrecking" and stock speculation by authorizing agreements for the division and apportionment of net and gross earnings among carriers themselves and also by allowing carriers to divide and apportion them among "others" who were not carriers. Under these provisions stockholders would be as much at the mercy of railroad managers as would the public. The Standard Oil Company and the "Dressed Beef Combine" and other monopolies could obtain rebates by contracts enforceable in the courts instead of by stealth and concealment as previously. The report further stated that railway transportation was a natural monopoly and that the element of competition was wanting except between terminal points and between trunk lines carrying the products of the West to the Seaboard. This natural competition the amendment proposed to stifle. The competition of water routes had always been a thorn in the side of traffic associations and pools; and the amendment authorized contracts between water routes and all rail carriers for a division of traffic and gross and net earnings. This section was stricken out at Lind's suggestion.[5]

Lind was among the "radicals" who saw the disastrous consequences to the public that resulted from watered railroad stocks. On January 5, 1892, he introduced a bill requiring the Interstate Commerce Commission to ascertain and report the actual

[4] *Congressional Record*, 52d Congress, 2d Session, pp. 147-48, 1291-92.
[5] *Congressional Record*, 52d Congress, 2d Session, pp. 709-12.

cost of construction of all railroads in the United States over which interstate commerce was carried.[6]

The close of Lind's third term was marked by a most persistent and successful fight in behalf of the Automatic Car Coupler Act, a measure requiring railways to adopt the use of safety appliances in the coupling of freight cars. This was one of the planks in the Populist platform of 1892. Lind said:

Not only is it competent for Congress to regulate the size of cars; it is competent for it to regulate the frequency of trains and the charges for transportation. It is competent to provide the pay of engineers who run the locomotives . . . just as we have since the organization of the government provided for the compensation of sailors on vessels under certain circumstances. We have prescribed regulations in regard to food and clothing of sailors. It is equally competent for us to make regulations as are now proposed in regard to interstate commerce. The question of expediency we are not now discussing. I do not mean to say that I am in favor of everything which may be proposed within the bounds of our constitutional power, but the legislation now proposed is constitutional; we do not want this constitutional bugbear brought up.[7]

In reply to a member who assailed his motives in supporting the bill and characterized his action as that of a self-constituted champion of labor, Lind denied that he had ever posed as such: "I have advocated what I believed to be right . . . and if I have assisted labor, that certainly was no objection to it." He was not entirely satisfied with the bill as amended by the Senate, "where there are more men interested in railroads than here," but he believed it was a good beginning in that it committed the government to the policy of preventing indiscriminate slaughter and the manufacture of cripples.[8]

[6] *Congressional Record*, 52d Congress, 1st Session, p. 132. On the same day he introduced a bill prohibiting discrimination in the interstate transportation of property by rail. He defeated, by parliamentary maneuver, an amendment giving special privileges to commercial travelers. *New Ulm Review*, March 3, 9, 1892.

[7] *Congressional Record*, 52d Congress, 2d Session, February 21, 27, 1893, pp. 1966–67, 2245.

[8] *Congressional Record*, 52d Congress, 2d Session, p. 1978.

One accomplishment of which Lind was very proud was his part in the initiation and furtherance of the movement to promote the improvement of the waterway from the head of Lake Superior by way of the Welland and St. Lawrence canals and the St. Lawrence River to the sea. In view of the importance this project has assumed in recent months, the resolution introduced by Lind on January 5, 1892, may be quoted here:

Resolved by the Senate and House of Representatives of the United States of America in Congress assembled, That the president of the United States be, and he is hereby, requested to invite negotiations with the government of the Dominion of Canada to secure the speedy improvement of the Welland and Saint Lawrence canals and the Saint Lawrence River so as to make them conform in depth and navigability, so far as practicable, to the standard adopted by the government of the United States for the improvements now in progress within the United States of the waters connecting the Great Lakes; and to that end the president is hereby authorized, if he deems expedient, to appoint three commissioners to negotiate on behalf of the United States with the representatives of the government of the Dominion of Canada the terms and conditions of any agreement which may be entered into between the two governments in pursuance of any proposition submitted in that behalf by the government of the Dominion of Canada.[9]

On Lind's motion the resolution was referred to the Committee on Interstate and Foreign Commerce; and on February 8, 1892, on behalf of that committee, he submitted a favorable report.[10] The committee believed it was time to take proper steps to secure a deep-water outlet for the commerce originating in the states bordering on and tributary to these waters. The report asserted that the impracticability of deepening or improving the Erie Canal to admit the passage of ocean-going crafts was admitted on all sides. In the St. Lawrence River nature had provided an outlet that needed comparatively little improvement to make the Great Lakes as available to the commerce of the

[9] *Congressional Record*, 52d Congress, 1st Session, p. 132.
[10] House Report no. 185, 52d Congress, 1st Session.

world as they were to the internal commerce of the United States and Canada.

A similar resolution was introduced by Senator Vilas of Wisconsin and adopted, thus paving the way for the appointment of the Deep Waterways Board. The desire on the part of the West for an outlet to the sea persisted, and the Great Lakes–St. Lawrence Tidewater Association, with executive offices at Duluth, was organized. In later life Lind maintained an interest in this project. He corresponded with Charles P. Craig, the executive director of the Tidewater Association, who expressed himself as sensible of the honor of helping to carry into effect the "idea of so distinguished a Minnesotan." [11] He also urged the importance of the project upon Senator Frank B. Kellogg, who responded favorably to his communication and assured him that he himself and Senator Lenroot of Wisconsin had been the leading men to push it against the opposition of New England and the eastern states. [12]

In a letter to Craig on August 27, 1924, Lind dealt caustically with the millers who denounced the scheme. "It has always been the misfortune of society that when it undertook to establish a new trade route, it invariably stepped on the toes of somebody who enjoyed a monopoly or private graft under conditions as they existed." He granted that it was difficult for a miller to see the advantage he had enjoyed slipping out of his hand; but he could not shut his eyes to the fact that there were almost as many people interested in farming as there were dollars interested in milling.

Seriously in the case of the miller, the opening of the waterway would indirectly at least be a blessing to him as well as to the rest of us, though it may appear now as a menace. If he would stop to reflect (if he can reflect), he would appreciate that if Minneapolis or Duluth or any other lake port should want cargoes of coffee or other products from distant shores, he would get outward rates on his flour that he cannot possibly get now.

[11] Craig to Lind, September 4, 1824.
[12] Kellogg to Lind, November 30, 1921.

Early in 1926 Lind was invited to address a meeting of the Great Lakes–St. Lawrence Tidewater Association in St. Paul, but to his regret was unable to do so because of an accident that had befallen him a few days before. By a rising vote the one thousand delegates from fourteen states expressed their regrets at his absence and acknowledged the indebtedness of the movement to his pioneer efforts of more than thirty years before.[13]

About a year before his death, Lind occupied a seat on the stage of the Garrick Theater in St. Paul at a meeting sponsored by the Ramsey County Democratic Club, where Senator Thomas J. Walsh of Montana made a ringing plea for support of the waterway. Walsh recited the history of the movement and expressed regret that it had not evoked the sustained interest of those most directly affected, though more than twenty states had indorsed it by resolutions of their legislatures and had leagued themselves in the Great Lakes–St. Lawrence Tidewater Association.[14]

Contemporaneously with the disappearance of free lands and the rise of Populism arose the agitation to restrict immigration and to abandon the free-handed, laissez faire policy of the nineteenth century. In the early nineties three main proposals as to the method of restriction were before Congress: (1) a head tax, (2) a literacy test, and (3) consular inspection. Only the second appealed to Lind. He believed consular inspection would defeat the purpose of restriction, namely, to secure a better class of immigrants. Those who make the best citizens, he said, are the young men who wish to escape military service; consular inspection would advertise that fact and cause measures to be taken in the country of origin to prevent emigration. He favored the literacy test as the best guarantee of a favorably selective emigration from Germany, Sweden, Norway, Denmark, England, France, and Ireland. He suggested that every immigrant should

[13] Craig to Lind, December 1, 1925, January 9, 1926; Lind to Craig, February 6, 1926; A. D. Moreaux to Lind, January 8, 1926.
[14] The meeting was held on August 30, 1929. Walsh's address is published in full in the *Minneapolis Tribune* of August 31, 1929. In 1934 the Senate rejected the treaty submitted by President Roosevelt.

be compelled to write a brief history of himself, stating where he came from and where he intended to go and answering all questions with reference to nativity and health. A copy of this should be filed in the office of the secretary of state, and the immigrant should be required to present another copy to the officer to whom he made application for citizenship.[15]

Some thirty years later, when racial antagonism was boiling furiously and the country was agitated by the alleged menace of foreigners, and when it appeared that drastic immigration restriction was about to become a reality, Lind as a "hyphenate" set down on paper his observations on the problem of immigration — conclusions which he had arrived at as a congressman and which, as he said, had stood the test of time.

My parents knew no language except their own (Swedish) but they were not illiterate. They had grown up under a system of public schools and compulsory training. When they reached our state and found a similar system in operation they felt at home in that respect. There was no question mark in their minds on the subject of public schools. Many relatives of my parents arrived about the same time. Their attitude on the subject of popular state education was the same as that of my parents. The older immigrants of that period have passed away. Their descendants have entered into the life and activities of our state as part and parcel of our population. In name they are still "Swedes" especially outside the state, but not in allegiance. They have perpetuated the tradition of descent and ancestry in some degree but these traditions are weakening. Cousins on my mother's side have intermarried with descendants of Welsh, German, French, Norwegian and Anglo-Saxon immigrants. . . . Now the term "hyphenate" except when used to designate "Anglo-Saxon" descent implies a certain degree of opprobrium. . . . Circumstances over which the great mass of hyphenates have no control are responsible for this condition. The great majority of them do not take the matter to heart, they regard it as a mere appellation, like "gophers," "badgers" or "suckers.". . . I am entirely reconciled to the designation in [this] sense, but if the term is to stand for illiteracy, opposition to our public schools and inability to coalesce in

[16] *New Ulm Review*, February 8, 1893.

American life and ideals then the application of the term to citizens situated as are the great majority of the people of this state is a manifest injustice.

He favored the literacy test because it was the only practical one that had been suggested that was just to the immigrant as well as to America. He admitted that ability to read and write was no test of either economic or moral efficiency in an individual, but denied that it was not a test as applied to a nationality or a class. "Our whole system of government, state and national, is predicated on the intelligence and political efficiency of the individual," he wrote. "Illiteracy and ignorance are not synonymous, but illiteracy and political inefficiency are."

But it is not the illiterate condition of the individual immigrant that constitutes the menace; his illiteracy could be overcome, if not in his case, in the next generation. . . . If he settles in a community where his race or nationality dominates this attitude is encouraged by his spiritual leaders and we have in that community not only illiteracy but a hostile belligerent spirit of opposition to our public schools that it may take many generations to overcome. . . . Our state on the whole is exempt from these deplorable conditions. . . . We have a few plague spots, however, that illustrate the untoward conditions which I have outlined and I regret to say that there has been little improvement in the nearly half century that I have observed them.[16]

Lind lived to see the enactment of the drastic percentage law of 1924 and the still more drastic national origins provision that became effective in 1929. In 1925 he wrote, "Immigration has in a manner ceased — for which I am thankful." [17]

As a member of the Committee on the Post Office Lind gave postal matters considerable study and came to the conclusion that very little advancement had been made in the facilities for handling mail during the last quarter of a century. On Lind's recommendation Postmaster-General Wanamaker decided to

[16] From an uncorrected draft of an undated document that may have been delivered as a speech. It was written between 1914 and 1916.
[17] Lind to Dr. Mayo, September 21, 1925.

make a test of the free delivery system in the village of Fairmont in 1891. Lind was of the opinion that unless the next
Democratic Congress was possessed with a mistaken streak of
economy, all towns of the size of New Ulm would be given
free delivery. He also predicted that within the next fifteen
years the system would be extended to the rural districts.[18]

He introduced an amendment to the post office appropriations
bill providing that the government should furnish a stamped
envelope for the price of the stamp. He favored the reduction
of the rate from two cents to one cent, the elimination of the
postal card, and the regulation by law of the size of envelopes in
order to get uniformity — one size for legal cap and another for
notepaper. Once this was accomplished, "some Yankee could
invent a machine through which these letters could be run and
come out all stamped and ready for transmission." "The idea of
a man standing before a pile of 2,000 or 3,000 letters and cir-
culars and pounding each one with an old stamp is a hideous
thing for me to contemplate," he said, "and a still worse sight is
an old man trudging about a city with a pack of mail that would
weigh down a Jew peddler, while the time he made in his distribution of mail would fall below the peddler." [19]

The free envelope proposal met with the disapproval of a
number of newspapers. It was stigmatized as a species of class
legislation and as an interference by the government in private
business which would destroy the business of people engaged in
the manufacture of envelopes. It was argued that the government might just as legitimately furnish its customers with free
stamps, free ink, and free pens.[20]

On the eve of the presidential election of 1892 Lind was appointed by the Democratic speaker as a minority member of a
select committee to investigate the Pension Office. The commissioner of pensions, Green B. Raum, had been appointed by

[18] *New Ulm Review,* April 8, 1891.
[19] *New Ulm Review,* December 21, 1892.
[20] Clipping in the Lind Papers; *St. Paul Pioneer Press,* quoted in the *New
Ulm Review,* December 14, 1892; *Mankato Daily Free Press,* December 10,
1892.

President Harrison. He had appointed his son, Green B. Raum, Jr., as chief clerk of the Pension Office and acting chief of the Appointment Office. The majority report declared Raum, Sr., incompetent and corrupt and recommended his removal. Lind wrote the minority report, which avowed that General Raum had inherited certain difficulties and abuses that had grown up under his predecessor; that certain employees who were not loyal to Raum had furnished false information to the newspapers in order to discredit him, and had therefore been dismissed. Lind praised Raum for introducing and perfecting reforms in business methods, and criticized the majority for failing to hold a meeting of the entire committee to discuss and weigh the evidence. "Nothing in our judgment but the supposed necessities and exigencies of an impending political campaign can account for the action and report of the majority," was the verdict contained in Lind's report. In the process of taking testimony Lind was a keen and sarcastic questioner and sometimes made witnesses wince.[21]

The retirement of John Lind from Congress and from public life at the close of his third term would be difficult to explain were it not for the unimpeachable character of the documents that give his reasons. In spite of the unpopularity of the Harrison administration and Lind's dissatisfaction with it, there was every reason for him to expect renomination and re-election. He had grown in political stature; he had won the respect of his associates in Washington; he was the ranking minority member of the powerful Committee on Interstate and Foreign Commerce; and he had committed no serious mistakes.

Politicians are given to rationalizations in explaining or justifying their conduct, and there is no reason to suppose that Lind was exceptional in that respect. Neither is there reason for the historian to doubt the truth of what he wrote to his son thirty years after the event. "My constituents were well satisfied with

[21] *Report of the Select Committee of the House of Representatives, Investigating the Methods and Management and Practices of the Bureau of Pensions, under Resolution of the 10th Day of February, 1892* (House Report no. 1868, 52d Congress, 1st Session, serial nos. 3049, 3050, Washington, 1892).

my work. I quit Congress so as to save my law practice. I did not want to become a pauper dependent on politics for a living." [22]

The announcement of his retirement was made public in the spring of 1891, before the Congress to which he had been elected convened. It was conveyed by a special dispatch from Duluth and published in the *Minneapolis Journal* of May 18, 1891. Senator Frank A. Day of Fairmont was quoted as saying: "Lind is entirely out of politics. I dined with him only a few days ago and he told me that he would never enter politics again because he had all he wanted of public life. . . . It will be no use to try to run him for governor, for I am positive he would not accept the nomination. His wife and family are urgent in their requests that he should return to private life and he has promised to do so." Fred W. Johnson, a close friend of Lind and the editor of the *New Ulm Review*, appended the statement that he had talked with the congressman in regard to the Day interview and had learned that all he had to say was that for the present he was out of politics. Johnson added the significant comment that the expression on his face was full of meaning and did not indicate by any means that the present was going to last any great length of time. [23]

Further light on the Duluth interview is shed by a letter from Lind to L. P. Hunt of the *Mankato Free Press*, dated June 3, 1891. In it Lind stated that he had not seen the original interview, but some of the comments that had come to his notice were such that he felt in duty bound to report what had passed between him and Day in order that no injustice be done to the latter. "On my return from Washington I met Mr. Day at the Merchants Hotel in St. Paul," he said. "In the course of our conversation I stated to him that I would not be a candidate for any office at the close of my present term, and that I had determined to withdraw from politics, so far as seeking or accepting

[22] Lind to John Lind, Jr., September 15, 1921.
[23] *New Ulm Review*, May 20, 1891. Mr. Johnson kindly accorded the author an interview on October 10, 1931.

any office was concerned, for some years to come. While the above was said privately, it was in no sense confidential and I need hardly add that it was said seriously and in sincerity." To this the editor of the *New Ulm Review* added the comment that it was fully in keeping with what Lind had repeatedly said to him.[24]

About the middle of the following July Lind was in Duluth and confirmed the report of his retirement. "I shall retire from politics for the present. I am yet a comparatively young man, and it would be looking too far into the future to say that I shall retire from politics permanently. I do not want, nor will I accept, any public office when my present term in Congress expires."[25]

The Day interview called forth many comments in the press of the state expressing regret that Minnesota was to lose the services of a man of such commanding ability, pure character, and fidelity to duty. The following letter from Frank J. Mead, Washington correspondent of the *St. Paul Daily News*, is representative:

From various and sundry signs it is evident that Hon. John Lind actually desires to retire to the shady walks of private life at the expiration of his present term in Congress. He wants to plow the furrow and draw the elusive brief. Bucolic pursuits for physical exercise intermingled with the practice of law for intellectual motion is what he personally desires. Therefore he is not a candidate for governor in the sense of seeking the nomination, or even of saying to any friend that he would like to be elected.

But there are also evidences that Mr. Lind would not peremptorily decline to be the Republican candidate for governor if the convention, when assembled, shall consider that he was the man who could best lead the party to victory in the North Star state.[26]

[24] *New Ulm Review*, June 10, 1891.

[25] *New Ulm Review*, July 29, 1891. In its issue for September 9 the same paper reported an interview Lind gave the *St. Paul Pioneer Press* upon his return from a trip to the Pacific Coast in which he made a statement to the same effect.

[26] *St. Paul Daily News*, February 28, 1892.

William W. Folwell on October 1, 1892, wrote to Lind that he did not know whether or not he ought to congratulate him on getting out of politics, because he had rendered a great deal of valuable service and had never been so well qualified to act the part of legislator.

The editor of the *Rock County Herald*, in a long editorial eulogizing the New Ulm statesman, concluded with the following prophecy, which was signally fulfilled but in a manner that neither editor, politician, nor John Lind could foresee.

Much as he may desire to remain in private life, it is morally certain that he will not be permitted to do so. The public interests need and demand such men as John Lind, and the call to higher responsibilities, which he cannot well refuse to obey, will come to him in the near future.

VII

FROM REPUBLICANISM TO FUSION, 1892–1895

WHEN John Lind made his surprising decision to retire, he not only was regarded as a sound Republican but he *was* a sound Republican, notwithstanding the fact that, like thousands of others, he made little effort to conceal his dislike for Benjamin Harrison. He publicly stated his preference for James G. Blaine.[1] There was at that time no reason why he should favor the Democratic party; there was nothing in its record in Congress that would cause him to think that the fortunes of the country were safer in Democratic hands. Cleveland's latest biographer says, "For the discontented agrarian interest between the Wabash and the Platte, the grain-growing farmers who intermittently hummed like a hive of angry bees, the administration did little." [2] There was as yet nothing unorthodox in his preference for free coinage of silver and his vote for the Silver Purchase Act. It was a Republican measure and passed both houses by a strict party vote. Minnesota Republican conventions had adopted silver planks, and such leading Republicans as Senator Cushman K. Davis had paid just as glowing tribute to the Silver Purchase Act as had John Lind.[3]

The Populist party had been formally launched at a great mass convention in Cincinnati in May, 1891, but the uncertainties of a third party did not at that time appeal to a man with

[1] Interview in the *New Ulm Review*, July 29, 1891; Lind to Knute Nelson, March 22, 1892, in the Nelson Papers.

[2] Allan Nevins, *Grover Cleveland* (New York, 1933), p. 361. Quoted by permission from the publisher, Dodd, Mead, and Company.

[3] James H. Baker, *Lives of the Governors of Minnesota* (St. Paul, 1908), pp. 382–83. Lind voted against free coinage bills from 1891 to 1893 because he believed the Silver Purchase Act should be given a fair trial. *New Ulm Review*, March 2, 1892.

Lind's background. He had seen the Farmers' Alliance at close range; most of its members were Republicans. He was in sympathy with a number of their ideas, but, as his analysis of the causes of the political overturn of 1890 shows, he had little faith in the effectiveness of the Alliance as a political party.

If there had been anything seriously heretical in his record, it is inconceivable that his name would have been prominently mentioned for the Republican nomination for the governorship and even for a seat in the United States Senate.

The quality of Lind's Republicanism and his attitude toward the Farmers' Alliance at the time of his retirement from office may be judged by two public addresses. In a Fourth of July address at Sherburne in 1891 he said that he had no respect for the calamity orator, but the fact of the existence of the Alliance movement, embracing thousands of intelligent, sincere, and patriotic men who were dissatisfied with existing conditions and were honestly seeking a remedy, merited careful and candid scrutiny.[4] He recited the conditions that had given rise to the movement in Dakota and then launched upon the money question. He asserted that the notion that the quantity of money fixed the rate of interest was fallacious and dangerous. "A dollar of money represents an aliquot portion of the wealth of the country," he said. "The larger the number of dollars, the smaller the portion each represents. . . . Hence the aggregate amount of money affects the rate of interest but slightly and if at all it is usually in the opposite direction to that contended for by some of our Alliance orators." What was needed, he said, was a dollar that represented and measured as much property in the fall of the year as it had in the spring. His concluding thought was that what had led the farmers to join the Alliance movement was neither poverty nor want but their settled conviction that those who carried and handled their products got an unfair share of the profits. But this state of affairs, he said, could never be adjusted by any single class of citizens.

In addressing the Blue Earth Agricultural Society on Septem-

[4] Manuscript in the Lind Papers.

ber 23, 1892, on the question "Why Do Farmers' Sons and Daughters Flock to the City?" Lind expressed his belief that the cause underlying the migration of thousands from Europe to America was also to some extent the cause of migration from country to city — the desire to get a better living. He believed that for twenty years the chances for success had been better in the city than in the country. This he attributed to the changed conditions brought about by the invention and introduction of agricultural machinery and to some extent to the opening of vast areas of new and fertile lands. Population and the consumption of foodstuffs had increased, but not sufficiently to make up for the change. On the other hand, there was scarcely any limit to the consumption of manufactured articles. The consumption of food was limited by the capacity of stomachs; the consumption of industrial products was limited only by desires, tastes, and means. There was no limit to the consumption of industrial products and luxuries except the inability to buy, and there was absolutely no limit to production. "It will continue to increase, and cease only when the very bowels of the earth have been 'turned inside out,' the elements have lost their properties and the human brain and hands their cunning."

Lind was nevertheless of the opinion that a state of equilibrium had been reached; that the cities had ceased to grow at the expense of the country population. Labor was scarcer on the farms than in the cities; on the whole the price of agricultural products had ceased to fall; the area of new lands capable of cultivation was beginning to be circumscribed. The limit of production was in sight, except as it might be increased by scientific methods of farming, which would not do much more than enable production to keep pace with population. Farming had seen its low tide; labor was more remunerative on the farm than in the city.

The rest of the address was devoted to possible means of stemming the tide of migration from rural to urban communities. The advantages of rural life as contrasted with the lot of the city dweller were portrayed: fresh air, freedom of movement, easier work, fewer temptations, and better moral environment. The advantages of the city lay in social intercourse, entertainment, and intellectual satisfaction. In order to supply these deficiencies in the country, a spirit of rivalry among the young people should be encouraged. Every township should have a good town hall, with a kitchen and dining room, where meetings of all sorts could be held. It would be just the place for holding "spelling down" contests, for debating and singing societies, and for Alliance meetings. The band could meet for practice, and oyster suppers and fairs might be additional attractions. Concerts and plays could be given. The park should have a baseball diamond and a small track for training colts.

Boys could be interested in raising flowers and planting shrubbery, vines, orchards, and trees, in cultivating a pride in fine corn, choice grain, and a love for domestic animals. If a boy was fond of chickens, he should be given a dollar or two for eggs with which to experiment with new varieties. "Don't lock up your tools against him unless he has some of his own. Make the girl think that she can beat her mamma in cooking some particular dish, and she will soon excel in cooking many." Farmers should let their sons and daughters have Saturday afternoons to themselves regularly, just as employers in the city are compelled to give their employees a weekly half-holiday.

You say you could not get your work done in shorter hours. So did the manufacturers. But they found themselves mistaken. . . . I firmly believe that your experience would be the same on the farm. If field work were commenced regularly at 7:30 with an hour and a half at noon, to end promptly at 5:30, you would see better results on the farm. It is not hard work but endless work that kills. The same is true of cares and responsibilities such as woman's. It is not the great trials that break her down. It is the thousand little cares and worries that constantly weigh on and worry her mind that often make the farmer's wife break down. . . . Every step you save her, every unnecessary care and worry you keep from her will save her strength and add to the happiness of the family. Inventions and machinery have done little for her. The sewing machine and the clothes wringer is about all she can boast of. You can save her many steps and much care by having a good cellar and a good sized and well arranged kitchen with a sink and hot and cold water. Pressure can be secured by having a small tank above the kitchen and pumping it full once a week.

This speech brought congratulatory letters from such distinguished Minnesotans as William W. Folwell and Senator Cushman K. Davis. Dr. Folwell thought Lind was "very sound on the matter" and expressed the hope that he was correct in the suggestion that farming had touched its low-water mark. The senator thought he had contributed a new idea about the limit of food production and the illimitability of the production of manufactured articles. "Your explanation of the causes which have impelled the youth from the country to the city is the best I have seen," he said.[5]

It seems clear that at the time the Farmers' Alliance movement was at its height and the Populist party was getting under way, Lind was in an optimistic frame of mind and took little stock in legislation as a cure-all for the ills that beset the man who followed the plow and tended the machine. In reply to a farmer who asked him if it was true, as some Democrats alleged, that the McKinley Tariff was responsible for the Homestead strike, a bloody contest between labor and capital in the steel works near Pittsburgh, he replied: "Yes, the tariff is responsible for the Homestead strike just the same as the farmers are responsible for potato bugs; you grow potatoes and this gives the bugs something to live and thrive upon; if you raised no potatoes, there would be no bugs. The tariff encourages and fosters manufactories; take away the tariff and there would be no factories; and if there were no such great industries, there would be no strikes."[6] This was just such an answer as might have been given by William McKinley himself.

At this stage of his career Lind gave vent to aspersions on the Democrats such as were the stock in trade of Civil War Republicans. They were to plague him in the years to come. He be-

<hr />

[5] Folwell to Lind, October 1, 1892; Davis to Lind, November 11, 1892.
[6] *New Ulm Review*, December 21, 1892.

lieved, or pretended to believe, that there was no possibility of fusion of Democrats and Alliance people in Minnesota. The Democrats, he said, favored a "let alone" policy in legislation and adhered to the English idea of a single gold standard. The Alliance, on the other hand, believed with the Republicans that federal and state governments were not mere police bureaus to keep the peace but agencies through which the people ought to guard and protect the economic and social interests of the whole body.[7]

While there is no reason to doubt that Lind refused the nomination for the Fifty-third Congress in the interest of his law practice, there is reason for thinking that his disgust with the Harrison administration, and with the Merriam administration and state politics in general, were contributing factors. It is also true that he had had a narrow escape in his third campaign. Yet in 1892 his political fences were in good repair; his following had increased measurably since 1890. The fact of the matter is that on occasion he showed an amazing indifference to his own political fortunes. This may have been due in part to an independence that sometimes took the form of contempt, thinly concealed, if concealed at all, for his political associates. In private conversation he was outspoken in airing his opinions of members of the political fraternity. Up to this time, however, his public utterances were usually guarded, probably because as between the politicians he had to deal with in Washington he preferred the Republican. He saw red every time he thought of Tammany Hall and its chieftains and braves. If he ever had an admiration for that "man of courage," Grover Cleveland, there is no record of it.

In praising the plain-spoken, blunt, courageous president, historians have often forgotten that there were others equally plain spoken and courageous who differed from his policies because they were convinced that he was "in bad company" and had a narrow vision of social justice. Cleveland could be obtuse and stubborn and sometimes fatally wrong-headed. It was

[7] *New Ulm Review*, March 23, 1892.

courageous of him to take the tariff by the horns in 1887, to demand the repeal of the Silver Purchase Act in 1893, to protect the gold reserve, to veto the Dependent Pensions Bill, and to bring the United States and Great Britain to the brink of war over Venezuela. But it was equally courageous for his opponents to run the risk of political oblivion, to look Wall Street straight in the eye, and to denounce the money sharks who feared neither of the dominant elements in the major parties. Lind was a crusader in behalf of the politically ineffective element in the population, the people whose influence usually carried no further than the election clerks.

We may turn now to the political situation in Minnesota in 1892. In the late winter of that year public sentiment on the subject of the Republican nomination for the governorship appeared to be crystallizing around three men — Knute Nelson of Alexandria, John Lind of New Ulm, and Gideon S. Ives of St. Peter — Nelson and Lind standing better chances than Ives. Nelson's strength was in the northern part of the state; the Lind and Ives followers divided the southern part.[8] Although Lind had said repeatedly that he was not a candidate for any office, the governorship bait was tempting; and if the nomination had come without effort on his part, he would have accepted it. His election would have been practically certain. His independence and aloofness from the factions that divided the Republican party would have insured a united party in the campaign, in which the prospects for Republican success appeared to be none too good. He was treated in a flattering manner by his fellow Republicans, who were anxious to draw him out on the governorship. To all these inquiries he replied that he was not a candidate, had never thought seriously of being one, and would not be one under any circumstances. He studiously refrained from giving public expression in favor of any candidate, but it was suspected that Nelson was his man.[9]

[8] *St. Paul Pioneer Press*, quoted in the *New Ulm Review*, March 16, 1892.
[9] Interview in the *Minneapolis Tribune*, printed in the *New Ulm Review*, May 11, 1892. The *New Ulm Review*, April 27, 1892, printed statements by about thirty prominent New Ulm citizens favoring Lind's nomination.

In the meantime Knute Nelson was playing a shrewd game. His interests were furthered by several astute politicians, including Robert C. Dunn of the *Princeton Union*.[10] There was, however, a great deal of talk that his Republicanism was not sound — that he was too much of a free trader and that his course in Congress had not come up to the expectations of Republican leaders.[11] On the other hand, in the event of his nomination the fact that the Democrats had said nice things about him would be a source of strength to the ticket. There was prejudice against him because of his foreign birth, but this was offset by the probability that he would draw back into the fold the Scandinavians who had gone into the Farmers' Alliance.[12] It was not a secret that no love was lost between the Washburn and the Nelson interests. Washburn feared Nelson and tried to cultivate him. In a letter to Nelson, dated April 10, 1892, which was prompted by an interview with Nelson published in the *Pioneer Press*, the senator expressed great surprise and wondered "what in the world" had led Nelson to say about him what he was reported as having said. He denied that he had ever been unfriendly to Nelson or jealous of him, and stated that either someone had lied to him or he was a victim of morbid suspicion without the slightest cause.[13] The Alexandria statesman was also unpopular in the McGill camp.[14] A certain element among the reformers in the Republican party did not approve of Nelson's coming out publicly for Merriam and "his monied gang" in 1890. They preferred Lind, who was immune to "ring dictation."[15] If Lind had chosen to make a bid for the gubernatorial nomination, Minnesota might well have been the

[10] Letters in the Nelson Papers. See especially Dunn to Nelson, March 8, 1892.

[11] "I believe in a tariff for revenue only. I think I am alone in that position among our entire delegation." Nelson to Gudmund F. Johnson, January 7, 1884, in the Nelson Papers.

[12] William Bickel to Nelson, August 18, 1892, in the Nelson Papers.

[13] Nelson Papers. See also letters from Washburn, August 10, 1892, and from Charles A. Pillsbury, May 6, 12, 1892.

[14] Nelson to H. G. Stordock, March 21, 1892, in the Nelson Papers.

[15] Stordock to Nelson, March 19, 1892, in the Nelson Papers.

arena of a battle royal between the "little giant" and "Honest John."

The personal relations between the two most distinguished Scandinavians in the state appeared to be harmonious, though Nelson was jealous of his rights and suspicious of the motives of others. They had served together in Congress from 1887 to 1889 and, according to Lind, their relations were pleasant.[16] At the time of Nelson's voluntary retirement from Congress, however, rumors were abroad that all was not well. The *St. Paul Globe*, which was friendly, or pretended to be friendly, to Nelson because of his vote for the Mills bill, and which was more than willing to sow discord in Republican ranks, quoted a "gentleman well posted on official life in Washington" as saying that Nelson had suffered severely from the indirect discourtesies aimed at him by three of his Minnesota colleagues — Senators Davis and Sabin and Congressman Lind. According to all congressional courtesies, he said, Lind should have come to Nelson for direction in his official course, since he was the senior representative. Instead he ignored him and ran "under the coattails of Sabin and Davis for protection." The gentleman could not vouch for the statement, but he had heard that the only comment Nelson had ever passed on the trio was, "Davis has too big a head to perceive his own littleness; no man fears Sabin who knows him, and as for Lind — well, he is ignorant and can't help it."[17]

The letters written by Lind to Nelson in 1892 tell a somewhat different story. On March 22 he wrote from Washington that he had seen it reported in the papers that Nelson was contemplating a trip to Norway, in the event of which there would be no opportunity for them to meet. He therefore felt in duty bound to write in order to explain certain matters. He assured Nelson that whatever impression he may have had, there had never been a moment since he had first learned to know him that he had entertained an aspiration inimical to his interests.

[16] Lind to Folwell, September 17, 1923.
[17] Clipping in the Lind Papers.

It is the dictate of my judgment and pride as a Scandinavian quite as much as the result of the personal regard I have always entertained for you. Both of us have had obstacles to overcome that we alone can appreciate. We have many things in common. Both of us are burdened to a certain extent not only with the responsibility of our individual success, but by reason of the peculiarity of our situation with maintaining and furthering the good name of a great people in a strange land. . . . We cannot afford to stand in each other's way and I don't propose to be in yours.

He then went on to say that Nelson might have inferred from the "silly effusions" in the press that he desired the nomination for governor; but he assured him that he was not seeking it, did not want it, and would not accept it if tendered in opposition to him. "If you are not a candidate, and do not want it, I am not prepared to say that I would refuse the nomination if tendered me. If you want it I am at your service and will state my position publicly so as to prevent the possible use of my name to 'club' you. If you do not desire the nomination I should be glad to know it so as to govern myself accordingly."

The *Minneapolis Tribune*, which was unfriendly to Nelson, played up Lind's proposed nomination as a master stroke and reported that inquiries were pouring in from parties who were desirous of knowing his wishes and were enrolling themselves among his adherents. With reference to this Lind expressed himself to Nelson as follows:

The mention of my name in the Minneapolis Tribune is not out of love for me. I have no love for Harrison's administration which fact I have not concealed. It may have been thought that any special activity on my part would be unpleasant as the convention is held in our state. To head me off and tickle me into "innocuous desuetude" the Tribune as the administration organ has several times put my name in big type as a candidate for governor. I may not know much about politics but I do not bite on a hook for gudgeons. The two cities are not crying for either of us to be the gubernatorial candidates.[18]

[18] This letter is in the Nelson Papers. The Republican national convention which renominated Harrison was held in Minneapolis.

Lind may or may not have divined the true motive of the *Tribune* in booming him for governor, but it is a fact that the Twin City papers were not happy over the prospect of having to plead the cause of the "little Norwegian" as the Republican nominee for governor and undoubtedly preferred to sing the praises of "Honest John." It is equally true that people who did not like Nelson were attracted to Lind. For one thing, Minneapolis and St. Paul had a monopoly of the two senators from the state, and it was strongly suspected that in his quest for the governorship Nelson was looking for bigger game. In order to weaken Nelson's chances and to destroy the Nelson-Merriam alliance, a man from the country districts was the best bet, and none was better than Lind. The *Tribune* published a report that Merriam and Lind had formed a coalition, but in a private letter from one of his supporters Nelson was assured that there was nothing whatever in it.[19] There was no doubt, however, that the anti-Nelson forces were concentrating on Lind; and if both Washburn and Davis joined hands, Lind might be forced into the game in spite of himself.[20] To divide the Swedes and Norwegians was another consideration.[21]

Notwithstanding the temptations that were dangled before his eyes and the machinations of the politicians, which perhaps even Lind did not fathom, there is no reason to doubt that he was "Honest John" when he stated his position to Nelson. One of Nelson's strongest supporters, S. E. Olson, a Minneapolis merchant prince and a mutual friend of the two Scandinavian politicians, informed Nelson in a letter of February 26, 1892, that sometime in 1890, Lind, while staying in his home, had given him "positive assurances" that he would loyally support Nelson in the event that he desired the gubernatorial nomination in 1892 and even pledged himself to deliver the delegation from the second district. In a private conversation at his home

[19] *Minneapolis Tribune*, April 11, 1892; S. E. Olson to Nelson, April 12, 1892, in the Nelson Papers.
[20] S. E. Olson to Nelson, March 3, 1892, and M. O. Hall to Nelson, May 9, 1892, in the Nelson Papers.
[21] M. O. Hall to Nelson, April 15, 1892, in the Nelson Papers.

in Washington in January, 1892, he "practically confirmed" what he had said on the previous occasion. Olson reminded Nelson that he had once expressed himself as fearful that if he ever permitted his name to come out, he would encounter serious opposition from Washburn and his brigade of "high joints." Olson assured him that there was nothing to fear from that source. On May 11, 1892, Olson told Nelson that Lind was positively out of the race and was openly advocating his nomination.[22]

Testimony to the same effect came to Nelson from M. O. Hall of Duluth.[23] He made it a point to see Lind immediately upon his arrival from Washington to attend the Republican state convention. A year earlier he had corresponded with Lind urging him to become a candidate for governor, but he had positively refused, and on the present occasion he sought to draw him out with reference to Nelson. Lind was the most sought-after man at the convention, but Nelson's friends, according to Hall, "got in their work on him." Hall sent Albert Berg of Chisago County, Peter G. Peterson of Nicollet County, Alfred Söderström, Joseph E. Osborn, and C. A. Smith of Hennepin County, and Soren Listoe of Ramsey County to buttonhole Lind, and to each he promised that he would not be a candidate and would support Nelson. Peterson and Lind were old personal friends, and Peterson assured Hall that Lind's word was good. On May 21, 1892, Hall jubilantly reported to Nelson that upon his return to Washington Lind had stated in an interview that the contest had narrowed down to Nelson and Ives. "Good for Lind!" he added.

Upon his return to Washington Lind wrote Nelson in reply to a letter which had arrived during his absence. He stated that when he had passed through Minneapolis on May 16, he had not had time to stop over. He felt, moreover, that for Nelson and him to have been seen together at that time might have given rise to talk. He expressed regret that Nelson did not attend

<hr>

[22] Nelson Papers.
[23] Letters of May 9 and 21, 1892, in the Nelson Papers.

the convention, because he would have received royal treatment and an enthusiastic reception. He took occasion to do some scolding, he said, because as a free lance he could afford to indulge in luxuries. The rest of the letter is significant.

> I hardly know what you refer to in your letter. There was *nothing* I wanted at the state convention. I accept your assurances of confidence with pleasure, but want you to feel, however, that I have never imagined that I had any grievance against you. On the contrary I have had none but the kindliest feelings toward you — except in respect of one thing: When I stepped up to your desk in the House and told you that Washburn had been nominated, you gave an answer that "cut to the quick." It did me a grievous injustice and I smarted under it for some time. I shall never think of it again and I trust that explanations will never be in order in the future.[24]

This letter is significant for two reasons: It confirms the rumor of friction or coolness between Lind and Nelson reported by the *Globe's* Washington correspondent; and it is most illuminating in view of what happened in the famous Washburn-Nelson senatorial contest of 1895. There must have been something about Lind that repelled Nelson. In spite of letters from Lind offering most cordial support, Nelson insisted on keeping old sores open. Fundamentally the two men were different. Lind's methods were direct and open; Nelson was the shrewd politician with a finesse that Lind never acquired. Nelson made use of his nationality in a way that Lind never did. In their early political careers Nelson was more independent than Lind; but while Nelson was becoming more and more regular, Lind was tending toward independence.

After Nelson's nomination Lind wrote a very friendly letter extending his congratulations and assuring him that his time and best efforts were at his service. He kept his promise and made speeches in his behalf, as well as in behalf of the Harrison-Reid ticket.[25] Nelson's opponents were Daniel W. Lawler, the Demo-

[24] Lind to Nelson, May 28, 1892, in the Nelson Papers.
[25] Lind to Nelson, July 29, 1892, in the Nelson Papers. See the *New Ulm Review*, October 5, 1892.

cratic nominee, and Ignatius Donnelly, the Populist candidate. Nelson's plurality over Lawler was almost 15,000. It was in this campaign that the Populist party, with Weaver as its presidential candidate, startled the country by polling over a million popular votes and twenty-two electoral votes.

From January 4, 1893, to January 31, 1895, Knute Nelson was governor of Minnesota. It was a stormy period. Lind practiced law in New Ulm and kept in touch with politics as a bystander who must have had many battles within himself in order to come to a decision as to what course he should pursue. He was by no means dead politically.

In the interval between Nelson's election and inauguration it was widely reported in the press that Lind was to be "near the head of the administration," but the reports did not agree as to what position he would occupy. Governor Nelson offered him a place on the Railroad and Warehouse Commission, but Lind declined because he could not afford to discharge the duties while he was trying to get back into harness as a practicing lawyer. He accepted the appointment to the Board of Regents of the University of Minnesota "with pleasure and appreciation." [26]

In the preconvention campaign it had been alleged that Nelson's nomination for the governorship was a step to defeat the re-election of Cushman K. Davis for the Senate in 1893. Be that as it may, it was expected that a supreme effort would be made to defeat him; and Lind came from Washington to attend the senatorial caucus in order to hold his friends in line for Davis. Lind was disgusted with what he called the "dastardly and corrupt" attempt to defeat his good friend. Senator S. D. Peterson of Brown and Redwood counties voted for Lind instead of Davis, in spite of the fact that the convention that nominated him had instructed him to vote for Davis. Peterson justified his vote for Lind on the ground that he was a man of "pure and spotless character." When Lind learned that Peterson had dis-

[26] *Minneapolis Tribune*, quoted in the *New Ulm Review*, October 28, 1892; Lind to Folwell, September 17, 1923.

regarded the instructions of the convention, he dispatched the following telegram to him: "I am advised that you voted for me. Such action, though well meant, does violence to the good faith that we both owe our party, as well as Senator Davis as a friend. I beg of you not again to embarrass me by action that will not be construed to the credit of either of us." Lind thought the victory of Davis meant a great deal not only because it assured the continuation of the services of an able senator but because it ought to awaken the conscience of the people to the necessity of electing to the legislature men of unquestioned integrity.[27] In order to make sure of Washburn's re-election in 1895, Lind and his allies saw to it that Peterson was defeated for renomination and a senator and representative pledged to Washburn were elected.

The Washburn-Nelson senatorial contest of 1895 is famous in the annals of Minnesota, but certain phases of it are clouded in obscurity. There is a hiatus from 1892 to 1898 in the Knute Nelson Papers in the Minnesota Historical Society. The most controversial incident in the senator's career is thus enshrouded in mystery, though Nelson's biographer has attempted to peer through the clouds.[28] Lind's part in the affair has also received some mention, but that has not been cleared up either.

John Lind and William D. Washburn were good friends. In 1889 Washburn defeated D. M. Sabin for re-election. Both men had solicited Lind's support. Through a mutual friend, William C. Corbett of Minneapolis, Washburn sought to cultivate closer relations with the New Ulm congressman, but at that time Lind was unresponsive, probably because he had already pledged his support to H. B. Strait of Shakopee in the event of a deadlock between Washburn and Sabin.[29]

In 1894 Knute Nelson was triumphantly re-elected governor. During the campaign it was rumored that Nelson would contest

[27] New Ulm Review, January 25, 1893; Lind to Folwell, September 17, 1923. As early as September, 1891, in an interview with the Pioneer Press, Lind had expressed the hope that Davis would be re-elected. New Ulm Review, September 9, 1891.

[28] Martin W. Odland, The Life of Knute Nelson (Minneapolis, 1926).

[29] Letter from Washburn to Lind, November 23, 1888; from Sabin, December 21, 1888; from Strait, December 28, 1888; from Corbett, January 3, 1889.

Washburn's seat, and, if successful, would resign the governor-ship. In the absence of an undisputed record of what Nelson said on a famous occasion during the campaign, it is impossible to say what his plans were. Washburn and his followers after-wards maintained that Nelson broke his promise; Nelson in-sisted that he entered the contest only after it was clear that Washburn could not be elected. Lind's version of the affair was written on September 17, 1923, twenty-eight years after the event, in response to an inquiry from William W. Folwell, who was collecting material for his *History of Minnesota*. Despite the fact that Lind's memory played him false in the matter of chronology, there is no reason to doubt that his version is sub-stantially correct as far as it goes.[30]

Lind was a member of the House when Washburn came to the Senate. He was under the impression that Washburn was an austere and unapproachable man of aristocratic tastes. He was shy of him until in the course of their official relations he came to have respect for his ability and admiration for his fear-less courage on economic and political questions. Lind knew, of course, that Washburn was prominent in railway and milling circles; that he had built the Minneapolis and St. Louis Railroad and was largely responsible for the building of the Soo Line.[31] Washburn was equally cognizant of Lind's attitude toward the railways. He knew also that Lind's name had figured as a possi-bility in case of a deadlock in 1889.

Some time after Nelson's re-election to the governorship, Professor J. S. Carlson of Gustavus Adolphus College spent an evening in the Lind home, and in the course of the conversa-tion urged Lind to become a candidate for the United States Senate. Lind became suspicious that the suggestion was not wholly prompted by Carlson's own wishes and succeeded in obtaining the admission that his visitor had come at the request of Governor Nelson. Before Carlson left, he was in no doubt

[30] A copy of this document is in the Lind Papers. The Folwell Papers are in the possession of the Minnesota Historical Society.
[31] Edgar, *The Medal of Gold*, pp. 60–61.

about Lind's attitude toward Washburn. Lind told him that he had retired from public life for personal reasons; that he liked and respected Washburn; and that his re-election was for the best interests of the state and nation. On reflection Lind became convinced that Nelson intended to become a candidate for the Senate, and the next day he wrote his resignation on the back of his commission as a member of the Board of Regents and mailed it to the governor. The sequel may be related in Lind's own words.

After the legislature had convened and it became evident that Nelson was a candidate, Senator Washburn wired me to come to St. Paul, which I did. I arrived at the Windsor Hotel early in the morning. I do not recall the date. The breakfast room was not open and I sat down in the writing room to look over the morning paper. In a few minutes I saw the senator from Redwood and the member of the House come through the hall from a little room in the rear of the office. I do not know whether they saw me; if they did they slunk away without speaking. Shortly afterwards Senator Buckman came out of the same room. I asked him how things were going and he told me that Governor Nelson would surely be elected. Within a couple of days the senatorial election was held, the two members of the legislature mentioned both voted for Nelson, and there was much talk about an investigation. Senator Buckman left for the South and as I recall it did not come back to the state during the session. Of this, however, I am not positive.

Out of the murk of the senatorial contest of 1895 at least two things are clear. Lind was in favor of Washburn's re-election and opposed to Nelson. Washburn was the Minneapolis candidate; the *Tribune* and *Journal* were bitterly opposed to the "little Norwegian." The *Pioneer Press*, edited by Joseph Wheelock, one of the most influential papers in the Northwest, leaned toward Nelson. Lind did not like this paper, as he made clear on several occasions. When Washburn's chances appeared to be hopeless, his cohorts held a meeting to decide upon a candidate who could hold the Washburn men together and attract the Populist members, as well as those who had been voting for candidates other than Washburn and Nelson. Lind was the man selected, but he gave to the press the following statement: "I have at no time entertained any proposition to be a candidate under any circumstances. That was my announced determination from the beginning of the contest, and I have never thought of abandoning it." [32]

There are several interesting angles to the senatorial battle. The man who started the landslide for Nelson was Frank A. Day of Fairmont, who, when his name was called, stated that he believed that Washburn was entitled to re-election but cast his vote for Nelson because the Washburn cause was lost. Day was a warm friend of Lind and later became his ardent supporter when Lind, like himself, deserted the Republican fold. William H. Eustis, who was to become Lind's opponent for the governorship in 1898, worked for Washburn. Lieutenant Governor Clough, who had rendered service in behalf of Washburn in 1889, "lined up the boys" for his opponent in 1895. The following year Clough, who succeeded to the governorship upon Nelson's resignation, contested the governorship with Lind, at which time the Washburn people left no stone unturned to defeat the man who had done so much to return their candidate to private life. And, curiously enough, in 1898 it was Governor Clough who urged Lind to become a candidate for governor and used his influence to defeat Eustis, whose nomination was "put across" by the anti-Clough faction. And, finally, Tams Bixby, Lind's boyhood friend from Red Wing days, was Governor Nelson's private secretary and employed every device known to the political game to build a winning team for his man. It was the same Bixby who by a trick defeated Governor Lind for re-election in 1900. [33]

What bearing the Washburn-Nelson contest had on the

[32] *Pioneer Press*, January 23, 1895. The *Pioneer Press* story was headed "Lind as Legatee" and gave the impression that Lind wanted greater assurances than the Washburn men were willing to give. The reporter may have used his imagination.

[33] For an account of the "Washburn-Nelson Senatorial Campaign," see Martin W. Odland, *The Life of Knute Nelson*, pp. 195–223, and William W. Folwell, *A History of Minnesota*, 3:489–99 (St. Paul, 1928).

political future of John Lind is impossible to determine definitely. That he was disappointed, not to say disgusted, over the outcome is a settled fact; but that it was the deciding factor which caused him to leave the Republican party, as many said at the time, cannot be proved by documentary evidence and is highly improbable. Although Lind did on occasion act on impulse, he was far too shrewd a politician and too honest with himself to make such an important decision out of personal disappointment. Moreover, the important part he had played in the senatorial contest must have shown him how powerful he was in the counsels of the Republican party, if he had had doubts about that. In October, 1896, when Lind was campaigning for the governorship on the Fusion ticket, Senator Nelson told John A. Johnson of St. Peter that if Lind had waited two years, the Republican party would have nominated him unanimously for governor.[34] It was the very certainty of Lind's future as an adherent of the Republican party that made it difficult for conventional politicians with an eye to the main chance to understand why he should have sacrificed the good things the future had in store for him as a loyal Republican. It is this very fact that suggests, if it does not prove, that his decision must have been on a higher plane than disappointment over the treatment he had received at the hands of the Republicans or the hope for better things in some other political camp. The logic of the situation compels the historian to search for other causes of Lind's defection from Republicanism — and fortunately the documents are extant.

The election of Grover Cleveland and an overwhelmingly Democratic majority in Congress in 1892 was followed shortly after Cleveland's inauguration by the panic of 1893. Only the circumstances of a shortage of wheat in Europe and a bumper crop in the United States, which converted Europe from an exporter of wheat to an importer, saved the United States from a panic before Harrison rode down Pennsylvania Avenue with Cleveland. Business failures, unemployment, declining prices,

[34] *St. Peter Herald*, October 30, 1896.

and a falling gold reserve impelled Cleveland to call a special
session of Congress to repeal the Sherman Silver Purchase Act.
The president's recommendation was carried out, but only
after a long and acrimonious debate and in the face of the bitter opposition of Silver Republicans and Silver Democrats.
The wrath of the bimetallists was centered on Cleveland, who
was denounced as the tool of Wall Street. Many of them could
indorse the sentiment of Governor John P. Altgeld of Illinois,
who said in 1895, "To laud Clevelandism on Jefferson's birthday is to sing a Te Deum in honor of Judas Iscariot on Christmas morning." [35]

Lind joined in the chorus. He believed that the repeal of the
Silver Purchase Act was the last act in the drama begun in 1873
that brought the country to its depressed condition. "The repeal was principally important to the gold advocates," he said,
"because it removes the last vestige of legislation that recognized silver as money, and to the bimetallists because it dealt
a final blow that destroyed silver as a money metal." [36]

One of the bitterest opponents of the repeal of the Silver
Purchase Act was William Jennings Bryan, then a youthful
member of the House of Representatives from Nebraska.
Lind's lifelong friendship with the eloquent Nebraskan began
when they served together in the House from December, 1891,
to March, 1893. Bryan was just entering public life, and Lind
was shortly to retire. They became well acquainted when Bryan
cooperated with Lind in the passage of the automatic coupler
legislation — an acquaintance pregnant with great events in the
life of the Minnesotan, one of them many years in the future,
when the Great Commoner was secretary of state. [37]

Bryan's sense of social and economic justice, his fight in behalf of the "under dog," his brilliancy as a speaker and debater

[35] *In Memoriam: John Peter Altgeld* (Chicago, 1907). This memorial volume contains a tribute to Altgeld from Lind's pen.

[36] Letter to the *Murray County Advocate*, printed in the *Willmar Tribune*,
July 21, 1896.

[37] Memorandum in the Lind Papers, probably written after the death of
Bryan in 1924.

had already marked him in Lind's mind as a coming leader of men. In the turmoil of the Cleveland administration Lind turned to him as a man who saw clearly what the times demanded. It is significant that more than a year before Bryan captivated the Democratic convention at Chicago — when he was as yet a comparatively unknown man — Lind on May 11, 1895, addressed the following letter to him:

DEAR SIR: In a frank non-partisan spirit I want to express to you my sincere admiration for the courageous fight that you have made agst. the regime of selfishness and corruption now in control of our government. I have watched your work with a great deal of interest and have only regretted that I couldn't lend you a helping hand.

I sometimes wonder whether the time is not near at hand when the younger men — such as you and I, who have much in common except party name — can consistently get together and work shoulder to shoulder for the accomplishment of those reforms we deem so essential for the return of a fair degree of prosperity to the portion of our population that earns its living by labor. Did such thoughts ever occur to you? If so, what answer does your judgment suggest? It would seem to me that you and I might find as much comfort in each other's company as we would respectively in that of the Hon. Secy. of Agriculture [Julius Sterling Morton of Nebraska] or of Sen. Sherman.

I quit politics because I wished to and I think I acted wisely. I have no desire to re-enter — certainly not until I feel that I am in full accord with the party with which I act on all vital questions. I still take a very lively interest in political questions. My views on the financial question are a thorn in the side of the "sound money" men. They fear and hate me but they haven't had courage enough to read me out of the party as yet. What do you think of the situation? [38]

This letter was written about four months after the election of Knute Nelson to the Senate and more than a year before Lind broke publicly with his party. It states unequivocally that

[38] Lind to Bryan, May 11, 1895, in the Bryan Papers in the Library of Congress. For permission to use the Bryan Papers the author is under obligations to Mrs. Ruth Bryan Owen.

he was not in full accord with his party, and it makes over-
tures to a member of the opposing party to disregard party
labels and to work in harmony with men of whatever party
for the accomplishment of essential reforms. It furnishes conclusive evidence that John Lind was already a political orphan,
although the leaders of the Republican party had not as yet
mustered courage to drive him out from under their roof. The
final act of separation between Lind and the Republican party
awaited the outcome of the national conventions in the following year. After these events "Honest John" and the "silver-
tongued orator of the Platte" could "consistently get together
and work shoulder to shoulder."

VIII

THE FIRST BATTLE

IF THERE had been any doubt that John Lind was at variance with the Republican party on the eve of the presidential campaign of 1896, it was dispelled after the Republican national convention in St. Louis had pledged the party to maintain the existing gold standard until an international agreement with the leading commercial nations of the world should provide for the free and unlimited coinage of silver. Shortly after this convention and before the capture of the Democratic national convention in Chicago by the Silverites, Lind joined with fifteen Republicans in an address "To the Republicans of Minnesota," in which was reviewed the record of the Republican party on bimetallism. It cited the fact that in 1888 the Republican national platform had condemned the policy of Cleveland to demonetize silver; that in 1892 the platform declared in favor of both gold and silver; that in 1894 the Republican party in Minnesota affirmed its belief in bimetallism; and that in the same year nearly every state convention condemned the single standard. The convention of 1896 had thus repudiated a fundamental doctrine of the party. "Gold monometallism means the obliteration of the great middle class, the yeomanry of the nation, and the division of the people into the very rich and the very poor." [1]

John Lind thus publicly displayed the Silver Republican badge. He had already started on his pilgrimage to the silver shrine. With what emotions he read Bryan's great "Cross of

[1] The address was published widely in the press of the state. The present writer copied it from the *Martin County Sentinel* of July 10, 1896. The editor of this paper, Frank A. Day, was one of the signers. The names of John B. Sanborn, Charles A. Towne, Frank M. Nye, and John Day Smith were also on the list.

Gold" speech we do not know, but the birds must have sung more sweetly than usual in New Ulm on the morning of July 11, 1896, when the papers heralded the nomination of the "boy orator of the Platte" on a platform declaring for the free and unlimited coinage of silver in the ratio of 16 to 1, without waiting for the aid or consent of any other nation.

During the exciting days of the national conventions Lind's correspondence grew enormously; from every quarter of the state came urgent requests that he announce himself an independent candidate for governor.[2] Twin City papers sent staff correspondents to New Ulm to interview the man on whom the eyes of the "reformers" were turned. The best the reporters could do was to send dispatches that he would not accept the nomination; but the papers persisted that he might consent. His friends admitted that he was honest in stating that he was through with politics — that he was no office seeker — but they pinned their hope on the belief that he would go where the people called.

In the meantime the *Minneapolis Journal* and the *Minneapolis Times* were making a bitter fight against Clough's nomination by the Republicans. In the first days of July they had the disagreeable duty of announcing his nomination by a wide margin over Samuel R. Van Sant and William H. Eustis. The machine had worked smoothly. The wounds that had been inflicted would be hard to heal before election day, however, and many disgruntled Republicans vowed that they would wreak vengeance upon the "Merriam-Clough-Hill machine." John Lind would be just the man to defeat the "tool of James J. Hill and the Great Northern Railway."

On the day after Bryan's nomination a staff correspondent was compelled to admit that after having talked with Lind for more than an hour, he was unable to quote "one single word of his which could seem to point a change in his position." Yet he had a feeling that a change had taken place.[3] In response to

[2] Staff correspondence from New Ulm, *Minneapolis Times*, July 5, 1896. These letters have been destroyed.

[3] *Minneapolis Times*, July 12, 1896.

a telegram from the *Minneapolis Times* asking him if he would under any circumstances consent to be a candidate in view of Bryan's nomination, Lind sent the following telegram:

You ask me whether under any circumstances I would run for governor. My answer to this question has appeared in the Times three times. Nothing has transpired to change my views since its publication. In answer to your reference to Mr. Bryan permit me to say, that in his nomination the American spirit has found expression and worthy leadership. His character, courage and ability, his vigor, devotion to purpose and broad humanity appeal to the patriotic sentiment of American manhood. If the citizens of our country and of our state who are opposed to foreign domination and class rule have been sufficiently disciplined by the enforced idleness, waste, privation, and losses which the gold standard has brought upon our people to make them forget past differences and party bickerings, and to bring them together to make common cause against a common enemy and for government by the people and for the people, such a movement will not be hampered for want of instrumentalities to carry out its decrees. If one man cannot respond to the call a hundred others equally good will be found ready and able to assume the task and lead the cause of the people to victory. The duty of the hour is with the people. Their united expression will find an organ.[4]

On the evening of July 15 Lind arrived in Minneapolis to attend the mass convention of Republican bimetallists on the following day. He spent the evening in the home of Senator S. B. Howard, which became the mecca of the Silverites. It was reported that the local managers used their efforts to keep newspaper men away from Lind because they were afraid he would declare positively that he would not accept the nomination.[5]

At the convention the appearance of the "spare figure" of Lind was the signal for an ovation; he was easily recognized as the leader of the free silver forces. He was introduced by Senator D. F. Morgan. In his speech Lind declared that he did not desire to become a candidate for any office; but he believed that

[4] *Minneapolis Times,* July 12, 1896.
[5] *Minneapolis Times,* July 16, 1896.

the cause of bimetallism was the people's cause, and he would therefore be content to contribute his energy and ability. But he dreaded putting on the political harness again more than he could say.[6] From his speech it is evident that his friends had prevailed upon him to accept the nomination, which was duly tendered that very day. He undoubtedly wrote the truth to his son twenty-five years later when he said, "I did not want to become a candidate but foolishly allowed some friends to persuade me. I had really quit politics to devote my time to my profession."[7]

As had been predicted, Lind was nominated by the Democratic state convention, held at Minneapolis on August 4. According to the report of the conference committee, presented by H. J. Peck of Shakopee, Lind was to be the nominee for governor; Democrats were to be named for the offices of treasurer and secretary of state; and the Populists were to select their men for the offices of lieutenant governor and attorney-general. The electoral ticket was to be apportioned among four Democrats, four Populists, and one Silver Republican.

What action the Populist convention would take on August 26 was not so easily predictable as that of the Democrats had been, for the leaders who were carrying the banner of Populism in Minnesota were at odds among themselves. The great leader was, of course, Ignatius Donnelly, the "Sage of Nininger," but he had returned from the Populist national convention at St. Louis disgruntled at the way he had been treated; and he aired his grievances in his paper, the *Representative.* Donnelly and Sidney M. Owen were at "outs"; other Populists were anxious to repair the rifts in their ramparts. Lind and Donnelly were personal friends, but the Sage shared the fear of others in his party that there was danger in nominating Lind because he was not an avowed Populist and because Fusion might destroy the party that had made its début only four years before.

One of the strongest opponents of Lind's nomination was Dr.

[6] *Minneapolis Times* and *Minneapolis Journal*, July 17, 1896.
[7] Lind to John Lind, Jr., September 15, 1921.

Christian Johnson, "special editorial contributor" and part owner of the *Willmar Tribune*, which he had established as a Populist organ in February, 1895. Shortly after the paper had been established, Victor Lawson, editor of the *New London Times*, was appointed manager, and before the campaign opened he was promoted to the position of editor and business manager. Lawson was an enthusiastic Populist and very friendly to Lind. Thus the columns written by Lawson and Johnson did not agree.

After Lind had been nominated by the Democrats, Johnson wrote to Donnelly that it was necessary to have a People's party administration and that he did not propose to elect a governor and have "Bill" Washburn and his wheat ring fill the office for him. "The more we look at this Lind wave," he wrote, "the more we see the fine Italian hand of Bill Washburn." [8] Two days later he wrote that if it became necessary to take Lind, he must be pledged in some way to the Populist party; to leave him in the control of "Owen and Co." would be tantamount to leaving him entirely in the hands of the Democrats. The ultimate end would be the destruction of the People's party in the state. He did not deem it advisable to fight Lind openly, however. He proposed to test the strength of the anti-Lind crowd by proposing Donnelly for chairman of the convention. [9]

In the *Willmar Tribune* Johnson argued that the Populist party ought to have the right of naming the Fusion nominee for governor, in view of the fact that the Populist national convention had indorsed Bryan without even requiring him to agree to the platform. "The People's party of Minnesota will not vote into power a Free Silver Republican or Democratic administration even though gilded by a John Lind," he said. He lamented that the Populist convention was to be held last. He had suggested that the Democratic convention should merely recommend Lind and allow the Populists to nominate him. [10]

In his paper, the *Representative*, before the mass convention

[8] Johnson to Donnelly, August 7, 1896, in the Donnelly Papers.
[9] Johnson to Donnelly, August 9, 1896, in the Donnelly Papers.
[10] *Willmar Tribune*, August 11, 1896.

of the Silverites in July, Donnelly stated that he had urged Lind's nomination by the combined free silver elements; but in view of his refusal to become a candidate, the People's party could not afford to get down on its knees to him.[11]

Johnson's attitude was disturbing to members of his own party, and it was suspected that Knute Nelson was back of him. T. J. Meighen, chairman of the State Central Committee of the Populist party, wrote to Donnelly that Johnson's denunciation of Lind would sow discord between Populists and Democrats and might endanger success at the polls. Meighen said he would have a talk with Lind. Democratic leaders also saw the danger and sought to pour oil on the troubled waters. On August 11 Lind had a conference with Donnelly.[12]

When the Populist convention was called to order in Minneapolis on the morning of August 26, all was harmony on the surface; and both Donnelly and Johnson accepted the Fusion nominee with good grace – outwardly at least. In an editorial indorsing the action of the convention, Donnelly wrote: "Eloquent, able, thoughtful, penetrating, John Lind is a kind of Gothic Lincoln." The echo in the *Willmar Tribune* was, "If the farmers and shippers of Minnesota do not elect John Lind governor over Jim Hill's man, Clough, then they deserve the fate they have received in the past."[13]

Lind made his acceptance speech before the Populist convention. He accepted the nomination "not as a Democrat, not as a Populist, nor a Republican, but as a citizen of our great state in hearty sympathy with the aims and endeavors of the united reform forces." He stated that he had been a Republican through all the early years of his manhood and regretted that he could not be a Republican now. The state needed an executive who would enforce the law, one who would resuscitate the anti-trust

[11] *Representative*, July 15, 1896.

[12] Meighen to Donnelly, August 11, 1896, in the Donnelly Papers; telegram from Lind to Donnelly, August 11, 1896, and Thomas D. O'Brien to Donnelly, August 12, 1896, in the Donnelly Papers.

[13] *Representative*, September 2, 1896; *Willmar Tribune*, September 22, 1896.

law, "now decaying and putrefying among the statutes of the state." [14]

In his speech of acceptance following the formal notification of the committee appointed by the Democratic convention, Lind covered the whole field again. Even the Democratic *St. Paul Globe*, which bolted the Bryan ticket, admitted that the document was a paper of "unusual, we might say extraordinary, force and ability. . . . Although we disagree wholly with its principal contention . . . it is, nevertheless, the most plausible and forceful presentation that we have seen of the wrong side of the financial issue." It praised its candor and dignity of expression and stated that it placed the candidate for governor of Minnesota head and shoulders above the candidate for the presidency. "The only doubt of his sincerity," it continued, "is conveyed by the fact that he is too intelligent to blunder on the money question." [15]

Lind's nomination was a tribute to his integrity. Though he did not have the unqualified support of the Twin City dailies, they joined in paying tribute to his ability and honesty. In reply to a communication from "A Palmer Democrat" inquiring as to its candidate for governor, the *St. Paul Globe* stated that there was no Democratic candidate for the office and that the choice lay between two men who had been thoroughgoing Republicans all their lives. It complimented both men and said of Lind that "personally he is a man of high character and admirable qualities." [16] Even the vitriolic *St. Paul Dispatch* recognized his ability, but played up the danger of electing a Populist because of the effect it would have on business. Capitalists and investors, it said, would withdraw their money and Minnesota would be spoken of in the same breath with Oregon and Colorado. [17] Democrats paid tribute to the fairness of the *Minneapolis Times* in reporting the campaign. This paper had urged Lind to be-

[14] *St. Paul Dispatch*, August 27, 1896.
[15] *St. Paul Globe*, September 12, 1896.
[16] *St. Paul Globe*, October 23, 1896.
[17] *St. Paul Dispatch*, September 28, 1896.

come the nominee and really advocated his election by its jibes against Clough.[18]

There was a curious inconsistency in the attacks of the *St. Paul Dispatch*. While pretending to shiver over the collapse of business in the event of Lind's election, it branded him a tool of one of the greatest business interests of the state. "John Lind is neither a Republican, a Democrat, or a Populist. He is just a plain Millers' Association man," it asserted. It attributed his acceptance of the nomination to the "Washburn Vengeance Committee," to whom he was alleged to have stated that he was not in accord with the Democratic or Populist party on any principle except the free coinage of silver. The declaration that he was as good a Republican as ever, said the *Dispatch*, was intended for a certain market. "He was, in that respect, like certain brands of Washburn flour. He was politically branded for certain purposes." And after his nomination the mask came off and he stated that he was in accord with the Democratic party on many points.[19]

It is true that Lind's record in Congress had won high praise from the *Northwestern Miller*, which spoke of him as a "bright and shining star," an energetic, capable, and most intelligent representative, who had shown common sense of the highest order.[20] It is also true that on March 20, 1894, he had been tendered a complimentary dinner by the millers of the Northwest. In his speech before the Populist convention Lind admitted that he had been the attorney for millers in two cases, once for a New Ulm firm and the other time for a firm in La Crosse, the issue on both occasions being a reduction of shipping rates. In Congress, he said, he had gone after the foreign transportation companies in the interest of the Millers' Association — referring to the Harter Act.

The efforts to frighten voters into voting against a "radical" lest the credit of the state should suffer and capital would shun

[18] *St. Peter Herald*, November 13, 1896.
[19] *St. Paul Dispatch*, August 15, 16, 1896.
[20] Quoted in the *New Ulm Review*, January 4, 1893.

the commonwealth was in line with the Mark Hanna campaign throughout the country, in which the kindly and benevolent face of Bryan was made to appear a mask for the menace of Altgeldism, anarchism, and the collective forces of evil. The Republican methods in Minnesota in 1896 are suggestive of those employed to defeat Floyd B. Olson, the candidate of the Farmer-Labor party, in 1930, 1932, and 1934. The *Minneapolis Journal* on October 31, 1896, published a full-page advertisement with ornamental borders headed "Lind's Success vs. Minnesota's Credit," signed by representatives of forty-six business firms of the Twin Cities and of Chicago and the East. On the same day the *St. Paul Globe* ran on its front page a statement signed by prominent business men of that city alleging that the election of a Populist governor would destroy the credit of Minnesota. In a speech delivered at Little Falls on September 19, Knute Nelson said that to elect Lind governor would be to give Minnesota the blackest eye it ever had. Minnesota would be regarded in the East as the abode of wild, long-haired Populists.[21]

It was inevitable that the speeches Lind had delivered as a Republican candidate should have been resurrected. There was little in them that was inconsistent with his acceptance speeches in 1896 except the chaff that was a customary part of the make-up of campaign speeches of those days. The *St. Paul Dispatch* published a cartoon showing the crumbling walls of a penitentiary, with escaping convicts labeled "Democrats." The cartoon bore the caption: "Now he is their candidate for governor." Below was printed an extract from a speech alleged to have been made by Lind in New Ulm in October, 1888: "Tear down the walls of every state prison in the land and you will find that 98 per cent of the population which you would release are Democrats. All Democrats are not murderers and horse thieves, but pretty near all the murderers and horse thieves are Democrats."[22]

Among the Democrats except the Gold Democrats, some of

[21] Copy of statement to L. A. Rosing, Lind's campaign manager, dated October 28, 1896, signed by J. M. Van Camp, C. H. Vining, and William H. Hall, in the Lind Papers.
[22] *St. Paul Dispatch*, August 22, 1896.

whom had been unseated as national committeemen by the state convention, the rejoicing over the capture of Lind was enough to cause them to forgive his former strictures against their party.[23] There was, however, some misgiving over his votes against free coinage bills in Congress. To a small coterie of malcontents who nominated Dr. A. A. Ames of Minneapolis, Lind's support of bimetallism was suggestive of Knute Nelson's vote for the Mills bill. Personally they expressed a liking for Lind, but politically they believed him to be a "reformer à la Knute Nelson." They alleged that Senator "Steve" Howard, who managed the Washburn campaign in the contest with Nelson, went to New Ulm to persuade Lind to alter his determination not to accept the gubernatorial nomination. Ames asked why the People's party should be "controlled by a few attorneys in Temple Court and allow itself to become the tail of a political monstrosity having a free silver Republican head, a Democratic body, and totally lacking in all convictions of what the people really want to accomplish?" What had a governor to do with the money question, when this lay wholly with Congress and the president? What had national finance to do with the washing of "Washburn's dirty linen"? [24]

In a letter to William R. Dobbyn, dated August 6, 1896, Lind explained his vote against free coinage when the Silver Purchase Bill was pending. He said that word came from the White House that the free silver bill would be vetoed. He also stated that the Democrats knew the bill would not become a law and introduced it for political purposes only.[25]

John A. Johnson in his St. Peter Herald repudiated the free silver plank of the Chicago platform and stated that it would not stand the test of the campaign; but he supported the entire Democratic ticket and asserted that as between Lind and Clough

[23] Daniel W. Lawler of St. Paul, Democratic candidate for governor in 1892, was among those unseated.

[24] Sixteen-page pamphlet, For Governor, Dr. A. A. Ames. Let the People Rule. Down with Party Machines. Reasons for the Independent Battle Now On.

[25] Printed in the Representative of August 12, 1896.

he did not see how a Democrat could vote for the Republican nominee.[26]

Lind emulated the example of his idol Bryan and took a very active part in the campaign. His speeches featured the money issue and contained little about parties. In the early part of September he was accompanied by Major J. M. Bowler on a tour of the southern part of the state. "John Lind walks so fast that I have to start to the train a half hour ahead of him," he said to a reporter.[27]

An interesting feature of the campaign was a joint debate between Lind and Professor James T. McCleary, who had succeeded Lind in Congress. The debate was staged in Tetonka Park near Waterville in Le Sueur County, on September 22. The *Minneapolis Times* and the *Journal* reported the speeches in full. Lind opened the debate with a speech that lasted an hour; McCleary held forth an hour and a half; and Lind's rebuttal consumed thirty minutes.

Anticipating McCleary's "yardstick argument," Lind placed several boxes on the table and asked the audience to imagine that each represented a half bushel. He said he remembered the time when a half bushel and a peck measured a dollar of wheat; the time when it took two half bushels to measure a dollar; and the later time when it took three half bushels to measure a dollar; and now, he said, it took four half bushels. He asked the audience if there was any sense in saying that money was a measure of value in the sense that a yardstick was a measure of length. He inquired if McCleary filled his pockets with yardsticks when he went to make a purchase. Money measured by comparison, he said; it was not only a measure of value but it was itself a commodity. There was no such thing as absolute value to a dollar. The speeches of the debaters were interrupted by questions and remarks from the audience, as well as by comments of their own.

At Red Wing Lind "exposed" Governor Clough's transac-

[26] *St. Peter Herald*, June 17, July 24, 1896.
[27] *St. Paul Globe*, September 12, 1896.

HOW CLOUGH GOT THROUGH
[From the *Minneapolis Journal*, November 5, 1896.]

tions in connection with the lands of the Hastings and Dakota Railway Company and criticized his signing of a deed conveying the land to the company instead of securing the forfeiture of the grant.[28]

When the returns of the election were in, the results were startling. McKinley's plurality over Bryan was unexpectedly large — 62,768. Lind lost to Clough by only 3,552 votes, a remarkable showing for the Fusion candidate in view of McKinley's large vote. During the campaign it had by no means been certain in Republican circles that Clough would be the winner, partly because Lind's ability as a vote-getter was conceded and partly because it was expected that Bryan would give McKinley a close battle. But the disparity between McKinley's and Clough's vote was surprising and evoked various explanations. The *Minneapolis Journal* saw in it an ample vindication of its own protest against Clough's nomination and asserted that if McKinley had not carried the state by more than twice the majority anybody had had a right to expect ten days before, Clough would have been beaten "out of sight." A month before, the paper said, Lind would have been elected; it was the free silver issue that defeated him. What had turned the tide was the fear of business men that capital would shun Minnesota as a Populist state.[29]

The *St. Paul Globe* thought there were powerful forces at work within the Republican party to secure the defeat of Clough. Lind's personal popularity and the fact that Republicans had voted for him in the past were also factors. To Tams Bixby, one of the shrewdest political generals in the country, more than to anyone else, Clough owed his election, according to this Gold Democratic organ.[30]

Dr. Christian Johnson in the *Willmar Tribune* made a somewhat different diagnosis. He reminded his readers that he had expressed the fear that if Lind came before the Populists of the

[28] See the reply of James A. Tawney to Lind's speech in the *Red Wing Daily Republican*, October 5, 1896.

[29] *Minneapolis Journal*, November 5, 1896.

[30] *St. Paul Globe*, November 6, 1896.

seventh district labeled a Democrat, thousands would refuse to vote for him. In spite of Lind's magnificent campaign, he said, in all old Republican towns he lost Populists enough to "dump us with a great thud." It was the same story all over the district, he said; the Democratic label seemed to have scared the Scandinavian farmers everywhere.[31]

Lind himself attributed his defeat to irregularities in the northern counties and in St. Paul, but he had neither the time nor the means to carry on a contest; he was grateful to the people who were uninfluenced by appeals to religious and nationalistic prejudice.[32]

The reference to religious and nationalistic prejudice merits careful examination, in the light of Lind's victory at the next election, and of the persistent impression that the Scandinavian vote elected him. Undoubtedly the fact that Lind was a Swede was a political asset to him; but the explanation that his nationality accounts for his large vote in 1896 and his election in 1898 is too simple.

In the eighties and nineties the Scandinavians — more especially the Swedes — were sometimes referred to as "voting cattle." It was said that they voted the Republican ticket in fair weather or foul. The Republicans fixed their slates accordingly, mostly ignoring the Swedes, who needed no inducement to mark Republican ballots. About the only thing that could induce a Swede to vote for a candidate of any other party was some such issue as temperance or the personal character of the candidate. The Swedish immigrants who came after the Civil War followed the leadership of their countrymen already in residence in the United States. The nativistic and puritanical tinge of the Republican party was not objectionable to the intensely Protestant sons of Sweden. With few exceptions, throughout the nineteenth century the Swedish-American press was Republican. The Swedes were lacking in political instinct and were not par-

[31] *Willmar Tribune*, November 11, 1896.
[32] Statement dictated in St. Paul on November 11 and published in the *Martin County Sentinel* of November 13, 1896.

ticularly successful in the political arena. Though individual Swedes aspired to public office, their countrymen did not follow the example of the Irish and make politics a profession. They were satisfied to do their duty at the polls by voting for the candidates of the party of Abraham Lincoln. In hundreds of Swedish communities a Democrat was a curiosity, a strange being, who, if not demented, surely concealed a cloven hoof. And if a Democrat was dangerous, a Populist was infinitely more so. The only bad thing that could be said about John Lind was that he was a Populist — but that was enough. On the other hand, there was food for thought in the circumstance that a man of such good report as "Honest John," a former Republican, had deserted the Republican party. Possibly not every Democrat was a horse thief or a murderer.

At the time of Lind's entrance into politics, however, the Scandinavians, particularly the Norwegians, were showing signs of dissatisfaction with the party that had held undisputed sway in the state since the election of Governor Ramsey. Political observers reported that the Norwegians were going into the Farmers' Alliance, whereas the Swedes remained loyal to their old allegiance. In the early nineties there was a Scandinavian Union League and a Swedish American League of Hennepin County. These organizations adopted resolutions setting forth their special interests and indorsed men of Scandinavian blood for public office. The existence of these organizations is itself an indication that their members, though loyal to the Republican party, were self-conscious and proposed to have a voice in the counsels of the party.

More pertinent to the campaign of 1896, however, were indications that Scandinavian voters were infected with the free silver heresy. The Swedish Lutheran clergy were almost one hundred per cent Republican, but even among their number was one, the Reverend Gustaf Wahlund, who wrote a pamplet advocating bimetallism. Bryan clubs were organized in Swedish communities where in the past no Democratic votes had been cast. The Swedish papers circulating in Minnesota were, how-

ever, overwhelmingly Republican. The only influential one
among them that supported Lind in 1896 was *Svenska Amerikanska Posten* of Minneapolis, published by Swan J. Turnblad.[33]
Among the less influential papers was *Fria Ordet*, a radical sheet
published in St. Paul, which shortly met the fate of all Swedish
publications that strayed from the straight and narrow conservative path. The *Minneapolis Veckoblad*, the organ of the pietistic
Mission Friends, avowed that it could assist in crushing the
Clough-Merriam machine by supporting the able and honest
Swede, without aiding the Democratic party.[34]

The Swedish vote included, of course, a churchly and non-
churchly element, but except on issues that involved the saloon
or some other "moral" principle the two groups were equally
loyal to Republican principles. *Svenska Amerikanska Posten*
was Democratic on principle — advocating bimetallism and a low
tariff — and was not in good standing with church people, for
Turnblad, though a staunch prohibitionist, had antagonized
them by his "liberal" attitude toward secret societies.

The most influential paper in the state was the *Minnesota
Stats Tidning* of St. Paul. This weekly was the mouthpiece of
the Swedish Lutheran church and reflected the conservatism of
the clergy, always staunchly Republican and strait-laced on
questions of temperance and Sabbath observance. Its Minneapolis correspondent admitted that Lind had the right to change
his political affiliations, but stated that "no loyal and thoughtful
Republican dared to vote for such a newly baked Democrat."
The editor deplored the fact that Lind had fallen into the company of Bryan and advised his readers not to vote for McKinley
and Lind. He explained the friendly attitude of the *Minneapolis
Times* toward Lind on the ground that it reflected Washburn's
hatred of Clough and Nelson. He predicted that after election
it would be shown that the "millers' ring" had no greater love
for the Swedes than before.[35]

[33] Lind to Turnblad, October 13, 1896, in *Svenska Amerikanska Posten*, October 17, 1896.
[34] *Svenska Amerikanska Posten*, September 15, 1896.
[35] *Minnesota Stats Tidning*, August 12, September 30, October 21, 1896.

The Swedish editor of the *Willmar Tribune*, who was also a member of the Lutheran church, alleged that *Minnesota Stats Tidning* was on intimate terms with the ring that ruled the G. O. P. and cited the fact that it had refused to publish an article favorable to Lind from the pen of the Reverend Lars G. Almén. The Willmar editor called upon the Swedish Lutherans to repudiate the paper that purported to represent them.[36]

As the campaign progressed it became clear to the Republicans that heroic efforts would have to be employed to stem the tide for the Fusion candidate. The Swedes might not "stay put." Accordingly, the big oratorical guns of Swedish America were moved up to the line of battle in Minnesota. They were Dr. Carl A. Swensson, the energetic and popular president of Bethany College at Lindsborg, Kansas, Professor J. S. Carlson of Gustavus Adolphus College, and William Widgery Thomas, Jr., of Maine, former minister to Sweden and Norway, who had sought in vain to induce Congressman Lind to support his appointment to that diplomatic post. Swensson declared that Lind was merely bait on a silver hook to catch Swedish votes; he deplored his defection from the old party because he had thereby thrown away his political future.[37]

Undoubtedly a number of Swedish votes were cast for Lind — how many can never be determined — but the election statistics do not bear out the statement of the *St. Paul Dispatch* that the Swedes without exception voted for him.[38] Lind carried Hennepin County, Clough's home, by a substantial majority; and the first ward in St. Paul, the Swedish ward, gave him a majority of 144 and McKinley a majority of 1,200. But over against these figures may be cited the returns from the almost solidly Swedish Chisago County, where Clough led by 1,500.[39]

[36] Victor E. Lawson in the *Willmar Tribune*, reprinted in *Svenska Amerikanska Posten*, November 3, 1896.

[37] References to these men may be found in the *Willmar Tribune*, September 15, October 6, 1896; *Minnesota Stats Tidning*, October 14, 1896; and *Svenska Amerikanska Posten* of November 3, December 1, 1896.

[38] *St. Paul Dispatch*, November 10, 1896.

[39] The author has talked with Swedes who have told him that in some congregations a man who expressed a preference for Lind was virtually ostracized.

Perhaps it would be more correct to say that what prevented Bryan and Lind from carrying Minnesota was the conservative German, Swedish, and Norwegian voters, to whom Bryan's free silver remedy for the ills that beset the state was so radical that they believed it bordered on dishonesty. Even so, Lind's personal popularity, the dissension within the Republican party, and the conviction of voters of all classes that Clough did not measure up to the standards of the governor's office, were almost enough to overcome the handicap of McKinley's large majority.

To the *St. Paul Dispatch* must be awarded the credit or the discredit, as the case may be, for Lind's defeat. Harry Black, managing editor, discovered the vulnerable joint in the Lind armor. He raised the religious issue in order to reduce Lind's strength among his countrymen as well as among the church people generally. The association of Lind's "atheism" with Bryan's "anarchism" presented attractive possibilities. Accordingly, this militant and relentless journalist sent a member of his staff, one J. S. Vandiver, to New Ulm to collect material for a series of articles on Lind's alleged agnosticism or atheism.[40]

This episode in Lind's life is interesting and important not only because it profoundly affected his political fortunes but also because it reveals the methods that have been, and still are, used to attract the attention of the electorate away from the real issues of campaigns. The whole affair throws considerable light on what manner of man John Lind was; it proves his rugged honesty, and shows his utter disregard for his own political fortunes when principles were at stake. He dearly loved a scrap and would go out of his way to invite controversy. The professional politician would say that he was lacking in prudence and judgment.

During Lind's last term in Congress and after he had publicly announced his retirement from politics, in 1892, the village of New Ulm was the scene of one of those unfortunately bit-

[40] For Vandiver's early journalistic career, see a letter from R. C. Dunn of Princeton to Knute Nelson, May 22, 1892, in the Nelson Papers, and the *St. Paul Globe* of February 6 and 9, 1901.

ter controversies that sometimes disturb the tranquillity of a community and usually leave their mark in divided families, schismatic churches, and bad blood in lodges and political parties.

One wonders why a man of Lind's background selected the village for his residence. The population is strongly German. The first settlers were members of the *Turnverein*, and for some years there were no churches. In the course of time Roman Catholic and Lutheran churches belonging to the Missouri Synod were established. These ecclesiastical organizations lay great stress on doctrine and are very zealous in shielding their members from all forms of heresy. Leagues removed from one another in doctrine and polity, the Roman Catholics and Missouri Lutherans of New Ulm stood shoulder to shoulder in matters pertaining to parochial schools, Bible reading in the public schools, and laws regulating the sale of liquor and Sabbath observance. There was a marked cleavage between the Turners and the church members.

It so happened that in 1892 the superintendent of schools was Robert Nix, a man of outstanding ability, who was a member of the *Turnverein*.[41] He made no secret of the fact that he harbored agnostic views, but he was wise enough to know that he had no right to impose his agnosticism on the school population. It was inevitable, however, that opposition should arise against a superintendent whose teaching staff was composed largely of members of the *Turnverein*. The fight against him resolved itself into a campaign to elect a school board that would be unfavorable to him. The excitement was so great that it attracted the attention of the Twin City papers. At the election some people tried to vote who were not qualified, and others were hurriedly naturalized to enable them to qualify. Both sides enlisted supporters from outside. Prominent educators of the state paid high tribute to the quality of the New Ulm schools under the superintendent. Dr. William W. Folwell

---

[41] William W. Folwell in writing Lind on October 1, 1892, asked, "Is Robert Nix doing anything with the extraordinary gifts with which he is endowed?"

stated that any persecution of Nix was a discredit to the town
and he pronounced him a man of extraordinary gifts and ac-
quirements. "Such men as Nix are scarce," he said. But Nix lost
his position.[42]

Lind jumped into the fray; the integrity of the public schools
was close to his heart. He had been superintendent of schools,
and the character of the campaign waged against his friend Nix
aroused his contentious nature and moral indignation. A man
afraid of jeopardizing his political future would have fought
shy of the whole unsavory mess, but he threw the weight of his
influence on the side of the unpopular superintendent.

When the *Dispatch* reporter boarded the train for New Ulm
to investigate Lind, there can have been no uncertainty in his
mind as to what he was to look for and what he would find.
He spent two days in the town interviewing business men and
public officials and examining the files of the local papers for
material on the school controversy.

In his opening paragraph the *Dispatch* reporter referred to
an address delivered by Lind the day before in the Swedish
Lutheran Emanuel Church of Minneapolis, the occasion being
the twelfth anniversary of its establishment. His subject was
"The Church as a Power of Civilization" and his theme was
the fatherhood of God and the brotherhood of man.[43] When
John Lind was on the platform in Minneapolis addressing a
body of Christian believers and making a mockery of the religion they professed, "your correspondent" was making inquiry
into the life and character of the man among those to whom
his life was an open book and to whom he had been known for
a dozen years as an avowed atheist. He then discoursed on the
"utter hypocrisy" of Lind and referred to his part in the school
fight and his "infidel lectures" delivered on Sunday evenings

[42] For details see the *New Ulm Review*, July 5, 19, 20, August 17, 24, 1892.
The editor of this paper staunchly defended Nix.

[43] The address was delivered on August 23, 1896. In reporting extracts from
it the *Minneapolis Journal*, in its issue for August 24, 1896, stated that "His
address was short, but pointed, and was received with close attention." There
was not a word of criticism in the *Journal* story.

before the Turner society. He included an extract from one of these speeches, which he alleged had been published in an infidel paper in Indianapolis. The gist of the articles may be summarized in the following sentence: "No one in New Ulm has ever made any pretence of denying the fact that John Lind has been an avowed agnostic, materialist, infidel, or whatever name may be used to designate a person who does not believe in the divine origin of the Bible or the efficacy of the Christian religion."[44]

In a separate article following the New Ulm dispatch it was stated that when Lind carried his hypocrisy so far as to enter the pulpit of a church, the *Dispatch* felt justified in ending his public hypocrisy. It asserted that at the conclusion of Lind's address in Emanuel Church, Dr. Olof Olsson, president of Augustana College and Theological Seminary at Rock Island, Illinois, took the platform and declared that it was not fit to be delivered before a Christian audience.[45]

The charge of atheism was used extensively in the campaign. *Minnesota Stats Tidning*, the mouthpiece of the Swedish Lutheran church in Minnesota, echoed the charges of hypocrisy and alleged that the Minneapolis address was designed to counteract his reputation as a materialist and rationalist and to gain the favor of the churchly Swedes.[46]

In his acceptance speech before the Populist convention, delivered a day or two after the publication of the *Dispatch* articles, Lind stigmatized them as the "most damnable, false fabrication ever put in black and white";[47] and in a speech in St. Paul, delivered in the closing days of the campaign of 1898, he attributed his defeat two years before to the slander.[48]

[44] *St. Paul Dispatch*, August 24, 28, 1896.
[45] In the account of his visit to Minneapolis and the program at the Emanuel Church published in *Augustana* on September 10, 1896, Olsson stated that "the unpretentious, straightforward, honest Swede delivered a good speech." *Augustana* was the official organ of the Swedish Lutheran church.
[46] *Minnesota Stats Tidning*, September 2, 1896.
[47] *St. Paul Dispatch* and *Minneapolis Journal*, August 27, 1896.
[48] *St. Paul Globe*, November 4, 1898. Frank A. Day's *Martin County Sentinel*, November 4, 1898, asserted that the infidel story defeated Lind. See also

After the election Lind determined to allay for all time the charge that he was an atheist. He brought suit for libel against the Dispatch Printing Company in the Ramsey County District Court. On February 16, 1897, the case was called for trial before Judge Bunn and a struck jury in the presence of a large crowd, including a number of lawyers. Lind sat behind his attorneys, Thomas D. O'Brien and S. L. Pierce. The plaintiff was the first witness. He denied that he had delivered the Indianapolis address cited in the *Dispatch* and further denied that it represented his views. He testified that he had not at any time expressed views opposed to Christianity nor had said that there was no God. He admitted that he had joined the Turners when he was about twenty years of age. With reference to the school controversy he stated that its origin had always been a mystery to him. He had never known Nix to teach infidelity and wished to have him retained for the best interest of the schools. On cross examination he admitted that most of the Turners were agnostics and some were atheists. He knew Nix to be an atheist.

The testimony of witnesses for the defense was to the effect that Lind's reputation in the community was that of an agnostic; that it was generally understood that he was a Turner, and that this was taken as an indication that he was an unbeliever; that he did not attend church and was not affiliated with any religious body. Asked to name individuals who had stated that Lind was an agnostic, the witnesses were unable to name more than one, and one witness admitted that he had seen the plaintiff in church. J. S. Vandiver, the writer of the libelous articles, admitted that the words were not exactly those spoken by the gentlemen he had interviewed. In loud and angry tones Attorney Pierce interrupted: "No. They are your own words; that is very plain."

In rebuttal the plaintiff placed two clergymen on the stand.

Lind's letter to Swan J. Turnblad, October 13, 1896, published in *Svenska Amerikanska Posten,* November 13, 1896. Editorial in the *St. Paul Globe,* November 8, 1898. According to *Svenska Folkets Tidning* (Minneapolis), October 12, 1898, a circular charging that Lind was an A. P. A. was distributed in Catholic communities in 1896.

Their testimony, which was corroborated, was to the effect that, although Lind was a Turner, it was understood that this organization did not represent his views. A Roman Catholic testified that he had contributed to the erection of a Catholic church. The defendant was unable to prove that the alleged atheistic speech had been either delivered or published.

The trial lasted four days and resulted in a disagreement of the jury after an all-night session.

The second trial was called in April. As in the first trial, the *Dispatch* relied upon Lind's reputation as an atheist, but was unable to furnish specific proof. The court instructed the jury to bring in a verdict for the plaintiff, and on April 14, 1897, he was awarded six hundred dollars compensation. Lind expressed satisfaction with the verdict, though he had brought action for twenty thousand dollars. His name was cleared from the charge that had undoubtedly turned voters away from him.[49]

The legal battle in the St. Paul courthouse was not to be the last passage at arms between Black and Vandiver and Lind. Vandiver got sweet revenge as manager of the Republican Press Bureau in the campaign of 1900, when Lind went down to defeat before Samuel R. Van Sant. As managing editor of the *Dispatch* Black could stay within the law and still by innuendo and journalistic sleight of hand snipe at Governor John Lind until the day of reckoning came in January, 1901, when Private Citizen John Lind elected to employ extra-legal methods, as we shall see.

In view of the misapprehension that still prevails about Lind's religious views, an attempt to throw light on the subject may not be out of place here.

In acknowledging the receipt of a diploma commemorating his fifty years' membership in the American Turnerbund, on

[49] The trial was reported in the Twin City papers. The present author has relied chiefly on the *St. Paul Dispatch*, the *St. Paul Globe*, and the *Minneapolis Tribune*. *Svenska Amerikanska Posten*, June 8, 1897, devoted almost three columns to the second trial and quoted liberally from the speech of Thomas D. O'Brien. Several documents, including the text of the Emanuel Church address, are in the Lind Papers. Munn, Boyeson, and Thygeson were the attorneys for the defendant.

November 20, 1926, Lind gave the reasons that impelled him to affiliate with the society.

> At the time of my admission, the Turnverein was not only the sole liberal association in that part of the state, but it was the repository and exponent of what there was at New Ulm of culture and education. I was then and there a young man, almost a stranger among you and without companions or social standing. While I did not agree with the society in all of its views, the language, and the Weltanschauung of its members opened to me a new world of thought and reflection. The sympathy and kindness of the members — the Nixes, Roos, Pfaender, Boesch and a score of others now gone — contributed the stimulus of thought and social contact that I needed.[50]

Lind was reared in a home where the parents were professing Christians. Like practically all immigrants from Sweden, they had been confirmed in the Lutheran church. Offended by the heartless and unauthorized expressions of a Swedish Lutheran minister at the time of the death of their unbaptized infant shortly after the arrival of the family in America, they had left the Lutheran church, however, and had become devout members of the Swedish Methodist church.

In his mature years John Lind was not an orthodox believer. His views were those of a man given to speculation and deeply interested in human nature and in those forces that mold character and influence conduct. In the early seventies, while he was superintendent of schools and practicing attorney, he subscribed to the *Religio-Philosophical Journal*, a Spiritualist magazine published at Chicago. From the beginning he read widely and was open to different points of view. In his formative years he was repelled by the narrow, puritanical frontier pastors, and he never affiliated with any church. Fraternal organizations did not appeal to him. Though as a young man he joined the Odd Fellows, he seems to have taken little interest in the order. Formal religion, with its ritual, liturgy, and creed, did not interest him. In his Thanksgiving Proclamation of 1900 he designated the

[50] Letter to Captain Albert Steinhauser.

day as one of "public thanksgiving," but made no mention of the deity. It was inevitable that a man holding these views should have gained the reputation, among certain groups, of being an atheist.

Nevertheless, Lind was a man of fine emotions and spiritual insight, qualities that found expression on many occasions. The death of his daughter Jenny in 1922 was a heavy blow. To his son Norman he wrote: "If Jenny continues conscious of this world and of the family she will be happier than ever." Like many men of liberal views, Lind preferred the teachings of Jesus to the philosophy of Paul. He was somewhat interested in Christian Science and was fond of discussing it with his friend Darwin Schuetz of Everett, Washington. After a hasty reading of Steinmetz' lectures, he wrote to him that he had gained only what he regarded as a confirmation of views he had arrived at twenty years earlier: "That in the final analysis there is no line of absolute demarkation between 'matter and spirit,' that the unity 'oneness' is the secret of the universe, that the variety of manifestations that our senses and intellect perceive are only different phases of the final reality."

There is something false about reducing a man's life to a formula. The same may be said about a man's religion, for, as Lind said to the present writer during the last year of his life, "In religion, as in everything else, you have to use good, common sense." Perhaps Frank A. Day said about all that can be said with positiveness about Lind's religion when he wrote in the *Martin County Sentinel:* "They may accuse John Lind of being an infidel, but they cannot call him a hypocrite."[51]

[51] Dr. John E. Bushnell, minister of the Westminster Presbyterian Church of Minneapolis, referred to his conversation with Lind at the time of his daughter's death in his address at Governor Lind's funeral. In a conversation with Dr. E. E. Ryden, pastor of the Gloria Dei Lutheran Church of St. Paul, on March 24, 1933, the present writer learned of a conversation between him and Lind at the home of A. E. Nelson of Minneapolis, about five years before Lind's death. Governor Lind sought Dr. Ryden out in order to engage him in a discussion of religious questions. Dr. Ryden's impression was that Lind had a deep and positive faith, though not orthodox. See also Lind to Norman Lind, October 6, 1922; to F. L. Anderson, April 26, 1924(?); and to Darwin Schuetz, August 31, 1923; also the *Martin County Sentinel*, September 4, 1896.

IX

SOLDIER AND POLITICIAN

THE DEFEAT of Fusion and the cause it represented was naturally disappointing to Lind. But he accepted it with good grace, and settled down to resume his law practice and to enjoy his home in the southwestern part of New Ulm, near the crest of the slope over which the town spreads its network of broad streets lined with tidy homes. "Defeat has not shaken our confidence. It has but taught us a lesson and disciplined us for the great struggle before us," he said at a banquet given by the Silver Republican Club of St. Paul in February, 1897.[1]

It was inevitable that the man who had come so close to breaking the succession of Republican governors dating from 1859 should have been mentioned as the standard bearer of the Fusion forces in the next campaign. Even before the close of the year 1897 political prognosticators flooded the press with speculations about the future of the New Ulm crusader. It was almost unanimously conceded that if he desired the nomination, it was his.[2]

At this early date it was predicted that the outcome of the election would depend largely upon the character of the Republican nominee. Would the convention select a man who could unite the various factions in the Republican party? Some were confident that if Lind ran as an independent, without any party label, he would be elected over any man the Republicans might name. They suggested that the Populists, the Democrats, and the Silver Republicans should hold separate conventions and leave the governorship candidacy blank, with the understand-

[1] *St. Paul Globe*, February 13, 1897.
[2] The Lind Papers contain hundreds of clippings from the press of the state dating from November, 1897, on this subject.

ing that Lind would run for the office independently of party
indorsement.

On December 3, 1897, Lind spoke at a meeting sponsored by
the John Ericsson Memorial Association in the Swedish Taber-
nacle of Minneapolis to raise funds for the erection of a monument in honor of the inventor of the "Monitor." Captain Hans
Anderson, the sole survivor of the crew of the famous "cheese-
box on a raft," was one of the speakers. Lind was introduced by
Judge Andrew Holt. As the applause subsided, his first remark
was "This is not election time." At the conclusion of Lind's
address, William H. Eustis opened his remarks by saying, "I
recognize in John Lind's voice the sweetness of the famous voice
of Jenny Lind and this same sweetness of voice will, without
doubt, soon make him governor" — a prophecy that was fulfilled
at the expense of the speaker's own political ambition.[3]

On December 19, 1897, Lind presided at an informal meeting of the leaders of the Minnesota reform forces in Minneapolis. In the course of the conference speakers referred 'to the
nomination of Lind as a matter of course. As soon as he had the
opportunity, Lind stated that the references to himself as a
gubernatorial candidate were very distasteful to him; he hoped
that they would cease. If they did not, he added, he would be
obliged to say something he hoped he would not be compelled
to say.[4]

The reactions to this announcement, which was promptly
taken up by the press, were varied. One country editor commented that it was "certainly a knock-out blow for those who
abhor the machine political and who would like once — just once
— to see an honest man in the governor's chair."[5] Another
thought it "probable that Mr. Lind sees the handwriting on the
wall and is satisfied with one defeat."[6] The comment of the
Winthrop News was to the effect that "John Lind has already

[3] *Minneapolis Times*, December 4, 1897.
[4] *Minneapolis Times*, *Minneapolis Journal*, and *St. Paul Pioneer Press*, December 20, 21, 1897.
[5] *Eden Valley County Line*, December 24, 1897.
[6] *Moorhead Independent*, December 24, 1897.

begun declining nominations. This early start will give him a chance to break his record of two years ago." [7]

Aside from the opportunity it afforded the newspaper paragraphers, Lind's statement had little significance so far as his actual decision was concerned. He knew it was too early to speak with finality. He could await the outcome of the Republican convention. He had merely deprecated a premature announcement of his candidacy. [8]

By the beginning of the humorous and tragic year 1898 the stage was set for political meetings of momentous importance. On January 4 and 5 the Mid-Road Populists held a winter meeting in St. Paul. Ignatius Donnelly was the leader. He declared himself opposed to Fusion because it meant disintegration. In spite of this, however, he announced that he would support Lind if the Populists saw fit to nominate him, even though he had not enrolled himself in their ranks. Dr. Christian Johnson sounded a different note. He thought the mistakes of Fusion two years before ought to teach the Populists to avoid it in the future. Fusion with the Democrats had driven the Republicans back into the party. He was a friend of Lind and proud of him as a Swede, but he did not think the Populists could win in the country districts as an appendage to the Democracy. At this meeting the Fusionists were conspicuously absent. [9]

One of the greatest events in the annals of the Democratic party in Minnesota was the meeting held in the Exposition Building in Minneapolis and the Jackson Day banquet in the West Hotel on January 11, 1898. The meeting and program were arranged by L. A. Rosing, chairman of the Democratic Central Committee and manager of the campaign of 1896. The great feature was the presence of the "peerless leader," William Jennings Bryan, who gave several addresses in the city. Lind was scheduled to speak at the banquet on "Politics, Ideal and

---

[7] Quoted in the *St. Paul Dispatch*, December 27, 1897.

[8] *Minneapolis Tribune*, December 24, 1897.

[9] *Representative*, January 12, 1898; *St. Paul Dispatch*, January 4, 1898. See also the *Minneapolis Journal*, December 20, 1897; *Minneapolis Times*, December 26, 1897.

Practical," but he was obliged to remain at home owing to the serious illness of Mrs. Lind and their children Norman and Jenny. Father J. M. Cleary spoke in Lind's place. But Lind's influence was everywhere present. Chairman Rosing, referring to his absence, said the people stood with him in spirit to reform the state government, "to restore to the people the lost power, to defeat the corrupt rings now in control." Lind's telegram expressing regret over his absence was received with an ovation that could not be mistaken.[10]

The most significant outcome of the banquet was the decision that there was to be Fusion in Minnesota in 1898 and that John Lind was to be its candidate for governor.[11] The Silver Republicans and Populists went away rejoicing. Both Bryan and Rosing declared for Fusion in no ambiguous terms, as did other speakers, and the applause that greeted their sentiments could not be misunderstood. The only questions that remained unanswered were: Did Lind desire the nomination? Who would the Republicans nominate — Van Sant, Eustis, or Judge Collins? Would the Republicans win in an "off year" with such a popular man as Lind running on the Fusion ticket?

The excitement over the sinking of the "Maine" in the harbor of Havana in February, 1898, and the war with Spain relegated political news to the inside pages of the Minnesota newspapers; and John Lind, together with his fellow citizens, put aside whatever political ambitions he may have had to do his "bit" in the war the people believed to be a crusade against Spanish tyranny and cruelty in Cuba. In the first days of March, Lind passed through Minneapolis on his way to Salt Lake City. He gave out the following interview to the *Minneapolis Times:*

You ask me about politics. Well, I don't know how it is here in Minneapolis but out in the country there is no interest in politics now. Everyone is thinking and talking of nothing but the Cuban situation and the Maine disaster. The farmers come into town every

[10] Extended accounts of the meetings were published in the Twin City papers, January 11, 12, 1898.
[11] L. A. Rosing to Lind, January 14, 1898; *Minneapolis Journal*, January 12, 1898.

day and wait for hours for the daily papers to get the latest news. There is no excitement, but a fixed determination that the time has arrived when something must be done. If the Maine was blown up by Spain, or by Spanish subjects, it is time to call a halt. If Spain wants war, then let us have war. That, I say, is the general feeling.[12]

Yet it was a great surprise when Lind enlisted, for it was mostly the younger men of the state whom the slogan "Remember the Maine" was bringing to the recruiting offices. The press was filled with speculations as to why the New Ulm lawyer had left his home and profession to assume the prosaic duties of quartermaster in the Twelfth Regiment of Minnesota Infantry Volunteers. The impending political conventions kept these speculations alive. The most plausible of the rumors was that Lind and Governor Clough had entered into a deal by which the former was given a commission, thereby eliminating him from politics, allowing him to retire gracefully, and removing a source of embarrassment to the governor.

The Republican *Minneapolis Tribune* observed that the salary of a quartermaster was small and that there was no chance for glory. The only explanation of the mystery was, therefore, that he had adopted this method of getting out of politics.[13] E. A. Twitchell, assistant editor of the *Representative*, was of the opinion that Lind knew the people of the state would never sanction a combination that would give the United States senatorship to the Democrats. He preferred to face the yellow fever rather than the requirements of such a campaign.[14]

Dr. Christian Johnson, in a letter to Ignatius Donnelly, uncovered what he believed to be a deep-laid plot. Lind's enlistment meant one of two things. Either he saw the folly of running on the Fusion program because he knew the Populists would not go to the polls like voting cattle at the call of Captain Owen; or else it was a scheme on the part of the Fusion

[12] *Minneapolis Times*, March 5, 1898; Lind to Norman Lind, Salt Lake City, March 7, 1898.
[13] *Minneapolis Tribune*, April 27, 1898.
[14] *Representative*, April 4, 1898.

crowd to get him out of the way during convention time, so that he might not be forced to subscribe to any platform pledge. Johnson professed to believe that the first was the true explanation.[15] But in a letter to Donnelly that was published in the columns of the *Representative*, he asserted that he had "reliable information" that Lind had pledged himself to Clough not to run for governor. The Fusionists knew this, he said, but the plan was to have Lind "keep still" until the convention had nominated him, after which it would be too late for the Populists to do anything. When Lind declined the honor, a joint committee would place a Democrat in nomination.[16]

The version of the same story that came from the pen of W. W. Jermane, the resourceful and usually well-informed political reporter of the *Minneapolis Journal*, was that Lind did not care to run because silver had ceased to be a live issue, and he did not care to run on state issues. Colonel Bobleter had suggested Lind to Clough, who made the appointment in return for a promise that he would not accept the nomination.[17] Others, like James A. Tawney of Winona, said it was a shrewd political trick to make Lind more popular.[18]

Naturally Clough's denial that a "deal" had been made was not convincing to those who were searching for a political motive for what to them appeared to be Lind's strange action; and when Lind did accept the nomination, there was a way out by alleging that Clough had released Lind from his pledge after the Clough machine had been smashed at the Republican convention by the nomination of Eustis.[19]

Lind was under no obligation to give his reason for wearing the uniform of his country, and he paid no attention to the gossip other than to state at the time of his enlistment that he was

---

[15] Johnson to Donnelly, April 30, 1898. Donnelly Papers.
[16] *Representative*, July 27, 1898.
[17] *Minneapolis Journal*, July 27, 1898.
[18] *Minneapolis Journal*, May 6, 1898.
[19] The *Minneapolis Journal*, April 27, 1898, published Clough's denial. The *Red Wing Republican*, August 16, 1898, accepted the *Minneapolis Journal* version and elaborated on it.

glad of the opportunity to serve his country, having always regretted that he had been unable to serve in the Civil War because of his youth.[20] Doubtless his motives were mixed, and he must have weighed the consequences to himself and to the cause for which he had fought in 1896. His biographer can do no better than to give the substance of a letter written by T. D. O'Brien of St. Paul on June 6, 1898, before the conventions.

O'Brien told Lind that it was a matter of common gossip, emanating almost entirely from Republicans, that he had accepted the commission for the purpose of reinstating himself in the Republican party. This had been repeated so persistently that O'Brien had been tempted to make public the conversation between Lind and himself in the latter's office just after he had accepted the commission.

According to O'Brien's recollection, Lind had stated that he was so situated that he was able to give his time to the duties of quartermaster and felt it his duty to do so; that he did not accept the commission either to escape or to secure the nomination for governor; that his friends must be the judges as to whether or not he should be nominated, but that in no event would he resign his commission to make a campaign. "You then said you would give me carte blanche as to whether you should be nominated or not." O'Brien attempted to have further conversation with Lind before he left the state, but on the occasion of their last meeting Lind was so averse to an extended conversation that he refrained from troubling him further.

Lind assured his family when he enlisted that the war would be over in time to enable him to return before September. The prophecy was fulfilled.[21] Had it been made to reassure his family and to assuage the grief of parting, or was he thinking of the political campaign? The events of the next few weeks may furnish the answer.

[20] *Minneapolis Times*, April 27, 1898.
[21] Manuscript of a speech delivered some time after 1901 in the Lind Papers. Minnesota's part in the war is related in William W. Folwell, *A History of Minnesota*, 3:231-40, and in Franklin F. Holbrook, *Minnesota in the War with Spain* (St. Paul, 1923).

Lind's part in the Spanish-American War need not detain us for long. After about a week spent in clothing, equipping, and drilling the troops at Camp Ramsey on the State Fair Grounds, the Twelfth Minnesota Infantry Volunteers were transported via the Minneapolis and St. Louis Railroad to Camp George H. Thomas at Chickamauga Park, Georgia. The running time of the train was irregular, and the regiment was on the train from May 16 to May 19. The regiment had but recently been mustered into service, and Lind had been unable to obtain blanks or any specific information about the method of discharging his duties.[22]

Upon its arrival at Chickamauga Park the regiment was directed to make camp at a point near the old Alexander House, about ten miles from the station at Rossville, where the troops were unloaded. The regiment was not supplied with wagon transportation, nor was it possible to procure teams for the immediate transportation of the commissary stores. The men did not reach camp until long after dark, and they were without food, fuel, or shelter. Fortunately Lind was able to pick up a couple of teams to carry baked beans, hard-tack, and coffee to the camp grounds.

The demoralized condition of the staff, quartermaster, and commissary departments in the Spanish-American War is well known, and Lind's regiment suffered with the others. "Everything from hay and oats for horses to food for men was underweight," Lind said. "Shoes gotten for the recruits did not last nearly as long as those purchased in St. Paul for the men who had left the state earlier in the year." [23]

Lind was very proud of his men and was correspondingly popular with them. As a token of appreciation for his services each of the Minnesota regiments — the Twelfth and the Fourteenth — presented him with a sword.[24] The adjutant general

[22] The reports and letters from Lind are in the Lind Papers and in the manuscript collection of the Minnesota Historical Society.

[23] *Minneapolis Journal*, September 17, 1898.

[24] Letter from Private A. A. Caswell of the Fourteenth Regiment, printed in *Svenska Amerikanska Posten*, September 13, 1898.

complimented him on his economy in purchasing supplies. "Your bills amount to considerably less than those of other regiments," he wrote.[25]

Lind fared very well in the hot southern climate; he lost weight, but he escaped the ravages of malaria that laid low so many of his men. Mrs. Lind, who had difficulty in reconciling herself to her husband's adventure, accompanied him to camp and remained until the middle of July. She visited the camp frequently and accompanied her husband on "sightseeing" tours on horseback.

The naval victories at Manila Bay and Santiago were especially gratifying to Lind, who prided himself that his predictions about the efficiency of the navy had been fulfilled; but he was disappointed, as were his men, that the speedy termination of the war would deprive them of the thrill and glory of driving the enemy out of Cuba and Porto Rico. "I am not anxious to go to the front; at the same time it seems almost a pity that the regiment should have undergone the hardships that it has endured without getting a little of the glory," he wrote to Norman. He thought it likely, however, that if the war did not end before the middle of July, his "crack" regiment would be the first to go to Porto Rico.[26]

The surrender of General Toral's forces to General Shafter at Santiago, followed by the signing of the protocol, assured the early return of the boys; and in the last week of August they were transferred to Camp Hamilton at Lexington, Kentucky, to remain there until the order to return home was given. By the middle of September the regiment was encamped at Camp Mueller near New Ulm — after much ill feeling had been generated between New Ulm and Winona over the location of the camp. The merchants of the respective towns anticipated a thriving business with the troops and their visitors.

During the hot summer weeks the people of Minnesota were not especially interested in Lieutenant John Lind; his political

[25] Hermann Muehlberg to Lind, May 23, 1898, in the Lind Papers.
[26] Lind to Norman Lind, June 12, 14, July 12, 1898.

fortunes gave them far more concern. The Republicans feared he would accept the Fusion nomination, and the Silver Republicans, Democrats, and Populists feared that he would not. He was pestered with correspondence and with visitors who sought to draw him out. To Norman, who was preparing for admission to the University of Minnesota, he wrote on June 12: "I do not want to run — and have said so publicly and privately but I think that they will nominate and run me or rather my name whether or no and I do not see what I can do about it." Two days later he wrote: "They understand perfectly well that I do not want the nomination and that I shall under no circumstances make a campaign. If, however, they nominate me, what can I do? To forbid them the use of my name would subject me to the suspicion that I had betrayed them and bartered my convictions. My present impression is that I will do nothing, at least at present. Let the situation solve itself. I have enough cares without fretting about politics."

How the "situation solved itself" is the theme of the next chapter.

X

THE SECOND BATTLE

THE CAMPAIGN of 1898 is a landmark in the political history of Minnesota; it marks the triumph of the Fusion forces and the election of the first governor after 1858 who did not carry the indorsement of the Republican party. The Republican monopoly of the governor's office over a period of forty years was thus broken; during the years since that time three Democrats and one Farmer-Laborite have been elected.

Aside from the unusual outcome, the campaign was dull and unexciting. A strange apathy seems to have seized upon the voters. The total vote for state officers was 92,069 less than it had been in 1896, and the number of registered voters was 55,850 less; 72,392 registered voters did not take the trouble to go to the polls. Lind defeated his Republican opponent, Eustis, by 20,184 votes, but his own vote was 30,274 less than it had been in 1896. Eustis' vote was 54,110 less than Clough's had been. August T. Koerner of Meeker County, candidate for state treasurer, received the largest vote cast for a state official; it exceeded that of Lind by 9,227. Lind was the only state official elected who did not wear the Republican badge. The explanation of his victory seems to be that more Republicans stayed at home than Silver Republicans, Democrats, and Populists.

We have seen that in the early part of the year 1898 the comments of the press showed clearly that Lind was expected to be Fusion candidate for governor, despite speculations about the meaning of his enlistment in the Spanish-American War. The Fusion leaders were fully aware that he was strangely indifferent to the nomination, but they knew also that he would not return to the Republican party, that he was loyal to the principles for which he had fought, and that pride, if nothing else, urged him to make another run if the chances of success were reasonably good. In any event, he was in a strategic position. He knew that he was the unanimous choice of the leaders of the allied forces and that there was nobody who cared to contest the nomination. He could therefore bide his time and await the outcome of the conventions. He could name his own terms because he was far more powerful than the parties that wished to nominate him.

In 1896 there had been dissatisfaction among the Populists because the Democrats had nominated Lind first and had in that way gained an advantage over the other parties to the alliance. In 1898, however, the leaders saw to it that there was no cause for dissatisfaction on that score. It was arranged that Democratic, Populist, and Silver Republican conventions should all be held in Minneapolis on June 15. Except in the Populist convention, the proceedings were cut and dried and everything went through as scheduled. Conferees from each body made up a slate which was submitted to the respective conventions. Lind was, of course, the nominee for governor, but each party adopted separate platforms, which in the main reaffirmed the position that had been taken two years earlier.

The discordant note in the Fusion chorus was struck in the Populist convention. As in 1896, the Mid-Roaders sought to save the identity of the party. Friction between them and the Fusionists had been evident ever since a meeting of the Populist State Central Committee in Minneapolis on February 16, at which Marion Butler, James B. Weaver, and former Senator Dubois were present. Trouble arose over the attempt to secure the appointment of a committee to invite Lind to address the gathering, and the invitation was not issued.[1]

From that time on the Mid-Road faction, led by Ignatius Donnelly and Christian Johnson, tried to head off Lind's nomination by the Fusionists as the best way of keeping the Populist party from disintegrating. On April 21 Donnelly sent out a cir-

[1] See the *Minneapolis Times* and other Twin City papers.

cular letter asking Populists to write letters for publication in
the *Representative* in opposition to Fusion and Lind's nomination.[2] At the Populist convention on June 15 a dramatic scene
took place between Ignatius Donnelly and Sidney M. Owen
which stirred the convention with excitement. The Sage of
Nininger made statements that brought Owen to his feet with
a heated reply, and the scores of many years were given a public airing.[3] The upshot of the long debate was the secession of
the Mid-Roaders and the nomination of an independent ticket
on the following day, with Lionel C. Long, editor and publisher
of the Magnolia *Initiator*, as the nominee for governor. Donnelly was indorsed for the United States Senate.

The quartermaster of the Twelfth Minnesota stationed at
Camp George H. Thomas was apprised of the action of the conventions not only through the official communications of the
committees appointed for that purpose but also through letters
from individuals who gave their views of the political situation
and urged his acceptance of the nomination. While he perused
these letters and the clippings from the newspapers whose editors sought to read his mind, he calmly awaited the news about
the Republican state convention, which was to be held in St.
Paul on June 30.

Clough's narrow escape from defeat in 1896 was a warning
to the Republicans that he was an impossible candidate to succeed himself and that the people were restless under what the
Fusionists were pleased to call the "ring domination" of the Republican party. What proved to be the controlling element in
the party was determined to overthrow the "Clough machine"
and nominate a man who was not dominated by the so-called
professional politicians. The results of the first ballot were as
follows: William H. Eustis, 520; Samuel R. Van Sant, 401;
Judge Loren W. Collins, 248. The second ballot showed a gain
for Eustis, and on the third he was declared the nominee. According to the *St. Paul Dispatch*, Eustis was the first man to

[2] This letter is in the Donnelly Papers. Several letters in response to it are
printed in the *Representative*, June 1, 8, 1898.
[3] *Representative*, June 15, 1898.

break through the ranks of the professional politicians and wrest the nomination from the men who had previously controlled the conventions.[4] Be that as it may, the fight for the nomination was extremely bitter, and Eustis' victory was won over the supreme efforts of the Clough followers to name Van Sant.

At the beginning of the campaign the choice of Eustis appeared to be a happy one. He was a man of outstanding ability and fine public spirit, and an excellent speaker. He was born at Oxbow, New York. At the age of fifteen he was stricken with an affliction that lamed him for life, but by dint of hard work and an indomitable spirit he obtained a good education, spent a few years in teaching, and was admitted to the bar. In 1881 he moved from New York City to Minneapolis and immediately took an active part in business and in the affairs of the city and state. He was instrumental in getting the Republican national convention to meet in Minneapolis in 1892, and at that convention made a speech in behalf of James G. Blaine. The same year he was elected mayor of Minneapolis. His aggressiveness and independence met the usual opposition from various elements of the population, and he left office with a record that was used with good effect against him in the gubernatorial campaign.[5]

Eustis and Lind were good friends and remained good friends to the end of their days. After his nomination Eustis made a speech before the convention in which he paid a neat compliment to Lind by referring to him as an honorable gentleman now serving his country at the front. He said he envied his opponent because he could serve his country in a capacity that was closed to him. Throughout the campaign Eustis spoke respectfully of Lind. Not so some of his supporters. Donnelly, for instance, wrote to Eustis requesting him to employ someone to "dig up" evidence that on more than one occasion Lind had been the attorney for the "millers' ring" and the elevator men, in order that he might make use of it in a speech to be delivered

[4] *St. Paul Dispatch*, November 9, 1898.
[5] The "Autobiography of William Henry Eustis" was published in the *Minneapolis Journal*, December 22, 1929–January 28, 1930.

before the Mid-Road Populist meeting in Minneapolis. Eustis replied that he had no knowledge of these matters and had no way of ascertaining the facts without a thorough search of the records, which he did not have time to make.[6]

In nominating Eustis the Republicans honored a man of ability and character, but politically his record was vulnerable, as we shall have occasion to show. His greatest handicap, however, was the opposition of powerful men within his own party and the apathy of a still larger number.

By the beginning of July the conventions had done their work, and the stage was set for the campaign, except for one detail — Lieutenant John Lind had not accepted the nomination. The letter of acceptance was delayed until July 20. During the weeks of suspense Lind and a few intimate friends were the only ones who were in no doubt as to the answer that was forthcoming from Camp George H. Thomas.

The long delay, the circumstances under which the letter of acceptance was written, and certain events that took place both before and after the nomination and acceptance conspired to strengthen the "theory" that Lind's decision hinged upon the approval of Governor Clough. If circumstantial evidence is accepted, the theory is plausible enough. The following is the hypothetical chain of events: Clough had given Lind a commission in order to eliminate him from the campaign of 1898; Clough's candidate was defeated at the Republican convention; Clough was "singularly bitter" against Eustis; Clough sent an emissary to assure Lind of his support; Lind sent a message to Clough giving assurance that he would run. On July 22 Clough gave out an interview in which he paid high tribute to Lind's character and ability and all but predicted his election; and after election Clough sent the following telegram to Lind: "Allow me to congratulate you from the bottom of my heart. There is still a God in heaven."[7]

[6] Donnelly to Eustis, September 21, 1898, and Eustis to Donnelly, September 24, 1898, in the Donnelly Papers.

[7] See Folwell, *A History of Minnesota*, 3:244–45, and James H. Baker, *Lives of the Governors of Minnesota* (St. Paul, 1908), pp. 385–86. The Clough inter-

Unfortunately, the documents do not bear out the theory, and the events do not necessarily fit into the scheme. Moreover, the theory leaves out of account the possibility, even probability, that Lind's enlistment was a shrewd move to disarm his opponents in the coming campaign of the opportunity of capitalizing the war as a Republican achievement. It is not even necessary to accept Lind's statement in a letter to Zadok H. Austin of Duluth that there had not been a moment since the conventions adjourned when he had thought of any other course than to accept.[8] His letters to Norman, written even before the nomination, place him in the attitude of a "receptive candidate" and prove that his loyalty to principles and supporters precluded the possibility of declining. Twenty-three years after the event he wrote to his son John that after his defeat he decided to become a candidate again. "I did not want to quit as a loser," he said.[9] When he sent the cryptic message to a friend of Governor Clough (if he did send it), "The business is done, and we are all well," he was merely informing the governor that the decision had been made. The implication that the decision was made only after Clough's support was assured is unwarranted.[10]

In his letter of acceptance Lind said that although he would prefer to return to private life, the renewed evidence of confidence "so unanimously expressed" convinced him that it was his duty to cooperate in the task of wresting the state from the "dominion of personal greed and ambition to which it has so long been subject." He refrained from an extended discussion of the issues of the impending campaign, partly because his views had been "fully expressed by my acts and in my utterances in public life, as well as in the late campaign." He could not, however, forbear from expressing his appreciation of the wisdom of the conventions in not permitting the "shimmer of a

view was published in the *Minneapolis Times,* July 22, 1898, and the congratulatory telegram in the Twin City newspapers of November 10, 1898.

[8] This letter was dated July 20, 1898, and was published in a number of papers. See the *Staples Tribune,* August 11, 1898.

[9] Lind to John Lind, Jr., September 21, 1921.

[10] Folwell bases his statement on an interview with Judge John Day Smith on October 4, 1914.

proposed imperial policy in distant lands to blind the eyes of the people to existing abuses at home."

The candidate thus capitalized his unique and independent position by confining his letter to state issues and by refraining from a discussion of specific ones. By not accepting the nomination of any party by name he also emphasized his independent position, a fact that caused the *Fairmont Independent* to comment as follows: "It is said that Lind wrote his letter of acceptance to the succotash party on a box of hard tack." [11] The terms "succotash party" and "mock turtle nomination" as applied to the Fusion forces gained considerable popularity in the newspapers.

The letter of acceptance assured the allied forces that they had captured the prize that for weeks and months had seemed uncertain. Though the leaders had little or no hope of electing the other candidates indorsed by the Fusionists, they were certain of electing Lind. The nomination of Eustis, they thought, had insured that.

In a letter dated August 1, Leonard A. Rosing of Cannon Falls, chairman of the Minnesota Democratic State Central Committee, outlined to Lind the plan of campaign which was followed in the main. The strategy took into account the fact that the electorate was primarily interested in state issues and that the personality and record of the candidates gave a heavy advantage to Lind. In the campaign of 1896 the Twin City papers (with the exception of the *Minneapolis Times*) had either actively supported Clough or, like the *St. Paul Globe*, refrained from expressing a preference. In 1898, however, a rather amusing situation developed, in which the only Democratic paper, the *Globe*, expressed a willingness to give cordial support to the ticket, and the leaders feared to accept the offer. The editorial comment of the *Minneapolis Journal* after election contained more truth than is usually found in squibs emanating from rival editorial sanctums: "The Globe plumes itself on the fact that it was the only English daily in Minneapolis and St.

[11] August 4, 1898.

Paul which supported Mr. Lind. But we have yet to hear that Mr. Lind took any pride in the Globe's performance." [12]

The skepticism as to the *Globe's* effectiveness as a campaign organ rested partly on the fact that it was alone in persistently opposing the war and in exposing the inefficiency and corruption in the conduct of the war, and partly on the fact that, by its jibes at the vagaries of the Populists and Silver Republicans in 1896, it had offended those elements in the Fusion.[13] Early in 1896 James J. Hill had purchased the *Globe* to keep it from becoming an organ of the advocates of the free coinage of silver.[14] Naturally the reform forces were suspicious of the editor, "Colonel" George F. Spinney, who was said to be drawing a princely salary from a party of New York capitalists.[15] Rosing wrote to Lind as follows:

I met Spinney of the "Globe" several times while in the city and he gave us the most cordial assurance of support throughout the campaign, telling us that he will be guided entirely in his editorial policy by the desire of the executive committee. There seems to be something strange about this and I confess that I am not as yet satisfied as to the reason for it. Hill undoubtedly still has financial interest in the "Globe" and sometimes I feel almost afraid of the support of the "Globe." The information has come to me that Hill has absolutely refused to contribute to the Eustis campaign fund and that he is very much opposed to Eustis. Whether this is simply for the purpose of scaring Eustis and keeping aloof from him until the campaign gets good and hot and thereby compelling him to make satisfactory pledges or not it is hard to tell. I talked to some about it, who would be apt to know Hill's feelings and they said that Hill does not trust Eustis, even if he does make pledges — that he has such an unlimited ambition that he feels that, if he once gets to be governor and if he feels that he can make political capital by crushing the railroads or injuring them in any way, he would not hesitate

[12] November 11, 1898.
[13] Several editorials published in the *Globe* during July, 1898, especially "Disillusion Beginning," in the July 22 issue.
[14] James J. Pyle, *Life of James J. Hill* (New York, 1917), 2:382–84.
[15] See the *Martin County Sentinel* (Frank A. Day's paper) for February 3 and March 24, 1899.

to do so, if he could thereby land himself in Knute Nelson's place. While on the other hand he feels that if you are elected governor, the worst the railroads can expect at your hands is absolute justice.

From Fairmont Frank A. Day wrote that he mistrusted the *Globe's* motives and honesty in coming into their camp. He did not like its silence under the charge of the *Minneapolis Times* that Hill owned it "body, soul, and breeches" and feared the effect of its course under such circumstances.[16]

In spite of misgivings, the campaign committee made good use of the columns of the *Globe*, centering its attacks around Eustis' record as mayor of Minneapolis. The *Globe* had, in the person of Rehse, one of the best cartoonists in the country and his talents were used with withering effect. The vulnerable joints in the Eustis political armor were these: 1. His part in the "hospital site deal," in which one of his intimate friends was alleged to have profited at the expense of the public. 2. The alleged "Guaranty Loan swindle." In 1893 the Northwestern Guaranty Loan Company had closed its doors, with the inevitable loss of thousands of dollars to investors. Eustis as a director was charged with having had a part in what was played up as a great fraud. A cartoon was circulated showing Eustis in the foreground and the Guaranty Loan Building and the hospital in the background, and labeled "Guaranty Loan Steal — $9,000,000. City Hospital Steal — $100,000." [17] 3. Eustis' veto of the street railway transfer ordinance on the ground that the railway company should be consulted. Governor Eustis, it was charged, could be depended upon to take the side of the railroads in the battle between the people and the "railway combine" to obtain fair rates and uproot extortion. 4. Mayor Eustis was alleged to have used the police force to coerce the strikers in the Great Northern strike and in the strike of the millers. Rightly or wrongly, organized labor felt it had a grievance. 5.

[16] Day to Lind, August 26, 1898.
[17] *St. Paul Globe*, November 3, 5, 1898; *St. Paul Dispatch*, November 1, 1898; *Svenska Amerikanska Posten*, October 4, 11, 25, 1898; *Willmar Tribune*, August 10, September 28, 1898.

HELP!
[From the *St. Paul Dispatch*, November 9, 1898.]

The Good Citizenship League of Minneapolis had criticized the mayor's enforcement of the liquor laws.[18] 6. Eustis' connection with the lumbering and grain interests made him suspect as an exponent of the claims of big business.[19] 7. The enmity of the G. A. R., dating from his term as mayor. In letters Lind was assured that the "G. A. R. boys" were bestirring themselves for an onslaught against Eustis.[20] 8. The hostility of many Scandinavian voters – a topic that merits more extended treatment.

Contrasted with the previous campaign, Lind's part in the campaign of 1898 was minor. The Twelfth Minnesota did not return to the state until the middle of September and was not mustered out until November 5. Naturally Lind did not have much time for campaigning, but he did manage to make two speaking tours in which he stressed such issues as honesty in government, mentioning specifically grain inspection and weighing, the administration of the public lands, the operation of the twine plant in the Stillwater penitentiary, railway regulation, the independence of the judiciary, and the control of corporations.

Lind's most important speech was delivered in the Exposition Building in Minneapolis on October 10. He maintained that national issues had nothing to do with his campaign. Free silver was not an issue, he declared. The people in 1896 had declared for the gold standard, and time would tell whether or not the decision was wise. "To be frank with you, my friends, I will say to you that I don't know that I have any party," he said. "Perhaps it might be said of me that I am a political orphan." [21] From that time the paragraphers in the Republican and Mid-Road Populist papers busied themselves with the "orphan candidate." The Mid-Roaders seized upon the speech as proof that the Populist convention was packed with Democrats who nominated Lind. Donnelly wrote in the *Representative*: "What a

[18] See the *St. Paul Dispatch*, April 4, 1897.
[19] Lars M. Rand to Lind, July 14, 1898.
[20] O. J. Johnson to Lind, July 23, 1898; W. E. Gooding to Lind, August 3, 1898.
[21] Twin City papers, October 11, 1898.

shameful declaration! Parties represent principles; and when a man says, 'I have no party,' he says in effect, 'I have no principles.' " [22] Despite attempts to ridicule the "orphan" speech, it was good politics; it divorced the speaker from what many voters thought were vagaries of Populism and Bryanism. The Republicans sought to capitalize national issues by waving the flag and shouting that a vote for Lind was a vote for Sagasta and Spain. In an interview given at St. Cloud on his way from Washington to his home in Alexandria, Senator Knute Nelson stated: "There ain't going to be any Spaniards elected to office in Minnesota this year. God's people are all going to be elected this year." [23] The loyalty issue made little appeal to an electorate that knew that Lieutenant John Lind had promptly answered the call of his country. Even the Republican *Minneapolis Journal* censured the vitriolic *St. Paul Dispatch* for running a cartoon representing Lind sitting in his tent, with his heels cocked upon a box of hard-tack, reading the letter of notification of his nomination. In the center of the tent was a hole in the ground, and sticking up through the opening was the end of a ladder. The opening was labeled "For use in case of a Spanish attack." The *Journal* commented that it was a very poor kind of humor which attempted to make Lind appear a coward. He was entitled to immunity from such disrespectful treatment in view of the fact that he had enlisted in the only position he could fill owing to the loss of his hand.[24]

Lind followed up the reference in his letter of acceptance to the "shimmer" of imperialism in speeches condemning the incompetency of Secretary of War Alger and opposing the retention of the Philippines. Porto Rico he hoped to see admitted as a state, however, because of its proximity to the United States and because the inhabitants of the island were more like the Americans. Replying to Eustis' assertion that the moral effect

[22] October 19, 1898. See the report of Donnelly's speech in St. Paul in the *St. Paul Dispatch*, October 15, 1898.
[23] *St. Cloud Journal-Press*, quoted in the *Willmar Tribune*, July 27, 1898.
[24] Editorial reprinted in the *St. Paul Globe*, July 13, 1898. See also the *St. Paul Dispatch*, July 21, 1898.

of Lind's election in the capitals of Europe would be bad, the
"orphan" said: "I say to you that the moral effect in the capitals
of Europe . . . was produced on that May morning in the
harbor of Manila, at El Caney, and on San Juan Hill, when Cer-
vera's fleet was sunk, and when hundreds of thousands of our
citizens responded to the call of the president and tendered their
lives in defense of American honor and human liberty." [25]

In almost every political campaign there are a variety of issues
that appeal to a variety of voters; and after election a variety of
explanations of the outcome are forthcoming. But in the Minnesota campaign of 1898 the result was so extraordinary — the
defeat of a Republican gubernatorial candidate after an un-
broken succession of victories since before the Civil War — that
the explanation was reduced to the simplest terms. John Lind,
a Swedish immigrant, defeated William H. Eustis of good New
York–New England stock. What could be plainer than that
nationality turned the trick?

In a letter to the chairman of the State Republican Committee
Eustis attributed his defeat to the defection of the Swedish
vote, and in his autobiography, written more than thirty years
after the event, he expressed the same opinion.[26] Ignatius Donnelly made the same diagnosis.[27] It is true that both sides played
on the chord of racial loyalty and antipathy. For example, the
St. Paul Dispatch proclaimed that the time had come to tear the
mask of hypocrisy from the Democratic campaign. "It simply
meant that the Democrats, knowing that fully 90 per cent of
the Swedish vote of the state was Republican, believed they
could nominate a Swede on the Democratic ticket who would
alienate a large portion of this Republican vote by reason of his
race connection." This editorial was followed by a cartoon
showing Charles XII of Sweden pointing the finger of scorn at

[25] St. Paul Globe, November 4, 1898; Minneapolis Times and Minneapolis
Journal, September 17, 1898; New Ulm Review, September 21, 1898. See comments in the St. Paul Dispatch, July 23, 1898, and Svenska Amerikanska Posten,
September 27, 1898.
[26] See St. Peter Herald, December 2, 1898.
[27] Representative, November 9, 1898.

John Lind and saying: "How dare you traffic in my people's name!" [28]

It must be admitted that the Republicans were unfortunate in having a candidate who could be accused with some justification of being a "Swede hater." This charge dated back to the mayoralty campaign and was embodied in an affidavit of Adolph Peterson, sworn to on October 31, 1898, and published on the first page of the *St. Paul Globe* on November 1, 1898. Peterson swore that after the election he went to Eustis and asked him to assist the Scandinavian Republican Club of the eleventh ward to pay for the rent of a hall it had used during the campaign. According to Peterson, Eustis replied "in an angry, rude, and boisterous manner" that he had never asked the Scandinavians to organize and vote for him, exclaiming: "I wish to God that you Scandinavians had never voted for me." Throughout the campaign the *Svenska Amerikanska Posten* played up Eustis as a "Swede hater" and charged that as mayor he had discriminated against the Swedes. In a letter to the press Eustis denied that he had ever said anything derogatory to the Scandinavian people.[29]

It is perhaps safe to assume that where there was so much smoke there was some fire: that Eustis, inadvertently or otherwise, had offended certain individuals of Swedish blood; but it is hazardous to affirm that the Swedes who voted for "Honest John" were influenced solely by racial pride and solidarity. It is equally untrue to say that the Swedes stampeded the polls to cast their votes for their distinguished countryman. For example, the political editorials in *Minnesota Stats Tidning* of St. Paul, the mouthpiece of the Swedish Lutheran church, were very different in tone from those that had appeared in 1896 — so different, in fact, that *Svenska Amerikanska Posten* com-

[28] *St. Paul Dispatch*, October 22, 27, 1898. See also the issue for November 11.
[29] *St. Paul Globe*, August 7, November 1, 1898; *St. Paul Pioneer Press*, October 30, 31, 1898; *St. Paul Dispatch*, October 27, 29, 1898; *Svenska Amerikanska Posten*, August 2, October 25, 1898; *Minnesota Stats Tidning*, October 5, 19, 25, 1898.

mented that its heart was with Eustis and its head partly with Lind.[30] The editor of the St. Paul paper predicted that Lind would run strongly with the Swedes and was of the opinion that the "16 to 1" issue would not cut so great a figure as it had in the first campaign. He avowed that he could wish the candidate well if he would only come out for what he was, namely, a Republican.[31] A prominent Swedish Lutheran minister, L. G. Almén, assailed the editorial policy of this paper and denounced Eustis as a tool of Thomas Lowry, the street railway magnate.[32] The *Minneapolis Veckoblad*, the organ of the Swedish Mission Covenant, though admitting that it was better to vote for a good Irishman than for an incompetent Swede, rejoiced that in Lind the Swedes had a countryman who was democratic, honest, unassuming, and of good morals. Moreover, the editor thought it would be a novel satisfaction to vote for a man who had not raised a finger to obtain the nomination.[33] *Svenska Folkets Tidning* of Minneapolis, a paper that had not supported Lind in 1896 because of his stand on the silver issue, advocated his election in 1898 on the ground that a change would be wholesome, the Republican party having been in power so long that it had built up a clique.[34]

The election statistics do not prove that Lind was elected on the nationality issue; they do show that compared with the election of 1896 his vote fell off less than did the Republican vote for governor and also that some who had voted for Clough in 1896 voted for Lind in 1898. The most striking fact revealed by the statistics is that Eustis ran far behind his ticket in Hennepin and Ramsey counties; the loss in Hennepin County alone was more than enough to elect Lind. In Minneapolis James Gray, the Fusion candidate for mayor, was elected — another significant fact. It would be difficult to prove that he was elected

[30] *Svenska Amerikanska Posten*, November 15, 1898.
[31] *Minnesota Stats Tidning*, July 13, 27, September 14, November 16, 23, 1898.
[32] *Minnesota Stats Tidning*, August 10, October 5, November 2, 1898.
[33] *Svenska Amerikanska Posten*, September 20, 1898.
[34] *Svenska Folkets Tidning*, October 5, November 2, 1898.

because of a Scandinavian surname. Certainly the Swedish voters as a group did not vote for Lind.[35]

A combination of circumstances was responsible for the election of Lind, and it would be idle to deny that his nationality and his personal popularity exerted their influence; but what counted more heavily was the dissension among the Republican leaders.

It will be recalled that Eustis was nominated after a bitter factional fight against the Clough–Van Sant cohorts, which caused Clough to oppose Eustis openly, though Van Sant accepted defeat gracefully. Clough, however, was not the only Republican who rejoiced in the fact that the "orphan" had found a home in the Capitol, though he was less politic in his declaration.[36] Eustis was feared by prominent Republicans as a man who would eventually contest the United States senatorship with the incumbents, Knute Nelson and Cushman K. Davis. It was even suspected that Nelson's remark that no Spaniards would be elected to office was deeper than it appeared to most people; that it was made to irritate fair-minded people and drive them into the Lind camp.[37] Over against this, however, it should be said that in some quarters Lind's election was regarded as a blow to Nelson's aspirations for re-election to the Senate.[38] We are able to peer behind the scenes through the Hubbard episode.

[35] Between the elections of 1898 and 1900 a pamphlet was published which gave the election statistics for 1896 and 1898 and purported to prove that the Swedish Republican vote elected Lind. The pamphlet is headed "It being of prime importance that Republicans should know, what Republicans voted for Lind both in '96 and '98, and what the prevailing cause that influenced them so to vote, the following statistics are given to aid a correct solution." In his "Autobiography" Eustis analyzes the election statistics for 1896 and 1898 to prove that he was defeated on the nationality issue. As a corrective to this, see an analysis of the vote in three towns in Martin County in the *Martin County Sentinel*, November 18, 1898. With reference to the vote in Hennepin County, see letter from James A. Peterson to Knute Nelson, November 26, 1898, in the Nelson Papers.

[36] J. B. Wakefield to Nelson, November 11, 1898, in the Nelson Papers.

[37] W. E. Gooding of the Hennepin County Democratic Committee to Lind, August 3, 1898.

[38] There are several letters in the Nelson Papers to this effect. Nelson wrote a letter of congratulation to Eustis on his nomination and offered his services in the campaign. Eustis to Nelson, August 2, 1898.

Lucius F. Hubbard, governor of Minnesota from 1882 to 1887, was prominently mentioned in 1897 as the likely appointee to the ambassadorship to Italy. It appears that President McKinley had decided upon the appointment when as a result of charges against Hubbard's business integrity the matter was dropped. A biographer of the governors of Minnesota asserts that the allegations came from a "noted intermeddler" in state and national politics, a member of a political party not in sympathy with Hubbard.[39] The former governor was vindicated, but too late to obtain the coveted appointment.

The political sequel to this episode is found in the Lind Papers. On January 6, 1898 — when the press of the state was absorbed in speculation about the political future of Lind — Mrs. Hubbard wrote a strictly confidential communication to Lind requesting an appointment with him at the Hubbard home in Red Wing or preferably at either the Ryan Hotel in St. Paul or the West Hotel in Minneapolis. She confided to him that she wished to give him information that might be of benefit to him in the near future. The meeting was held, and on March 11 Mrs. Hubbard sent the "papers I promised" in the hope that Lind would find them useful and that they would give him an idea of the "manner in which Mr. Hill is controlling politics in this state." The letter concluded with the request that the papers be returned to her, "as the Gov. does not know that I have sent them." On April 1 she wrote again acknowledging the return of the papers and giving Lind the liberty of using them at his discretion. "I hope Mr. Towne will have an opportunity to see them," she wrote. "I consider Mr. J. J. Hill a man who has lost his soul — a 'whitened sepulchre.'"

In due time Charles A. Towne of Duluth, chairman of the National Committee of the Silver Republican party, was acquainted with the contents of the papers. On July 9 — about a week before Lind's letter of acceptance was made public — Towne wrote to Lind as follows:

Now, John, I regard this a very important matter. We must by

⁹⁹ James H. Baker, *Lives of the Governors of Minnesota*, pp. 273–74.

all means handle it effectively and carefully. . . . Of course neither you nor I must actively appear in the actual disclosure. The method by which it shall be put before the people, the means for making the showing absolutely conclusive and indisputable, and other incidents, ought to be decided carefully and in due season. My judgment is that with all the overt and admitted blemishes on Davis' [Senator C. K. Davis] associations, with this particular matter to give them point and force, and with a hard, well-directed fight against the rings, the trusts, the railroads and combinations, etc. etc.[40]

What specific information was contained in the Hubbard Papers is not revealed in the Lind Papers, but it is obvious that all was not well in the Republican camp and that the party machinery was not functioning smoothly during the campaign of 1898.

However acrimonious the contest between Lind and Eustis may appear to the historian who examines the newspaper files, the personal relations between the two men remained most respectful. Neither deigned to throw mud at the other. Frank A. Day, editor of the *Martin County Sentinel*, commented as follows: "Mr. Eustis' telegram of congratulation to John Lind was most gracious and manly and Gov. Lind's reply could not have been improved upon by Lord Chesterfield in his palmiest days." [41] At a reception for Mr. and Mrs. Lind in the Press Club parlors in Minneapolis on November 17, 1898, the rival candidates met for the first time after the election and clasped hands most cordially.[42]

Many years of life remained to Lind and Eustis, and both men were able to render valuable services to city, state, and nation. Twenty-five years after the political campaign in which they had played the principal parts, Lind had the pleasure of writing a letter to his friend expressing appreciation of his generous donations for the medical care of crippled children.

[40] See letter from Henry N. Somsen to Lind, July 27, 1898.
[41] November 11, 1898. See comment in the *Minneapolis Journal*, November 11, 1898. The telegrams were published in the latter paper on November 10 and 11, 1898.
[42] *St. Paul Globe*, November 18, 1898.

I have had it in mind a long time to express to you formally my high appreciation of the noble, generous spirit which has actuated you to devote the earnings of a long and successful career to the aid of the unfortunate. This is the kind of charity that is worth while. Your monument need not be erected by the taxation of your fellows. It is already builded in the minds of those who now know you and it will survive forever in the grateful remembrance of the generations you have helped.[43]

After the election the Lind home in New Ulm was besieged by friends and politicians bringing congratulations, advice, and applications for office. Mrs. Lind wrote to Norman, who was a student at the University of Minnesota: "I wish you could see some of the flowers we have, roses, carnations, chrysanthemums, a houseful of beautiful flowers from Minneapolis — and about two hundred telegrams from all over the state, also different states. Have been serenaded every night, city band, regimental band, mandolin club, and now the little boys in town with sticks and pans." Norman was advised to write a letter to his father to offer congratulations on the first victory over the Republican party in forty years, but he was admonished not to show his elation to his Republican friends.[44]

[43] Lind to W. H. Eustis, December 29, 1923.
[44] Mrs. Lind to Norman, November 11, 1898.

XI

GOVERNOR OF MINNESOTA

THE WEEKS intervening between the election and the inauguration of the "orphan" governor were crowded with activity. After winding up affairs connected with the quartermaster's office, the governor-elect faced the infinitely more difficult task of mapping out a course that would satisfy the demands of the leaders of the several groups of the alliance. He had the advantage, however, of being one of the most popular governors the state had ever had, a fact that was abundantly demonstrated by the unusually large attendance at the reception given for Governor and Mrs. Lind at the Ryan Hotel in St. Paul on the evening of January 3, 1899. Lind was averse to holding an inaugural ball, though he agreed to attend if it were arranged. Accordingly the committee arranged a reception, which was in accord with his wishes. Former Governor Ramsey and Governor Clough were conspicuously present; and one of the agreeable surprises was the appearance of William H. Eustis. His loyal greeting to the governor-elect was rewarded by Mrs. Lind, who plucked a rose from her bouquet and handed it to him. The following day the inaugural ceremonies were held.

If Lind's triumph was a cause for alarm in conservative circles, the governor's message quickly allayed the fear of the "menace of radicalism." It was greeted with a chorus of praise; Republicans, Democrats, and Populists vied in acclaiming it one of the most level-headed documents ever written by any governor. Yet it was far from colorless; on the contrary, it was specific and pointed in its recommendations, which looked toward fundamental reforms in government and changes in governmental policies.[1]

[1] In several issues during January, 1899, the *St. Paul Globe* published press comments on the message.

The *Duluth News-Tribune* rejoiced that "instead of turning out a screeching creed worthy of a Kansas populist, Gov. Lind wrote a sensible, well-tempered, sharply pointed message — a rattling good document, worthy of the careful attention of the state's lawmakers."[2] The able political reporter of the *Minneapolis Journal*, W.W. Jermane ("Jerry J."), found the message in striking contrast to the speeches made by the Fusionists during the campaign. "Lind is trying to be decent," he wrote, "but it will be hard work in his present company." His paper said editorially that the document "is remarkably free from demogoguery and claptrap. It is nearer the product of statesmanship than any message delivered by a Minnesota chief executive for a good many years."[3] The editor of the *Luverne Herald*, Herbert J. Miller, a Republican member of the Senate, commented as follows: "Without committing itself to the indorsement of all its recommendations, the *Herald* has no hesitancy in saying that it considers Gov. Lind's inaugural message one of the ablest and most noteworthy of all the state papers that have come under its notice."[4] And the *St. Paul Globe*, with inevitable irony, said, "Mr. Lind talks more like a hard-headed Western business man than a Spaniard. Eh, Pioneer Press?"[5]

As legislator and as governor Lind was influenced by his work as teacher and superintendent of schools. His message, while eminently practical, reflected somewhat the academic point of view. As governor he frequently attended educational meetings and addressed gatherings of teachers. His address at the meeting of the Minnesota Education Association in the winter of 1900 was pronounced the most educative part of the program.[6] Perhaps the best commendation of the forward looking quality of the message came from Professor Richard T. Ely, director of the School of Economics, Political Science, and His-

[2] Quoted in the *St. Paul Dispatch*, January 11, 1899.

[3] *Minneapolis Journal*, January 7, 1899; *Martin County Sentinel*, January 7, 1899.

[4] Quoted in the *Martin County Sentinel*, January 20, 1899.

[5] *St. Paul Globe*, January 5, 1899.

[6] *Practical Education*, quoted in the *Martin County Sentinel*, September 9, 1900.

tory of the University of Wisconsin. "I like particularly what you say about forestry, and also about mineral reservations, especially with respect to the reservation of rights to the states," he wrote. The professor informed the governor that he intended to read to his class in the distribution of wealth extracts from the message to illustrate the fortunate drift of opinion on the part of those who truly had the public welfare at heart.[7]

With such unanimity about the excellence of the message, it might be supposed that the legislature would respond readily to the "long catena of matters for the consideration of that body"; but a legislature with a strong Republican majority in both houses was not enthusiastic about carrying out the recommendations of a Fusion governor. For the most part it ignored his demands for reform in the state administrative machinery, for a more equitable system of taxation, including a tax commission, for the regulation of trusts, for a different method of caring for the insane, for a board of control to supervise penal, charitable, and correctional institutions, for the prohibition of free passes on railroad trains, and for the free printing by the state of school textbooks.

The governor's appointments were promptly confirmed by the Senate. Even the Republican state auditor, Robert C. Dunn, admitted in his newspaper that fitness for office appeared to be the first consideration, though some of the governor's staunch followers thought he went too far in rewarding old soldiers. Frank A. Day had no fault to find with the war veterans, "but there is such a thing as having too much Smith," he said.[8]

Leonard A. Rosing of Cannon Falls, Lind's campaign manager in his three gubernatorial campaigns, was appointed as his secretary. A committee from the Farmers' Alliance, headed by Ignatius Donnelly, called on the governor to urge the appointment of farmers to certain important posts. The following Populists were awarded important offices: E. M. Pope of Mankato,

[7] Bulletin of the Reform Press Bureau, St. Paul, printed in the *Martin County Sentinel*, March 24, 1899.

[8] *Martin County Sentinel*, January 27, February 24, 1899; *St. Peter Herald*, March 24, 1899.

public examiner; P. M. Ringdal of Crookston, railroad commissioner; and J. M. Bowler of Renville, dairy commissioner. Fred W. Johnson of New Ulm, a Silver Republican and brother of John A. Johnson, who was an intimate friend of Lind and one of the incorporators of his gubernatorial boom, was made state librarian. An appointment gratifying to organized labor was that of Martin McHale of Minneapolis, a member of the Stonemasons' Union, as commissioner of labor.[9]

Before the legislature convened there was much speculation about the mutual attitude of the Democratic and Populist parties. At a conference attended by members of both parties it was decided to join in a complimentary vote in the organization of both branches and to cooperate as far as possible in legislative matters. In both houses, however, the Republican majorities were so large that the minority was almost powerless to further the program of the governor.[10]

In the House of Representatives there was no question about the leadership of Jacob F. Jacobson of Madison and C. F. Staples of Dakota County. Jacobson, a bluff, unpolished native of Norway, was dean of the House and a unique character. He was said to be the only member who talked almost all the time without talking himself to death. But his sterling honesty and character won for him the sincere regard of his colleagues. Lind and Jacobson were acquaintances of long standing, the latter having been a delegate to the Republican congressional convention that nominated Lind in 1886. Jacobson's adherence to the Republican party was destined to be rewarded with the nomination for governor in 1908, but in 1899 it was said that he and Lind were working together; and the *St. Paul Dispatch* even alleged that he was a Populist. The *Martin County Sentinel* paid the following tribute to him: "Representative Jacobson has tackled the corporations with his old-time vigor. . . . 'Jake' is a power in the land and if the Republicans had a few more like

[9] W. W. Jermane in the *Minneapolis Journal*, January 6, 1899.

[10] *Minneapolis Journal*, January 7, 1899; John A. Johnson's letter in the *St. Peter Herald*, January 6, 1899.

him in the state there would be no excuse for the existence of a Populist party." [11]

In the Senate there was an almost total lack of leadership, but the Republicans had several able members in Bert Miller of Luverne, Fred B. Snyder of Minneapolis, Allen J. Greer of Lake City, Timothy D. Sheehan of St. Paul, Edward T. Young of Appleton, and John J. Ryder of East Grand Forks. Among the minority members was S. A. Stockwell of Minneapolis, a Democratic-Populist, who in a sense was the minority leader. He usually supported the governor's nominations and policies.

Serving his first term of civil office was Senator John A. Johnson of St. Peter, then thirty-six years of age. The future governor, running on the Fusion ticket, had defeated an orthodox Republican, Professor J. S. Carlson of Gustavus Adolphus College. Johnson wrote a weekly "Capitol Letter" for his newspaper. These weekly reports were not only informing but they reflected the spirit and attitude of both the man and his paper. The paper was gentlemanly and in no sense rigidly partisan; during the campaign it spoke well of Eustis and his Republican supporters. Johnson's independent course was not to the liking of the *St. Paul Globe*, which stated that he seemed to find more or less delight in annoying the administration, despite the fact that he had received more recognition than most of his colleagues. [12]

The most important measure of the session, which was introduced by Jacobson, provided for an increase in the tax on the gross earnings of railways from three to four per cent. In his inaugural message the governor recommended to the legislature the amendment of the gross earnings tax so that railway property would no longer escape its fair and proportionate burden of taxation. He presented statistics to show that railways in

[11] *St. Peter Herald*, January 6, 1899; *Martin County Sentinel*, January 27, May 12, 1899.

[12] *St. Peter Herald*, March 10, 1899; *Martin County Sentinel*, March 24, April 28, 1899; *St. Paul Globe*, February 23, 1899. The best job of political reporting during this session of the legislature was done by W. W. Jermane ("Jerry J.") of the *Minneapolis Journal*.

Minnesota were taxed less heavily than in neighboring states, and he had not the slightest doubt, he said, that well-considered legislation to that end was constitutional.

The Republican opposition to the bill was based on its alleged unconstitutionality. It was stated that some railways were operating under territorial charters which provided that the companies should pay a three per cent gross earnings tax in lieu of other taxes and that these provisions amounted to contracts between the territory and the companies. Hence, it was argued, it was not competent for the legislature, without the consent of the companies, to increase the rate to make it approximate the general rate of taxation; the territorial legislature had contracted away the power of taxation, and subsequent legislatures were bound by the terms of the contract for all time to come. In a letter to Senator Charles Halvorson of Dawson the governor disposed of this argument as follows:

To make this point clear to you, let me reiterate that there is not a railroad company doing business in this state today, with the single exception noted, that has ever paid a cent of gross earnings tax to the state in pursuance of the provision of any territorial charter; that the companies themselves repudiated the taxation provisions of the territorial charters, and that all the gross earnings taxes that have been paid to the state have been paid under and in pursuance of legislation enacted since the admission of the state. . . . These various acts passed by the legislature in 1865 and accepted by the companies were a complete revocation of the provisions of the old charters and established new "contracts," which were accepted and acted upon by the companies.[13]

The Jacobson bill passed the House on February 7 with only five negative votes, but it was killed in the Senate by a close vote, after Fred B. Snyder, one of the ablest lawyers in the Senate, had made a masterly speech in its favor. There was great indignation throughout the state, and it was freely charged that unfair methods had been used to defeat the bill. The governor publicly expressed his belief that it was killed by the corrupt

[13] Letter dated March 25, 1899.

use of money. Senator Bert Miller's *Luverne Herald* stated that it was defeated by a "damnably rotten railroad lobby and the men who served its purpose for their own private gain." The veteran Republican editor of the *Windom Reporter* censured the "fool Republican Senate" and predicted that Lind would be re-elected unless the Republicans shelved the old and conservative members. "Jerry J.," the correspondent of the *Minneapolis Journal,* referring to the errors of the Republicans, said:

Lind's record in the office of governor will be another strong campaign argument. He is the shrewdest politician in public life in the state. The Republicans are continually crying about his "mistakes," when they know, if they know anything, that from the point of view of the people, he is giving as satisfactory an administration as the state has had for years.

The reporter praised the governor's stand before the State Board of Equalization and his administration of the dairy and food department, which raised him head and shoulders above his Republican predecessors. The *Journal,* however, was the only Twin City daily in favor of the Jacobson bill.[14]

Though defeated on this major item of the tax reform program, the administration made some progress toward such reform. The governor kept in touch with state boards in a way that few, if any, of his predecessors had done. Under his direction the Board of Equalization raised the assessment of the street railway companies of St. Paul and Minneapolis by about $2,000,000 and that of the mining companies in St. Louis County by $1,600,000, as well as those of the lumber syndicates. The railway commissioners investigated freight rates and in some cases reduced them as much as four and one-half cents per hundred.

As when he was administering the Tracy land office, Lind threatened to return to the Department of the Interior clear lists

[14] *Minneapolis Journal,* February 8, March 29, April 12, 18, 1899; *St. Paul Dispatch,* October 18, 1900; *St. Peter Herald,* March 31, April 21, May 19, June 2, October 20, 1899; *Martin County Sentinel,* February 10, March 24, April 14, 28, March 19, 1899.

for the benefit of the Hastings and Dakota land grant. In this he did not have the cooperation of the Department of the Interior, however, in spite of the fact that in 1895 the legislature had attempted to forfeit the Hastings and Dakota grant.[15] The governor signed the Somerville bill placing foreign corporations on an equal footing with Minnesota corporations and requiring them to pay fees equal to those paid by other corporations. This law brought a considerable revenue to the state. The governor vetoed the Miller bill, designed to make findings of fact in the proceedings before the Railroad and Warehouse Commission official court records. Bert Miller, the author of the bill, charged that the veto was made at the instance or demand of the Great Northern Railway; but in a letter addressed to Miller, in which he displayed sound legal knowledge, clear reasoning, and righteous indignation, the governor proved that the proposed law would have worked to the advantage of the railroads, and he demanded that the charge be retracted. This demand the senator was gracious enough to comply with.[16]

It is strange that the man who had staged many a fight against railroad companies, and who as governor had recommended the prohibition of railway passes to state employees, should have made bold to address a letter to James J. Hill, president of the Great Northern Railway, suggesting that his company grant free transportation to state officials. In a long letter to the governor Hill pointed out that his road paid a tax to the state in excess of one thousand dollars a day, and that apparently for the reason that it was a Minnesota corporation subject to "all manner of indignity and imposition and calls for gifts for objects in which it has not the slightest interest." "The state of Minnesota," he continued,

is not a pauper and it collects from its citizens taxes enough to more than pay fair wages to all of its employes. . . . I feel the time has come when the railway companies should absolutely refuse to do more for the state than to discharge their legal obligations as citizens

[15] Britton and Gray to James A. Tawney, September 12, 1900, in the Tawney Papers in the Minnesota Historical Society.
[16] *Luverne Herald*, June 9, 22, 1899; *St. Peter Herald*, July 7, 1899.

of the state. . . . I am sorry to refuse any request that you may make; at the same time, the principle involved is an important one and the time has come when the state of Minnesota, so far as this company is concerned, must pay its own bills.[17]

Governor Lind vetoed two other bills, both of which were passed over his veto. Before his inauguration he had visited Wisconsin for the express purpose of acquainting himself with the details of the Wisconsin plan for caring for the insane. In his inaugural message he recommended a system by which the more tractable patients would be farmed out in colonies and thus made to contribute to their own support. In such small communities, he thought, these unfortunate wards of the state would fare better than in large institutions where they would be idle most of the time. Friends could visit them, and it would be possible for some of them occasionally to visit their near-by homes. Both county and state would contribute to the support of these communities. Dr. William W. Folwell of the University of Minnesota and Dr. S. G. Smith of St. Paul favored a modified plan by which the insane would be cared for in the larger county hospitals in Hennepin and Ramsey counties. The State Board of Corrections and Charities also favored some such plan. The governor recommended that the extreme cases be cared for in well-equipped hospitals for the insane. The governor's plan was defeated by the demands of the cities of Anoka and Hastings, which contended that they had not received their share of state institutions. They were backed by the commercial interests of St. Paul and Minneapolis and the northern part of the state. Accordingly a bill was passed establishing insane asylums at Hastings and Anoka, which was vetoed and passed over the veto.[18]

[17] James J. Hill to Lind, June 23, 1899. In his biennial message the governor stated: "Our state enjoys the peculiar distinction of being the only one whose laws expressly authorize the issuance of railroad passes. . . . I repeat the recommendation [of former governors] that the practice be abolished root and branch."

[18] Folwell, *A History of Minnesota*, 3:247–48; *Minneapolis Journal*, January 3, April 7, 18, 1899; *St. Paul Globe*, January 5, March 9, 1899; *St. Paul Dispatch*, April 7, 1899; *St. Peter Herald*, March 31, April 14, 21, 1899.

In 1897 a law was enacted by the legislature providing for the payment of a bounty of one cent a pound on sugar manufactured in the state. A sugar factory was founded in Minneapolis, and a claim subsequently made to a bounty of about $20,000. When the officials of the factory applied to the state treasurer for this sum, they were told that it could not be paid without a special appropriation of the legislature. The appropriation bill was duly passed. It was vetoed by the governor, but passed over the veto. Lind objected to the bill because no time limit was fixed by the bill and no limit to the amount that could be paid to any one producer. Moreover, he doubted the wisdom of legislation that took property from one taxpayer and gave it to another. He did not question the obligation of the state to pay the bounty already accrued, but he objected to a permanent policy of taking property from one taxpayer and transferring it to another to enable him to carry on an industry which but for such aid would not be profitable or self-sustaining. The legislature repealed the law, but the appropriation was paid.[19]

The *St. Paul Dispatch* was indignant over the "insolent tone" of the message and condemned it in the following words:

The veto was merely a cheap piece of political buncombe that confessed itself on its face, and simply shows that the governor felt his democracy was under suspicion, and that he must do at least one silly and unpatriotic thing to establish his party standing. He hasn't been a Democrat long enough to have become thoroughly imbecile, but, under the circumstances, he is making encouraging progress.[20]

The sugar bounty veto message was pointed at another bounty, the so-called Lalbourne bill, which provided for a bounty on pig iron smelted in the state. The veto message was read just before the House voted on the Lalbourne bill, which was defeated. The message was credited with contributing to the negative vote.[21]

[19] *St. Paul Dispatch*, February 17, 18, 21, May 18, 1899; *St. Paul Globe*, February 19, 1899; *St. Peter Herald*, February 24, March 3, 10, 1899.
[20] *St. Paul Dispatch*, February 20, 1899.
[21] *St. Paul Dispatch*, February 8, 27, 1899; *St. Peter Herald*, February 24, 1899.

During the campaign the Fusionists had made a great deal of noise about the incompetency of state officials; the management of the Stillwater prison twine factory was singled out for special attention, some papers going so far as to demand the removal of Warden Henry Wolfer, who had held the position since 1892. A few days after Lind's inauguration, Wolfer was offered the position of warden of the Connecticut state prison, with a considerable increase in salary. The board of managers of the Stillwater prison and Governor Lind held an informal conference at which Wolfer was asked to be present. The governor spoke kindly of the warden's administration and told him that he was in no position to advise him about the Connecticut offer; he promised, however, that if the legislature appropriated money to raise his salary, he would have no objection, though he would not take the initiative in recommending it. The upshot was that Wolfer remained in his position. Three months later a joint legislative committee made a report indorsing Wolfer's work and praising conditions in the twine factory. Before the end of the year, however, Wolfer resigned to accept a position with a commercial firm at a much larger salary than the state had paid him. His successor was General Charles McCormick Reeve, an officer of the Thirteenth Minnesota Regiment, which had seen service in the Philippines. Reeve's administration came under fire in the campaign of 1900; and shortly after Van Sant's inauguration in 1901, Wolfer was reappointed to the Stillwater post.[22]

During his first month of office Lind removed John S. O'Brien from the board of prison managers, after a stormy interview in which the governor charged him with making unworthy suggestions in the matter of appointments. The *Minneapolis Journal* said the governor had acted vigorously and promptly and had added to his reputation.[23]

[22] *Willmar Tribune*, July 20, 1898; *St. Paul Globe*, January 12, 17, February 7, 16, 1899, February 8, 1901; *St. Paul Dispatch*, January 11, 1899, August 14, 1900; *Minneapolis Journal*, April 17, 1899; *Minnesota Stats Tidning*, January 25, 1899; *St. Peter Herald*, August 3, 10, 1900.

[23] *Minneapolis Journal*, January 31, 1899; *St. Paul Globe*, January 31, February 1, 1899; *St. Paul Dispatch*, January 31, February 16, 1899.

In a special message the governor suggested that the prison board be authorized to extend the facilities for manufacturing binding twine, in view of the fact that it had become a source of profit to the state and had made the prison self-sustaining.[24] The Fusionists had also charged during the campaign that the Department of Grain Inspection was corrupt and that inspection was conducted in the interest of buyers and against the interests of the shipper and producer. Lind did not disappoint his followers who demanded that he institute a searching investigation of grain inspection and weighing. Before his inauguration he was apprised that on December 12 the Hennepin County delegation to the legislature had been forced to have a conference in the Chamber of Commerce in Minneapolis with representatives of the grain inspection department. In the course of the meeting the legislators were informed that the Minneapolis grain men had decided to stand by the grain inspection department; and it was demanded of them that they oppose all attempts by the governor to obtain legislation changing the existing order of things. The governor's informant stated that this information would probably not get into the daily press.[25]

During the first three weeks of the legislative session the Jacobson resolution directing a joint committee of nine to investigate the grain department and to rectify abuses with respect to grades was unanimously adopted. The committee reported that grading of wheat had not been uniform; that some of the inspectors had been careless and incompetent; that the weighing of grain at terminals had been done in a loose manner; and that farmers had suffered heavy loss by shipping unclean wheat and by loading wheat into dirty cars. Ignatius Donnelly said in the *Representative* that under Lind's new inspection bureau practically another grade of wheat had been added, thereby placing hundreds of thousands of dollars into the pockets of the farmers which had formerly gone into the hands of the wheat

[24] *St. Paul Dispatch*, April 8, 1899; *St. Paul Globe*, April 9, 1899.
[25] L. C. Hodgson to Lind, December 13, 1898, in the Lind Papers in the Minnesota Historical Society.

ring. The governor signed the Torson bill providing for the popular election of members of the Grain and Warehouse Commission.[26]

The governor's recommendation that the state print its own textbooks for use in the public schools was defeated in the House by a vote of 57 to 46. The bill was supported by the typographical unions, but it was opposed by various other interests, including Catholics and Lutherans, who argued that they ought not to be compelled to assist in publishing books that would not be used in their parochial schools.[27]

The achievements of the Lind administration, judged by the actions of the legislature, are not impressive. Only three or four of the governor's recommendations were acted upon favorably. On the other hand, the record is bare of legislation detrimental to the state. Lind's presence in the executive office was a guarantee that the bills would be carefully scrutinized. In his final message to the legislature in 1901 he repeated his recommendations for tax reform, including an income tax in lieu of the personal property tax, an inheritance tax, an increase of the gross earnings tax, and taxes on foreign and domestic corporations.[28]

Lind was one of the few governors of Minnesota who have had the opportunity of appointing a United States senator. In January, 1899, the legislature re-elected Cushman Kellogg Davis for a third term, his services having been so satisfactory that there was no doubt of his choice by the Republican majority. The Fusionists, however, had some difficulty in agreeing to whom should be given the complimentary vote of the minority. The Populists were jealous of the supremacy of the Democrats and sought to resist the process of absorption. For this reason the complimentary vote was given to Charles A. Towne of Duluth, a Silver Republican, much to the chagrin of the Gold

[26] *St. Peter Herald*, January 20, October 10, 1899; *Minneapolis Journal*, April 17, 1899.
[27] *St. Paul Globe*, January 22, February 3, 1899; *St. Paul Dispatch*, March 23, 1899.
[28] The *Minneapolis Journal* for April 18, 1899, has a comprehensive review of the legislative session.

Democratic *St. Paul Globe,* which complained that the tail of the dog undertook successfully to wag the dog. "Cut off this tail that assumes to wag the dog," it said. "The dog will look and act all the better. T'ell with Towne and the Silver Republicans, anyway."[29]

Shortly before election in 1900, Senator Davis became critically ill. Governor Lind sent his kindest regards to his good friend, to which the senator responded: "Give the governor my best wishes and say to him that I consider him one of the very best governors the state of Minnesota has ever had. Also, tell him that I regret that political differences prevent me from supporting him."[30] The popular senator died on November 27, 1900, and Governor Lind issued a suitable proclamation.

During the campaign of 1900 Republicans and Democrats had predicted that in the event of Davis' death, the appointment to fill the vacancy until the legislature elected a successor in 1901 would go to Towne, who, though a Silver Republican, had won the good will of the Democrats by working like a Trojan for Fusion and by declining the Populist nomination for the vice-presidency in 1900. Apparently Towne surmised that the governor was in doubt about appointing him, and so he addressed a long letter to him in which he urged his claims to the distinction and implored the governor to appoint him.[31] In due time his uneasy hour was ended, and he became the first senator from Minnesota without the Republican label in many years.

One event that occurred during Lind's administration brought him considerable anxiety as well as criticism, namely, the question of the return of the Thirteenth Minnesota Regiment from the Philippine Islands. During the weeks between the signing of the protocol and the ratification of the treaty with Spain, opposition on the part of anti-imperialists within both parties to the establishment of a colonial empire, with its attendant problems, became pronounced. While the ratification of the

[29] *Minneapolis Journal,* January 13, 1899; *St. Paul Globe,* January 19, 1900.
[30] *St. Peter Herald,* November 9, 1899.
[31] Charles A. Towne to Lind, November 18, 1900. The letter was written in anticipation of Davis' death.

GOVERNOR AND MRS. LIND

treaty was pending in the Senate (it was ratified on February 6, 1899), Senator Stockwell of Minneapolis introduced in the legislature a resolution opposing the annexation of the Philippines.[32] The resolution was defeated by overwhelming votes in both houses, but it was favored by the governor. By no twist of words could Lind be called a pacifist, but he had consistently opposed large appropriations for the army and navy and he was adamant in his opposition to the imperialist policy of the McKinley administration. In a speech delivered before the united patriotic societies in the Peoples Church in St. Paul on Washington's birthday, 1899, the governor made some pointed remarks against the administration. "The regular has no place in our Constitution," he said. "A navy has a place there, but the Constitution says that Congress shall have power to raise armies and to provide for their maintenance for no period longer than two years. There is no such limitation as to the navy." He said the fathers had implicit confidence in the volunteer. "We have always had and must have a standing army on the same lines as we have peace officers in every community." The cavalry and artillery were of necessity permanent, but they should be merely a nucleus for other forces. "As our country grows there is necessity for a standing army, but not in the sense of standing armies of Europe."[33]

With the papers publishing casualties among Americans engaged in the war against the Filipino insurrectionists, mass meetings were held all over the country protesting against imperialism. In Minnesota the opposition took concrete form in the demand for the speedy return from the Philippines of the Thirteenth Minnesota Volunteer Infantry. There had been great rejoicing among the men of this regiment when, on May 12, 1898, it received orders to join the expeditionary forces against the Spaniards in the remote islands; but after the Spaniards had laid down their arms, the Minnesotans thought the purpose for which they had enlisted had been accomplished.

[32] *Minneapolis Journal*, January 19, 1899.
[33] *St. Paul Globe*, February 23, 1899.

The longing of the soldiers for home and the desire of their relatives and friends to see them took the form of demands on the governor, congressmen, and senators that they bend every effort to have the necessary orders issued. On April 4, 1899, at a meeting of the Thirteenth Regiment Auxiliary Association in St. Paul, it was voted with only two negative votes to use every effort to bring the regiment home. Two weeks later the governor received the following cablegram from the officers of the regiment: "The regiment must be ordered home and mustered out of service immediately." [34]

In a communication to the legislature on April 17, 1899, the governor expressed disappointment because he was unable to report a definite time for the return of the regiment. He had telegraphed President McKinley about the matter, but had received no reply. He left it to the legislature to determine what action should be taken. Within a few days the governor had an audience with McKinley and officials of the War Department and received assurance that the regiment would start for home not later than June 1. [35]

Some Republican papers seized upon the governor's efforts in behalf of the regiment to denounce him as a renegade, a copperhead, and an ally of Aguinaldo. The *St. Paul Dispatch* said that it was due to him and some others that the regiment had become the laughingstock of the country, and it accused the "spineless governor" of playing godmother to a few weakling officers. [36]

The embarkation of the regiment was delayed until August 10. In San Francisco, in the early part of September, Governor Lind and his staff, with representatives of civic associations, welcomed the returning heroes; and on October 12 no less a personage than the president of the United States in the presence of a large concourse of people welcomed their return to Minneapolis. In the reviewing stand on Nicollet Avenue were Presi-

[34] *St. Paul Globe*, April 5, 20, 1899. The Knute Nelson Papers contain letters and papers asking that the regiment be mustered out.
[35] *St. Paul Dispatch*, April 17, 25, 1899; *St. Paul Globe*, April 29, 1899.
[36] *St. Paul Dispatch*, May 2, 1899; *St. Paul Globe*, April 27, 1899.

dent McKinley, Governor Lind, Secretary of the Navy Long, and former Senator William D. Washburn.

On this gala occasion "Honest John," with characteristic blunt honesty, delivered an address that endeared him to thousands and furnished a welcome opportunity to newspapers for loosing their shafts at him. The governor's breach of hospitality consisted of an address at the Exposition Building, following McKinley's welcome to the soldiers, in which he failed to make any direct reference to the presence of the president of the United States. McKinley's speech was a justification of his policy of acquiring territory; he cited the objections that had been made to it and showed how they had been disproved by events. The regiment having been welcomed by the people of the Twin Cities and by the president of the United States, the governor proceeded to bid it welcome on behalf of the people of the state. He rejoiced over the happy reunion of friends and relatives and congratulated the soldiers on their valor; but he went on to say that to the thoughtful citizen it was also a solemn occasion because the state had reached a stage in its development that eliminated the volunteer soldier from the sphere of national activity and influence in the future.

By our growth and development the mission of the American volunteer soldier has come to an end. For purposes of conquest and subjugation he is unfit, for he carries a conscience as well as a gun. The volunteer soldier has always stood for self-government, liberty, and justice. With your generation he will pass from the stage of our national life. His fame and his example will continue the heritage of our people — the theme of story and song. May the spirit which has actuated him ever guide our people, and temper the strength of the nation which has outgrown him, with the eternal principles for which he has fought and died.[37]

It may be true, as the *Minneapolis Journal* commented, that the governor's "nose was out of joint" and that he was ignorant of what the proprieties of the occasion demanded, but with re-

[37] *Minneapolis Journal*, October 12, 1899. See comments in the *Minneapolis Journal*, October 13 and 14, and in *Svenska Folkets Tidning*, October 25.

gard for what was in the minds of the soldiers of the Thirteenth Regiment and of their friends and relatives plain John Lind spoke the unadulterated truth and did not allow politeness to gloss over what every reporter present knew were the facts in the case. Many years later, while acting in the capacity of personal representative of the president of the United States in Mexico, Lind had occasion to remember more than once his experience with a volunteer regiment reluctantly engaged in a war of conquest.

XII

THE THIRD BATTLE

A T THE beginning of the year 1900 the Fusionists were not on the anxious seat over a nominee for governor as they had been in the two preceding campaigns. They were almost unanimous that John Lind was one of the ablest and most popular chief executives in the history of the state; and privately — even publicly — influential Republicans admitted that he had shown courage, ability, and good judgment. The hope of defeating him depended upon the ability of the Republicans to nominate a man satisfactory to the various factions and the possibility that in a presidential election year in a Republican state their candidate might be swept into office on the crest of the presidential vote, despite the fact that in 1896 Clough had narrowly escaped defeat at the hands of Lind. The nomination of Samuel R. Van Sant of Winona was a good choice. He was a politician of the old school, loyal to his party, pleasing in personality, and very popular with the G. A. R., of which he was a prominent and active member. McKinley, Roosevelt, and Van Sant buttons were popular all over the state.

When Lind called himself an orphan in 1898, he virtually cut loose from the three parties that nominated him, and many voted for him as an independent in preference to Eustis. As governor, however, he followed the leadership of Bryan, his idol, and his experience with a Republican legislature which blocked his comprehensive reform program convinced him that he had little in common with a party dominated by such men as Mark Hanna, Matthew S. Quay, and Henry Cabot Lodge, and men of that stripe. He awaited an auspicious occasion to announce to the people of the state that his political orphanage was at an end. The occasion was the Jackson Day banquet held at the West Hotel in Minneapolis, on January 10, 1900, at which Bryan and Towne were present. At the meeting following the banquet both guests made great speeches, but at the banquet Lind made a tremendous impression. In the words of the *Minneapolis Journal* reporter, "The climax of the most successful festal day in the history of the Democratic party in Minnesota was reached when pale, nervous, dry and nervous-lipped John Lind arose to make a speech which had been anxiously awaited for days. All eyes were turned on the careworn governor." [1]

He began by telling the banqueters that as they were sitting at the table, Bryan had remarked: "Lind, this is a pretty good looking lot of Democrats, isn't it?" The governor reported his reply to the Great Commoner as follows: "That is getting to be an old remark up here. A year ago, and prior to that, it was everyday talk; then we were anarchists, but now we are antis. I don't know whether it is that the Republican party has receded in virulency or that we have advanced in grace. Perhaps it is a little of each."

In the course of his speech the governor declared himself an out-and-out Democrat. He said he was not only an anti-imperialist but also an anti-Republican and avowed that he did not want to be elected again because he was John Lind; he wanted his principles to win with him.

I don't propose hereafter to be in public office or be a candidate for public office so long as I cannot feel . . . that the majority — that the political sentiments, the political ideas, the public opinion of the great majority of the constituency, of the citizenship of the state — is back of me. I don't feel that it was at the last election.

God forgive me if I will ever again enter a political contest simply as a contest for office. My manhood rebels against it, as yours does, I know, when you think about these things. I said in a letter to a friend of mine the other day that on this occasion I should announce my determination not again to be a candidate for public office. I make that announcement.

He then declared that he "didn't want to be the state's hired

<hr />

[1] *Minneapolis Journal*, January 11, 1900.

man another two years, even if I could be elected" and referred to the fact that he did not have the cooperation of the legislature.

The reporter confidently wrote that this speech had made it futile for any other name than Lind's to be mentioned as the Democratic candidate. For the moment, he wrote, the factions, the petty politicians, the schemers, the intriguers sank out of sight. "John Lind and his principles stood before the seven hundred assembled Democrats as indispensable to party success. Everything, it was felt, should be sacrificed for the sake of such a leader. . . . The Republicans of Minnesota have a fight on their hands." [2]

Notwithstanding the speech that was music to Democratic ears, notwithstanding the interpretation of the enthusiastic reporter, John Lind had not sold his body and soul to the Democratic party. In a speech at Sioux Falls, South Dakota, on February 12, he said:

I waited a good many years for reform through the Republican party. Finally, I concluded it was not worth while to wait any longer. I was growing old, and I said that I would step out and see what could be done outside. I do not talk to you as a Silver Republican. I do not talk to you as a Populist or a Democrat; simply as a citizen from an adjoining state, and I am rather glad I am here without any party label on my coat, and for all I know I am going to continue that way for some time to come. But I expect to travel with the people who are going in my direction, and it is not with the Republican party. [3]

Notwithstanding this disclaimer, the entire address was an attack on the policies of the Republican party; and it may be taken as the governor's confession of political faith and as a prototype of the speeches he delivered in his campaign for reelection. He stated that events since 1896 had justified the position of the Bryanites on money and that better times had come in spite of the monetary policy of the McKinley administration.

[2] *Minneapolis Journal*, January 11, 1900.
[3] Manuscript in the Lind Papers.

The trusts came in for the same castigation they had received in 1896, and Hannaism, of course, was coupled with these iniquities. The remedy proposed was the revision of anti-trust laws, judicious taxation, and the prohibition of watering stocks. He reaffirmed his belief in the income tax. Paying his respects to imperialism, he said:

Now in England and the European countries they have had imperialism always. It is a natural condition there. It has been class rule or gang rule from the beginning, but there is a certain benignity, a certain kindness, a certain moral responsibility, a certain element, a certain portion of the milk of human kindness in the European imperialism that is entirely, radically wanting in the Standard Oil, the Commercial, the American imperialism. . . . Here it is an imperialism imposed solely by corporate interests, by commercialism, by the commercial spirit for gain.

The portions of the address dealing with the war against the Filipinos, increased appropriations for the army and navy, and the greed of the commercial classes coincide with Bryan's utterances in the same campaign.

In the first week of September Lind was accorded a unanimous nomination by the Democrats, Populists, and Silver Republicans. The Populist party was rapidly going the way all third parties have gone. In Minnesota Dr. Christian Johnson of Willmar, who had been an ardent crusader against Fusion and a defender of the integrity of the Populist party, announced his intention to vote for McKinley because the Populists had been swallowed up by the Democrats. Ignatius Donnelly, however, supported the Mid-Road Populist ticket, on which his name appeared as the vice-presidential candidate with Wharton Barker. S. M. Fairchild of Minneapolis and E. G. Wallender of Duluth were the Populist nominees for governor and lieutenant governor, respectively. The fact that the conservative *St. Paul Globe* supported Lind convinced Donnelly that Lind had deserted his principles.

Lind's acceptance speech was delivered in the St. Paul Auditorium on September 6. He stated that he had not had the opportunity to read the platform, but he assumed that it was in line with the past endeavors of the party, both in the state and the nation. He then proceeded to stress the issues he believed to be vital in the impending campaign. In his judgment the trusts, imperialism, and militarism were the paramount national issues. First and foremost among the issues peculiar to Minnesota was taxation. He renewed the recommendations contained in his inaugural address and censured the legislature for failing to carry them out.

As a citizen of the state, I feel humiliated to think that the legislature, elected by the people, sworn to support the Constitution of our state, which imposes equal burdens upon all, and permits special privileges to none, should refuse to pass a law enabling us to tax the Standard Oil Trust, which transacts millions of dollars worth of business in the state annually, or the Federal Steel Company, which owns nearly all the valuable mining properties in the northern part of the state, to say nothing about the lucrative business of the various loaning companies, machine companies, and other corporations that enjoy the advantage of our trade, protection of our laws, and the fruits of our industry.

He called attention to the inadequacy of the gross earnings tax and condemned the Senate for refusing to afford the taxpayers relief from unjust discrimination in favor of railroad property. Former legislatures and executives were taken to task for failing to husband the public lands. They had frittered away millions of acres of this magnificent domain by grants to railroad companies, instead of retaining it to endow institutions and public schools. He pointed out that suits had been instituted under his administration to recover portions of the domain. High praise was awarded the policy of the Railroad and Warehouse Commission, which since January had had a majority of members in sympathy with the aims of his administration and had eliminated abuses in grain inspection and had reduced railroad rates. Never in the history of the state had its finances been in better condition and never, he said, had its credit stood so high. "I confess that I take some pleasure in referring to this fact, in view of the claim made by the opposition two and four years ago that my election as governor of this state would ruin its credit and destroy the business of the people."[4]

In contrast to his course in the previous campaign, Lind made extensive speaking tours up to the day before election. On the last evening he addressed seven audiences in Minneapolis. In the beginning of October Bryan invaded Minnesota, and Lind joined his party and appeared on the same platform with the Great Commoner. On October 2 the two candidates spoke at St. Peter, on which occasion the governor was introduced by Senator John A. Johnson, the man who had nominated him in the Democratic convention. Lind recalled how he had made the acquaintance of the young Nebraskan in Congress and how they had fought together against the twine and lumber trusts. At that time, he said, they differed politically, but now they were fighting under the same political flag. Bryan paid tribute to Lind's ability and devotion to the interests of the people. "If elected I can never hope to make a better president than Lind has made a governor," he said.[5]

The Republican campaign followed the beaten path of previous campaigns by exposing the dangers of Populism. The masterly skill of Tams Bixby was again in evidence, and it was through a trick of this seasoned political field marshal that Lind again tasted defeat as the result of questionable methods. In 1900 the game was more subtle than the *coup* engineered by the Vandiver-Black combination of 1896.

The day after election the *St. Paul Globe* headline announced Lind's re-election and stated that his plurality would probably reach eighteen thousand.[6] On the morning of the next day the *Dispatch* reported Lind as saying that he would be entirely satisfied whatever the outcome might be.

It looks as if the trend was toward Van Sant, but not enough returns have been received upon which to base an exact opinion. The

[4] The acceptance speech was published as a pamphlet.
[5] *St. Peter Herald,* October 5, 1900.
[6] November 7, 1900.

vote for governor will be very close, probably 2,000 or less. If I am elected, I will continue to serve the people without fear or favor, as I have in the past. If I am defeated, I will feel relieved and retire from office feeling that I have striven conscientiously to do my duty.[7]

When the returns were in, Van Sant had 152,905 votes to 150,651 for Lind, with the latter running about seventy thousand votes ahead of his ticket. While Van Sant was perhaps legally elected, Lind was undoubtedly the choice of the people. Lind himself said he was counted out by a trick, but Frank A. Day was more specific in his language. He said that Tams Bixby's "rascally trick" of placing Tom Lucas on the official ballot as the Social-Democrat candidate for governor cheated Lind out of twenty thousand votes.[8] It is a fact that from fifteen thousand to twenty thousand ballots obviously intended for Lind were invalidated because they were marked for both Lind, designated as "People's-Democrat," and Thomas H. Lucas, designated as "Social-Democrat." It appears that this number of voters, in glancing down the list of candidates, placed a mark opposite every candidate designated as a "Democrat," as Bixby intended they should, thus invalidating the portion of the ballot pertaining to the governorship. In the official returns Lucas received only about three thousand votes—proving that the ballots marked for both Lind and Lucas were intended for Lind.

There was talk of contesting the election, and in a public letter to Captain Charles C. Whitney, chairman of the Republican State Committee, L. A. Rosing, chairman of the Democratic State Committee, proposed that the Democrats should select four counties and the Republicans a like number for a recount. If Lind did not gain at least five hundred votes in a recount of

[7] St. Paul Dispatch, November 8, 1900.

[8] Martin County Sentinel, November 23, 1900. This charge was made by other papers. See, for example, the Hutchinson Independent, Benson Monitor, and Litchfield Independent, quoted in the Martin County Sentinel, November 30, 1900, and in the St. Paul Globe, January 4, 1901. Peter G. Peterson, a member of the Nicollet County Republican Committee, wrote to Knute Nelson that if Thomas H. Lucas had not been on the ticket, Lind would have won. Letter dated November 16, 1900, in the Knute Nelson Papers.

these eight counties, the Democrats would not ask for a recount of the state.[9] The members of the Democratic State Committee favored a recount, and at a meeting called to consider what action should be taken, Lind was asked to state his opinion. Lind responded by asking Victor E. Lawson of Willmar, chairman of the People's Party State Committee, the only Populist present, to state his view of the matter. Lawson advised against making a recount, because it would be difficult to prove irregularities with the county machinery controlled by Republicans. Thereupon Lind said: "That's just what I think. Good day, gentlemen." With that the governor left the room.[10] No plan of action was decided upon.

In view of the fact that Lind ran far ahead of his ticket, polled 18,671 more votes than in 1898, and would have been elected but for the invalidation of several thousand ballots intended for him, it is rather futile to seek the explanation for his defeat. Nevertheless, it may be worth while to attempt an analysis of the vote. If Lind had held his own in Hennepin County, he would have been elected. The Republicans presented a far more formidable line of battle than in 1898, when the nomination of Eustis fell like a wet blanket. The G. A. R. voters, normally Republican, returned to the fold when the opportunity of voting for one of their number wearing the Republican badge presented itself. It was said that Lind sacrificed his strength as an independent when he announced at the West Hotel banquet that his orphanage was at an end. It was also said that if he had confined his speeches to state issues, instead of preaching Bryanism, the outcome would have been different. The Swedish Republican newspapers stated that many Swedes who had voted for Lind in 1898 voted for Van Sant in 1900 because they knew he was lost forever to the Republican party. *Minnesota Stats Tidning* accorded high praise to Lind's administration and to his speech of acceptance, but lamented the fact that a man of his ability should follow Bryan in national politics. This attitude

[9] *Svenska Amerikanska Posten*, November 27, 1900.
[10] Conversation of the author with Senator Lawson, January 6, 1933.

gave Republicans the opportunity to say that it was not the Lind of 1898 who was running in 1900.[11]

It was inevitable that the Republicans should appeal to the Swedes by alleging that Lind had failed to give them their fair share of appointments — that he had discriminated against them in favor of the Irish. There was an element of truth in the allegation. The governor's Swedish appointments were largely from the non-church element, for the natural reason that the church people were hostile to him.[12] A politician makes his appointments from among those who support his policies and cast their votes for him. It was even charged that the support of Swan J. Turnblad's *Svenska Amerikanska Posten* was detrimental to Lind because the paper was in bad odor with the churchly Swedes.[13] Swedish counties like Chisago, Goodhue, Isanti, and Kandiyohi went for Van Sant, though Lind's vote showed an increase over that of 1898. Isanti and Kandiyohi were in the Lind column in 1898, but they went to his opponent in 1900. In the latter county, where McKinley had a majority of 1,139, Van Sant's plurality was only 55. Lind carried Ramsey County by a close vote and lost Hennepin County by a still smaller margin.

It is a curious paradox that the defeated governor had never been more popular than when he returned to private life. Prominent Republicans stated publicly that Lind was the best governor the state had ever had. The editor of the Republican *Alexandria Post* said that the election showed the people believed in him. "Lind is aggressive and does things," he said, "and people like aggressive action." [14] The *Princeton Union*, owned by Robert C. Dunn, the Republican state auditor, stated that the people trusted Lind and that he was popular with all classes of

[11] *Minnesota Stats Tidning*, September 12, October 31, November 14, 1900; *Svenska Amerikanska Posten*, October 9, November 27, 1900; *Svenska Folkets Tidning*, November 14, 1900; *St. Paul Dispatch*, September 11, November 10, 1900.
[12] *Svenska Amerikanska Posten*, October 23, 1900.
[13] Letter from L. A. Rosing to Swan J. Turnblad in *Svenska Amerikanska Posten*, November 27, 1900.
[14] Quoted in the *Martin County Sentinel*, November 23, 1900.

voters.[15] At Red Wing Judge N. O. Werner, one of the owners of *Svenska Folkets Tidning* and a leading Republican, said in an interview: "Lind is the best governor Minnesota ever had. There is no denying that John has made a good governor. He would have been senator before this if he had chosen to stay in the party. Governor Lind was never so strong as he is today." [16]

Twenty-four years after his defeat Lind wrote to a friend as follows:

During the Republican domination of the state we had timber and timber lands, iron bearing lands and mining. These resources were largely gobbled up by industries and groups who dominated the Republican party absolutely, and who continued in the saddle until I succeeded by the help of the Democrats and liberal Republicans and the then Populist movement to break the combine. Since that time we have had two Democratic governors.

We were all elected, not because we were Democrats, but because a majority of the people had confidence in us and deemed it necessary to break up the Republican oligarchy. In this we succeeded in a measure, and the result was to reinstate the Republicans by a new, and, on the whole, a better class of Republicans.[17]

On January 9, 1901, in the presence of the legislature and Governor-Elect Van Sant, Governor Lind read his final message, which in the main reiterated the recommendations of his inaugural address. Referring to the desirability of incorporating labor unions, he took occasion to say that since the "wager of battle" had given way to the settlement of personal disputes by arbitration, it was logical to adjudicate labor disputes by compulsory arbitration. He also suggested the necessity of having some method of reviewing election returns, but expressly denied that he wished it to be applied to the late election. The address was warmly applauded, and when Representative John Pennington of Dakota County offered a resolution commending his ad-

[15] Quoted in the *Svenska Amerikanska Posten*, December 11, 1900, and the *St. Paul Globe*, January 3, 1901.
[16] *St. Peter Herald*, July 20, 1900.
[17] Lind to J. A. Edgerton, September 9, 1924.

ministration, and a Republican called for the yeas and nays, the latter suggestion was met with a chorus of disapproval. The original resolution passed unanimously.[18]

The ceremonies attendant on the change of administration having been concluded, John Lind put on his overcoat and walked down the steps of the Old Capitol. Pedestrians on Wabasha Street might have seen the tall, one-armed man, wearing a determined look, glancing neither to the left nor right until he reached the office of Harry Black, the managing editor of the *St. Paul Dispatch*. The story of what happened in the editorial sanctum has been told in different ways, but there is unanimous agreement about the main item of business that was transacted.

It appears that during the summer of 1900 the *St. Paul Dispatch* had stigmatized the governor as a traitor.[19] Through the medium of a reporter the governor had demanded from Black a retraction of the statement, but none ever came. Upon entering Black's office, the former governor informed the managing editor that he was now a private citizen and demanded to know whether or not a retraction was forthcoming. Upon Black's refusal to comply with the demand, the governor's good right arm avenged the insult, and he calmly left the office, leaving the managing editor and two reporters wondering whether or not Private Citizen John Lind was not more to be feared than the governor. Two days later the *Pioneer Press* published a cartoon by Rehse, the same artist who had rendered yeoman service to Lind in 1898 on the first page of the *Globe*, in which the governor was pictured as leaving newspaper row, wearing a boxing glove on his right hand. Attached to the lapel of his coat was a tag reading: "John Lind. Private Citizen at Large." The

[18] *St. Paul Dispatch*, January 9, 1901. The farewell message is printed in full in this paper.

[19] On July 18, 1900, the *Dispatch* published a cartoon with the caption: "The Minnesota soldier is anxious to go. What will the governor's associations prompt him to do?" The cartoon represented a Minnesota soldier as anxious to fight against Chinese boxers and Filipinos and Lind ready to kick him. See also the cartoon, "Which is the Tin Soldier?" in the issue for August 20, 1900.

caption of the cartoon read as follows: "It is said that the Ex-Governor has quit suing the newspapers." [20]

With the exception of a few hostile editorial comments from brethren in the profession employed by Twin City newspapers, the press warmly applauded the former governor for his method of dealing with "Black Harry," as some of the editors called him. If one may judge by the comment of the press and the letters that came to him, the affair in the editor's office greatly added to the popularity of the already popular former governor. There is such a thing as fairness even in the newspaper business, and the commendation of Lind's action seems to indicate that he had selected a good subject for the purpose of teaching a lesson to unscrupulous journalists. In the words of one editor, "If the Dispatch editor would be slugged for every mean thing he has said he would soon resemble a piece of raw beefsteak." [21] The reaction of the *Martin County Sentinel* was as follows: "Gov. Lind has done a great many things to win the approval of the people but no act of his received more general commendation than that of thrashing the villainous villifier who called him a traitor. Bravo, John Lind!" [22]

The editor of *Svenska Amerikanska Posten*, always a staunch defender of the governor, thought "that kind of leather needed just that kind of oil." "There is a point at which patience ceases to be a virtue," he wrote, "and this paper had long since passed it." [23] The mouthpiece of the Swedish Lutheran church, *Minnesota Stats Tidning*, a paper that had withheld its support from Lind in his three campaigns, thought that though Lind's action did not exactly follow the letter of the law, "the general opinion is that this action, like his administration, was not so bad." The editor stated that if Minnesota had nothing blacker on its

<hr />

[20] *St. Paul Pioneer Press*, January 11, 1901. There were many editorial comments in the press.

[21] *Elk River Star-News*, quoted in the *Martin County Sentinel*, January 25, 1901.

[22] January 18, 1901. See comment of the *Winnebago City Press News*, quoted in the same paper.

[23] January 22, 1901.

register of sins, it need have no fear of the day of judgment.[24] A newspaper man of long experience, at the time serving as adjutant of the Minnesota Soldiers' Home, Frank J. Mead, wrote to Lind: "I want to congratulate you on licking a cur. You did just right." [25]

But it was not only members of the profession that claimed Harry Black who approved of the governor's "red-blooded Americanism." From men and women in all walks of life came letters of commendation. D. H. Evans, who many years later was the Farmer-Labor candidate for governor, wrote that while he was present at the Minneapolis Board of Trade the governor's conduct was the topic of discussion, and that among the hundreds there, who were nearly all Republicans, not one was found who did not commend his action. Some expressed their approval in the most emphatic manner.[26] A member of the staff of the *St. Paul Globe* had heard the act highly commended as "both proper and just by people from whom the opposite expression might be expected." [27]

From a future mayor of Minneapolis came hearty congratulations upon the "very fitting manner" in which he had closed his administration and the "vigorous fashion in which you resumed your duties as a private citizen." [28] And an instructor in the University of Minnesota wrote that he and his wife were elated at the "first righteous revenge of your unofficial life." [29] From a judge of probate [30] and from one of the most illustrious editors and writers on the scroll of the state came equally cordial sentiments.[31]

Many years later, in the presence of several members of the Board of Regents of the University of Minnesota, Lind expressed

[24] *Minnesota Stats Tidning*, January 16, 1901. See also a quotation from this paper in the *Svenska Amerikanska Posten*, February 5, 1901.
[25] January 10, 1901.
[26] January 14, 1901.
[27] James B. Wootin to Lind, January 10, 1901.
[28] J. C. Haines to Lind, January 10, 1901.
[29] Harlow Gale, January 10, 1901.
[30] W. G. Gresham, January 10, 1901.
[31] W. C. Edgar to Lind, January 10, 1901.

regret that he had chosen to use physical chastisement to punish the editor;[32] and his biographer prefers to regard his second thought, rather than his state of mind at the time of the affair, as characteristic. Nevertheless, it must be said that even today as one scans the files of the *St. Paul Dispatch* for the years when Lind was governor, the diabolical innuendo of its editorials arouses indignation. What brought the chastisement of the editor was a slander which Lind pronounced "the vilest that could be uttered against a citizen."[33] But throughout his administration the *Dispatch* pursued him with editorials that overstepped all bounds of decency; and the public approval of Lind's act proves that even his political enemies were outraged by them. For example, following Lind's speech in which he stated that the Twin City Rapid Transit Company had offered him a bribe, the *Dispatch* ran a headline across the first page in red ink as follows: "Gov. Lind confesses that a corporation indirectly offered him a bribe. When before was it ever dreamed to bribe a Governor of the State of Minnesota? Let us elect a governor whom no corporation would even dare to think of bribing. Vote for Van Sant."[34]

At all events, in 1901 Minnesota approved of what the *Pioneer Press* was pleased to call "another exhibition of frontier ruffianism." This paper added: "He prefaced his assault with a remark which implied that as he was no longer governor he felt free to chastise his too severe critics. There is, however, nothing in the constitution of the state which requires a man to cease to be a gentleman when he ceases to be governor."[35]

[32] Interview with Mr. C. G. Schulz of St. Paul.

[33] Draft of a letter written by Lind.

[34] *St. Paul Dispatch*, November 5, 1900. Lind's speech was reported in the *St. Paul Globe* for November 3, 1900.

[35] *St. Paul Pioneer Press*, January 10, 1901.

XIII

POLITICS, 1902-1913

MUCH as John Lind enjoyed the excitement of a political campaign and the activity connected with public office, he accepted defeat gracefully and looked forward to the resumption of his law practice. He had the satisfaction of knowing that on the official returns he was defeated by a small margin and would have been elected but for the invalidation of thousands of ballots intended for him. He immediately opened a law office in Minneapolis and formed a partnership with Andreas Ueland, which within a few years became the firm of Lind, Ueland, and Jerome. He transferred his residence from New Ulm to Minneapolis, and in 1907 the family moved into a new house which remained the governor's home until his death. The summers were spent at Minnewashta, until it became the lodge of the Minneapolis Campfire Girls.

It was inevitable that the man who had brought victory to the Democrats after so many years of waiting should have been their favorite for the gubernatorial nomination in 1902; but the "Minnesota Cincinnatus," as a cartoonist pictured him, refused to be called from his legal plow. Said the *Minneapolis Times* editorially:

Mr. Lind has positively declined the nomination, and in such terms as to make it a stultification of himself and his party should he yield to the importunities of his admirers and signify his acceptance at the last moment. He has declined because he does not care to sacrifice his law practice — or neglect it, at least — in a forlorn hope, and because nothing would be added to his political fame if by any chance he should be elected. Doubtless he feels that he has made sacrifices enough for the present.[1]

[1] *Minneapolis Times*, June 24, 1902.

With the same persistency that he showed when engaged in an argument, Lind did not want to quit public life a loser. He became the Democratic candidate from the fifth congressional district, which included the so-called "silk stocking" seventh ward of Minneapolis, and defeated his Republican opponent, Loren Fletcher, by a comfortable margin. As usual, his opponent attributed Lind's election to the "Swede vote," in spite of the fact that L. A. Rosing, the Democratic candidate for governor, a man of the same stock, lost Hennepin County by almost 7,000 votes and Lind carried it by 2,000.[2]

Whether it was because Rooseveltian strenuosity had captivated the country, assuring the continuation of Republican ascendancy for at least another presidential term, or because of the strange faces in the House of Representatives, or because of the unsatisfactory committee assignments that fell to him, Lind took little interest in Congress and shortly after taking his seat announced that he would not seek re-election. He was quoted in the press from Maine to California as saying that he found Congress a much less interesting body than it was when he served before. He learned that the House of Representatives did not have the power in legislation it formerly had, and what power it did possess was lodged in the hands of a few. "As at present constructed the House does not offer much opportunity for a man of ideas and judgment," he was reported as having said.[3]

Among the members of the Minnesota delegation in the Fifty-eighth Congress, which convened in December, 1903, were James A. Tawney, James T. McCleary, Andrew J. Volstead, and J. Adam Bede. Prominent Democrats in the House were Oscar W. Underwood of Alabama, Joseph T. Robinson of Arkansas, John Sharp Williams of Mississippi, Champ Clark of Missouri, Gilbert M. Hitchcock of Nebraska, Albert S. Burleson of Texas, and Carter Glass and Claude A. Swanson, both of

[2] Telegram from Loren Fletcher to Knute Nelson, November 5, 1902, in the Nelson Papers. See the *Minneapolis Journal*, March 2, 1904.

[3] See, for example, the *Chicago Chronicle*, January 28, 1904; *Los Angeles Herald*, February 14, 1904; and *Chattanooga Times*, January 26, 1904.

Virginia. Lind cast one of the 167 votes for John Sharp Williams for speaker against 198 for "Uncle Joe" Cannon, the famous speaker who made "Cannonism" a symbol of the tyrannical rule of the majority.

The unsatisfactory nature of Lind's committee assignments gave rise to newspaper insinuations that the relations between him and John Sharp Williams, the leader of the minority, were strained. Before Congress convened, Williams wrote to Lind that he was afraid he was going to be very much disappointed, because there were twenty-nine more Democrats in this Congress than in the last and no more places. He regretted that he was unable to do more in the nature of a large committee than to assign him to the Committee on Claims, though the place was "totally incommensurate with your abilities and past services." "If I am any judge of human nature at all," he wrote, "you are the sort of man who takes his public duties seriously. . . . For a man of your abilities the floor is the place for influence in moulding the general policy of the country. I shall take pleasure, whenever I can, in giving you the floor for that purpose." [4]

Lind took public notice of the insinuation of the *Minneapolis Journal* that all was not well between him and the minority leader, and on the floor of the House stated that he had assurances from both Williams and Speaker Cannon that he had been recommended for assignment to the Committee on Labor and the Committee on Naval Affairs, in which recommendation the Republican speaker did not concur.[5] During the first session Lind resigned from the Committee on Claims, and after the resignation of Carter Glass from the Committee on Public Lands, Lind took his place.[6]

Lind took little part in debate. His speech on Canadian reciprocity was made at the request of the minority leader and received considerable notice in the press. Republican presidents — Arthur, Harrison, McKinley, and Roosevelt — had recommended the principle of reciprocity, and the Republican platforms of

[4] John S. Williams to Lind, December 1, 1903.
[5] *Congressional Record*, 58th Congress, 2d Session, p. 287.
[6] *Congressional Record*, 58th Congress, 2d Session, p. 4110.

1896 and 1900 had indorsed it. Moreover, the American Protective Tariff League was active in disseminating literature in favor of reciprocal agreements with foreign governments. There was, therefore, nothing inconsistent with protection in advocating reciprocity with the northern neighbor, though in the agricultural states of the West there was fear of competition with products raised on the cheaper land of Canada. President Taft learned as much, to his sorrow, in 1911, when a combination of western insurgents and regulars waged a bitter battle against the treaty with Canada, which was ratified only with Democratic support.

The Minnesota branch of the National Reciprocity League was sponsored largely by commercial and manufacturing interests; and such Twin City dailies as the *Minneapolis Journal* and the *St. Paul Dispatch* were favorable. Lind as a representative from an urban district found himself at variance with his Republican colleagues from rural districts, who argued that reciprocity with Canada would benefit only the milling and manufacturing interests. At the time Lind made his speech, on December 14, 1903, Canada was in a receptive frame of mind, and he could not foresee that within a decade a political victory in Canada would be won with the slogan "No trade or traffic with the Yankees."

It will be recalled that during his previous service in Congress Lind subscribed to the principles of protection and voted against the Democratic Mills bill and for the McKinley bill, though the latter was far from satisfactory to him. In his maiden speech delivered from the Democratic side of the aisle he declared that under existing conditions a tariff for any purpose was necessarily protective to a greater or less degree.

We hear a great deal said on both sides of the chamber in regard to a protective tariff and a revenue tariff, as though the two terms represented distinct and opposed policies. They may have in the past, but there is little ground for distinction any longer. What is imposed today as a revenue tariff is also a protective tariff, and from this time on, when our industrial activity covers almost the entire field of human endeavor, any tariff levied upon the commodities that we produce within our own domain – and we produce everything – is necessarily protective to its extent. In the future it will be more accurate to speak of the tariff as "high" or "low" than to speak of a revenue tariff or a protective tariff.

He conceded to the Republicans that there was "every reason to believe that the protective policy has had a beneficent effect" in stimulating industries in a young country like the United States. He laid down the proposition that "a fiscal policy is useful to any country in connection with its industrial development to the extent to which it tends to develop and extend the demand for domestic products without unduly burdening the consumer." The existing Dingley Tariff, he said, had ceased to bring forth the greatest industrial activity and to make the largest, broadest domestic and foreign market for American products, and he cited instances to support his contention.

Addressing himself specifically to Canada, the speaker pointed out that her southern boundary was largely imaginary; that her population was drawn from the same source as that of the United States; that Canadians and Americans spoke the same language, read the same literature, held the same ideals, and had the same standard of living. His travels in Canada had convinced him of the possibilities of the future. Notwithstanding these conditions, he said, "with a wanton shortsightedness . . . we have shut ourselves by a tariff barrier from participating in the development and the trade of that magnificent country." He foresaw a large exodus from the northwestern states to participate in the development of the Canadian domain. Though he presented statistics to show that the value of American exports to Canada far exceeded the value of the raw materials imported into the United States, he urged a broad view of the whole question; and in reply to an interruption from his colleague Davis, who feared reciprocity would lower the price of American wheat and would benefit only the Minneapolis millers, he pointed to the folly of imposing a tariff on commodities of which there were large exportable surpluses.

Lind's speech was one gun fired in the Democratic attack on the Republican "stand-pat" tariff policy. The campaign was planned by John Sharp Williams. In the many newspaper comments on the Lind speech it was recognized that the Democratic congressman had stolen thunder from Albert B. Cummins, the Republican governor of Iowa, whose exposition of the tariff was known as the "Iowa idea." The strategy of the Democratic minority was based on the belief that victory in the presidential campaign of 1904 depended on abandoning free trade, indorsing protection, and assailing the administration for failing to redeem its pledge to revise the tariff downward.[7]

Lind sought to "smoke out" the Republican members of the Minnesota congressional delegation by demonstrating that in his own state reciprocity was a Republican as well as a Democratic doctrine. Since the "stand-patters" controlled the House, the Minnesotans found themselves in a very uncomfortable position. Both Tawney and C. R. Davis interrupted their Democratic colleague, and Volstead essayed the task of replying in a set speech. The *St. Paul Dispatch* congratulated Lind on having made a very clever argument and said that it proved that his immersions in Populism and Democracy had not washed all Republicanism out of him. "It will be a queer contretemps," this paper said, "if the fact that a former Republican now posing as a Democrat, who advocates a policy Minnesota Republicans have always been in favor of . . . should make six or seven Republican representatives and two senators turn tail and run away from their party. We must say that it would be either a tribute to Mr. Lind's sagacity and strength, or a display of their asininity, that would very much surprise Minnesota Republicans."[8]

[7] *Chicago Chronicle*, December 16, 1903; *Milwaukee Sentinel*, December 30, 1903; *New York Times*, February 15, 1904; *Brooklyn Times*, February 22, 1904; *Burlington Hawkeye*, February 26, 1904; *Boston Herald*, February 28, 1904; *Buffalo Enquirer*, March 4, 1904; *Independent* (New York), February 18, 1904; *American Economist*, February 26, 1904.

[8] Clipping in the Lind Papers. For a digest of press comments on Volstead's speech, see the *Minneapolis Journal*, February 20, 1904.

In his last term of Congress Lind's special interests were similar to those that claimed his attention when he wore the Republican livery: interstate commerce, public lands, and the Indians. He attacked the Philippine policy of the administration and advocated the early independence of the islands on the ground that they were a source of heavy expense without yielding adequate returns in the form of trade. He condemned the tariff barrier the Republicans had erected between the United States and the islands and compared the value of American trade with Canada with that of the Philippines.

With the approach of the state and presidential campaigns in 1904, Lind was again prominently mentioned for the gubernatorial nomination, as he was to be in future campaigns. In the Republican party there was a fierce contest between Loren W. Collins and Robert C. Dunn in which the laurels of victory fell to the latter. The nomination of the Princeton man proved to be very unpopular, and a large anti-Hill and anti-Dunn element among the Republicans favored Lind's nomination by the Democrats.[9] But running on the Democratic ticket for governor in Minnesota in a presidential election year — especially with Roosevelt the Republican candidate — was not inviting. It could not be foreseen that Republican dissension and a candidate with a vulnerable record, together with a major mistake in tactics, would assure the election of another Democratic governor of Swedish blood from Lind's own part of the state. The reluctant and successful candidate was John A. Johnson of St. Peter. On October 17, 1904, in a speech delivered in the St. Paul Auditorium on behalf of the candidate he had known since childhood, Lind made the following statement:

I come before you tonight not to ask your votes as on former occasions, but to discuss according to my best light and judgment our mutual duties and obligations as citizens of this great nation and of our beloved state. On the 3rd of March next my political career will end. I will never again seek or accept public office. I have no

[9] Lind's name figured prominently in the press, and he received a number of letters urging him to become a candidate.

political ambitions ungratified — no desire except as a citizen to aid and assist my fellows in furthering the cause of good government.[10]

This promise was kept, in spite of friends and editors who from time to time urged him to become a candidate for the United States Senate and in spite of the gubernatorial nomination tendered by the Democratic convention in 1910, up to the time when he became Woodrow Wilson's personal representative in Mexico, in 1913.

The defeat of Lind's idol, Bryan, in two successive campaigns left him out of the picture in 1904, and by the middle of April the nomination of Alton B. Parker was practically assured. Among the Minnesota Democrats there was a faction working for the nomination of William Randolph Hearst. Lind's old friend, J. M. Bowler, was one of the Hearst boosters. Lind, however, as an irreconcilable foe of Tammany, threw his influence in favor of Parker, and, as it turned out, was elected delegate at large to the St. Louis convention.[11] In the campaign in which "T. R." carried everything before him, Lind was a member of the subcommittee on literature of the Democratic Congressional Committee.[12]

In the presidential campaign of 1908 Lind again had the pleasure of addressing voters in behalf of Bryan's candidacy. He indorsed the Democratic platform, which included such progressive planks as tariff revision, guarantee of bank deposits, postal savings banks, exemption of labor unions from the anti-trust law, and other legislation in the interest of labor. He paid high tribute to both Bryan and Taft as men who typified the best in the respective parties. As usual on his many visits to Minnesota, Bryan was entertained in the Lind home.

The tremendous popularity of Governor Johnson assured his renomination in 1906 and 1908 and made it unnecessary for Lind to decline nominations. But after the untimely death of the state

[10] The speech was printed in pamphlet form.
[11] Lind to Norman Lind, June 27, 1904; *Minneapolis Times*, April 13, 1904; interview with Lind in the *New York Tribune*, April 20, 1904.
[12] W. S. Cowherd to Lind, May 14, 1904.

idol in the fall of 1909, and the succession of Lieutenant Governor Adolph O. Eberhart, a Republican, eyes were again turned to "the leading Democrat of the state" as the one man who could unite the progressive forces and assure the election of another Democratic governor.

The outlook for Republican success in Minnesota in 1910 was anything but hopeful. Progressive ideas were in the ascendancy. The unpopularity of the Taft administration had been abundantly demonstrated by the overthrow of "Cannonism" by a coalition of Democrats and western insurgents, by the fight against Secretary Ballinger's administration of the Department of the Interior waged by the friends of conservation, by the fiasco of promised downward revision of the tariff in the Payne-Aldrich Act, which passed over the opposition of the two Minnesota senators, Knute Nelson and Moses E. Clapp, and the almost solid congressional delegation, and by the chilly reception accorded Taft in Minnesota following his ill-fated Winona speech in defense of the tariff. These events made the election of Eberhart dubious, if Lind could be persuaded to head the state Democratic ticket.

From Republicans and Democrats, from men of prominence as well as from the plain people, came letters assuring Lind that all over the state he was acclaimed as the one man who could rescue the state from domination by the "interests." One prominent state official wrote that he had knowledge that Jacob F. Jacobson, the Republican gubernatorial candidate in the previous election, and other leading Republicans had refused to attend the state convention because they did not wish to be bound by it and desired to be free to support the candidate of their own choice.[13] A member of the Board of Control wrote:

I hardly think, my dear governor, that you have any conception of the intensity of feeling that exists in relation to your much desired nomination. This is not confined to Democrats, although the rank and file of the Democracy are unanimous on the proposition, but I believe you would be astonished if you knew how far this feeling

[13] Charles Halvorson to Lind, June 28, 1910.

"I DON'T SEE ANYTHING OF THOSE COUNTY
OPTION TEETH!"

[From the *Minneapolis Journal*, July 28, 1910.]

extends among the Republican masses. . . . It is not a matter of Democratic politicians here and there who may have horizons bounded by offices they desire who want your nomination. It is the people themselves, who are not worrying over offices, but who want to see Minnesota in safe and able hands.[14]

Friends wrote appeals and one county delegation after another was instructed for Lind, but the former governor steadfastly adhered to his decision not to accept public office and serenely departed for the Pacific Northwest before the state convention met. Three days before the delegates convened at Minneapolis he received a telegram at Portland from R. T. O'Connor, which read: "Developments among delegates indicate very strong sentiment against county option. Proposition to nominate you notwithstanding this. Is there any chance that you will accept?" To which the following laconic reply was dispatched: "No, nor will I accept on any platform."[15] Lind's friends in the Hennepin County delegation wired that they were attempting to prevent his nomination and requested a "strong statement" that he would not accept;[16] others, on the other hand, advised against answering telegrams, hoping against hope that he would accept, regardless of the liquor plank.[17]

From Fred B. Lynch, one of the powerful leaders for whom Lind had high regard, came the information that a straight fight had developed between the liquor interests and those who believed in government of the people; that the nomination of anybody else would be a victory for the liquor interests; and that the party would be rightfully stigmatized as the tool of these interests. "It remains for you to say if the brewers shall control the Democratic party in Minnesota as they control the Republicans." To this Lind replied: "Any public service of which I am capable I owe the University. My duty is there now. I cannot accept the nomination if tendered."[18]

[14] Charles E. Vasaly to Lind, June 18, 1910.
[15] Telegrams dated July 25, 1910.
[16] W. M. Jerome to Lind, July 25, 1910.
[17] C. A. Quist to Lind, July 26, 1910.
[18] Telegrams dated July 26, 1910.

When the convention met in Minneapolis on July 28, John Lind, two thousand miles away, dominated it. His personality was bigger than any issue. The country delegates arrived full of determination to nominate him and "shouted down" those who attempted to state his position. Notwithstanding the defeat of the county option plank, before the close of the first day it was certain that Lind would be nominated. After the nomination was an accomplished fact, W. M. Jerome and E. S. Corser asked the nominee to wire his refusal before the convention adjourned, but Lind was en route from Portland to Everett, Washington, and the telegram failed to reach him before the convention adjourned.

"What will John Lind do?" was the question uppermost in every Democratic mind. Most of the delegates cherished the hope that he would accept, otherwise it is hardly conceivable that they would have nominated him. The wires were hot with fervent pleas for a favorable answer,[19] the following message being typical: "Sentiment from every part of state so overwhelming for you for governor that the delegates to state convention did not dare nominate anyone but you. Your friends will relieve you from annoyance making campaign unless you desire."[20] From the editors of the Minneapolis and the St. Paul *Daily News* came the assurance that their papers would support him.[21] Frank A. Day added a postscript to his letter stating that he "would bet 10 years of my life and my hope of the hereafter that you can beat Adolph O. Eberhart 75,000."[22] Another message said his best friends had fought loyally to prevent the nomination and would deeply deplore his acceptance.[23]

When the news of his nomination reached him, Lind was visiting his son Norman in Everett and making preparations for a trip to Alaska with his family. To a newspaper reporter he

[19] Telegrams from D. H. Evans, July 27, and from F. B. Lynch and Frank A. Day, July 28, 1910.
[20] A. C. Weiss and others to Lind, July 28, 1910.
[21] W. G. McMurchie and W. A. Frisbie, August 18, 1910.
[22] Letter dated August 17, 1910.
[23] Telegram from E. S. Corser and W. M. Jerome, July 28, 1910.

gave out the following statement: "No, I shall not accept. I told my friends, one and all, before I left Minneapolis, that I was through with politics and I meant it. Of course, I am duly grateful for the honor bestowed on me, but under no circumstances can I accept that honor, nor shall I. This is final." [24]

Letters and telegrams being of no avail, it remained for the Central Committee to exercise the authority intrusted to it by the convention, and James Gray, who had been elected mayor of Minneapolis at the same time Lind had triumphed over Eustis, was placed at the head of the ticket. ·

It is doubtful if in the history of the country a man could be found who could match Lind's record of dodging nominations and proposed nominations. This is partly explained by the fact that throughout he was far stronger than his party, whether Republican or Democratic, and partly by the dire necessity of the Democrats to nominate a man with Lind's independent position and reputation for integrity. Undoubtedly, with Lind the nominee, the chances for Democratic success were excellent. As in 1898, the Republican party was torn with dissension; and Eberhart, the Republican candidate, had a vulnerable record as a member of the legislature and as lieutenant governor. He made no secret of his opposition to county option and prohibition, and his committee appointments as president of the Senate were open to attacks from progressives. Why, then, did Lind refuse to enter the lists with him?

Aside from his public announcement that he would never seek or accept another public office, there were valid reasons. In 1900 he had made his "West Hotel mistake" when he announced that he had no desire to be elected simply because he was John Lind. He wanted his principles to triumph with him. In 1910 he knew that a Democratic legislature could not be elected; and a Republican legislature would tie the hands of a Democratic governor, except in the matter of filling a number of appointive offices. The most that could be expected was that

[24] *Minneapolis Tribune,* July 28, 1910. This paper contains a great deal of material on the convention.

a coterie of professional politicians would ride to positions and power on the strength of his popularity. Three years later, on June 13, 1913, in a letter to Postmaster General Burleson he expressed his opinion of the Democratic party in Minnesota in terms that help to explain his position in 1910.

We have in this state a bunch of guerillas who call themselves Democrats and who divide their time between mischief making and trailing flesh pots or swill barrels as opportunity affords. At times they use Bryan's name to conjure with, but their loyalty to any cause is only skin deep. They care no more for Bryan than they do for any other man that does not promise profit. In 1904 they had some of Hearst's money and howled themselves hoarse for "Hearst and reform," so long as the money lasted. Last year they got some brewery funds and yelled for Clark and "true democracy." Fortunately there are not many of them. When the decent patriotic elements in the party become aroused, it's an easy matter to handle them. . . . Many of us have devoted our time, and to some extent our means, zealously and unselfishly to make the Democratic party in the state reputable and respectable. Under the splendid leadership of Mr. [F. B.] Lynch we have succeeded in both respects. . . . He is the most unselfish man that I ever saw in politics.[25]

In 1910 Lind had arrived at the stage in his political pilgrimage where party labels meant little, provided there was an organization effective enough to turn out progressive legislation of the brand for which he had fought throughout his life. In 1910 he made a speaking tour in behalf of the Democratic candidate for governor, but he also took care not to lend his influence in favor of anybody who was not in good standing with the progressive forces. Thus it was that he gave hearty indorsement to the re-election of Senator Clapp, one of the progressive Republican senators who had exposed the iniquities of the Payne-Aldrich Tariff. He paid tribute to the rugged senator for his fearless and able service and said the progressive Democrats in the legislature would vote for his re-election to a man. "Senator Clapp," he said, "is doing the work that I should endeavor to do

[25] See also Lind to Bryan, November 25, 1912.

if I were in his place, and he is doing it better, I believe, than I could. This is no time for 'swapping horses.'"

In his speech at Albert Lea he referred to the "good beginning" that had been made in the first congressional district by defeating in the primaries James A. Tawney, veteran congressman in whose behalf President Taft had spoken at Winona. Tawney was the one Minnesota representative who had voted for the Payne-Aldrich bill. Lind took no chance of spoiling the liberal tone of his speech by expressing a preference between the Democratic and Republican candidates for Congress, since both were opposed to the Taft administration.

After paying his respects to the "stand-patters" in Washington, he launched an attack on the same school of politicians in Minnesota. He charged that Eberhart was silent on such issues as the initiative and referendum and county option. In his opinion it was no answer to say that the governor would sign a county option bill if passed. "The people do not pay a governor $7,000 a year for his autograph," he said. "They are entitled to the benefit of his judgment and his conscience on public questions." [26]

Public indignation over the enactment of the Payne-Aldrich Tariff, the repudiation of the Taft administration manifested in the defeat of Republican "stand-patters" in the primaries, and the election of a Democratic majority in the House of Representatives were naturally gratifying to Lind and inspired hope for a Democratic victory in the next presidential election.

As a loyal supporter of Bryan and progressive measures, Lind from the beginning was active in behalf of Woodrow Wilson's nomination and was opposed to the factions that sponsored Champ Clark and Judson Harmon. Under the leadership of men like John Lind, A. C. Weiss of Duluth, T. D. O'Brien of St. Paul, Congressman Winfield S. Hammond, and Fred B. Lynch of St. Paul, the Wilson forces controlled the state convention and defeated the efforts of the Clark cohorts to have an uninstructed

[26] The Albert Lea speech was reported in full in the *Minneapolis Journal*, October 12, 1910.

delegation sent to the Baltimore convention — which, as it proved, might have prevented Wilson's nomination. The James J. Hill interests were back of Clark, and the genuine Bryan men formed the backbone of the Wilson movement.[27] It was Lind's belief that had it not been for the factional fight in the party, coupled with the nomination of Daniel W. Lawler of St. Paul for the United States Senate, Wilson would have carried Minnesota. In precincts where Lawler polled a good vote, Wilson lost. St. Paul, which had always been considered reliably Democratic, went against Wilson.

During the summer of 1912 Mr. and Mrs. Lind, their daughters Jenny and Winifred, and their son John, Jr., visited Europe and attended the Olympic games in Stockholm. This was the only visit the governor made to the land of his birth. He returned in time to cast his vote for Wilson and, after election, to call a conference of prominent Wilson supporters to lay plans for the future.[28]

Shortly after election Lind wrote a letter to Bryan, who was expected to be the new secretary of state. Wilson's announced purpose to call a special session of Congress, he thought, augured well. "The people expect tariff revision downward," he said, "and they want it right away." Next in importance to the tariff, in his judgment, was the selection of members of the cabinet. If another position was to be awarded to the Middle West, as appeared likely from the press, he suggested Fred B. Lynch.[29]

During the first days of January, 1913, before the new administration was ushered in, Lind was in Washington, and, armed with a letter of introduction from Senator F. P. Gore, he called on Colonel Edward M. House, whose close relations with President Wilson earned for him the designation of the "Third House."[30] Lind did not come to the capital as a seeker for office, but within a few weeks after Wilson's inauguration he was in-

[27] Lind to Postmaster General Burleson, June 13, 1913; F. B. Lynch to Burleson, June 3, 1913, copy in the Lind Papers.
[28] Martin O'Brien to Lind, November 21, 1912.
[29] Lind to Bryan, November 25, 1912.
[30] F. P. Gore to Lind, January 3, 1913; telegram from Colonel House.

vited to accept the assistant secretaryship of the interior, a position he did not for one moment consider. Congressman Hammond wrote that he did not know of the offer until after it had been made and added that Lind could not think of accepting it.[31] Another proffered appointment was that of minister to Sweden, but the president was informed that personal and family considerations made acceptance impossible. Lind added the following judicious observation:

Reflection convinces me that it would be questionable policy for one of foreign birth to accept a resident appointment to the country of his nativity. Complications might arise in which the most prudent conduct would not avoid criticism and embarrassment. Furthermore I prefer to be at home where I may be able to contribute something toward the redemption of our state and the realization of the policies of the administration.[32]

The president stated that the appointment was a "very deliberate and thoughtful choice" on his part; and though Lind could not foresee a European situation that would probably have complicated his position in Stockholm, he enunciated a sound principle, one that had been followed by previous administrations with respect to that diplomatic post. The appointment was, of course, suggested by Bryan. Its chief significance, however, lies in the fact that it disproves the idle gossip that Wilson had never even heard of John Lind until Bryan suggested his appointment to a diplomatic mission of infinitely greater importance and delicacy. John Lind was to have greater influence in shaping and realizing the policies of the Wilson administration than he had ever dreamed. Mexico — not Sweden — was to furnish his schooling in diplomacy.

[31] W. S. Hammond to Lind, June 23, 1913.
[32] Lind's telegraphic reply to a telegram from Wilson to Lind, June 11, 1913.

XIV

THE MEXICAN MISSION : THE FIRST PHASE

I HAVE never written a letter that I was not willing to have made public at the time it was written or at any future time and I do not propose to. — Lind to Wilson, January 10, 1914.

I have done or said nothing that I am not willing the world should know in due time. — Lind to Bryan, July 14, 1914.

In the first days of August, 1913, newspaper headlines announced the appointment of John Lind as personal representative of President Wilson and adviser to the American embassy in the City of Mexico. If the appointment was a surprise to the American people, it was not less so to Lind himself. On July 28 he received the following telegram from Secretary of State Bryan: "If convenient please come to Washington for consultation on important matter. Confidential." The following day from the same source came another telegram: "Please come at once prepared to remain several weeks." At the time Lind was busy in court and requested the postponement of the trip for a few days. It was only after his arrival in Washington that he learned why he had been summoned.[1]

Lind left no record of his conversations with the president and the secretary of state, and he refused to reveal them before a Senate committee seven years later. On August 4, 1913, accompanied by Mrs. Lind, he left Washington for Galveston, Texas, bearing his instructions and a letter of credence signed by the president of the United States:

August 4, 1913.

To Whom It May Concern: This will introduce the Honorable John Lind, who goes to Mexico at my request and as my personal

[1] Lind's testimony before the Senate committee, April 27, 1920, in Senate Document no. 285, 66th Congress, 2d Session, pp. 2317 ff.

representative, to act as advisor to the American Embassy in the City of Mexico. I bespeak for him the same consideration that would, in other circumstances, be accorded a regularly accredited representative of the Government of the United States.

WOODROW WILSON
President of the United States

The form of Lind's credentials, addressed "To Whom It May Concern," is no less extraordinary than the appointment itself and the errand on which the bearer was sent. On this mission of unusual delicacy the president sent a man without diplomatic experience, unfamiliar with the Spanish language, and possessed of only such knowledge of Mexico as could be obtained from general reading. He did, however, have one qualification essential in a diplomat, and that in far higher degree than the American ambassador to Mexico who had just been recalled, namely, the ability to keep silent. He had not been in Mexico many weeks before the paragraphers were writing squibs about the "silent man." A famous cartoonist portrayed Uncle Sam selling tickets to a side show, with a poster featuring "The man mystery of Mexico — John Lind — who holds the record for the longest continued silence at a diplomatic post. Never known to talk for publication. See him! (You can't hear him.)"[2]

Of the press comments — and they were legion — many criticized the choice of the "plain-spoken man" and expressed doubt whether his mission could be successful. Perhaps the most charitable comment came from the Nation, which, in answer to the sneer of English newspapers about intrusting diplomacy to "amateurs," said that for the past two years England had had her finest professional diplomat in the Balkans, and the world knew what a "fine mess" he had made of it.[3]

The reader may welcome at this point a brief survey of the Mexican situation as it had developed up to the time Lind departed on his mission. In 1910 the long dictatorship of Porfirio Diaz ended with the Madero revolution. Diaz had for thirty-five

[2] *Washington Evening Star*, January 10, 1914.
[3] *Nation*, September 4, 1913. See also the issue for August 7, 1913.

years ruled Mexico with an iron hand, and in 1910, in spite of his eighty years, it appeared that his government had never been stronger. But it fell like a house of cards.

The man whose name is associated with the greatest social and economic upheaval in Mexico's history is Francisco I. Madero. Opinions concerning him differ violently. Like all reformers, Madero was the victim of the most savage and unscrupulous abuse, especially from the press, which was largely controlled by the old régime. Though the Diaz government had fallen, the old clique remained in control in strategic places. The City of Mexico, always hostile to reform, and the foreigners in the capital, most of whom were representatives of mining and oil interests, were determined to destroy Madero. He was called, among other things, an idealist, a visionary, a fool, a knave, a fakir, a spiritualist; and yet he had the courage and the ability to take up the cause of the people and overthrow the supposedly invincible Diaz.

The student of history knows, of course, that a revolution so profound and so prolonged as the one inaugurated in 1910 does not depend upon the personality of a single man. For some time forces had been operating to undermine the Diaz oligarchy. Although the American people did not understand the basis of the Diaz supremacy, American business knew that Diaz was through and that a dependable successor had to be found.[4] Diaz had been very cordial to foreign investors, and at the time of his overthrow American investments totaled several hundred millions. Americans had more money invested in mines, smelters, oil, and rubber than all the other foreigners combined — even more than the Mexicans themselves.[5] The Mexican Petroleum Company under American ownership was the greatest oil interest in the country.[6]

[4] Two recent books are indispensable to an understanding of the Mexican revolution and the forces behind it: Carleton Beals, *Porfirio Diaz : Dictator of Mexico* (Philadelphia, 1932), and Frank Tannenbaum, *Peace by Revolution : An Interpretation of Mexico* (New York, 1933).

[5] Beals, *Diaz*, p. 346.

[6] Ray Stannard Baker, *Woodrow Wilson : Life and Letters* (New York, 1931), 4:246.

In 1910 the combination of army, church, and capital, the pillars of the Diaz structure, were in danger of being pulled down by the arms of youth, democracy, labor, and a down-trodden landless people rising to self-consciousness. Diaz esteemed the foreigner; the new Mexico hated, feared, and distrusted him.

With an unstable government in Mexico, President Taft was confronted with problems similar to those that had confronted several presidents before the Diaz régime. Pressure was brought to bear on him to protect American lives and property, and public opinion was stirred by the inevitable reports of outrages upon men, women, and children. Little, if anything, was said of the ruthless persecution of Mexican political refugees in the United States from 1904 to 1910 — the longest and blackest chapter, according to the latest biographer of Diaz, in American "misadministration of justice and immigration laws." [7] Feeling toward the United States in Mexico was not improved when, shortly after the downfall of Diaz, President Taft ordered the mobilization of troops on the Mexican border.

The American ambassador in Mexico City was Henry Lane Wilson of Indiana. The part played by this gentleman in the Mexican capital will probably be a matter of dispute as long as Madero is remembered. Suffice it here to say that he represented perfectly the foreign colony in Mexico City, and his services were understood and duly appreciated. On November 28, 1910, he telegraphed the Department of State that the revolutionary movement had failed, whereas it had scarcely begun.

On November 23, 1910, Madero proclaimed himself provisional president of Mexico, and on October 1 of the following year he was elected president. A year later, however, another revolution broke out, and on February 19, 1913, General Victoriano Huerta deserted Madero and was proclaimed provisional president. The deposed Madero was held prisoner in the National Palace until the night of February 22, when he and the deposed vice-president, Jose Pino Suarez, were transported in

[7] Beals, *Diaz*, p. 408.

two automobiles to the penitentiary. Exactly what happened on that night is a matter of dispute, but there is no doubt that Madero and Suarez were killed in cold blood. Huerta's part in the crime is not entirely clear. He was probably opposed to killing Madero because of the effect it would have in the United States; but there is little doubt that he was privy to the plans for the murder, and he shares the guilt for not opposing it and for doing nothing to prevent it. The moral responsibility for the crime rests on him.[8]

During these tragic days Henry Lane Wilson was both secretly and openly hostile to the Madero government. For this attitude he was applauded by the Americans in Mexico City, who with few exceptions favored recognition of the government set up by the assassins who had betrayed the principles of the revolution. It was in the American embassy itself, in the presence of Ambassador Wilson, that General Huerta and General Felix Diaz, after a protracted conference, on February 18 drew up an agreement that brought the crisis to an end. Louis d'Antin, Wilson's clerk, was the only other person present, and the full details of the meeting have never been revealed. From that day to this, however, it has been charged that Madero was murdered with the knowledge, if not the consent, of Henry Lane Wilson. This has never been proved; but the ambassador's extraordinary activity in behalf of the Huerta government and his bombardment of the State Department with misleading dispatches lent color to the indictment.[9] According to Wilson's own statement, Madero was at the time of his assassination simply a Mexican citizen, and his death, however repugnant to all codes of civilization, should have concerned the American

[8] Letter, with inclosure, from Captain W. A. Moffett, commander of the "Chester," to Lind, June 11, 1914. See Herbert I. Priestly, *The Mexican Nation* (New York, 1923), p. 417.

[9] Lind to Bryan, March 31, 1914; Priestly, *The Mexican Nation*, p. 415; Baker, *Woodrow Wilson*, 4:240–41; Juan Sanchez Azcona, "A Tragic Chapter in Mexican History : The Conspiracy against Madero," reprinted from *El Universal* in the *Living Age*, April 20, 1926. The ambassador's version is given in Henry Lane Wilson, *Diplomatic Episodes in Mexico, Belgium, and Chile* (New York, 1927), pp. 252–88. A copy of the agreement between Huerta and Diaz is in the Lind Papers.

government no more than the death of any other Mexican citizen.[10]

Unfortunately for Ambassador Wilson, the Taft administration was within a few days of its end when these events were taking place in Mexico City; and with the termination of the Taft administration Philander C. Knox, the exponent of "dollar diplomacy," left the Department of State. According to Ambassador Wilson, Secretary Knox told him some years later that if the Huerta government had acceded to his demands for the settlement of certain long-standing differences, he would have recommended to President Taft as late as ten o'clock on the morning of March 4 that recognition be given.[11]

With the inauguration of Woodrow Wilson on March 4, 1913, a "new deal" in the relations between the United States and Mexico was inaugurated, though for a time Henry Lane Wilson remained at his post. The "two Wilsons" were as different as men can be in what they conceived to be the duty of the United States in the Mexican imbroglio. The ambassador had a profound contempt for Wilson's and Bryan's knowledge about Mexico,[12] and from the beginning President Wilson had deep distrust of the ambassador. In the deposition and murder of Madero, the ambassador saw only another incident in the long procession of Mexican revolutions; the president saw beneath the contest between ambitious and selfish men the smoldering embers of a revolt against oppression. To the president the drunken usurper was the "unspeakable Huerta." Mistrusting the reports that came to him from the embassy, he sent William Bayard Hale and other agents to Mexico to report on conditions. Hale's reports increased Wilson's suspicion of the ambassador, who resented Hale's presence.[13]

[10] Testimony of Henry Lane Wilson, April 16, 1920, in Senate Document no. 285, 66th Congress, 2d Session, p. 2278.

[11] H. L. Wilson, Diplomatic Episodes, p. 297.

[12] Wilson, Diplomatic Episodes, pp. 321-22; Wilson's testimony in Senate Document no. 285, 66th Congress, 2d Session, pp. 2289-91.

[13] Baker, Woodrow Wilson, 4:238, 243-44, 253-55, 257-58; Henry Lane Wilson's testimony in Senate Document no. 285, 66th Congress, 2d Session, pp. 2289-91.

In the meantime conditions in Mexico were rapidly becoming worse; the Department of State and the embassy were working at cross purposes; sporadic revolts against Huerta were springing up; public opinion in the United States was becoming restless; and there were ominous signs of impatience in Congress. Henry Lane Wilson was called to Washington "for consultation," and on July 28 — the same day Lind was summoned to Washington "for consultation on important matter" — he met the president at the White House. On August 4 — the day that Lind received his credentials — the ambassador was informed by Bryan that the president had decided to accept his resignation.

It is important to remember that before Lind's appointment the president had reached the decision that Huerta, the symbol and tool of the vested interests in Mexico, must go; and Huerta had publicly announced that he would not resign.[14] It was this impossible situation that caused many informed people to say that Lind went on a fool's errand; that it was preposterous to expect Huerta to agree to a proposition that eliminated him from the picture. "The sole object of my trip, as I understood it," said Lind, "was to secure peace under a constitutional, orderly form of government."[15] Undoubtedly the appointment of the crusader against imperialism and "big business" from Bryan's section of the country was partly to reassure the country of the president's good intentions and allay the incipient revolt in Congress.

While the "personal representative" was proceeding on his errand, a debate in the Senate was precipitated by a resolution introduced by Clarence D. Clark of Wyoming to authorize the Committee on Foreign Relations to investigate the conditions of American citizens in Mexico. President Wilson was criticized for not taking the Senate into his confidence, but there was no criticism of Lind's appointment. The hostile attitude of such Republican senators as Albert B. Fall of New Mexico and William Alden Smith of Michigan was plain, but Crawford of

South Dakota and Kenyon of Iowa, both progressive Republicans, declared that they voiced the sentiments of a large number of Republican senators when they expressed confidence in Wilson and Bryan. They agreed that the situation was too serious to be discussed from the standpoint of small advantages to anybody.[16]

Step by step Lind made his way while newspapers were publishing dispatches that he would not be allowed to land; that he would be expelled from the country; and that he would be denied means of communication with the Foreign Office. At Galveston he and Mrs. Lind boarded the battleship "New Hampshire." Before landing at Vera Cruz, on Saturday, August 9, the envoy was transferred to the battleship "Louisiana" in order to confer with Rear Admiral Frank F. Fletcher and William Bayard Hale, the latter having come down from Mexico City. At five o'clock in the afternoon the Lind party landed at Vera Cruz, where a cordon of twenty Mexican police stood ready on the dock to give protection. On Sunday morning, August 10, accompanied by Hale, Consul W. W. Canada, and Mrs. Lind, he departed for Mexico City and arrived without incident in the evening.

The situation was very delicate, and Lind decided not to attempt to communicate with the Mexican Foreign Office for a couple of days. Hale agreed that it was prudent to delay publishing Lind's instructions for some days after delivery, in order to give the Mexican officials time for reflection and to allow diplomatic pressure to make itself felt. Lind reported that the office-holders, and public opinion in Mexico City, would force an immediate negative answer. While waiting for a favorable moment to present his demands, he conferred with representatives of foreign governments, resident Americans, and prominent Mexicans.[17]

[16] *Congressional Record*, 63d Congress, 1st Session, August 7, 9, 1913, pp. 3171–76.
[17] The account of the negotiations between Lind and the Mexican Foreign Office at the time of Lind's first visit to Mexico City is based on undated drafts of his dispatches to the State Department.

On the evening of August 12 Lind was entertained at a dinner given in his honor by members of the foreign colony. The next day he received an anonymous postal card informing him that the "bunch" he had had the "honor" of dining with was responsible for Ambassador Wilson's "nervous prostration." He was told that they were the greatest gang of crooks in the world and was cautioned to take a "lime bath" and keep out of their company. The correspondent thought there were few honorable men among those who "ran" the foreign colony.[18]

We may make allowance for the questionable reliability of information transmitted upon an anonymous postal card, but the fact remains that throughout his Mexican sojourn Lind lived in an atmosphere surcharged with intrigues and troubles. President Wilson was far away and could view matters calmly and, fortunately perhaps, read his representative's heated dispatches and reports with a detachment that at times exasperated the writer. After he had exhausted the possibilities of politeness and had learned to know the character of the men with whom he was dealing, he used vigorous language and suggested action to bring Huerta to terms.

While Lind was on his way to Mexico, Secretary Bryan sent several diplomats in Washington notes requesting that they ask their respective governments to instruct their representatives in Mexico City to put pressure on Huerta in order that a respectful hearing might be accorded the president's proposals, a request that was responded to with varying degrees of cordiality.

On August 13, the day after he had been received unofficially by Federico Gamboa, Huerta's foreign minister, Lind was instructed by Bryan to present the president's proposals. Accordingly, on August 14, accompanied by Nelson O'Shaughnessy, the American *chargé d'affaires*, Lind delivered his message to the foreign minister. President Wilson directed him to "press very earnestly upon the attention of those who are now exercising authority or wielding influence in Mexico" that the government of the United States did not feel at liberty any longer

[18] "Georgian" to Lind, August 13, 1913.

to stand inactively by while it became daily more evident that no progress was being made toward the establishment of a government in the City of Mexico which the country would obey and respect. The government of the United States tendered its good offices because the powers of the world expected the United States to act as Mexico's nearest friend. The government pledged itself to pay the most scrupulous regard to the sovereignty and independence of Mexico and to give every possible evidence that it was acting in the interest of Mexico alone, and not in the interest of persons who had property claims to press. The situation that existed in Mexico was said to be incompatible with the fulfillment of international obligations and with the best interests of Mexico itself.

A "satisfactory settlement" would include (1) an immediate cessation of fighting throughout Mexico, a definite armistice; (2) security for an early and free election in which all would agree to take part; (3) Huerta's promise not to be a candidate for president of Mexico at this election; and (4) the agreement of all parties to abide by the results of the election.

From August 12 to 16 Lind had several conferences with Gamboa and at least one meeting with Huerta. With his characteristic gesture of earnestness — that of tapping with his right hand on his left wrist — he expressed to the foreign minister, not by way of threat but as his personal conviction, that the rejection of these proposals was a grave and perilous step; that any hope for division among the American people along partisan lines, such as Gamboa had hinted at, was utterly futile; that after the president had communicated to Congress and to the American people all the incidents accompanying the change of government in Mexico, no American in or out of office would dare to defend publicly the character of the Huerta government. He offered as an example the effect on Congress of President Harrison's message on the Chilean trouble.

Speaking wholly without instructions, Lind ventured the opinion that though the president might wish to pursue some less drastic policy one of three courses would be forced on him:

(1) the modification of American neutrality laws; (2) the granting of belligerent rights to the rebels; or (3) intervention. O'Shaughnessy agreed with Lind that the first two alternatives made a profound impression, and the third in lesser degree. Gamboa expressed the hope that President Wilson would modify his views when he saw the full text of the forthcoming Mexican note.

Gamboa's main line of attack in the interviews was the argument in favor of recognition by the United States of the Huerta government. He cited the action of the American government in the case of Panama. Lind declined to discuss the action of his government in that affair, suggesting that it had no bearing on the present situation, which was in a class by itself by virtue of the fact that the embassy of the United States had unfortunately become a *quasi* party to an agreement which had resulted in the existing *de facto* government. He contended that although his government had not recognized or confirmed Ambassador Wilson's participation in the formulation of that agreement, nevertheless, in so far as that agreement constituted the basis of the *de facto* government, the government of the United States had the right to insist that Huerta must comply with its terms. Lind urged this consideration only in reply to the argument of precedent.

The vital point in the attitude of his government, Lind insisted, was that it would not recognize a *de facto* government which had assumed power by the means and under the circumstances the present one had done. On this point his instructions were final, he said.

Gamboa explained his own difficulties, the attitude of his colleagues and the almost total hopelessness of making them appreciate the American viewpoint. Lind inquired whether Gamboa had anything to suggest differing from his note, now that his formal record was made. He answered with regret that he did not. Thereupon Lind inquired whether he desired him to report that answer, to which the foreign minister replied most positively that he did not.

One morning Gamboa came to the embassy to inquire of Lind whether President Wilson would look with favor on his coming to Washington to discuss with him and the secretary of state the proposals contained in the note. Coming simply as a Mexican citizen authorized by the *de facto* government, he was confident that he could secure a modification of the president's proposals. Lind was certain that the suggestion was made in good faith, without intent to slight him personally, though he understood that it was also a scheme to gain time.

Lind had many inspired callers, Americans, Mexicans, and foreigners. The British minister, Sir Francis Stronge, urged that the recognition of Huerta was all that could save the country from anarchy, though he did not suggest a course of action. He tendered his good offices to arrange an interview with Huerta, which Lind courteously declined on the ground that he was in touch with Gamboa, through whom the invitation to call could be issued if Huerta desired it. The British minister explained that the resident representatives of foreign governments in Mexico City became charmed with the place and with the geniality of its inhabitants, and inevitably became sympathetic with the existing government. The minister deplored that he had been led by Ambassador Wilson to believe that he represented the policy of the United States.

Having expressed his willingness to see Lind, Huerta occupied most of the interview attempting to convince his visitor of the strength of his army, explaining the plans for increasing it, expressing optimism over the speedy pacification of the country, and outlining his program for reforms to be effected after peace was established. In reply to the inquiry how long he expected to remain, Lind stated that he had no instructions on that point. Thereupon Huerta expressed the hope that his stay would be extended and that he would soon be commissioned, so that he could be received in a manner befitting the greatness of the United States. Lind replied to this broad hint that he hoped the day was not distant when conditions would entitle the president to feel justified in sending an ambassador to Mexico.

Through the British minister, Lind was informed that Huerta was very agreeably impressed and pleased by his call. The minister then called Lind's attention to an item in the *Mexican Herald* stating that it had been proposed in Congress to afford rebels the opportunity to obtain munitions of war. The minister thought this a "horrible proposition." Lind thought it hardly worth while to discuss the proposition abstractly. The United States was confronted with a situation that demanded action, he said, and there was no telling what might happen if the question were relegated to Congress. Lind thought the "old gentleman tolerable only as a conduit for conveying Huerta's reflections."

The greatest difficulty Lind had to contend with was the conviction in the Mexican official mind that partisan opinion divided the American people; and no argument or illustration he could muster served to dispel it. He reported that nothing short of a demonstration in Congress such as would follow a communication setting forth all the facts in the case would make an impression.

The formal reply to Lind's proposals was made public in a note from Gamboa dated August 16, 1913. In this document, addressed to "Mr. Confidential Agent" and bristling with sarcasm and innuendo, the Huerta government absolutely refused the armistice. It asserted that "Mexico cannot for one moment take into consideration the four conditions which His Excellency Mr. Wilson has been pleased to propose through your honorable and worthy channel." [19]

In his note in reply to Gamboa, dated August 25, Lind refrained from discussing his "observations," since they were not deemed pertinent to the suggestions contained in his original proposals. He was authorized by President Wilson to submit, in the spirit of his original propositions, three suggestions: (1) The election called for on October 26, 1913, should be held in accordance with the constitutional laws of Mexico. (2) Huerta should bind himself not to be a candidate for election. (3) The

[19] The text of Wilson's instructions and Gamboa's two notes in reply were published in the *Mexican Herald*, August 28, 1913. They were also published in the American newspapers.

remaining propositions contained in the original instructions should be taken up later. He was further authorized to say to the *de facto* government that if it acted favorably, at once, on these suggestions, the president of the United States would inform American bankers that the government of the United States would look with approval upon the extension of an immediate loan sufficient to meet the temporary demands of the *de facto* government.

Previously to the presentation of this note Lind had suggested to the Department of State that Consul Canada should be instructed to come to Mexico City from Vera Cruz; and if no answer came from Huerta within a day or two, Lind should call on Gamboa, quietly bid him good-bye, and inform him that he desired to spend a few days at Vera Cruz before sailing. He would remain at Vera Cruz until President Wilson's forthcoming message to Congress had had time to "percolate Huerta's understanding." Then Lind would be within easy reach of Gamboa, who might call on him "for a change" if Huerta had anything to communicate. This course was suggested because it was dignified and because Lind had become satisfied that "silence and action at the opportune time are the most effective arguments." "Let the ultimatum be action," he said. "They discount words. Unless Huerta accepts and receives the good offices of the United States speedily, there will be a crisis. It may not be avoidable if he accepts. If positive action by the United States should become imperative, it must be speedy and efficient. It would not be a big task, at least in its earlier aspects."

Without waiting for the reply to his second set of proposals, Lind departed for Vera Cruz, where he arrived on August 26. That evening he reported to the State Department that the business interests were delighted with the moderate and helpful character of the president's suggestions. He saw a financial crisis in the offing. On the train he rode with the president of the National Bank of Mexico, who was of the opinion that nothing but the assistance of the United States would save the situation.

Lind did not have long to wait for Gamboa's reply. On

August 27 he received by a special messenger from Huerta, a document even more ironic than the first. The foreign minister began by taking notice of the "highly significant fact" that whereas the first note was addressed to "the persons who at the present time have authority or exercise influence in Mexico," the second made reference to "President Huerta" and to the "*de facto* government." With burning sarcasm Gamboa called attention to the fact that the laws of Mexico did not permit the provisional president, General Huerta, to become a candidate at the coming election and sneered at the "gratuitous suspicion" of President Wilson that he intended to be. With respect to the promise of the American government to use its influence with American bankers, he referred to it as "an attractive antecedent proposal, to the end that, moved by petty interests, we should renounce a right which incontrovertibly upholds us. When the dignity of the nation is at stake, I believe that there are not loans enough to induce those charged by the law to maintain it to permit it to be lessened."

President Wilson, when he had been informed that Huerta had rejected his proposals, postponed reading his message to Congress until August 27. Washington was tense with excitement. In a short, well-written message, accompanied by pertinent documents and delivered in a calm, conversational tone, the president recited the facts in the case and forecast the course to be pursued in the future, which was to be one of peace and good will. "We shall triumph as Mexico's friends sooner than we could triumph as her enemies," he said. He urged Americans to leave Mexico at once, not because the government intended to slacken efforts to safeguard their lives and their interests but because it was imperative that they should take no unnecessary risks. Lind, he said, had executed his mission with singular tact, firmness, and good judgment. At the conclusion of the reading of the address there was a tremendous outburst of applause from the packed floor and galleries.

When Lind returned to Vera Cruz he believed that his sojourn in Mexico was near an end. President Wilson, however, desired him to remain until he received further instructions.[20] The first phase of his Mexican mission was closed. He had failed to accomplish what he had set out to do. As the mouthpiece of Wilson's disinterested and idealistic proposals his words had fallen on the deaf ears of Huerta, who knew nothing of democracy and constitutional government; he had been trained in the army, which in Mexico offered the most lucrative rewards and was beyond the control of the civil authorities. Political democracy was nonexistent in Mexico. Huerta was a military dictator, and no argument based on constitutionality or international morality could dislodge him and his followers, who had employed the technique of previous presidents to rise to power and influence. Lind's instructions were specific and iron-clad, and his failure was Wilson's failure. If Lind had acted on the promptings of his innermost feelings, he would have accorded Huerta the same treatment that he did the editor of the *St. Paul Dispatch*. Wilson's indignation was deep, but he saw Mexican politics at long range; Lind's indignation grew deeper the longer he remained on the Mexican scene.

Lind's stay at Vera Cruz was lengthened until the first days of April, 1914, and during these long weeks and months he was the chief watchman of Wilson's "watchful waiting" policy — "Wilson's cloistered agent," some called him. It was on the whole a lonesome and trying existence, and there was more than one hint in his dispatches that he longed to return to Minneapolis. This feeling was usually dispelled, however, by a dispatch or letter from Wilson or Bryan expressing the deepest regard for and appreciation of his "indispensable services" and urging him to remain at his post.[21] Wilson assured him that he read his dispatches each day and took them very seriously. Bryan wrote that it must be lonesome work, but assured him that he was rendering great service and that the president appreciated it.[22] In October John Bassett Moore, acting secretary of state,

[20] Bryan to Lind, August 25, 1913.
[21] Wilson to Lind, January 28, 1914.
[22] Bryan to Lind, January 29, 1914.

reported that the president felt it highly desirable that he remain
and keep close watch on Mexican affairs, preferably, if he found
it possible, at Mexico City.[23] Many dispatches contained the
words "We approve of your course" and "Use your own judgment."

During the first weeks of the Vera Cruz vigil Mr. and Mrs.
Lind lived at the Hotel Terminus; but after Mrs. Lind's departure for the United States on November 1, 1913, Lind lived
in the consulate and became the favorite of the staff. For many
years afterwards he was to receive letters from Josephine Bonhomme, a clerk in the consulate, who told him about Mexico,
as well as about the doings of herself and *mamasita*. His visitors
— and they were legion — did not find it difficult to reach him.
No ceremony attended their reception. They were directed up
a flight of stairs, at the head of which his door stood open. His
room served for the reception of guests, the conduct of business, and sleeping. A lattice door opened on a balcony. In the
middle of the room stood a square table with green patterned
cover, usually littered with books and papers. His only trunk
was perched on a pine box in a corner, and in another corner
his plain iron bed. Admiral Fletcher, for whom Lind had high
admiration and affection, invited him to live on board the flagship "New Hampshire," but he preferred to stay on shore.

In spite of rumored threats on his life, Lind walked alone and
freely about the city and did not feel that he had at any time
been exposed to danger. About five o'clock every afternoon,
dressed in dark clothes and a pearl gray felt hat, he took his
walk — a very conspicuous figure in hot Vera Cruz. One of his
favorite walks was across the railway yards to the edge of the
city. Almost everybody recognized him, and as a mark of particular respect he was invariably given the inside of the walk.
The common people went out of their way to make it pleasant
for him, and some of them would take his hand and kiss it.
Though he could not speak their language, he was invited into
their homes for a cup of coffee. He played with the children

[23] Moore to Lind, October 10, 1913.

and pitched pennies with the boys. Huerta's spies usually followed him at some distance, and Lind never knew whether they were detailed to spy on him or to protect him. Sometimes Lind would wave his handkerchief, at which signal they would come up to have a glass of beer or a cigar.[24]

The American consul at Vera Cruz was William W. Canada, an elderly man who had been in the consular service in Mexico since 1897. He had great respect for Lind, although the two did not agree as to the policy of their government. Canada's sympathies were with Huerta, and he was not happy over the fact that Lind's room was a rendezvous where the Carranzistas and other revolutionists poured their plans into the ears of President Wilson's personal representative. Canada had acquired a sympathy with individuals and interests that Lind loathed, but he thought the old gentleman himself a "good American." [25]

During his stay in Mexico City, Lind lived for the most part in the American embassy, where he made the acquaintance of Nelson O'Shaughnessy, the *chargé d'affaires*. O'Shaughnessy and Lind were as different as Irish and Swedes can be. O'Shaughnessy had served as secretary of the embassy until, upon the recall of Henry Lane Wilson, he was made *chargé d'affaires*. He was thirty-seven years of age and Lind was fifty-nine. The former had entered the diplomatic service in 1904, whereas Lind was serving his apprenticeship. Lind drew up his papers and documents without the aid of the *chargé*, but at the time of his first visit to Mexico City he seems to have had confidence in him. O'Shaughnessy, however, had acquired the point of view of the professional diplomat in Mexico and was not enthusiastic about the appointment of confidential agents like Lind and Hale. He was out of Mexico at the time of the assassination of Madero, but he was as ardent for the recognition of Huerta as Henry Lane Wilson, and, as he later testified, thought the whole policy

[24] Lind to Norman Lind, September 1, 1913; Lind's testimony, April 27, 1920, in Senate Document no. 285, 66th Congress, 2d Session, pp. 2340–42; Admiral Fletcher to Mrs. Lind, January 14, 1914.
[25] Canada's testimony, April 30, 1920, in Senate Document no. 285, 66th Congress, 2d Session, pp. 2421–45; Lind to Charles A. Douglas, February 22, 1916.

of the administration from March 4, 1913, "brutal, unwarranted, and stupid."

O'Shaughnessy's attitude toward Huerta was most cordial, and the wily old Indian went out of his way to pay attention to the *chargé* and his attractive wife, whereas he hated the plainspoken, rugged Lind. O'Shaughnessy thought Huerta a strong character, and of all the public men he knew the most friendly to the Americans. When they met in public, Huerta would embrace O'Shaughnessy and call him either "Nelson" or "hijo" and lead him out to have a drink. O'Shaughnessy was as cordially distrusted by the Constitutionalists as Henry Lane Wilson had been; and he made no secret of his disagreement with the policy of the Wilson administration.[26]

Mrs. O'Shaughnessy was an interesting, clever lady, very courteous and kind to Lind, but in her heart disdainful of his ability as a diplomat and unforgiving of his indiscretion in coming to Mexico without a dress suit. At their first meeting at the Hotel Terminus in Vera Cruz, Lind appeared in shirt sleeves. She was much impressed with him and sized him up as a man of many natural abilities and much magnetism — tall, gaunt, sandy-haired, unmistakably Scandinavian, with the blue eyes of the Norsemen set under level brows. She found him very agreeable. "There was something Lincolnesque in his look and bearing," she wrote, "but his entry on the Mexican stage was certainly abrupt, and the setting completely unfamiliar, so some natural barking of shins has been the result. Looking at him, I couldn't help thinking of the 'pouring of new wine into old bottles' and all the rest of the scriptural text."[27]

The O'Shaughnessys were loyal Catholics and were of the opinion that the Catholic church in Mexico was the victim of persecution at the hands of the Constitutionalists. O'Shaugh-

[26] Edith O'Shaughnessy, *A Diplomat's Wife in Mexico: Letters from the American Embassy at Mexico City, Covering the Dramatic Period between October 8th, 1913, and the Breaking Off of Diplomatic Relations on April 23rd, 1914, together with an Account of the Occupation of Vera Cruz* (New York, 1916), pp. 23–24; O'Shaughnessy to Lind, November 20, 1913; G. R. Hackley to Lind, June 21, 1915.

[27] Edith O'Shaughnessy, *A Diplomat's Wife*, p. 2.

nessy later testified that in his judgment anti-clericalism was not only anti-Catholic but anti-Christian and that the Catholic church had always stood for law and order, whereas the revolutionary governments were founded on loot and graft.[28]

Lind did not conceal from O'Shaughnessy his conviction that the church was one of the bulwarks of the Diaz system and was opposed to the social reforms advocated by the rebels. He was on principles opposed to a privileged church, and he did not make an exception of Mexico. "What poor Mexico needs," he said later, "is education, schools, and to the extent that the church in Mexico opposes public schools I think it is a very unfortunate policy, and I think the same policy in the United States very unfortunate." [29] He regarded the reports of the persecution of priests and nuns and the desecration of churches as greatly exaggerated. Reports were soon abroad in both the United States and Mexico that Lind was violently anti-Catholic, and strong statements were attributed to him. For example, some years later three witnesses testified before the Fall Senate committee that in the presence of O'Shaughnessy, Lind had said that it was good news that several priests had been killed by the Carranza forces and that "the more priests they killed in Mexico the better it would suit him, and the more pleased the president would be." Before the same committee Lind denied having made such a statement, saying, "If any statement of that character has been made here it is absolutely and unqualifiedly false."

[28] O'Shaughnessy's testimony, May 3, 1920, in Senate Document no. 285, 66th Congress, 2d Session, pp. 2714-15; Louis d'Antin to Lind, January 5, 1915. For a judicious account of the position of the Catholic church in Mexico, see Frank Tannenbaum, *Peace by Revolution*, pp. 34-67. I. C. Enriquez, *The Religious Question in Mexico* (New York, 1915), is a pamphlet written by a man who took part in the revolution against Huerta. It defends the priests as against the high dignitaries of the Catholic church and states that the former are the friends of the reactionary forces. It cites letters purporting to prove that the high prelates supported Huerta.

[29] Lind's testimony, April 27, 1920, in Senate Document no. 285, 66th Congress, 2d Session, pp. 2332-33, 2361-62. In a letter to Woodrow Wilson, dated January 10, 1915, Lind wrote that nearly all the aristocrats who had called on him laid the present ills of the Mexican people to the loss of control by the church. Lind stated that the aristocratic element had used the church as its principal instrumentality in keeping the people in subjection and slavery.

O'Shaughnessy did not recall that Lind had included the president in his statement.[30]

The official relations between O'Shaughnessy and Lind were regular; and upon his return to Vera Cruz the latter wrote to Bryan that the *chargé* was loyal and kindly and was liked by everybody. In October, however, he wrote that he deemed it inexpedient to accept any solution suggested through the embassy without making an investigation of the origin of the suggestion. He reported that O'Shaughnessy had informed him that nothing could prevent a terrible civil war and armed intervention, to which Lind added: "The passage 'the voice of Jacob but the hand of Esau' occurred to me." The same sentiment, in the same language, he said, had been expressed to him by the political leaders of the church party on August 14.[31]

A month later, after his second visit to the City of Mexico, he seems to have lost all confidence in the *chargé*. He wrote to Mrs. Lind that Mr. and Mrs. O'Shaughnessy had done everything in their power to make it pleasant for him while he was living at the embassy; but that did not prevent him from saying that O'Shaughnessy was such a fool that it was almost impossible to work with him. Before leaving the capital, he wrote, he had told the Huerta government in the presence of O'Shaughnessy and the German and Belgian ministers that unless and until the Huerta government "had strangled that bastard Congress and notified me of the fact there would be no further parleying by the United States. I notified Bryan and he approved my action. I had hardly left Mexico City when Mr. O'Shaughnessy commenced to hobnob with them and send in all sorts of propositions of what they would do if the United States would do thus and so. It made me hot. If it had not been for his wife, I would have asked that he be disciplined."[32]

During the first days of January, 1914, while the O'Shaugh-

[30] Testimony of William F. Buckley, Father Francis P. Joyce, and Nelson O'Shaughnessy, in Senate Document no. 285, 66th Congress, 2d Session, pp. 812, 2661, 2716–17; Lind's testimony, p. 2334; Edith O'Shaughnessy, *A Diplomat's Wife*, p. 114.
[31] Lind to Bryan, August 28, October 11, 18, 1913.
[32] Lind to Mrs. Lind, November 11, 1913.

nessys were sojourning at Vera Cruz, Lind wrote to President
Wilson that, while he did not wish to cast reflections on
O'Shaughnessy's loyalty, he felt it his duty to say that his antecedents were different from his and that he was necessarily influenced by his environment and by the church, to which he was
strongly attached. There was, he said, no question but that
Huerta went out of his way to show his personal regard for
O'Shaughnessy. He went on to say that Huerta was shrewd
enough to see that O'Shaughnessy was in high standing with the
church and in touch with it as no other American, and he did
not believe for one moment that his preference for the *chargé*
was based on mere personal grounds.[33]

As early as September 9 O'Shaughnessy was aware that his
attitude and conduct were causing comment, for on that date
he wrote to Lind that the papers were saying that the Department of State and he were not working in unison; and on January 5, 1914, he informed Lind that a representative of the *New
York Journal* had shown him a telegram stating that there was
a rumor in New York that Lind had asked that he be ousted.
About a week later O'Shaughnessy received a warning from
Bryan that he should not be too cordial toward Huerta.

Though Lind distrusted O'Shaughnessy and his associates, he
refrained from saying so publicly. In reply to a communication
from an American lawyer residing in Mexico City, inclosing
copies of his communications to Washington authorities which
reflected on O'Shaughnessy's character, Lind wrote that he had
endeavored to keep from becoming involved in any differences
that might exist between American citizens, and least of all did
he feel justified in taking any step that tended to disturb the
pleasant relations between the embassy force and himself. He
therefore returned the documents unopened and unread, and
sent a copy of his letter to O'Shaughnessy. Lind's course of action in this instance may have been influenced to some extent
by the distrust he had for the correspondent.[34]

[33] Lind to Wilson, January 10, 1914.
[34] Lebbeus R. Wilfley to Lind, December 24, 1913, January 7, 1914; Lind to
Wilfley, January 29, 1914; Lind to O'Shaughnessy, January 29, 1914.

Lind's work at Vera Cruz consisted largely in collecting information and passing it on to Wilson and Bryan. There was both an advantage and a disadvantage in staying at Vera Cruz. The city was a kind of clearing house for people of every variety, Mexicans as well as foreigners, and scores upon scores called on him to give their views of the Mexican situation. There was in the floating population, however, a motley crowd of refugees and fugitives who, by their very presence, perhaps, gave a distorted view of the Mexican panorama.

One of Lind's most valued confidential informants was Loring Olmsted, with whom he became acquainted shortly after his arrival in Mexico. Olmsted was an American by birth and a man of good family and good education. He had left the United States on account of a love affair and had been a resident of Mexico for about thirty years. He spoke the language of the country fluently and had a wide acquaintance there. He was devoted to the Mexican people, and was one of the few Americans who sympathized with the Constitutionalist movement and with the policy of the Wilson administration. His position as manager of the British Club in Mexico City afforded him the opportunity of hearing the tittle tattle that went the rounds and of learning about the schemes that were hatched among the members of the foreign colony. He sent long reports to a friend in Vera Cruz, who delivered them to Lind. He also made secret trips to confer with Lind, for which he was paid nothing but his fare. Olmsted was indignant over the insulting treatment of Wilson's proposals and wrote that if Lind had understood Spanish as well as he, he would have been aware of the underlying sneers in every line of Gamboa's notes. Many of his Mexican friends wondered why these insults had not been resented.[35]

Another confidential informant, less reliable than Olmsted, was Louis d'Antin, first clerk and legal counselor to the American embassy. He was born in Texas of a French father and a Mexican mother. He spoke fluent Spanish and was a Mexican in his make-up. Lind made use of him, but accepted his judg-

[35] Loring Olmsted to Lind, October 16, 1913.

ment and information with the proverbial grain of salt. He had been employed by the embassy since 1911 and had lived through the troubled times of the Madero revolution and the Huerta *coup d'état*. Between him and the *chargé* there existed a mutual distrust. D'Antin thought O'Shaughnessy a procrastinator and derelict in putting up a stiff front against the Huerta officials. He breathed the wish that Lind might put the necessary stamina in O'Shaughnessy's backbone. "These curve-back, Frenchified, Anglicized diplomatic bamboozlers do not appeal to my taste," he wrote.[36]

Another man whom Lind came to know and to rely on as one of his most valued friends and assistants was George R. Hackley, an American business man, who, though it would have been more pleasant for him if he had aided Huerta, sympathized with the Constitutionalist cause. He was one of the few among his countrymen who comprehended and appreciated Wilson's policy.[37]

One of Lind's most constant correspondents was J. J. Slade, Jr., an American business man who had married into a Mexican family. He was well posted on Mexico and from first to last advocated the recognition of Huerta as the only man who could restore peace and order. He said it was preposterous for the United States to attempt to reform Mexican politics. He had the confidence of Huerta's men and sometimes conferred with Lind in their company. Though in disagreement with Lind on many points, he seems to have had wholesome respect for Lind's integrity and ability.[38]

Among the many Americans who agreed with Slade was Sloan W. Emery, a former member of the Board of Regents of the University of Minnesota and a manager of a hacienda – a large plantation on which the laborers were virtually slaves. The hacienda system had gained steadily in power and strength, and

[36] D'Antin to Lind, November 6, 15, 1913, January 5, 1914; d'Antin to Mrs. Lind, January 10, 1914; H. L. Wilson, *Diplomatic Episodes*, pp. 176–77.

[37] George R. Hackley to Lind, November 1, 1915; Lind to Ignacio Bonillas, December 20, 1915.

[38] J. J. Slade to Lind, August 29, 1913.

at the time of the downfall of Diaz was at its height. In company with Admiral Fletcher, Lind visited Emery's hacienda, and what he saw there and elsewhere convinced him that it was impossible to look for peace and orderly conditions in the country until the evils of the system were abolished. The laborers, who were virtually prisoners, were supervised in groups of ten by big burly drivers, armed with revolvers and blacksnakes. At the other end of the row in the field was a man stationed with a sawed-off shotgun. Lind thought the hacienda system intolerable.[39]

Fred Adams, an Englishman who represented the Lord Cowdray oil interests, became a warm friend and admirer of Lind, despite the fact that Lord Cowdray was Lind's *bête noire*. Adams conferred with Lind about the protection of the property of his company; and though he had no success in persuading the stubborn Minnesotan, he never forgot the "mental intimacy of our friendship when you were in Vera Cruz." Lind had high regard for Adams' ability and toward the close of his stay in Mexico wrote for him a cordial letter of introduction to Bryan.

Letters and cards in the Lind Papers indicate that there was no dearth of advice from diplomats, government officials, army and navy officers, clergymen, and business and professional men. Scarcely a day passed without the dispatch of one or more telegrams and letters to the president and the secretary of state. There were broad hints in the Mexican newspapers now and then that Lind ought to be grateful that he was living in a country where spies were not assassinated; but Lind felt that on the whole the Mexican press had treated him pretty well, though of course the American-Diaz subsidized *Mexican Herald* was one conspicuous exception.[40] In February an obscene and scurrilous journal entitled *Mister Lind* made its appearance, and the

---

[39] Lind's testimony, April 27, 1920, in Senate Document no. 285, 66th Congress, 2d Session, p. 2335; S. W. Emery to Woodrow Wilson, September 4, 1913, copy in the Lind Papers.

[40] Lind to Norman Lind, January 26, 1914; Lind to Bryan, November 5, 1913.

editor and publisher, a burlesque writer and habitual drunkard, was duly rewarded by Huerta for his caricatures of Woodrow Wilson and his personal representative.[41] The issue for March 27, 1914, portrayed Wilson and Villa standing in a pool of blood drinking a toast.

With his return to Vera Cruz after presenting Wilson's proposals, Lind's work had just begun. When he wrote to Norman, on September 1, that he expected to loaf there several weeks and did not intend to return to the capital until he was invited, little did he imagine the hectic months that were in store for him and the tragic train of events that followed hard upon his departure.[42]

[41] *El Pueblo* (Vera Cruz), March 21, 1915.

[42] On August 28, 1913, O'Shaughnessy wrote Lind that Gamboa had informed him that while his return to Mexico City would be personally agreeable, officially there would be no object in coming.

XV

THE MEXICAN MISSION : THE SECOND PHASE

BOTH Lind and Bryan were hopeful of the success of the Mexican mission during the first two weeks of September, but before the end of another month they were to learn much more about the character and the diabolical resources of Victoriano Huerta. At Lind's solicitation William Bayard Hale left for Washington on August 28 to lay the situation before the Department of State; and at the same time Lind wrote a letter to Bryan giving his impressions and suggestions.

I have seen enough of conditions here and learned enough of the Latin character to realize that we cannot expect to make them conform in any very great degree to our standards in the matter of government. They are incapable of understanding our viewpoints. The sense of cooperation in government and in business, which is a strong characteristic of the Teutonic race, is utterly lacking in them. Patriotism in the sense of sacrifice by the individual for the common weal is utterly lacking. They recognize only two forces in politics, in religion, and, I might say, in business, namely, power and "pull." Saint Peter holds the keys, the Padre has some "pull" with him; appease the Padre, make him well disposed and the chances for enjoying the good will of Saint Peter are fair. The man at the top who wields the sword is a fact. His good will must not only be insured but he is respected and obeyed as a matter of fact. If anyone deems him strong enough to contest the supremacy of the person in power he does it at his peril. If he wins he exercises the power in like manner as his predecessor. This philosophy is so ingrained in the Latin that it is almost hopeless to expect them to see anything else. Anyone who has had the misfortune to deal with the Irish of our cities in the matter of the distribution of offices and patronage has his mind prepared in a slight degree to appreciate the conditions in Mexico. Under these circumstances for any rational man to attempt to outline a policy in advance as to detail is little less than absurd. At present only two things command any respect, power and authority. It is beginning to dawn on them that the United States has power. The effect of non-recognition has been a good object lesson. It must be used discreetly but to the best advantage. . . .

Dr. Hale is more worried than I am in regard to the rumors about Huerta's resignation and the possibility of his being a candidate in spite of his protests. That does not worry me a bit. I think he understands that if he is a candidate at the election he cannot and will not be recognized whether elected in form or not. If he does not understand it I will have it conveyed to him in language that is capable of only one construction and I want to say right at this point that while I have endeavored to be extremely polite on paper I have not minced words or terms in my personal conversations with Gamboa and partisan interests.

When it comes to the matter of elections we simply cannot expect elections to be held in the same sense they are conducted in the United States. The law does not provide for elections like ours. Judged by our standards the elections here are a farce, nothing but the homage of a people to the forms of democracy. All we can reasonably expect is that homage be decently paid and that the laws be observed in form and in a reasonable spirit. . . .

The great stumbling block here is that you cannot find any two Mexicans who will really trust one another in the way that we trust our fellows. . . .

What can be done in the North is a problem. The situation in Mexico City is so kaleidoscopic that one cannot safely predict what it will be next week, but, assuming that I will have substantially the same factors to deal with in the future as I have had in the past, I foresee the absolute impossibility, or at least improbability, of accomplishing anything directly in the line of the president's suggestion for an armistice. It will have to be worked out along the line of "wiping the slate" and an amnesty law for certain individuals and military organizations to be guaranteed in one form or another by the United States.

There are a lot of rebels, especially in the South, but enough all over the country who are bandits pure and simple. It will not do for us to espouse their cause. They will have to be dealt with efficiently by any power that exercises sovereignty in Mexico. All that we can hope is that they will be punished according to the forms of law either military or civil and not in the surreptitious assassinating way in which the killing is committed under the present régime. No one in authority in Mexico can be squeamish about bloodshed, but it should be insisted on that life can only be taken according to the forms of law. The Mexican law is sufficiently elastic to gratify even a Huerta's lust for blood if he had the sense to use the law for executing his vengeance instead of the means that he employs.

It will be recalled that Gamboa, in answer to Lind's second set of proposals, had sneered at Wilson's ignorance of Mexico's laws in supposing that Huerta could be a candidate for the presidency at the impending election. Both Wilson and Bryan accepted the assurance at face value and sent hearty congratulations to Lind, though the president cautioned him against allowing the provisional authorities to infer that the government of the United States conceded that Huerta was president *ad interim* by the operation of law.[1]

Lind informed the State Department that the *de facto* government hailed with great satisfaction the announcement in Wilson's message to Congress that the government would prohibit shipment of munitions to Mexico, because its needs could be supplied from Europe. He suggested that no policy would solve the situation that was not equally effective against all combatants; and he asked whether or not the United States would be justified in regarding munitions of war destined for Mexico as contraband, whatever their origin. Bryan replied that he had forwarded the substance of Lind's telegram to Wilson, who was considering the suggestion, and added that the elimination of General Huerta had accomplished one of the main objects of his mission.[2]

In the meantime, with the City of Mexico seething with hostility toward the United States, Huerta and Gamboa began a new game of deception and procrastination by requesting that Manuel Zamacona be permitted to come to Washington in the

[1] Wilson to Lind, August 28, 1913; Bryan to Lind, August 27, 28, 1913.
[2] Lind to Bryan, August 30, 1913; Bryan to Lind, August 31, 1913.

same capacity that Lind had come to Mexico.[3] Bryan instructed
Lind to inform Gamboa that in view of the fact that Wilson's
proposals had been submitted to Huerta and had been rejected,
there was nothing further to communicate, unless it was desired
to renew negotiations with a view to securing an armistice and
to insuring free elections. In that case Lind could be invited to
return to Mexico City.[4] Nevertheless, since the object was to
gain time, Zamacona sailed for Washington, without even calling on Lind. Lind suggested that he be received, but that he be
informed that any adjustment must be arranged through him,
because any other course would be taken as a sign of weakening
and an indication that Lind's usefulness was at an end. "When
you set out to break bronchos, you must not relax your reins
or forget your spurs," he wrote. "If you do, there will be a
plunge in a new direction. We are headed on a line."[5]

When Zamacona arrived in Washington, he was informed
that he would be received on condition that the question of
recognition be considered settled; that it be understood that
Huerta would not be a candidate at the election; and that in the
event of a conference with him, the proposals would be communicated through Lind. Naturally, Zamacona did not see his
way clear to accept these conditions. Huerta and Gamboa pretended to O'Shaughnessy that they resented the refusal to receive their emissary; but actually they had accomplished the
purpose of his mission, namely, extension of time to work out
their plans.[6]

While Zamacona was in Washington, Huerta read his message to Congress on September 16. Lind interpreted the message
as leaving the way open for negotiations; and Bryan was encouraged because there was nothing in it to indicate a desire on
Huerta's part to be a candidate and because it promised free

[3] O'Shaughnessy to Department of State, September 1, 1913; O'Shaughnessy
to Lind, September 2, 1913.
[4] Bryan to Lind, September 8, 1913; O'Shaughnessy to Lind, September 9,
1913.
[5] Lind to Bryan, September 5, 1913.
[6] Bryan to Lind, September 15, 1913; O'Shaughnessy to Lind, September 22,
1913.

elections. The secretary again told Lind that his mission had been successful, and he thought it likely that he would be called to Mexico City before the election. Wilson thought it was so probable that there would be opportunity for further service, in addition to his valuable reports, that he desired him to remain for the time being.[7]

The events of the next five weeks were to disillusion Wilson, Bryan, and Lind: they were to learn that Huerta's promises were mere paper, and designed to throw them off the track in order to gain time. Before the end of September Lind received a communication from Loring Olmsted stating that he had reliable information that Huerta and Blanquet would be the next president and vice-president of Mexico and that the promise of free elections was a subterfuge. Gamboa's nomination for the presidency was a blind. On the strength of this information Lind reported to Bryan that whatever course might be pursued, Huerta would continue in the presidency.[8]

In preparation for his *coup d'état,* Huerta made certain shifts in his cabinet and appointed rabid anti-Americans and men who could be trusted to execute his plans. Lind went ahead as though in ignorance of Huerta's schemes and proposed through a mutual friend the lines of procedure to be followed in the coming elections. He also suggested that negotiations with the northern revolutionists be inaugurated. Wilson entirely approved the latter suggestion and instructed Lind to press it as strongly as possible, but nothing came of it; and on October 10 Lind sent the first of several dispatches suggesting that before long the United States would be compelled to land troops in Mexico.[9]

Up to the last moment Huerta pretended to negotiate with Lind. Then, on October 10, 1913, he dissolved the Chamber of Deputies and arrested 110 of its members. On the following day the diplomatic corps was received in uniform by Moheno, the

[7] Lind to Bryan, September 16, 23, 1913; Bryan to Lind, September 18, 1913.

[8] Olmsted to Lind, September 24, 1913; Lind to Bryan, September 25, October 2, 3, 6, 1913; J. J. Slade, Jr., to Lind, October 3, 1913.

[9] Lind to Bryan, October 7, 8, 1913; Acting Secretary Moore to Lind, October 9, 1913.

new minister of foreign affairs. The arrest of the deputies brought a strong protest from the State Department, transmitted through O'Shaughnessy. "The president is shocked at the lawless methods employed by Huerta and as a sincere friend of Mexico is deeply distressed at the situation which has arisen." This act of bad faith toward the United States, the president said, had destroyed all possibility of a free and fair election, and he would not feel justified in accepting the result of such an election or in recognizing a president so chosen.[10]

The ruthless action of the usurper so exasperated Lind that he became convinced that sooner or later troops would have to be landed in order to establish law and order, and he thought it desirable that the troops should come with the good will and friendship of the more efficient portion of the people. He shuddered to think what would happen when the Mexicans of the North reached Mexico City, unless a few brigades of American troops were there to temper the passions of the victors.[11]

The other exasperating feature of the *coup d'état* was what Lind believed to be the part played by the new British minister, Sir Lionel Carden. When Lind arrived at Mexico City, he conferred with Sir Francis Stronge, the British minister, who told him frankly that the best course would be to recognize Huerta. The British government withheld recognition until May, 1913, because Sir Francis suspected Huerta's culpability in the assassination of Madero. Sir Francis was not popular with the British colony and was displaced by Carden, a man who had had long diplomatic experience in Latin America and who had crossed the Taft administration during his sojourn in Cuba.[12]

Upon the arrival of Carden at Vera Cruz on October 7, Lind met him at a luncheon given in his honor by Admiral Fletcher. During the long conversation that ensued, the minister impressed Lind as a man of great ability. When the diplomat advocated the

[10] Bryan to Lind, October 12, 13, 1913; O'Shaughnessy to Lind, October 14, 1913.

[11] Lind to Bryan, October 13, 1913.

[12] Baker, *Woodrow Wilson: Life and Letters*, 4:240, 243, 261; O'Shaughnessy, *A Diplomat's Wife*, p. 15.

recognition of Huerta on the ground of expediency, Lind mentioned certain aspects of his career that did not indicate strength of character and suggested that the attitude of the United States was different from that of the governments of Europe. The United States was equally interested in the recovery of business, he said, but its policy had to take the future into account.[13]

Carden presented his credentials the day after Huerta's *coup*. Lind reported to his government that Carden's arrival at Mexico City was perfectly timed to strengthen Huerta in his new rôle of dictator; and from that time he blamed Great Britain for defeating the success of his mission and bent his efforts to "smoke" her out. He wrote to Bryan that England contended that it was largely through misapprehension that Huerta had been recognized as constitutional president *ad interim;* and later, after he had ceased to function in that capacity and had declared himself a dictator, Carden presented the greetings of his royal master and his credentials to Huerta. He believed the whole thing had been carefully planned, and he was convinced that the control and monopoly of the oil interests was the aim not only of the Lord Cowdray interests but also of the British government. The late minister had not been deemed big enough to accomplish this, and therefore Carden had been selected for the job, he said. One of Lind's informants told him that Carden had opposed Wilson's proposal in the second note with reference to assisting Mexico to secure a loan from American bankers. If Carden got the loan, according to this man, Huerta would belong to Carden.[14]

On October 26 the election was held. A day or two before Huerta had announced to the diplomatic corps that he would not be a candidate and that any votes cast for him would be null and void. But on the very day the announcement was made,

[13] Lind to Bryan, October 8, 1913; Acting Secretary Moore to Lind, October 10, 1913.

[14] Lind to Bryan, October 15, 23, 24, 27, 1913; J. J. Slade to Lind, October 16, 1913; Olmsted to Lind, October 16, 1913; O'Shaughnessy, *A Diplomat's Wife,* pp. 21–22, 24; Baker, *Wilson,* 4:256–67, 279. On October 31 Slade wrote Lind that Carden had nothing to do with Huerta's *coup*.

his men were circulating confidential instructions for the conduct of the election, and Huerta and Blanquet placards were posted. The confidential instructions, according to Lind, "would make a Tammany chieftain turn green with envy." The election was wholly a farce. The ballot was open, and every voter announced his choice publicly. Few voters had the courage to oppose the authorities. On election day Lind and Consul Canada took a walk around Vera Cruz, and the only poll they found was a Huerta official collecting ballots in a cigar box. He put a number of ballots in the box, and, so far as they could discover, they were the only votes cast in the city.[15]

The upshot of the farcical procedure was that Huerta declared the election void, and he sat in the saddle as securely as ever.

After this affair Lind was more than ever convinced that there was no hope for a peaceful settlement; it was either intervention by the United States or the triumph of the revolutionary leaders of the North. He wrote to Bryan that "to hope to establish peace and to work the regeneration of a nation by men so utterly devoid of truth, honor, and decency as Huerta and his whole entourage is absurd."[16] Wilson himself gave up hope of doing anything with Huerta and set himself unalterably in favor of eliminating the usurper. Through Lind's eyes he saw the distinct possibility of armed intervention. Such was the state of affairs when the president gave his memorable address before the Southern Commercial Congress at Mobile, Alabama, at which many delegates from Latin America were present. The address was delivered on October 27, the day after the Mexican election.

The president was aware of the fact that in the countries of Latin America the feeling was abroad that he had refused to recognize Huerta because he was not satisfactory to the United

[15] Lind to Bryan, October 24, 1913; Bryan to Lind, October 24, 27, 1913; H. M. Boyd, Salina Cruz, Oaxaca, to Lind, October 26, 1913; Lind's testimony, April 27, 1920, in Senate Document no. 285, 66th Congress, 2d Session, pp. 2321–22.

[16] October 30, 1913.

States; and from this fact they drew the conclusion that in the future the United States would refuse to grant recognition to any government in Latin America that did not meet with its approval, in order to have a pretext for intervention. The truth is, of course, that Wilson regarded Huerta as the tool of unscrupulous foreign interests who wanted to perpetuate the Diaz régime. Wilson spoke to Latin America when he "took this occasion to say that the United States will never seek one additional foot of territory by conquest." "It is a very perilous thing," he said, "to determine the foreign policy of a nation in the terms of material interest." [17]

Lind's next objective was to prevent the assembling of the new Congress on November 14. He believed that with adequate encouragement the rebels could be thundering at the gates of Mexico City before that date. [18]

After Huerta's *coup*, rumors were abroad in the Mexican capital that a crisis was in sight, and that Huerta was about to resign. What gave rise to these stories, perhaps, was the arrival of more American battleships in Mexican waters and the rushing of box cars to the Mexican border. So persistent were the rumors of an impending crisis that Bryan gave a statement to the press denying that an ultimatum had been sent. The secretary informed Lind that Wilson would soon make a public announcement of his policy. Lind was gratified that Washington was showing signs of a stiff upper lip. [19]

The basis for these rumors was a note from Washington, dated November 1, to be submitted in confidence through the embassy to the minister of foreign affairs, informing him that unless Huerta retired voluntarily it would be necessary for President Wilson to insist on the terms of an ultimatum. The rejection of such an ultimatum would force him to propose very

[17] Baker, *Wilson*, 4:236, 280–84, 288; Policarpo Bonilla (ex-president of Honduras), *Wilson Doctrine : How the Speech of President Wilson at Mobile, Ala., Has Been Interpreted by the Latin American Countries* (New York, 1914).

[18] Lind to Bryan, October 29, 1913.

[19] Bryan to Lind, October 30, November 4, 1913; Lind to Bryan, November 3, 1913; Lind to Mrs. Lind, November 11, 1913; O'Shaughnessy, *A Diplomat's Wife*, pp. 32–33.

serious practical measures to Congress. The note stated that the United States was willing to do anything within reason to spare Huerta's feelings and to lend him personal protection. It was further suggested that some man or a group of elderly men then in retirement and identified as little as possible with the recent troubles should constitute a provisional government to arrange for a general election of a new Congress and an executive. The government declared itself firmly and irrevocably resolved to cut the Huerta government off from all outside aid and stated that it would leave the dictator only a few days longer to act with apparent freedom of choice. Any attempt to substitute Blanquet, whom Lind had reported as even more corrupt than Huerta, would lead to deeper irritation and the final rupture.[20]

With the situation at Mexico City tense, the Russian, German, and Norwegian ministers came down to Vera Cruz, ostensibly on a hunting expedition. Lind was very anxious to see them, but believed it prudent to give them the opportunity to call first, which they did. Lind's fluency in German stood him in good stead in the long conversation that followed. The ministers agreed that the situation was ominous and said that scores of Mexicans, speaking in confidence, had expressed the hope that the United States would not delay the rescue of the Mexican people. The German minister, Paul von Hintze, was the most emphatic of the three. He did not think the problem was serious from the military point of view. The army was virtually defunct, he said, and the better class of Mexicans would welcome intervention. He thought Huerta saw the hopelessness of the situation and would be willing to wipe out the congressional election. Lind was impressed with Von Hintze's fund of information. He was very cordial and listened eagerly to Lind's condemnation of the British policy, and he gave assurance that Germany had no political interests or aspirations in Mexico and had full confidence in Wilson's policy.[21]

[20] Bryan to Lind, November 1, 1913; Lind to Bryan, October 30, 1913.

[21] Lind to Bryan, October 31, November 1, 3, 1913; Lind to Mrs. Lind, November 5, 1913; Lind's testimony, April 27, 1920, in Senate Document no. 285, 66th Congress, 2d Session, pp. 2323-25.

With affairs approaching what he thought was a crisis, Lind on November 5 inquired of Washington whether or not it was the wish of the president that he go to Mexico City for a few days. The president replied that in view of the fact that Lind was in a position to know what the conditions were, he might use his own judgment. Accordingly, on the evening of the following day, accompanied by two army officers, Lind departed for the capital, where he was immediately besieged in the embassy by a swarm of newspaper reporters. According to Mrs. O'Shaughnessy, the whole town was whispering and wondering what the arrival of the president's personal representative might mean.[22]

Lind left for Mexico City in the hope that his government would fix a short and definite time for Huerta's compliance with Wilson's demands. So impatient was he for action that Mrs. O'Shaughnessy confessed that she had not drawn a peaceful breath. Huerta was equally determined that things should not come to a head, and he dreaded the publicity that would accompany an interview with Lind. During the three or four days of Lind's stay in the capital, the old Indian disappeared so completely that there were stories in the newspapers that he had fled the country. O'Shaughnessy was absolutely unable to find him, and one of his ministers told the *chargé* that he flew into a rage every time Lind's name was mentioned.[23]

While Huerta was in hiding and Lind was in waiting, the president's representative devoted some time to "smoking out" Carden. The British minister called on him and engaged him in conversation, after which he invited him to tea. Lind excused himself, however. His relations with the German minister were as cordial as ever. Mrs. O'Shaughnessy invited Von Hintze to luncheon in order to permit Lind to meet him informally. Lind made no secret of his hostility toward England and stated in the presence of Von Hintze that the government of the United

[22] Lind to Bryan, November 5, 6, 1913; Bryan to Lind, November 5, 6, 1913; O'Shaughnessy, *A Diplomat's Wife*, p. 40.

[23] Lind to Bryan, November 7, 1913; O'Shaughnessy, *A Diplomat's Wife*, pp. 41, 46, 47–48, 50, 54.

States would never allow the domination of British interests in Mexico.[24]

While Lind was in the capital, O'Shaughnessy was instructed from Washington to present the ultimatum and to say that unless Huerta complied with it, diplomatic relations would be severed. When Lind and O'Shaughnessy presented themselves at the palace on November 12, Huerta failed to keep his appointment. Lind departed for Vera Cruz that night, in the hope and expectation that the O'Shaughnessys would follow before the end of the week; and on arrival there telegraphed Washington that in his judgment if Congress was not terminated by Huerta or by its own action, O'Shaughnessy should be instructed to demand his passports. Lind left the capital hoping that his sudden departure would make an impression on Carden and the people of the city.[25]

In spite of the fact that Carden led a procession of diplomats to Huerta to advise him to yield to Wilson's demands, O'Shaughnessy was informed that Huerta could not accept the intervention of any foreign power in a matter that concerned only the people of Mexico, and that the Congress would meet for the purpose of deciding the validity or nullity of the presidential election and of transacting certain business that required congressional action. The Congress thus met on November 14, as originally intended.[26]

His second mission to Mexico City having failed to bring Huerta to terms, Lind thought his work was completed and expressed the wish to Bryan that he be permitted to return to the United States. He had no desire to "hang on" for the sake of a chance to "make good," but he would abide by Bryan's decision if the latter thought he might be able to perform some service.[27]

[24] Lind to Mrs. Lind, November 9, 1913; O'Shaughnessy, *A Diplomat's Wife*, pp. 40, 42, 44.
[25] Lind to Bryan, November 13, 14, 1913; O'Shaughnessy to Lind, November 13, 1913; O'Shaughnessy, *A Diplomat's Wife*, p. 53.
[26] Baker, *Wilson*, 4:288–90; O'Shaughnessy to Lind, November 14, 15, 1913; Lind to Bryan, November 15, 1913.
[27] Lind to Bryan, November 19, 1913. On November 30 Bryan telegraphed that he regretted that he was compelled to stay at Vera Cruz so long and that

In view of the fact that Huerta was not amenable to reason, Lind reported that two alternatives remained for the United States: (1) to take military possession of Mexico and to administer affairs as had been done in Cuba, or (2) to allow the Mexicans themselves to carry out the work of reconstruction under such restrictions and limitations as it might be necessary to impose. The latter choice appealed to Lind because he was convinced that Mexico City had to be humbled. This job he believed ought to be intrusted to the people of the North, since they were more progressive and better schooled and educated. "To make a dog feel that he really is a cur he must be whipped by another dog and preferably by a cur," he wrote. "Consequently, let this housecleaning be done by home talent. It will be a little rough and we must see to it that the walls are left intact, but I should not worry if some of the verandas and French windows were demolished. General Villa, for instance, would do the job satisfactorily." [28]

Thenceforth Lind was to bombard the State Department with telegrams and letters urging that assistance be granted to the rebels; and when their progress toward Mexico City seemed too slow, he suggested landing troops. He hoped armed intervention would not be necessary, but he warned Bryan against harboring the delusion that merely getting a new president would set things right. Hereafter, he said, we must be the "pillar of cloud by day and the pillar of fire by night and compel decent administration. . . . From this necessity there is no escape, unless revolution and anarchy are to continue the order of the day in Mexico." He held no brief for the methods of the rebels, but thought that "for every charge against the rebels there is credit plus on the federal side."

In Pancho Villa he believed the revolutionists of the North had an intrepid and resourceful leader, possessed of the highest moral, physical, and mental efficiency the conditions and en-

his efforts had been without results. The government was moving as rapidly as circumstances permitted, he said.

[28] Lind to Bryan, November 15, 1913; Lind's testimony, April 27, 1920, in Senate Document no. 285, 66th Congress, 2d Session, pp. 2329–30.

vironment could reasonably be expected to produce, but only a little better than the best of the federal generals. Life and fate had taught him to be cruel and avaricious. He was pictured in the American press as a demon, but Lind judged his acts by the Mexican standard and received reports of atrocities committed by rebels with stoicism, knowing that the ledger was double-paged.

Venustiano Carranza he thought was honest, a man of his word and of convictions, set in his views almost to pig-headedness, and possessing more merit and fewer objections than any other available Mexican in sight; but he insisted that the United States must have a definite understanding with him. Early in December Lind had reached the conclusion that it was a choice between Carranza (or his nominee) and military intervention and occupation by the United States.[29]

During November and December, while Lind was continually warning Wilson and Bryan of the probability of intervention, Wilson assumed a Micawber-like attitude, hoping that something would "turn up" to render such action unnecessary. Despite the fact that on December 10 he wrote that there was not the least likelihood of making war in Mexico, he knew, or ought to have known, that there was.[30] In his annual message to Congress he reported that "by a little every day" Huerta's power and prestige were crumbling and that "his collapse is not far away."

After reading Wilson's announcement of "Our Purposes in Mexico," transmitted to foreign governments on November 24, Lind expressed satisfaction to find that his reports were in line with it. "Our purposes," as stated by the president, were solely and simply to secure peace and order in Central America by seeing to it that the processes of self-government were not interrupted nor set aside. It was the purpose of the United States to discredit and defeat such usurpations as those of General Huerta. The present policy was to isolate him and force him out,

[29] Long telegram from Lind to Bryan, December 5, 1913.
[30] Wilson to Ralston Fleming, in Baker, *Wilson*, 4:294.

but if he did not retire by force of circumstances, it would be the duty of the United States to use less peaceful means.[31]

At this time Lind had no fear that Huerta would win out; he was convinced of the inherent weakness and viciousness of the elements upon which Huerta relied for success. He feared, however, that the longer the revolution dragged on, the more imminent became the danger of intervention. It was to forestall this that he urged his government to facilitate the progress of the rebels by assisting them to obtain munitions. "This is no time for fine spun theories about international law," he wrote. "The motives of the revolutionists may not be wholly above suspicion, but after all it is the only force in Mexico arrayed against the organized cruelty and corruption of this unfortunate country."[32] Lind was assured by Bryan that Wilson's attitude toward the revolutionists was substantially his own, but it took weeks of prodding before the president agreed to accept Lind's proposal to abolish the embargo on munitions.[33]

To see with his own eyes what the rebels were accomplishing, Lind accepted Admiral Fletcher's invitation to accompany him on a visit to Tampico and Tuxpam. When they arrived off Tampico on the "Rhode Island" on the morning of November 26, Lind immediately found another reason for venting his spleen on the British in notes and letters to the State Department. The presence of the British cruiser "Suffolk," commanded by Sir Christopher Cradock, raised the question of precedence by reason of the seniority of the British officer. Fletcher pointed out the significance of precedence in the event that troops were landed, and succeeded in persuading Cradock to make the first call. Lind absented himself for "obvious reasons."[34] Notwithstanding the amicable adjustment of this touchy question, it was not settled to Lind's satisfaction; he grieved that in matters

[31] Bryan to Lind, November 24, 1913; Lind to Mrs. Lind, November 26, 1913.
[32] Lind to Bryan, December 14, 1913.
[33] Lind to Bryan, December 9, 1913; Bryan to Lind, December 13, 1913.
[34] Lind to Bryan, November 24, 26, 1913; Bryan to Lind, November 24, 1913; Lind to Mrs. Lind, November 26, 1913.

other than political Cradock assumed that he was entitled to precedence. If Cradock needed prompting, Carden undoubtedly supplied the inspiration, he thought.[35] He wrote to Wilson that he hoped some means would be found to give Fletcher the rank of vice admiral.[36] Lind's feelings were not mollified when he learned that on December 2, 1913, Cradock in full uniform and accompanied by Carden called on Huerta at the palace, making it a most formal ceremony.[37]

Carden's attitude, and indeed that of the diplomatic corps at Mexico City, was exceedingly irritating to Lind. The diplomats openly expressed the opinion that Wilson's policy must fail because Europe could not see her material interests sacrificed to the "deluded altruism" of the United States.[38]

Another incident, similar to that of the arrival of Carden at Mexico City, was the report that the newly appointed Italian minister was on his way to take up his duties. O'Shaughnessy telegraphed Lind that the reception of the minister would be most unfortunate and would furnish a still greater incentive to resistance to the American demands than the reception of the British admiral. He did not believe the Italian government, if it knew the exact situation, would insist on the minister's being received. O'Shaughnessy saw in the incident the hand of Carden, who was in charge of the Italian legation. The minister tarried three weeks at Havana, but on December 29 was received with all honors. O'Shaughnessy appealed to Lind to bring the "Machiavellian intrigues" of the British minister to the attention of his government, for he could not believe that Great Britain, with the friendship of the United States at stake, could permit or connive at the checkmating of the policy of the United States by its representative.[39]

Lind needed no prompting from O'Shaughnessy to continue

[35] Lind to Bryan, December 13, 1913.
[36] Lind to Wilson, January 10, 1914.
[37] O'Shaughnessy to Lind, December 2, 1913.
[38] O'Shaughnessy to Lind, December 10, 1913.
[39] O'Shaughnessy to Lind, December 8, 15, 1913; O'Shaughnessy, *A Diplomat's Wife*, pp. 92, 97-98, 104, 115.

his purpose to "smoke out" Carden, but he was glad to learn that the *chargé's* eyes had been fully opened. On December 14 he telegraphed Bryan:

England may talk fair in Washington, but I tell you that in Mexico she is maneuvering every moment to get the advantage and to place us in an embarrassing light before the world so as to justify such steps as she is meditating to maintain her present political supremacy in the government of Mexico. The sending of a naval commander outranking any American officer in Mexican waters was not an accident. She expected control of naval operations here but failed at least in part in that respect. The constant ridicule by Carden of the American government and American policies and American military power has its baneful influence. Nor should it be overlooked that none of the European nations sympathize with the policy or attitude of the United States in fact, whatever they may say diplomatically. I get this on every side.

This strong indictment brought a request from Bryan that Lind mention concrete instances in which Carden had done or said things unfriendly or embarrassing to the American government.[40] Lind replied immediately that his evidence was not of a character cognizable in a court of justice. It was based on hearsay or obtained from confidential sources. He gave the names of his informants and gave assurance that he had not overstated facts.[41] During the weeks following he sent in several items bearing on the inquiry.[42]

At last came the welcome news that Carden had been asked to report to his government "à la Henry Lane Wilson"; but he did not depart before the British colony had made its point of

[40] Bryan to Lind, December 16, 1913.

[41] Lind to Bryan, December 17, 1913. See Baker, *Wilson*, 4:301–02.

[42] D'Antin to Lind, January 8, 1913; Lind to Wilson, January 10, 1913; Lind to Bryan, January 21, 24, 28, February 21, 25, 1913. On March 6 Lind reported to Bryan that he was confident that the "Japanese movement" in Mexico was inspired by Carden for political purposes. A number of Englishmen close to Carden had at different times called his attention to the presence of Japanese and to their popularity in Mexico City. Lind thought these men were inspired by Carden, who knew how susceptible Americans were to the Japanese bugaboo and who was aware of the friction growing out of the California antialien land legislation.

view clear by giving a banquet in his honor—with the real purpose, however, of censuring the government of the United States.[43] The recalled minister took his departure in the latter part of February, 1914, with the Mexican press featuring his prospective conference with President Wilson as a hopeful sign for Huerta. Bryan assured Lind that the president had not invited the minister; the interview had been arranged at the re-request of the British embassy. The interview proved to be quite formal, and Carden had no suggestions to offer.[44]

With the approach of Christmas, Lind longed to return to Minneapolis to be with his family and to enjoy the bracing atmosphere of the Northland instead of sweltering under the tropical sun in Vera Cruz. On December 19 he wrote to Bryan that he felt his time was not employed to much purpose and suggested that he be permitted to confer with him personally in Washington. Captain W. A. Moffett of the cruiser "Chester" had informed him that he could take him to a Gulf port in from twenty-four to thirty-six hours.[45] A "norther" made it impossible to send a ship's launch on Christmas Day, so Lind had to forego the pleasure of accepting the dinner invitation of the ward room officers of the flagship "Rhode Island." Instead a telegram came from Bryan suggesting that he meet President Wilson at Pass Christian, where he was spending the holidays.[46]

On January 2, 1914, on board the "Chester," the president and his personal representative held an extended conference. Neither left a formal record of the meeting, but it may be taken for granted that Lind urged the necessity of aiding the rebels, removing the embargo on munitions, and bringing the Mexican situation to a "showdown." Wilson told Bryan that he got nothing new, but relished the opportunity of seeing things nearer at

[43] O'Shaughnessy to Lind, January 13, 1914; Lind to Bryan, January 17, 1914; Olmsted to Lind, January 18, 1914.
[44] Lind to Bryan, February 14, 1914; Bryan to Lind, February 27, March 14, 1914.
[45] Lind to Bryan, December 19, 1913; Lind to Norman Lind, December 17, 1913.
[46] Lind to Norman Lind, December 25, 1913; Bryan to Lind, December 25, 1913.

hand. Lind wrote to Mrs. Lind that he was glad he had made the trip. "I now know how the president feels. I did not before. That is, I wasn't sure. I had kept firing in my stuff and made my views clear but I did not know whether he agreed with me. He does."[47] Norman, who came to Pass Christian to meet his father, found him in splendid spirits and health.[48]

When he returned to Vera Cruz, Lind was reconciled to a continuation of his vigil until April. From his letters it is reasonable to infer that he had promised Wilson he would remain that long.[49] Why this time limit should have been fixed is not clear; but as it turned out, he took his departure the first week of April — just in time to escape the stirring events that brought the crisis he had so long predicted and hoped for. After his return from his conference with Wilson, he devoted the month of January to sending a constant barrage of dispatches urging that the embargo be lifted and the belligerency of the rebels recognized.

At Lind's invitation Mr. and Mrs. O'Shaughnessy came down to Vera Cruz a few days after the Pass Christian conference. Lind made use of the opportunity to impress upon the *chargé* the impossibility of having further dealings with Huerta and the necessity of raising the embargo. Mrs. O'Shaughnessy was terrified at the thought of aiding the rebels, and her husband was still of the opinion that an understanding might be reached with Huerta, by which he would resign and take the field, and a good man be named as his successor in the presidency. A cabinet formed with due recognition to the rebels, and the understanding that Huerta might be a candidate at the ensuing election, completed the proposed arrangement.[50]

At the beginning of the New Year Lind wrote long reports

[47] Baker, *Wilson*, 4:299; Lind to Mrs. Lind, January 22, 1914; Lind to Bryan, January 15, 1914.

[48] Norman Lind to Mrs. Lind, January 3, 1914; Norman Lind to John U. Sebenius, January 8, 1914.

[49] Lind to George E. Vincent, January 7, 1914.

[50] O'Shaughnessy to Lind, January 5, 1914; O'Shaughnessy to Bryan, January 10, 1914; Lind to Bryan, January 8, 11, 1914; Lind to Wilson, January 10, 1914; O'Shaughnessy, *A Diplomat's Wife*, pp. 120, 130, 133, 135, 139, 149.

and letters to Wilson and Bryan in which he presented his view of the situation and recommended lines of action. He thought it would be helpful if the revolutionists of the North were to delegate a representative who would take up quarters at Vera Cruz and be in constant communication with Lind. To President Wilson he wrote on January 10:

It is very amusing to me, Mr. President, when I read the learned dissertations of men like Woolsey, Harvey and others covertly sneering at your Mexican policy as the dream of an impractical idealist who has no conception of the Mexican situation or of international politics. I had not been here more than a couple of weeks, as Mr. Hale will testify, before I became thoroughly convinced in my own mind that however justifiable and ideal your policy may be on ethical grounds its economic and political importance for the United States is greater in so far as one is justified in making any comparison at all between right and interest or expediency. If the Huerta government, or rather what the Huerta government stands for in principle, should prevail Mexico would continue to be a European annex, industrially, financially, politically and in sentiment except in the single industry of mining where American courage and resourcefulness has forged ahead, as you might say, by purely physical means. To illustrate: Every public work in Mexico during the last twenty years, of any consequence whatever, has been executed by English and European engineers and capital (this does not include some railroad construction which, at the time, was private enterprise). Lord Cowdray alone has received $125,000,000 for public works of different kinds from the Mexican treasury. I will not stop to specify the items but I have them. American contractors and bidders were turned down in every instance. There was no competition in fact. Besides this he has received concessions of inestimable value. French, Spanish and German promoters have also had a "look-in," but the United States, none. . . . However friendly Diaz may have been to the Americans in a political way, his whole government was essentially European in spirit and in sentiment and the worst type of European at that. . . . If the revolutionists win out, and we are so far committed, it seems to me, that it is incumbent upon us to see to it that they do win, then the tables will be turned and will have a Mexican régime that will be at least impartial and it is to be hoped friendly, on the whole. . . .

There is another subject that I must weary you with again. That is the regular army. It is probably the most corrupt and menacing factor in the whole Mexican situation. It has become and is an institution existing and conducting its operations wholly for its own ends. It does not regard itself as an instrumentality of the nation except to the very limited extent that a given national purpose may serve its own ends. I cannot in this letter go into details, or instance corruption and mendacity, and there is no vocabulary extant east of the Mississippi that could do justice to the subject. As to the rank and file, they are made up of criminals and conscripts. The latter are methodically and purposely converted into criminals, or, at least, into beasts as rapidly after their enlistment as circumstances permit. They are forced to attend and to execute the murder of prisoners. Besides, as you know, Huerta is capturing women as well as men for the army. Some of them are undoubtedly decent women, but many of them are vile. . . . In Mexico the word "army" is a synonym for "graft.". . . The army today is more vicious in its influence than was the church before the time of Juarez. . . .

My best judgment of the situation at this writing is that while the revival of the Huerta sentiment, to which I referred at the beginning of his letter, is a fact, that revival must not be overestimated. It is not based on confidence but prompted by the fear that something worse may befall if he should fail. It will not last long. There are forces in operation that, in connection with the situation in the North, are bound to undermine Huerta's power very soon.

Lind suggested that the recognition of the belligerency of the rebels would make it possible to aid them "in a proper way" to capture Tampico and other Gulf ports and to establish and maintain an effective blockade against munitions. Captain William Burnside, military attaché to the embassy, and Captain W. A. Moffett gave assurance that they would take care of the military side. Moffett told Lind he would like a short leave of absence from his command and promised to raise a full beard in double-quick time.[51]

[51] Lind to Bryan, January 29, 1914.

Lind wrote to Bryan that while he did not pretend to understand the Mexican mind, certain traits developed by centuries of force and oppression were obvious, the foremost of which was respect for force. It was risky to make a suggestion to a Mexican that savored of a direction or a command, he said, unless it was accompanied by a show of force adequate to follow it up. He went on to say that many of the communications he had conveyed to the Huerta government had been made public and were in their nature commands. The Mexicans had construed them as threats, and Huerta had been diligent in fostering the notion that they were ultimatums. Days and months had passed without anything happening, and the dictator had been able to say that the United States was afraid of Mexico, with the result that Mexicans, particularly in Mexico City, held the United States in absolute contempt. These considerations caused Lind to recommend that the United States should at the earliest possible moment take Tampico, Vera Cruz, and other Gulf ports.[52]

Bryan's disappointing reply to these promptings was, "We shall let Huerta fall. There is no doubt about that, but the president prefers that he shall be overcome by domestic force rather than by us." Lind, however, was permitted to assure his "inspired visitors" that the men of the North had the sympathy and the active support, if necessary, of the administration.[53] Thereafter he made no secret of the fact that the revolutionists of the North had the "sympathy and good will of my government" and that President Wilson had told him personally that he had satisfactory assurances from Carranza that American lives and property would be given protection by the revolutionists as far as lay in their power.[54]

On January 28 Bryan was reminded in a dispatch from Vera Cruz that nearly a month had elapsed since the Pass Christian conference without action having been taken along the lines discussed at that meeting. To this the secretary of state replied that

[52] Lind to Bryan, January 7, 15, 1914.
[53] Bryan to Lind, January 17, 1914.
[54] Lind to Benton Gibson and others, January 23, 1914; Lind to Joliet Plantation, Oaxaca, January 24, 1914.

the president appreciated Lind's services and had under consideration the raising of the embargo.[55] At last — on January 31 — came the welcome news that the embargo would be raised. A memorandum was sent to all American embassies stating that the government had received convincing information that there was more hopeful prospect of peace if Mexico were left to the forces now reckoning with one another than if a mere change of personnel were effected in Mexico City. The president no longer felt justified in maintaining an irregular position with respect to the contending parties in the matter of neutrality; he therefore intended to remove the prohibition on the exportation of arms and munitions from the United States into Mexico. "Settlement by civil war carried to its bitter conclusion is a terrible thing, but it must come now . . . unless some outside power is to undertake to sweep Mexico with its armed forces from end to end, which is the beginning of a still more difficult problem." [56]

The announcement of the raising of the embargo was received with greater equanimity by Huerta than it was by the O'Shaughnessys, and the wily old Indian was as friendly as ever to the chargé. Bryan reported that the Constitutionalist representatives were much pleased and that there was considerable ammunition on the border waiting to be sent over the line. He took occasion to say again that the president was pleased with the prospect and had given great weight to Lind's opinion in the move he had just made.[57]

Great as was Lind's satisfaction over the advantage thus gained by the revolutionists, he was disappointed that their progress in the direction of Mexico City was so painfully slow. Certain incidents, moreover, which occurred shortly after the president's proclamation, played into the hands of Huerta and gave enemies of the Wilson administration in the United States opportunities to argue that his policy was ill advised and destined to

[55] Lind to Bryan, January 28, 1914; Bryan to Lind, January 29, 1914.
[56] Bryan to Lind, January 31, 1914. Wilson's proclamation was dated February 3.
[57] O'Shaughnessy to Lind, February 3, 1914; Bryan to Lind, February 5, 1914; O'Shaughnessy, A Diplomat's Wife, pp. 165, 174, 175, 178, 193.

fail. In the latter part of February a New York paper published an article by James Creelman that received wide notice in the press of the United States and Mexico. This same Creelman at the time the Diaz régime was drawing to a close had hurried to Mexico at the call of the Diaz interests and published a series of articles designed to counteract the effect of the telling articles on "barbarous Mexico" by John Kenneth Turner, in which he exposed the unsavory conditions that afflicted the down-trodden masses under the Diaz system.[58]

Lind met Creelman in Vera Cruz before the latter visited Mexico City, and understood that his mission was undertaken in the interest of Huerta. Upon Creelman's return after a stay of about two weeks in the Mexican capital, on February 12, Lind got the impression that the newspaper man thought that Huerta was impossible and destined to fall at no distant date, and that the United States would be obliged to intervene before the end of the year. Lind was unable to judge how much of Creelman's contention was prompted by his desire to elicit his own views, but he found it did not require a great deal of tact to induce him to do most of the talking. When Creelman's article was published it breathed intense hostility to Lind, who was portrayed as sitting in the rear of the American consulate, as he had sat for seven months, smilingly waiting, "while Mexico and her 15,000,000 men, women, and children have moved to ruin." The Creelman article was very disturbing to Lind, but Bryan told him not to worry about it.[59]

On February 17 William S. Benton, a ranchman and British subject, was killed near Juarez by General Villa. In England public opinion was raised to a high pitch of indignation; and in the United States the incident was made the basis for criticism of the administration by those who wanted intervention. Senator Fall of New Mexico, one of the persistent and bitter critics of Wilson's policy, in a speech in the Senate on March 9 de-

[58] John Kenneth Turner, *Barbarous Mexico* (Chicago, 1911), p. 245.

[59] Lind to Bryan, February 2, 27, 1914; Bryan to Lind, March 3, 1914; O'Shaughnessy, *A Diplomat's Wife*, p. 217.

nounced the State Department for its inactivity. Naturally the Huerta press in Mexico used the opportunity to stir the population of the capital, whereas it had been silent after the killing of seventeen Americans and forty-one Mexicans on February 4 in a tunnel obstructed by Maximo Castillo, a Huerta follower.[60]

Bryan ordered an investigation of the Benton killing, but Carranza embarrassed the administration still further by denying the right of the United States to investigate the death of a British subject and appointed a commission of his own. Lind thought Villa's action most unfortunate at "this juncture," but believed it ought not to influence the general conduct that the administration had begun. Advices from the North indicated that Benton was a "quarrelsome, domineering Englishman, very abusive at times." Lind still had a good opinion of Carranza's character.[61]

During the remaining weeks of his stay in Mexico, Lind was in a most uncomfortable and agitated state of mind. The effect of the intense heat and the long strain of suspense, coupled with a steady stream of excited and disgruntled callers, showed in his dispatches and reports. The slump in the fortunes of the rebels and the Benton incident played into the hands of Huerta; the representatives of foreign governments were becoming increasingly restless; and there was talk of intervention. He feared that Huerta, with the secret help of the British, might succeed in pacifying the Tampico-Monterey district, which would give him such prestige that the United States could not refuse to grant recognition.[62]

In two long communications dated February 25 and March 8, addressed respectively to Wilson and Bryan, Lind warned them of the seriousness of the situation and recommended drastic action. To the president he expressed gratitude for his generous letters of appreciation and encouragement and apologized for the insistent mandatory form of his recent communications. His

[60] Bryan to Lind, February 22, 1914; "C. O. I. S." to Lind, February 22, 1914.
[61] Bryan to Lind, March 3, 1914; Lind to Bryan, February 23, 28, March 10, 1914.
[62] Lind to Bryan, February 23, 24, March 10, 11, 1914; Norman Lind to W. M. Jerome, March 28, 1914.

sole excuse was that he wished to impress in the strongest possible way that a point had been reached where "execution is as
important as judgment."

I have sincerely hoped that the liberation of Mexico might be
accomplished by indirect means, but there has been no moment
since September that I have not been conscious of the possibility
that this work may devolve on us. I have, however, been very solicitous that before such contingency be reached the ground should be
fully prepared so as to make the physical work as light as possible
and the political aspect of it a moral necessity — a necessity forced
upon us by the appeals of the Mexicans themselves and the united
voice of Europe. I prefer to have Europe clamor for us to do that
which our honor and our interest compel us to do even against her
protest. We have about reached that point. As to the political effect
of such action at home I have neither fear nor doubt. Our people
will fight for either right or interest. When the two, right and
interest, go hand in hand woe to the man who stands in the way.
That is our nature and that is our history.

In his highly confidential letter to Bryan, which was handed
to the secretary of state by a trusted friend, Lind presented a
gloomy picture. He regarded every day of Huerta's power as a
serious menace not only to the future welfare of Mexico but to
the relations between the American government and the nations
interested in Mexico. The situation was too serious, he said, to
allow Huerta to continue longer. Unless a decided change occurred by March 15, he believed Huerta should be eliminated
within forty-eight hours. The plans for the accomplishment of
this had already been completed at Lind's end of the line, and
he believed it would not entail the loss of a single American life.
A marine officer (who was named), accompanied by a railway
official, had just returned from Mexico City, where he had
posed as a railroad man in search of a railroad employee suspected of having been drafted. The missing man was not found,
but in his search the officer had located every gun and noted its
size and efficiency. Correct maps had been obtained, and no detail had been omitted. No civilian would be allowed to accom

pany the proposed expedition except Lind and his son Norman, who was staying at Vera Cruz. The railway official had picked his men. The expedition would arrive unheralded at Mexico City shortly before daylight, and would possess the city before noon. The object of the expedition was to maintain peace and to protect life and property, Huerta would be held in safe-keeping until such time as he could be turned over to the proper domestic authorities to be dealt with according to law. Suitable proclamations had been prepared by naval officers, whose names were given. No formal orders were wanted or needed except the president's authority to proceed.

In a subsequent telegram Bryan was assured that the sole purpose of the proposed expedition was to put a stop to Huerta's anarchical career and to afford the Mexican people an opportunity to resume orderly government. Lind did not believe that any resistance would be offered "this side" of Mexico City. There was no considerable body of troops south of Torreon, and if they should proceed south, the revolutionists would probably follow them up. If the expedition could be taken with the formal consent of Carranza, Lind thought it would be the shortest and surest way of restoring peace and would prevent war with Mexico, which at that time seemed imminent.[63]

The only reply Bryan made to the suggestion was a telegram stating that the president did not contemplate any immediate action.[64] The most charitable and obvious explanation for the conception of this plan is the effect of seven months of anxious waiting in hot Vera Cruz for something to turn up and the influence of naval and military officers, who were itching for a "scrap" with the "greasers." This influence, together with O'Shaughnessy's outspoken sympathy for Huerta and the growing tension between the *chargé* and Lind, was too much for the old fighter from Minnesota.[65] One of the most disheartening

[63] Lind to Bryan, March 12, 19, 1914.
[64] Bryan to Lind, March 14, 1914.
[65] Lind to Bryan, March 22, 24, 1914; Arnold Shanklin to Lind, March 24, 1914; Olmsted to Lind, March 25, 1914.

things was the attitude of the Americans in Mexico. "Every one, big or small, has his own little grab hook out," Norman wrote, "and because the United States does not go to war to pull his little minnow out, they all get right up and cry, wail, beat, and gnash their teeth." [66]

Hoping against hope that the rebels would capture Torreon, and daily urging the State Department to give them active assistance, Lind finally telegraphed Bryan on March 29 that Huerta would be able to continue indefinitely. In view of this situation, he expressed the desire to be allowed to return to the United States for some weeks, even though the State Department might wish him to return to Mexico. The president approved of the proposed visit and requested him to come to Washington that he might have the benefit of a conference. "We appreciate highly the service you have rendered and regret exceedingly the hardships you have suffered," Bryan wrote.[67]

On April 6 the "Mayflower" stood out to sea, with John Lind and his daughter Jenny on board. O'Shaughnessy's farewell was a wire expressing regret at his leaving, because he expected shortly to come to Vera Cruz. Mrs. O'Shaughnessy's entry for the day, however, expressed more nearly the *chargé's* feelings, as well as her own. "Lind leaves tonight for Washington, so exit from the tragic scene Don Juan Lindo (I sometimes feel like calling him Don Juan Blindo), who commenced life in a Scandinavian town as Jon Lind, and who has ended by dreaming northern dreams in Vera Cruz, in the hours of Mexico's agony." [68]

Lind did not expect to remain in Washington more than a few days, but before he arrived, on April 14, the arrest of the paymaster and seven sailors from the United States gunboat

[66] Norman Lind to W. M. Jerome, March 28, 1914. Norman and Jenny Lind arrived at Vera Cruz on February 8, 1914. Jenny returned to the United States with her father; Norman remained in Mexico until a few days after the capture of Vera Cruz.

[67] Bryan to Lind, March 30, 31, 1914; Lind to Bryan, April 1, 2, 3, 1914.

[68] O'Shaughnessy to Lind, April 2, 1914; O'Shaughnessy, *A Diplomat's Wife*, p. 250.

"Dolphin" by Mexican soldiers at Tampico started a chain of events that detained him weeks instead of days. Before Lind conferred with President Wilson, the latter had sustained the demand of Admiral Mayo that Huerta order the firing of a salute of twenty-one guns to the United States flag; and Huerta had replied that the apology for the arrest and punishment of the officer responsible for the arrest of the American sailors was sufficient and that no salute would be fired.

XVI

THE A. B. C. MEDIATION

WHEN Lind arrived in Washington, he found that city — and indeed the whole country — seething with excitement. Public sentiment was back of the president, but a number of Republican papers said the present situation proved the folly of his idealistic policy and insisted that the crisis would not have come if Huerta had been recognized in the first place. Huerta quibbled and dodged until on Saturday, April 18, 1914, Wilson issued an ultimatum giving him until six o'clock P. M., Sunday, to comply with the demand to salute the flag. On Sunday evening newsboys hawking papers containing the announcement that Huerta had refused to comply unconditionally with Wilson's terms were shouting "War extra!"

On the morning of April 14 Bryan brought Lind to see the president, but there is no record of the conversation. Later in the day, however, a huge battleship fleet was ordered to proceed to Mexican waters, and a sharp note was sent to Huerta. The time limit for Huerta's compliance having expired, Wilson read a message to Congress on the afternoon of Monday, April 20, reciting the events leading up to the crisis, asking Congress for authority to use the armed forces of the United States against Huerta, specifying that the United States had no quarrel with the Mexican people, and expressing the hope that the trouble would not lead to war.

On the evening of that day, while Lind was a guest in the home of Secretary Daniels, the conversation was interrupted by a summons from the White House. At the White House conference were Bryan, Daniels, Garrison, Lind, and the chiefs of staff of the army and navy. The question under discussion was what should be done to compel Huerta to make amends for insulting the American flag. Shortly after Lind's arrival the president called for a statement of his views. Lind suggested that Captain Moffett, who was at the time in the harbor of Tampico with the "Chester," should demand an apology; and that if the apology were not given promptly, the "Chester" should sink the "dinky" Mexican gunboats in the harbor. He thought the retaliation should be in kind. Admiral Blue objected that the "Chester" might be sunk, to which Lind replied that he had been all over Tampico and knew at first hand that there were neither guns nor ammunition to molest the American ships. He thought Moffett could sink the gunboat "Bravo" in five minutes.

Shortly after he had spoken, Lind was excused; and he knew nothing further until he read in the papers the next day (April 21) that Admiral Fletcher had been ordered to seize the custom house at Vera Cruz. Lind always felt that the capture and occupation of Vera Cruz was a mistake, and ten years later wrote to Secretary Daniels that he knew of no action by the American government that had been so generally misconstrued and misunderstood in Mexico.[1]

With the shedding of blood it was inevitable that jingoistic papers in the United States should demand a declaration of war before the various factions in Mexico could unite to oppose the American forces, and that papers in South America should take a hostile attitude toward the United States. While the public was reading about rumors of war, anti-American riots in Mexico, and orders for sending troops to Vera Cruz, the plenipotentiaries of Argentina, Brazil, and Chile on April 25 tendered the good offices of their respective governments to effect an amicable settlement of the imbroglio. The offer of mediation was promptly

[1] Lind to Daniels, November 24, 1925; Daniels to Lind, November 27, 1925; Lind's testimony, April 27, 1920, in Senate Document no. 285, 66th Congress, 2d Session, p. 2363; Baker, *Wilson*, 4:323. The *Minneapolis Journal* (October 31, 1915) published a Washington dispatch stating that Lind had recommended the occupation of Vera Cruz. In a letter to James Gray, the Washington correspondent of this paper, dated November 13, 1915, Lind called attention to the inaccuracy of the dispatch. *Mexico*, "a weekly to promote intelligent discussion of Mexican affairs" published in New York City, on April 25, 1914, published an article entitled "One Man" alleging that Lind had advised Wilson to take Vera Cruz.

accepted by Wilson. Previously to the acceptance of the so-called A. B. C. mediation, it had been decided at a conference attended by the president, the secretary of state, and certain members of the Senate Committee on Foreign Relations, that the negotiations should not be limited to Huerta but should include the rebel leaders Carranza, Villa, and Zapata.

These developments delayed Lind's departure from Washington until the early part of June. At the earnest request of Wilson and Bryan, who insisted that they needed his help, he remained in the capital, much as he longed for the cool breezes of Minnewashta.[2] During these weeks he had long and frequent conferences with the president and the secretary of state and presented formal reports and memoranda. He was also in constant communication with the revolutionary leaders and assisted them in drawing up documents. In addition to these activities he was bothered with telephone calls from people with axes to grind, who sought to use his influence on their behalf with the State Department. But their importunities were in vain.[3] Lind had few, if any, specific instructions from his government, but he knew that the administration wanted peace in Mexico without military intervention, and his efforts were bent to that end.[4]

Before leaving Vera Cruz, Lind had had a meeting with H. L. Hall, a Mormon American who had resided in Mexico for about twenty years and who represented himself as being thoroughly familiar with the Zapatista movement in the south of Mexico, where the agrarian movement was strong. Hall told Lind that the Zapatistas were not guilty of one-tenth of the atrocities that had been practiced against them. His errand was to learn whether or not the government of the United States would be willing to enter into relations with the Zapatistas through a Colonel Martinez, who was a friend of Arnold Shanklin, the American consul-general at Mexico City. Shanklin had suggested that Martinez visit the United States in order to get in touch with the revolutionary organization there and to cooper-

[2] Lind to Norman Lind, May 28, June 5, 1914.
[3] Lind to Norman Lind, May 26, 1914.
[4] Lind to Bryan, July 14, 1914.

ate with it. Lind promised to do his part to facilitate the journey because he thought it would be advantageous for the United States to have the good will of the Zapatistas in the event of a crisis with Huerta.[5]

Lind did not meet Martinez, but through Shanklin it was arranged that communication should be conducted by code. Lind was to be known as "Juarez," Shanklin as "Paz," Zapata as "Dix," Hall as "Clark," and Martinez as "Brady." [6] A number of "underground" messages passed among the principals to this arrangement during Lind's sojourn in Washington, and Hall later came to Washington. Lind reported to Shanklin that the administration had the warmest sympathy for "Martinez' friends" and would use its good offices in their behalf, but he hoped they would take no military action against Mexico City, because such action would upset all plans for their permanent relief. Bryan also gave assurance of his support.[7]

Zapata and Martinez, however, proved to be hard to handle; through Lind and Hall they attempted to obtain a sum of money as the price of denying themselves the privilege of advancing toward Mexico City. Lind informed Zapata, through Shanklin, that the government could not furnish money even for charitable purposes, but suggested the possibility that the Red Cross and private charity would lend assistance as soon as an avenue for delivery was open. Zapata must understand once for all, he said, that there had been no negotiations between him and the government of the United States. Unable to obtain funds through Lind and Hall, Zapata notified Shanklin that he would proceed as seemed best to him. Lind's distrust of Martinez was later verified.[8]

Lind's chief interest was in the fortunes of Carranza, upon

[5] Lind to Bryan, March 23, 1914.

[6] Hall to Lind, April 6, 1914; Lind's testimony, April 27, 1920, in Senate Document no. 285, 66th Congress, 2d Session, pp. 2350–52.

[7] Lind to Shanklin, May 15, 1914; Bryan to Clinton MacEachran, May 12, 16, 1914; Hall to Bryan, May 14, 1914; Bryan to Shanklin, June 20, 1914. There are many communications pertaining to this episode in the Lind Papers.

[8] Shanklin to Hall, May 23, 24, 26, 29, June 2, 1914; Lind to Shanklin, May 28, June 2, 1914; Hall to Lind, June 11, 1914; Lind to Bryan, July 4, 1914.

whom he had pinned his faith for some time. From first to last, previous to and during the sittings of the A. B. C. conference, he was the advocate of the Carranza cause.

On April 30, three weeks before the conference met, Lind submitted a memorandum to Wilson outlining his position with respect to the approaching conclave. After reading it, the president said to him, "I concur wholly." In part the document read as follows:

In dealing with Huerta it must not be lost sight of for a moment that we are dealing with a Frankenstein devoid of all moral judgment, ruled by appetite and passion, and guided by cunning. . . . Huerta is at the end of his rope. His army is destroyed. The reports about the possible understanding with Zapata are absolutely false and put forward only to affect American opinion. . . .

I think the revolutionists have shown more self control and more political capacity under trying circumstances than I deemed them capable of, in view of their limited political experience in the past. . . .

The proposed mediation by the A B C group was wisely accepted with the reservations expressed in the acceptance. Nothing else could be done. I am fully convinced, however, that the mediation will result in nothing. Its greatest value, so far as the Mexican situation is concerned, is the fact that it has afforded the Americans an opportunity to escape. The three ministers, in all human probability, hold the same views in respect to government as do the Huertistas in Mexico City. They will naturally regard the Huerta government as the principal factor in the Mexican situation. They will insist on a compromise. No compromise is possible; it is not a strife between individuals; it is a contest between the masses and the classes. As evidence in support of these suspicions, I call to your attention the fact that the three ministers are in the closest touch and in constant consultation with the class of Mexicans and foreigners who favor the continuance of the present system in Mexico but who are probably willing, and perhaps anxious, for a change of dictators. The mediation will drag along weeks without result. If the hands of the revolutionists are tied in the meantime, I believe you will find, at the end of the period, a public sentiment in the United States almost irresistible, and probably uncontrollable, that you proceed and complete the work of setting the Mexican house in order. In such contingency all our previous efforts to insure peace on a basis that will give promise of permanency will be wasted and lost. We will be face to face with war. On the other hand, if the progress of the revolutionists is not stayed the Mexican situation will be solved and Huerta will be eliminated before the mediators have completed their scheme of mediation. If the hands of the revolutionists are tied, Huerta will be afforded time to scheme and to devise new obstacles and combinations. He will try to drag in European interests, as evidenced by the despatches from England received yesterday. He will probably succeed. Now that Carranza has made his position clear and it appears that he and the forces which he controls have not only shown a willingness, but have actually demonstrated their ability to protect American lives and property, it seems to me that some plan should be devised to aid, or at least permit, the revolutionists to continue their work. They are doing our work as well as their own.

At the beginning Bryan and Lind differed as to the course to be pursued with respect to the revolutionists. Bryan leaned toward the support of Villa. Lind advised strongly against this, pointing out that the object of the supporters of Villa was to destroy Carranza, create chaos, and thus get back into the saddle. He was convinced that there was a deliberate conspiracy on the part of "big business" to bring about a split between Carranza and Villa, and he suspected that officials of the American government in Mexico, Special Agent George C. Carothers, who was with Villa, and Consul Felix Sommerfield were the instruments of the conspirators. "I still feel confident that the only solution that will insure peace on a promising basis and relieve us from the responsibility and hazard of intervention is the selection of Carranza," he told Bryan. "Carranza eliminated, Villa is probably the only man strong enough to compel acquiescence by force, if necessary. But the world will not accept Villa at this time. Hence I predict, as I have often said before, that it is Carranza or intervention." [9]

[9] Lind to Bryan, June 14, 1914; Charles A. Douglas to Lind, June 20, 1914; Lind to A. B. Farquhar, August 6, 1916.

The United States and Huerta having accepted the offer of mediation by the representatives of the A. B. C. powers, these plenipotentiaries invited Carranza as the chief commander of the Constitutionalist forces to accept their good offices. The "first chief" promptly accepted their good offices "in principle," leaving it for a later time to enter into the details of the negotiations.[10] This brought notes from the mediators requesting Carranza to suspend all hostilities and military operations and to appoint representatives to the conference.[11] In the communications that followed Carranza took the position that the mediators should define the scope of the conference, that the conflict between the United States and Huerta was independent of the internal struggle in Mexico for liberty and rights, and that suspension of military operations would only accrue to the advantage of Huerta.[12]

In assuming this attitude toward the Niagara Falls conference, the Carranza representatives in the United States, Rafael Zubaran and Juan F. Urquidi, had the advice of Lind, who was in constant communication with them and with their legal adviser in Washington, Judge Charles A. Douglas.[13] Lind assisted them in drafting communications to the mediators and to Bryan. The Constitutionalists were highly appreciative of these services.[14]

For example, before the meeting of the A. B. C. mediators, in a public statement to Secretary Bryan, Zubaran, the Washington representative of the Constitutionalists, assured him that the relations between the Constitutionalists and the United States were friendly and that Americans who found themselves in territory in possession of the Carranzistas would be granted every protection.

The first chief of the Constitutionalist army, fully realizing the

[10] D. D. Gama and others to Carranza, April 28, 1914, and Carranza's reply, April 29.
[11] April 30, May 2, 1914.
[12] Notes dated May 3, 1914.
[13] Lind to J. Acuna, secretary of foreign affairs, February 23, 1916.
[14] G. R. Hackley to Lind, June 14, 1914.

menace to the good relations between the people of Mexico and that of the neighboring republic, the United States, arising out of the wanton conduct of the usurper, Huerta, has delegated the undersigned to make clear the feeling and the attitude of the Constitutionalists, and, indeed, of the people of Mexico toward the United States. . . .

He also feels that the policy followed, and to be followed, in his struggle against the usurper Huerta is giving due protection to the lives and property of all American citizens and all foreigners who maintain strict neutrality and is a manifest assurance of both the purpose and ability of the Constitutionalists to discharge the international obligations of Mexico within the territory which they now, and will hereafter, control.

Lind drafted these two paragraphs of the statement, after which it was submitted to Carranza by Zubaran. Carranza then authorized his representative to deliver it to Bryan. Later Lind forwarded by cable to Consul Canada a translation in Spanish for circulation in Mexico.

Lind was fearful that the interests hostile to reform in Mexico would triumph at the conference and advised the Constitutionalists to be chary of committing themselves to a position that might ruin their cause. He warned Bryan that the Huerta representatives were masters of argument, diplomacy, and duplicity, whereas the American representatives labored under the disadvantage of having no firsthand knowledge of Mexican conditions. He thought the interests cooperating to defeat the objects of the revolution would make an effort to commit the United States to a plan designating three or more commissioners to administer the government of Mexico *ad interim* and to have the United States use its influence to compel the revolutionists to accept the plan. Failing in this, Lind anticipated that an effort would be made to commit the United States to the proposition that Carranza must not be permitted to assume the temporary administration of the government pending the election. The acceptance of either plan, in Lind's judgment, would defeat the reforms of the Constitutionalists and play into the hands of the

Huertistas who hoped to stalemate the revolution. He wrote as follows:

This is not a situation that demands a diplomat to conciliate. The problem we have to deal with is a victorious army with a score of politically inexperienced but ambitious chiefs — every one including Zapata a potential candidate for the dictatorship. . . .

I also think it worth while to reflect seriously whether it is prudent or good politics on our part to publicly become sponsors, by advocacy or otherwise, for any particular reform program in Mexico however meritorious it may appear. . . . The Mexicans of the North, as you already appreciate, are very sensitive about doing anything that smacks of taking orders from the outside. I am confident that they have a program of agrarian reform in view. I also have reason to believe that they will gratefully accept suggestions in this connection if communicated in the right spirit and unofficially.

In conclusion, it seems to me that the only safe course for us in the mediation proceeding is to remain listeners as long as possible, to allow all suggestions to come from other sources. In other words, to act negatively as long as possible. It will not be many weeks, perhaps many days, until it will be apparent to the world that to undertake any serious discussion of Mexican domestic affairs without the presence and cooperation of the constitutionalists would be utterly absurd. When that condition is reached I think it is incumbent upon our representatives to make that suggestion. The mediators can then, if it is desired to continue the mediation, again invite the Constitutionalists to participate. I think Carranza would be glad to send representatives to explain the attitude and program of the Constitutionalists.[15]

In another communication to Bryan, dated May 29, Lind presented an argument in opposition to a plan that was reported to be under consideration by the mediators to provide a new *ad interim* president on the theory that in order to have any status as head of the government, he must step into Huerta's shoes. After reciting the pertinent facts of Huerta's *coup d'état*, he wrote:

[15] This document bears no date, but it was presented to Bryan before Carranza appointed representatives to the conference held on June 11, 1914.

This recital of facts, known to all Mexicans, makes it apparent that nothing short of physical force will ever compel the Constitutionalists to assume the executive power of Mexico from Huerta's bloody hands. . . .

I almost wish that the mediators will turn down Carranza's request for representation. . . . In any event, whether representatives are received or not, I have little hope that any good can be expected from mediation. . . . There is really nothing to mediate. As between the United States and Huerta it is a question of national honor and dignity. Every one of your peace treaties excludes such questions from arbitration. . . .

The Huerta delegates have only one real object in view — to eliminate Carranza. If they succeed in that they will yield everything else. Naturally they are just as much opposed to the mediation of any domestic question as are the Constitutionalists, but you will find them willing to yield on this or any other point to accomplish their main end.

It seems to me that we should not worry about the succession. That will take care of itself. When Carranza goes in he will be a dictator for the time being and nothing else. This is the naked fact and why attempt to conceal it? It is only as a dictator that he can accomplish the reforms that are demanded. When he reaches Mexico City in the discharge of his sworn duty as governor to defend the Constitution, with the power and will of the nation at his back, what other Mexican citizen possesses as good a right to gather the shreds of that document and direct its restoration?

By the end of May Bryan was satisfied that the success of the Constitutionalists was inevitable and insisted that the provisional government must be in favor of agrarian and political reforms, not neutral, as the Huerta delegates proposed; and on May 29, the day of his conference with Lind, he urged that the provisional government must be disconnected from the Huerta régime.

In a statement made public on the last day of May, Carranza clarified his attitude toward the mediation conference. He expressed astonishment that there should be such apparent lack of understanding of the attitude of the Constitutionalists on the part of the mediators, the American government, and a portion of the American press. He avowed that the recent successes of the Constitutionalist army were conclusive proof of the waning power of Huerta, and still the mediators appeared to ignore this fact. It was made plain that the Constitutionalists would have nothing whatever to do with anyone friendly or previously connected with the Huerta government and that the "first chief" would be provisional president while the elections were verified and constitutional order restored. Agrarian reform was declared to be a wholly internal problem to be solved without outside interference.

Lind was gratified that Carranza's statement conformed so closely with his own communication to Bryan. He wrote to Norman: "My respect for Carranza grows. This statement is worthy of a statesman. It is hard to get some people here from meddling with things that do not concern them. But the situation is clearing. The president is all right." [16] Shortly after Carranza's statement was made public, Lind left for Minneapolis, but the Carranzista representatives at Washington continued to seek his advice. And when they were granted an interview with the American commissioners on June 11, they stood firm in denying the right of the mediators to attempt to settle the internal affairs of Mexico and affirmed that under no consideration would Carranza accept the results of mediation, no matter how much in his favor they might be. [17]

So far as the Carranzistas were concerned, the upshot of the A. B. C. mediation amounted to nothing. It was war to the knife between them and Huerta and anybody associated with him.

Lind's part in the tangled affairs attending the A. B. C. conference was severely criticized in some quarters. It was alleged that not only had he aided the rebels in landing ammunition but that he had taken the part of a man who was notoriously hostile to foreigners and to Americans in particular. It was also charged that he had received a retainer from Carranza. It is true that

[16] Lind to Norman Lind, June 2, 1914.
[17] Juan F. Urquidi to Lind, June 12, 1914; Douglas to Lind, June 12, 1914.

Judge Douglas, the counsel for Carranza, offered him a retainer, but Lind declined to accept it, giving as his reason that he was working for a cause that was close to his heart.[18]

Undoubtedly Lind overestimated Carranza's ability. In any event, for the time being he regarded him as representing a cause and discounted liberally the reports of his hostility toward the United States. He had been told by Mexicans that Carranza was fighting for a principle unusual in a rebel leader in Mexico.[19] Lind and Carranza had in common an undying hatred for Huerta. In denying the right of a foreign power to interfere in the internal affairs of Mexico, Lind believed Carranza but voiced the general public opinion of Mexico.[20] He also knew enough history to understand why Mexicans distrusted the humanitarian professions of the United States, even though spoken by the lips of so high-minded a man as Woodrow Wilson. The war of 1846–48 was too recent to have been forgotten by Mexicans; and Carranza had seen a spirit of contempt for Mexicans manifested by the Americans with whom he had come into contact along the border.

Moreover, Lind was favorably impressed with the men who represented Carranza in the United States. Many of the Carranzista leaders had been educated in the United States and were sincerely interested in intelligent reform. Urquidi, for example, was a graduate of the Massachusetts Institute of Technology; and Luis Cabrera was a man of intelligence whose hostile attitude toward Americans, in Lind's opinion, was greatly exaggerated. Cabrera, he thought, merely wanted foreign interests to bear their fair share of the burden of taxation.[21]

[18] Correspondence between Lind and Douglas. See also Lind's testimony, April 27, 1920, in Senate Document no. 285, 66th Congress, 2d Session, pp. 2360, 2364–66.

[19] Views on the Mexican situation expressed by Emeterio de la Garza in conversation with Rear Admiral Fletcher on board the U. S. S. "Louisiana," October 11, 1913, in the Lind Papers. Lincoln Steffens held a view similar to Lind's with respect to Carranza and his cause. Steffens to Lind, February 8, 1915.

[20] Lind to Bryan, July 23, 1914.

[21] Lind to Acuna, February 23, 1916; Urquidi to Lind, February 1, 1915; Lind's testimony, April 28, 1920, in Senate Document no. 285, 66th Congress,

By lending assistance to the shipment of arms and munitions
to the rebels, Lind dealt with certain shifty individuals and got
his fingers burned. It was inevitable that situations should arise
to plague him in the future. He was approached by Sherburne
G. Hopkins, an attorney who was consulted by the Carranzistas
at various times but at the time was interested in obtaining munitions for Villa. He stated that he had the assurance of the State
Department that it would not interfere with shipments of munitions to the rebels. At the time Lind was ignorant of the fact
that Hopkins was not in good standing with the department;
after he was apprised of that fact, he avoided him. Before the
Senate committee in 1920 Lind denied the truth of a story published in the *New York Herald* on June 30, 1914, purporting to
relate a conversation between Lind and Hopkins.[22]

Lind took his departure from Washington during the first
days of June, but his connection with the State Department was
not formally severed until the first week of August. He retired
with the assurance of Wilson and Bryan that they were duly
appreciative of the great service he had rendered through difficult and trying circumstances. "Your ability, fidelity, and industry have been such as to leave nothing to be desired," Bryan
wrote.[23] In view of the allegations in the press that Lind received
a "very generous sum" for his Mexican services, it is proper to
state that he received only the salary of an ambassador.

Though Lind was to have no official connection with the
State Department again, he continued to take an active interest
in Mexican affairs. Bryan was fully cognizant of his attitude and
encouraged him to continue his efforts to inspire confidence
among Mexican leaders with respect to the unselfish attitude of
the administration. The confidence of the Carranzista leaders in

2d Session, p. 2337; Luis Cabrera, *The Mexican Situation from a Mexican Point
of View* (Washington, 1913).
[22] Lind to Bryan, July 14, 1914; memorandum of Lind to the Department of
State, April 16, 1915; Lind's testimony, April 27, 1920, in Senate Document no.
285, 66th Congress, 2d Session, pp. 2411–19, 2359–60. See speech of William
Alden Smith in the Senate, August 9, 1913, with reference to Hopkins' activity
in behalf of the Madero government.
[23] August 5, 1914.

him burdened him with a large correspondence, and he could not set foot in Washington without being sought and importuned by them for aid and suggestions. In July, Bryan indicated to Judge Douglas that he and Wilson were considering asking Lind to join Carranza at once, to which Douglas replied that nothing wiser or timelier could be done.[24] In the many uncertainties of the months ahead, Lind was one of the most trusted counselors of Douglas and Carranza.

Lind lamented the fact that Bryan was surrounded by men who were out of sympathy with the administration; and he thought it especially unfortunate that the secretary of state was compelled to rely on reports from Mexico sent in by George C. Carothers, Felix Sommerfield, and Paul Fuller.

Carothers had lived in Mexico since 1889 and had served as American consular agent in Mexico from 1900 to 1913, after which he became special agent of the Department of State. He was friendly to Huerta, and after his cause was seen to be hopeless he took up with Villa and traveled with him on his special train. Lind sensed trouble ahead when Carothers began making appeals to the State Department to raise the embargo in order to obtain munitions for Villa, and he laid much of the blame for the split between Villa and Carranza at Carothers' door. The influence of Sommerfield was bent in the same direction. Lind also alleged that Paul Fuller was under the influence of the interests that had sustained Henry Lane Wilson. Despite the fact that Lind feared the State Department was misled by the reports of these agents, Carothers testified that his conferences with Bryan were unsatisfactory and that he never had the cooperation of the State Department.[25]

In any event, it is clear that powerful forces were at work

[24] Douglas to Lind, July 18, 1914; J. J. Slade to Lind, July 27, 1914.

[25] Lind to Bryan, September 28, 1914; memorandum from Lind to the Department of State, April 15, 1915; d'Antin to Lind, October 6, 31, 1914, January 5, 1915; G. R. Hackley to Lind, June 17, 1915; testimony of Carothers, February 28, 1920, in Senate Document no. 285, 66th Congress, 2d Session, p. 1775; Hugh L. Scott, *Some Memories of a Soldier* (New York, 1928), p. 502; *Angles of the Mexican Situation from Mexican Viewpoints*, a pamphlet containing

to sow discord among the rebels, and their efforts bore abundant fruit in the months to come, in spite of Bryan's instructions to Carothers to bring the leaders into hearty cooperation. Under these circumstances Lind suggested to Bryan that an investigation of Mexican affairs by a Senate committee might clear the atmosphere and give the American people a better conception of the issues at stake than the "Cowdray inspired press" gave them, but Wilson thought an investigation might delay settlement.[26]

The events of July and August in Mexico were bewildering to readers of American newspapers. The rebel armies marched on Mexico City, and on July 15 Huerta resigned and fled the country, leaving the government in the hands of Francisco Carbajal. Carranza, however, would treat with the Huertistas only on the basis of unconditional surrender. About a month later Carbajal retired in favor of Iturbide, who signed an agreement naming Carranza provisional president; and on August 20 the "first chief" of the Constitutionalists entered the capital and shortly set up his own government. The triumph of Carranza was of course gratifying to Lind, and the rugged Minnesotan was not forgotten in the capital. When the Washington statue was lifted to its pedestal from which a Huerta mob had unseated it at the time of the Tampico incident, it was short one arm, and immediately a peon in the crowd shouted: "Better without an arm; let's call it John Lind."[27]

Notwithstanding the inglorious ending of Huerta's government, there were dark clouds on the horizon which made the victory for Carranza less complete than it would have been had all the elements in the revolt against Huerta worked in harmony. A newspaper correspondent wrote Lind from Mexico City that he gravely questioned "if there is any sure remedy for

the opinion of General Alvardo in regard to Francisco Villa, published in "El Liberal," City of Mexico, November 18, 1914. On a visit to New York City, Lincoln Steffens learned that Wall Street was favorable to Villa. *The Autobiography of Lincoln Steffens* (New York, 1931), p. 715.

[26] Lind to Bryan, July 3, 1914; Bryan to Lind, July 4, 1914.

[27] Slade to Lind, September 20, 1914.

the Mexican cancer save the knife wielded by a celebrated surgeon with striped pants and benevolent whiskers." [28]

In the first week of October, 1914, a constitutional convention in Mexico City called by Carranza ended within a week in dissension between the two parties under Carranza and Villa, and the latter succeeded in having it removed to Aguascalientes, in territory dominated by himself. Here the Villistas and the Zapatistas made common cause against Carranza, who refused to attend on the ground that by doing so he would waive his office as chief of the army and thus incapacitate himself for performing the duties of chief of the Constitutionalist army. In his formal reply to the invitation Carranza stressed the dangers lurking in the ambitions of Villa and Zapata. His retirement, he said, might pave the way for a reactionary régime.[29]

Carranza refused to accept the choice of the convention for provisional president, Eulalio Gutierrez; and, hard pressed by the Villa and Zapata forces, the "first chief" evacuated Mexico City and established his headquarters at Vera Cruz the latter part of November, about the time the American troops were withdrawn from that city.

Thus a new revolution had started in Mexico, with Carranza, Villa, and Zapata at the head of rival armies striving for control of the government. On November 21, 1914, Judge Douglas wrote Lind that Huerta's revolution would pale into insignificance when contrasted with the new revolution, and he said he felt the need of Lind's advice when he thought of the problems ahead of them for the next six months or year.

[28] R. H. Murray to Lind, October 10, 1914; Juan F. Urquidi to Lind, August 16, 1914; Slade to Lind, September 20, October 2, 1914; "Memorandum of the Political Situation in Mexico, September 16, 1914," in the Lind Papers; Fred Adams to Lind, January 4, 1915.

[29] "To the Citizens of the Convention at Aguascalientes," Signed by V. Carranza; Manifesto Addressed by General Francisco Villa to the Nation, and Documents Justifying the Disavowal of Venustiano Carranza as First Chief of the Revolution (1914); Reply of Don Venustiano Carranza to the Chief of the Northern Division of the Constitutionalist Army, in Charge of the Executive Power, to the Mexican People. Refutation of the Manifest of General Francisco Villa. A Pamphlet Published Originally in El Liberal (Mexico City), October 25, 1914. These documents are in the Lind Papers.

XVII

THE RECOGNITION OF CARRANZA

WHILE these stirring events in and around Mexico City were taking place, Lind was attending to his law practice; and in October, 1914, he sought rest and treatment at a sanitarium in Battle Creek, Michigan. He was pestered by invitations to address gatherings of various sorts; but the Mexican situation continued to be so delicate, and Lind was known to be so close to the president, that he deemed it inexpedient to accept speaking engagements. A hostile press was eager to pick up almost anything he might say, in order to embarrass the administration.[1] Unfortunately he did not decline every invitation and in the fall he addressed the Traffic Club of Chicago on "The Mexican People." Still more unfortunately, he yielded to his friend W. C. Edgar, editor of the *Bellman*, and permitted him to publish the address in that weekly. It was also published as a separate. Lind later admitted that it was not prepared with the care he would have given it had he intended it for publication. As he had feared, an inaccurate statement was immediately seized upon, and he found himself under fire.[2]

About one-third of the address was devoted to a survey of the climate, resources, and people of Mexico. The remainder consisted of observations made by the speaker during the months he was stationed at Mexico City and Vera Cruz.

I felt then, as I feel now, that permanent peace in Mexico on the basis of the social and economic conditions that have exisited in the past is an impossibility. . . . The new leaven is at work, and no

[1] Lind to Bryan, June 14, July 3, 8, 1914; Bryan to Lind, June 16, July 4, 1914.
[2] Lind's testimony, April 27, 1920, in Senate Document no. 285, 66th Congress, 2d Session, pp. 2334-36.

Diaz, nor a thousand Huertas, with all the money in the world, could restore the peace of the old régime unless enough foreign soldiers were brought in to put the adult Mexican population underground. . . . When I saw and reflected over these things I asked myself, and I asked some of the critics of President Wilson's policy, whether it was not within the range of possibility that a people who within a brief generation had responded with such facility to the new social and economic environment, might make equivalent progress in the field of politics and government, if afforded a fair chance. I am hopeful, yes confident, that they will. I do not look for uninterrupted success. We have been administering our own affairs and practising self-government for nearly three hundred years and still we have problems, old as well as new, that have not yet been adequately solved.

The speaker thought it unreasonable to expect a high moral standard in respect to frankness and directness of speech in a people whose country had for generations been under oppression and tyranny; but if allowance were made for the concessions truth must always make to politeness, according to the Mexican ideal of politeness, he thought it might be fairly said that "the word of the Mexican may be taken with as much reliance as the word of men of other nationalities."

High praise was awarded the universal courtesy and kindliness in the daily life of the Mexican people. "My mission, at least in the City of Mexico, was not regarded by the press or by the leaders of public opinion as a friendly one," he said. "Nevertheless, I cannot recall one instance among the thousands of people that I met and came in contact with, or in my walks about the cities, or in the country roads, where the slightest mark of rudeness or disrespect was shown."

The address closed with a plea for efforts on the part of the American people to understand their southern neighbors and for closer cultural and commercial relations with them. "But these things to which I have alluded, the troubles which beset the unfortunate people, do not evoke the sympathy of men who have lost dividends from mines, or wells, ·or plantations. I do not belittle these losses — they have been great and grievous. But there are greater interests in this world than dividends." The speaker predicted that the Mexican people were emerging into the "light of a new and better day." "They may still stumble politically. They may fall at times. But I would rather have them stumble and fall travelling our way than to see them slide peacefully back into the bondage, the ignorance, the vice and the sloth of the sixteenth century."

What drew the fire of the critics of the address was the portion that dealt briefly with the illiteracy of the people: "Popular education, except in respect to religion and politeness, was forbidden by a papal bull for two hundred years, and is now opposed by the old régime; but it is one of the vital tenets of the Constitutionalist movement."

Shortly a letter arrived from R. H. Tierney, S. J., editor of *America*, a Catholic weekly published in New York, requesting Lind to cite the bull and to give the reference to the *Bullarium* in which it was to be found, as well as the name of the pope who issued the bull. "I should hesitate to make this request of a busy man, did not your ready and confident remarks about the document leave the impression that you have it at your elbow," wrote the editor. "This, I trust, is actually the case. For in this event you will not lose time, and I shall receive, I trust, a speedy reply to my letter, which I am making public in this issue of *America*." [3] Lind made no reply to this letter, nor did he take public notice of attacks in the Catholic press, which his unverified statement invited.

A controversy in its later stages often assumes a character somewhat different from that which it had originally. Lind was accused — not only by Catholics but by others — of having plagiarized the *Encyclopedia Britannica* in preparing the address; and the "deadly parallel" was employed to prove the allegation, as in the booklet prepared by the Reverend Francis C. Kelley and entitled *The Book of Red and Yellow*. The crime of "literary piracy" attributed to Lind consisted in incorporating

[3] R. H. Tierney to Lind, January 4, 1915.

in his address a few historical facts pertaining to the early period of Mexican history found in the *Britannica*. Inasmuch as the aggregate of this material was small in amount and incidental to the body of the address and the identical words of the reference work were not used and there were no references or citations to any other publication, historians and scholars with whom the present author has consulted have been unable to detect anything unusual or unethical in Lind's use of the encyclopedia. In reply to inquiries from friends about the truth of the charge, Lind conceded too much. "If the matter had been intended for publication I should probably have indicated the quotation, although I do not deem it necessary to give credit to a public encyclopedia for historical facts any more than it is to cite a dictionary for the authority of the language one employs in speaking." [4] To J. W. Crook of Amherst College he wrote:

While in Mexico the only historical work to which I had access was the official history of New Spain prepared by Solis in the reign of Carlos II. . . . I have observed that Prescott in his history of the conquest has accepted Solis' version of the conditions at the time of the conquest in most particulars, and the same is true of the article "Mexico" in the Enc. Brit. . . .

In preparing the historical portion of my address I had the Britannica before me and dictated to my stenographer such items as I wished to include. In the instance quoted by my Jesuit critic, I read the passages referred to from the volume without any attempt to paraphrase the language. I might as well have taken the matter from Solis and put it into English in my own words for the two texts agree, but the language of the Encyclopedia was already in English. The truth of the matter is I use these books as I use my dictionary. It never occurred to me to credit the facts taken from them. You will bear in mind also that I was preparing an address for oral delivery with no intention to have it published. To stop to quote Solis or the Enc. Brit. or Webster in the course of a speech is not customary, to say the least. And it never occurred to me to do so.

[4] Hugh T. Halbert to Lind, February 10, 14, 1915; Lind to Halbert, February 13, 16, 1915; J. W. Crook to Lind, November 26, 1916; Lind to Crook, November 28, 1916; Lind to A. B. Farquhar, February 24, 1916.

The address was well received and caused some comment. I kept it out of the Chicago papers, but my friend, W. C. Edgar, the publisher of "The Bellman" of this city, heard of it and expressed a desire to read it and publish it. I gave him the manuscript and the first thing I knew it was published in "The Bellman." I never saw the proof. If I had, it is doubtful whether it would have occurred to me to credit the historical data which I had included in that portion of my address. The next I heard of the matter was the receipt of the pamphlet, "The Book of Red and Yellow," of which I enclose you a copy. Quite a number have been mailed to me, as well as hundreds of scurrilous letters, most of them anonymous and apparently from priests. . . .

I also take the liberty to enclose a print of the address referred to and the text of Solis (pp. 220–221), which was evidently plagiarized by the editor of the article in the Britannica, for I observe that he does not mention Solis' name.

If it were not for the fact that the charge of plagiarism was publicly made and was even expanded (in testimony before a Senate committee in 1919–20) into the charge that Lind made use of the *Britannica* in preparing his reports to Wilson and Bryan, the incident would be too trivial to mention in these pages.[5]

From the maze of reports, documents, pamphlets, comments in the press, and letters addressed to Lind, it seems just and fair to conclude that both Lind and his adversaries erred in not making sufficient allowance for the fact that the Catholic church in Mexico was pretty much what the Mexican people were. The really important thing that stands out, however, is the fact that Catholic prelates and laymen in the United States opposed the recognition of Carranza because they were convinced that he was hostile to the interests of the Catholic church in Mexico. It is equally true that Carranza and his supporters in the United States and Mexico were convinced that in order to bring about

[5] Testimony of William F. Buckley, December 19, 1919, in Senate Document no. 285, 66th Congress, 2d Session, pp. 774–79. Buckley was engaged in real estate and oil leases in Mexico. In his testimony before the Senate committee, April 27, 1920, Lind stated that he did not care to discuss Kelley's booklet. Senate Document no. 285, p. 2336.

certain necessary reforms along social, economic, and political lines, the power of the church had to be curbed.[6] Carranza was only following the course charted by Juarez in the decade of the fifties, despite the fact that some of Carranza's advisers were Catholics and educated in the United States. Obregon, Cabrera, Zubaran, and Arredondo, who were close advisers of the "first chief," were men of high intelligence and ability.

Naturally Lind's address was pleasing to many Mexicans, and it was published in several papers as proof that Wilson and Lind were in sympathy with them and with their striving for a higher degree of liberty. In fact, Lind's correspondence indicates that Carranza, Cabrera, Zubaran, and Arredondo regarded Lind as a guarantee of the good intentions of the Wilson administration.[7]

The greatest handicap that beset the partisans of Carranza was the man himself. He was stubborn, pig-headed, lacking in diplomacy, jealous, and suspicious of his associates as well as of the sincerity of Wilson and his advisers. The Carranzistas could not divest themselves of the suspicion that the occupation of Vera Cruz by the American forces was not intended solely for their good. They did not doubt Lind's word, but they thought him mistaken in his judgment of Wilson. In a memorandum sub-

[6] The reader who has the inclination to delve into this phase of history is referred to the following: *Pastoral Letter of the Catholic Episcopate of the United States on the Religious Situation in Mexico* (published by the Committee of the American Episcopate, December, 1926); *Mexico, Bolshevism the Menace* (Supreme Council of the Knights of Columbus, New Haven, Connecticut, 1926); Francis C. Kelley, *The Book of Red and Yellow* (Chicago, 1915); A. Paganel, *What the Catholic Church Has Done to Mexico* (in defense of Carranza); Cardinal O'Connell Answered by Mr. Rafael Zubaran (Mexican Letter Bulletin no. 41, February 3, 1915, issued by the Mexican Bureau of Information, New York); I. C. Enriquez, *The Religious Question in Mexico. By a Mexican Catholic* (New York, 1915). The last work is a defense of the priests as against the high dignitaries of the church. It quotes from letters alleged to have been left behind by Urrutia, a member of the Huerta cabinet, to prove the political activity of the church. In the Lind Papers are letters from Catholics and clippings from the Catholic and secular press showing the attitude toward Lind and Carranza.

[7] Letters to Lind from d'Antin, January 5, April 1, 1915; I. C. Enriquez, December 18, 1914; J. J. Slade, February 24, 1915; Josephine Bonhomme, April 13, 1915; and Miguel D. Lombardo, April 17, 1915; *El Pueblo* (Vera Cruz), April 17, 1915; *El Dictamen* (Vera Cruz), July 30, 1915.

mitted to Secretary Lane on April 15, 1915, Lind presented some of the problems of the Carranza sympathizers:

Carranza was not wholly tactful. In the administration in Mexico his situation was difficult. Besides he attempted to go after the foreign looters too early in his administration. The Waters-Pierce interests in the Mexican National Railway expected the presidency of that institution which Huerta had given to Lord Cowdray. The general manager of Waters-Pierce in Mexico was slated for the position, a very good man by the way; I know him well. But Carranza to put a stop to the rivalry between the oil companies, disappointed both by appointing a Mexican, Mr. Cabrera. He also disappointed all of those interests with regard to concessions surreptitiously obtained which he proposed to cancel. The financial interests of the Madero family became apprehensive about some of their concessions. In fact all the foreign and special interests found that Carranza was too strict and honest. They feared that they could not work with him.

I first inferred the trouble ahead when Carothers commenced to make frantic appeals to the State Department for the raising of the embargo so that Villa might obtain ammunition from the United States, this at a time, bear in mind, when Carranza and the Constitutionalist forces had plenty of ammunition. . . .

The conspiracy to oust Carranza from that time on developed rapidly. . . . The Aguascalientes convention was a scheme to oust Carranza. . . . When the scheme succeeded Carranza and his friends wisely left Mexico City without precipitating any battle. They reasoned, and wisely, that all Villa would need was a little time and "rope" to convince, not only the Mexican people but the American people, of his utter incapacity to bring order in Mexico. I think we are all now convinced of that fact. Surely the majority of the Mexican people are.

The subterfuges resorted to by Carothers of reporting his wounding and assassination, which reports were undoubtedly intended to create renewed interest and sympathy in his waning career, fell flat.

Carranza is back in Mexico City. . . . I do not assume to predict how soon Carranza will be able to establish peace and order, or what other difficulties may arise before that is accomplished. But I believe that Carranza can accomplish the eventual pacification of Mexico without outside assistance if anyone can. He is absolutely honest, patriotic and patient, characteristics many Mexicans more tactful than he unfortunately do not possess. My confidence is based largely upon the good men by whom he has surrounded himself. I think also that it will be much easier to deal with Carranza in the future than in the past, for our government has now demonstrated its entire unselfishness so completely that even men of the Carranza type must see things in a different light from that in which they looked at the situation six months ago.

The suspicions and actions of Carranza and his advisers made it even more difficult for Lind and Douglas, and others who worked with them, to explain the aims of the revolutionists and to counteract the propaganda of the anti-Carranzistas. On June 15, 1914, Bryan cautioned the Carranza government as to the treatment of Catholic priests and foreigners, and this warning was followed by notes designed to admonish discretion.[8]

At the beginning of the year 1915 and for some time thereafter the situation in Mexico was most distressing, and it appeared that Carranza's hope for recognition was lost. About the middle of February, Douglas left for Mexico to discuss certain matters with Carranza and to present to him the American point of view. Upon his return he presented to Lind an autographed photograph of the "first chief."[9] Bryan wrote to Lind on February 18 that the situation was so difficult that he hardly knew what to expect. He thought Lind would be interested to know that he had a statement from the vicar-general to the effect that he did not know of a single case in which a nun had been violated. He had heard of such reports, but when he traced them down found they were not true. This seemed like a remarkable statement to Bryan, in view of the reports broadcast throughout the United States — reports that were the basis of very violent criticisms of the administration.[10]

[8] Douglas to Lind, December 21, 1914.
[9] Douglas to Lind, February 17, March 20, 1915.
[10] It may be pertinent in this connection to note that after the recognition of Carranza was so severely criticized because of charges of outrages upon priests and nuns, the president's personal secretary, Joseph P. Tumulty, himself a Catholic, replied to a public letter from Dr. James J. McGuire in which he stated that there was no official record of a single proven case of these

Lind constantly urged upon the Carranza representatives in the United States the necessity of getting under way a campaign of public education in order to explain to the American people the aims of their government and to counteract the hostility of its enemies. Many obstacles had to be removed before the goal of recognition was reached, but Lind never doubted the friendliness of Wilson. He understood that in view of the approaching presidential election the president had to play a game that would leave the impression on the public mind that his hand was forced and that recognition was the only way out. Bryan's sympathies were undoubtedly with Carranza, but when Robert Lansing succeeded him upon his dramatic resignation on June 8, 1915, at the time of the "Lusitania" crisis, a diplomat of the old school was at the head of the Department of State, although Wilson continued to be his own secretary of state.

Lansing would probably have refused recognition if his own inclinations had ruled; and the information that came to him from the special agents in Mexico was far from favorable to Carranza.[11] Moreover, the Brazilian minister, who was in charge of the American embassy in Mexico City, was an admirer of Huerta, and but for the fact that he was in charge of the embassy would have been expelled from the country by Carranza.[12] It is also true that the officials of the South American countries were not very friendly toward the revolution. The problems of those countries were somewhat similar to those of Mexico, and it was feared that the triumph of Carranza and his principles might bring a train of revolution elsewhere.

The army officers on the border were far more friendly to Villa than to Carranza. General Hugh L. Scott, chief of staff,

alleged crimes in the files of the Department of State. There had been many unsubstantiated reports of that nature, he said, but none of the special agents of the department and none of the consuls had been able to verify them. Tumulty's letter was dated November 27 and was published in the press on November 28, 1915.

[11] Lind to Lansing, July 23, 1915; Willard L. Simpson to Lind, August 19, 21, 1915; Douglas to Lind, October 8, 1915.

[12] Letters to Lind from d'Antin, October 12, 1914; Josephine Bonhomme, June 16, 1915; and R. H. Murray, June 30, 1915; El Pueblo (Vera Cruz), August 10, 1915.

288 JOHN LIND OF MINNESOTA

upon his return from the border to make his report, strongly advised Wilson against recognizing Carranza; and after recognition was an accomplished fact, the general, upon making inquiry from officials in the State Department junior to the secretary why it had been done, was told that they did not know the reason, for they had all advised against it as late as a month before recognition.[13]

Fortunately Great Britain and the United States were no longer at odds over Mexico, as they had been during Lind's sojourn in Vera Cruz. The World War made it necessary for British statesmen to remove every possible cause of friction between the two governments. There was ill feeling when American interests in Mexico were transferred from the British embassy to the Brazilian embassy, shortly after the Tampico incident; the British in Mexico attributed the transfer to the personal spite of Wilson against Carden.[14] However, Sir Cecil Spring-Rice, the British ambassador at Washington, favored the recognition of Carranza. Douglas conferred with him about various matters and was told that he had a high esteem for Lind. Fred Adams, a representative of Lord Cowdray's interests with whom Lind had conferred in Vera Cruz, visited Washington in the late winter, armed with a letter of introduction to Bryan from Lind. Adams had a conference with the British ambassador, who expressed the wish to meet Lind because he had learned what a staunch and conscientious seeker after truth he had been in Mexico. Adams also had a talk with Douglas. Lind told Douglas that Adams saw the handwriting on the wall and was con-

[13] H. L. Scott, *Some Memories of a Soldier* (New York, 1928), pp. 516–17; W. L. Simpson to Lind, August 19, 1915. In an article in the *New York Sunday American*, March 12, 1916, William Bayard Hale stated that in Mexico the recognition of Carranza was universally attributed to the alleged discovery in the archives of the Huerta government of receipts signed by Robert Lansing as an attorney and the threatened publication of these documents in the United States. Hale stated that Lansing as a private individual assisting his father-in-law, John W. Foster, acted as attorney of the junta which represented Huerta in Washington. In a letter to Lind dated August 30, 1915, R. H. Cole wrote: "We located in the Embassy today a paper showing the 'Secy.' signature, where he had represented the Mexican government during Feby. 1913."

[14] Loring Olmsted to Lind, May 6, 1914.

vinced that Carranza offered the best solution. He also informed Douglas that Adams was a favorite of the higher clergy in Mexico and could do more than any man to "pull off Archbishop Mora," whom Lind pronounced a great politician who had "stirred up this American Catholic trouble." [15]

In the first part of April, Lind conferred with Douglas and Arredondo preparatory to making a statement of the character and aims of Carranza to be submitted to Wilson and Bryan. In a long report to Bryan dated April 16, 1915, Lind reported the substance of his interview with Arredondo. He stated that Arredondo was a near relative of Carranza and that the two men had grown up together in the same environment and had read the same books and held the same political views. Arredondo lamented that there was a general misunderstanding of Carranza in the United States; that he had been represented as a senile egotist despised by the best men in the Constitutionalist movement. He denied that Carranza was hostile to the Catholic church.

Our whole family are Catholics. Carranza was married in the church — his children were baptized and we are all members of the church, but we are as determined as was Juarez, that church and state must be and remain separated. We have no quarrel with the church but our laws and the Constitution forbid monasteries, convents, nunneries and religious orders in Mexico, and the law must be observed. You Americans can hardly appreciate our feelings on this point. You have no Maxmilian, and I say to you, and I challenge contradiction, that during this whole disturbed period there has been no single instance where a priest or a member of a religious order has suffered loss of life or even banishment, though their political offenses have in many instances been aggravated. . . .

We have some good schools in the states but no facilities for popular education in the rural communities. "Next to peace," said Carranza to me, "we need teachers." One of his first acts of civil

[15] Fred Adams to Lind, February 16, 20, 26, April 15, 1915; Douglas to Lind, March 30, April 23, August 25, 1915; Lind to Douglas, March 29, April 2, August 27, 1915. On December 24, 1915, Douglas wrote to Lind that Adams had helped the Carranza cause toward recognition.

authority was to send a large number of promising young Mexicans to an American normal school in Massachusetts.

With respect to the land question, Arredondo told Lind that there had been no change in the Constitutionalist program. Certain fundamental reforms were necessary, but there would be no confiscation. The problem would be solved by the introduction of efficient administration and an adequate system of taxation of unoccupied lands. He stated further that after fundamental reforms had been inaugurated under a military administration, it was Carranza's firm determination to restore the operation of the Constitution, and free and fair elections would be held. Arredondo assured his American friend that Carranza and his supporters were confident that the relations between the United States and Mexico would be cordial in the future. "Your president," he said, "has put our present and future relations on a basis that appeals strongly to the sentimental side of our people."

You know and Mr. Carranza and all of his supporters appreciate that at all times Mexico needs the goodwill and friendly cooperation of the United States, but at this moment we need more than we can express in words also the neighborly sympathy and confidence of your government. With that aid peace and orderly government are in sight in Mexico. . . . I wish you could make it clear to your government how vitally we need your official support in the present crisis. We do not assume to suggest what form it should take but it is essential that Carranza's government should be recognized as the temporary organ of the Mexican people. By his military control such recognition seems fully justified.

In a memorandum dated April 19, 1915, and handed to President Wilson, Lind recommended the speedy recognition of Carranza for the following reasons: 1. Villa's complete military defeat would not only remove him as a factor in the military situation but would tend to insure the return to the Carranza fold of the Constitutionalist element that had sympathized with Villa. 2. It would make it difficult for General Angeles to consolidate the remnants of the Huerta army. 3. The recognition of the provisional government would at once command the respect and cooperation of the foreign representatives and foreigners in Mexico. 4. Under circumstances not unlike the present, the government of Juarez had been recognized when the latter had little more than a foothold at Vera Cruz. 5. There was no competitor of the Carranza government worthy of international consideration. His administration could be recognized without subjecting the administration to the charge of partiality.

While the newspapers were crowded with stories of the victories of General Villa, who by this time had committed himself entirely to the cause of the reactionaries, and with General Huerta's arrival in New York from Spain on April 12, to be followed shortly by his journey to the border with the intention of joining the forces fighting Carranza, Lind, Richard H. Cole of Pasadena, California, Joseph W. Folk of Missouri, Douglas, and Arredondo cooperated in drafting a decree to be issued by Carranza. A tentative form of the decree was submitted to Lind for criticism and revision; and after the revision had been made, Arredondo made it the basis of another dispatch to Carranza.[16] As a forerunner of the decree Carranza gave out an interview in Vera Cruz. All in all, during the month of May Judge Douglas had great hopes for the Carranzista cause and constantly solicited Lind's advice through correspondence and personal interviews.

While these negotiations were on foot in Washington, Henry Allen Tupper, a Baptist minister, and Richard L. Metcalfe, editor of the *Omaha Nebraskan* and formerly associate editor of the *Commoner*, were in consultation with Carranza, urging him to publish the decree at the earliest opportune moment.[17] In Washington the Carranzistas anxiously awaited the publication of the decree, and on June 2 Arredondo summoned Lind to the capital because, as he said, his presence was "of utmost importance." When the document arrived, it was translated and put

---

[16] Douglas to Joseph W. Folk, April 20, 1915; Carranza to Lind, April 23, 1915; Douglas to Lind, April 26, 30, May 6, 14, 29, 1915; Lind to Douglas, April 28, May 10, 1915; Arredondo to Lind, April 30, 1915.

[17] H. A. Tupper to Lind, May 31, 1915.

into proper form by Lind, Metcalfe, and d'Antin.[18] On June 11 Carranza's manifesto to the nation was issued. Despite warnings from the Department of State that indicated a skeptical attitude toward the "first chief," Douglas was assured that if Carranza strengthened himself there would be nothing in the way to prevent speedy recognition.[19] As a part of the publicity campaign Lind made a statement to the press while he was in New York, in which he gave his view of the situation and the reasons why Carranza should be recognized.[20]

On this visit to Washington Lind did not see Wilson, but from persons close to the president he learned that his attitude toward intervention had suffered no change, notwithstanding the language of his recent note; and from the reports of conversations between Lansing and Douglas, which were initiated by the secretary of state at Wilson's instance, he got the impression that the administration did not favor a compromise between Carranza and Villa, though it did desire some spirit of conciliation on the part of the former.[21]

The arrest and detention of Huerta on the border by federal officers on June 27 was gratifying to Lind, who wrote to Arredondo that this action ought to satisfy him that the administration was unequivocally with the Constitutionalists as against the old régime; and to Lansing he wrote that the arrest was most timely and fortunate.[22]

On July 11, 1915, Carranza was again in control of Mexico

[18] Arredondo to Lind, June 2, 1915; Douglas to Lind, June 2, 5, 7, 1915.

[19] Douglas to Lind, June 5, 1915.

[20] The interview was printed in the New York Herald, June 14, 1915. A copy of the paper was sent to Secretary Lansing and to Postmaster General Burleson. Douglas to Lind, June 11, 1915; Arredondo to Lind, June 12, 1915; Lind to Douglas, June 15, 1915.

[21] Lind to Samuel Untermeyer, June 17, 1915; Douglas to Lind, June 25, 1915. Josephine Bonhomme wrote to Lind from Vera Cruz, June 16, 1915, that President Wilson's note impressed her "as a little distressing because it stated that all the factions were fighting for the same principles." Duval West and other American representatives in Mexico, she said, held the same erroneous opinion. A letter to Lind from R. H. Murray, written in Mexico City, June 30, 1915, was very critical of the Americans in Mexico, "who are always damning their government."

[22] Lind to Arredondo, June 30, 1915; Lind to Lansing, July 1, 1915.

City; and this hopeful turn of events brought Lind another summons from Arredondo, Douglas being with his client in Mexico.[23] At Lansing's request Lind prepared a memorandum on the Mexican situation and on August 1 delivered it in person to the secretary.[24] Lind's statement was that unless the American government threw the weight of its influence with one or the other faction, the struggle would continue for a long time, and some catastrophe might occur at any moment to force military intervention. He thought Carranza would prevail, but it would be a long contest, with ever present danger of new complications. For the United States to set up another man would be to invite suspicion. On the other hand, if Carranza were recognized, the United States would be able to carry on negotiations with Mexico through the medium of better agents. The memorandum then went on to say that from knowledge Lind had as early as May, 1914, when Villa had professed loyalty to Carranza, his agents, Carothers and Sommerfield, were surreptitiously negotiating for arms and munitions from New York for Villa's account. All the American consuls in Mexico he had met, with the exception of John R. Silliman and Arnold Shanklin, were friends of Henry Lane Wilson and hostile to Carranza and to Wilson's policy.[25]

After a stay of three weeks, Lind left Washington in a very optimistic frame of mind. He communicated with Colonel Edward M. House for the purpose of sounding him out and of making use of his influence with Wilson. The colonel wrote that he had come to practically the same conclusion as Lind about the necessity for speedy action by the government, for in the event of Wilson's defeat the new administration would feel that

[23] Arredondo to Lind, July 12, 14, 16, 1915; Lind to Arredondo, July 14, 1915.
[24] Memorandum dated July 23, 1915. Lind wrote to Douglas (September 9, 1915), that when the memorandum was presented to Lansing, he intimated that he proposed to refer it to Paul Fuller for detailed consideration. This suggestion made Lind suspicious, and when he explained that he did not desire such reference, Lansing generously promised that it would not be made.
[25] See testimony of Consul W. W. Canada with reference to Silliman in Senate Document no. 285, 66th Congress, 2d Session, pp. 2427–28.

it had the warrant of the people to intervene. That would mean the upsetting, for the time being, of everything the Constitutionalists had fought for. He knew that Wilson and Lansing were sorely perplexed as to what action to take, because scarcely any two suggestions agreed. House expressed the fullest confidence in the purity of Lind's motives and the hope that the matter would work out in a way that met his cordial approval.[26]

At this time Lind was constantly watching the political barometer; like a boy who trusts and admires his father, he was greedy for any sign of approval of his course from the president. On August 2, 1915, he wrote to Wilson, who was summering at Cornish, New Hampshire, that in the memorandum he had submitted to Lansing he had omitted to point out the danger that lurked in a scheme outlined in the *New York Times*, according to which the administration favored a plan to have Vasquez Tagle assume the executive power of Mexico under the claim that the presidency devolved on him by operation of law, since he had been a member of the Madero cabinet. It was also alleged that he would be immediately recognized by the United States. Lind pointed out the consequences of this step and reminded the president that he still believed what he had reported to the State Department as early as December 5, 1913, that it was Carranza's success or American intervention.

To this letter Lind received the gratifying assurance that the president appreciated the legal difficulties of the plan Lind supposed was under consideration, and he begged him to discount and disbelieve absolutely everything he saw in the newspapers.[27]

Upon receipt of this letter, Lind immediately relayed to Douglas by wire and postal service the contents of the letters from his "Cornish correspondent" and from "Colonel Smith." He stated that the letter from Cornish was absolutely confidential and must not be revealed to anyone except Arredondo. It confirmed the hopes he had entertained right along, and he could not escape the conviction that the letters spelled victory.

[26] House to Lind, August 2, 6, 1915; Lind to House, August 4, 1915.
[27] Wilson to Lind, August 5, 1915.

He cautioned Douglas, however, to be prudent, to avoid raising controversial issues, and to refrain from attacking enemies at this stage. He did not doubt that Carranza's oil plan, which Cabrera had explained to him in detail, was wise, but "the better it is for Mexico the more opposition it will have from abroad and from interested Mexicans." He thought it better to keep the plan in the background until the situation was better defined. "We must be cunning as well as wise when we are fighting greed and prejudice combined," he wrote.[28] To other correspondents he wrote that "the president's sense of justice and his intuitive judgment are so strong that I have little fear but that any step which he takes will be well considered and for the best interests of the Mexican people, as well as our own." And he added: "I have stood so forlornly alone that I have at times questioned in my own mind the sanity of my conclusions."[29]

Douglas and Arredondo, however, were not so hopeful. Arredondo expressed the hope that Lind would find some "easy explanation" that would not injure his faith in the president's policy in the midst of the hubbub raised by the press, the movement of troops to the border, and the sending of battleships to Mexican ports; and Douglas was sure that the administration was hostile to Carranza and that war would come.[30]

This pessimism was caused by the action of Lansing in calling an informal conference of the diplomatic representatives of Brazil, Chile, Argentina, Guatemala, Bolivia, and Uruguay to confer with him with reference to an opportune time to recognize a responsible government in Mexico and to suggest that the political and military chiefs meet at a neutral place to effect an agreement. Carranza and many of his supporters in the United States believed that Lansing had made a mistake in calling this conference. Carranza was exceedingly suspicious of anything that remotely suggested outside interference in the internal affairs of Mexico. Lind had written that portion of the brief that

[28] Telegram and letters from Lind to Douglas, August 9, 1915; Lind to Hackley, August 12, 1915.
[29] Lind to W. L. Simpson, August 12, 1915.
[30] Arredondo to Lind, August 11, 1915; Douglas to Lind, August 14, 1915.

suggested a conference between the Carranzistas and the Villistas, and this was concurred in by Arredondo and Cabrera; but Carranza declined to accede to it, and his followers expected that he would reject the proposal of the joint powers for a conference. In this predicament Douglas requested Lind to take the "laboring oar" in urging Carranza to make some slight concessions and to take the initiative in arranging a meeting of Douglas, Lind, Cabrera, and Arredondo.[31]

Lind was perturbed at Carranza's refusal to permit his representatives to receive unofficially the emissaries of Villa. He thought the United States had the right to require that certain conditions be met as the price of recognition; that Carranza must pursue a course that would contradict the charges that he was determined to gain selfish ends at the expense of the peace and welfare of his country; that he must convince the president that he was not seeking to maintain himself in power by force; and that he must consider American views and prejudices.[32]

In these views Douglas fully concurred, and they were transmitted to Carranza through Arredondo; but Douglas had small hope of their acceptance and feared that Carranza would not answer the note at all, in which case it would be regarded as an intentional indignity and affront to the signers of the note, and especially to the United States. Douglas suggested that Lind send a telegram direct to Carranza.[33]

On September 5 Lind wrote to Arredondo that Carranza's refusal to answer the note might delay recognition indefinitely. He agreed with Carranza's attitude, but suggested that an explanation of that attitude couched in courteous and diplomatic language would settle the question for all time. If, in Arredondo's judgment, Carranza would like to have Lind's views, he was

[31] Douglas to Lind, August 14, 1915; *El Pueblo* (Vera Cruz), August 10, 1915; interview with Zubaran in *El Dictamen* (Vera Cruz), August 20, 1915. Zubaran was quoted as saying "Mediation accepted would justify subsequent intervention."

[32] Lind to Douglas, August 16, 1915.

[33] Lind to Douglas, August 16, 1915; Douglas to Lind, August 19, September 3, 1915; Douglas to Arredondo, August 17, 1915; Arredondo to Lind, August 21, 1915; Lind to Arredondo, August 23, 1915.

authorized to cable an inclosed communication over Lind's signature. The message, which was sent under date of September 6, stated that the situation was hopeful and that Lind knew better than any one else that Wilson was well disposed toward Mexico, but he had much to contend against in the execution of his policy of neighborly good will and the furtherance of democracy in Mexico. He had the opposition of "your clerical party acting through our own," likewise the *Cientificos* of both nations. These interests, he said, had used the press to create prejudice against Carranza's government, and it was being said that Carranza would not answer the note; that he did not want peace; and that he deliberately intended to insult the American republics and by that means attach the chauvinistic elements to his dictatorship. The "first chief" was admonished that it was imperative that the recent note be answered. Moreover, it would afford the best opportunity to get his views before the American people. On the strength of the answer and the showing it would make, a formal request for recognition could be made, and Lind was confident it would be granted.

To this Carranza sent the following reply:

I was pleased to take cognizance of your message dated the day before yesterday and trust that in view of the good disposition of President Wilson toward the Mexican people and the certainty that the Constitutionalist government will maintain peace and order in Mexico, closer relations between the two countries may be reached, hoping also that if the president has clearly noticed the perfect solidarity existing in the Constitutionalist party and that it is exercising control and authority over the greater part of the Mexican republic, he will accede to extend his recognition to the de facto government I represent. Mr. Arredondo will bring my reply to Secretary Lansing and the South American plenipotentiaries to your attention. I am very grateful to you for your good offices. Affectionate regards.[34]

The week beginning September 6 was expected to bring the crisis: the Pan-American conference was scheduled to meet, and

[34] The telegram was sent through Arredondo who was requested to transmit it to Lind.

Carranza's reply was awaited. Lind was of the opinion that Wilson was as well disposed to the Constitutionalist cause as ever, but he warned Douglas that Tumulty and probably some members of the cabinet were hostile. In order to make it as easy as possible for the State Department, Lind sent Douglas a copy of his dispatch to Carranza and a copy of his letter to Douglas and authorized the latter to send them to Colonel House if he deemed it wise to do so.[35]

While the fortunes of Carranza hung in the balance, the press blazed forth headlines announcing a break between Wilson and House and Lind. The president was alleged to have parted with "those marvels of reticence, Colonel House and John Lind, and the kitchen cabinet is shot to pieces." The gist of the story was that the two advisers had lost caste at the same time; that House and the president had broken over the former's espousal of Carranza's claims to recognition and that Lind had influenced House to insist upon recognition. Lind was alleged to have told House of his views, and House was alleged to have gone to the White House for the purpose of insisting on the recognition of Carranza. The story also included an item to the effect that Lind expected to be called into the conference with the representatives of the Latin American countries and was greatly surprised when he was completely ignored and Paul Fuller, an anti-Carranza man first and last, was requested to participate. Seeing that his presence in Washington was not wanted, Lind was said to have departed for Minnesota and had not been consulted by the administration since his departure.[36]

Lind made no public comment on the story, and House was reported as saying, "Mighty interesting, if true." Tumulty characterized the report as "absolute rot." Wilson took such offense that he sent out word by Tumulty that the authors of the reports were thereafter barred from the White House.[37] Lind was much

[35] Douglas to Lind, September 9, 1915; Lind to Douglas, September 9, 1915; Lind to Arredondo, September 10, 1915.

[36] The story "broke" in the papers on August 20 and was followed up with numerous editorial comments.

[37] James Gray, a Washington correspondent, to Lind, August 31, 1915.

chagrined to be placed in the public light as the "culprit who had seduced the colonel from his allegiance" and in a letter to Douglas dated September 2, 1915, recorded that he was satisfied in his own mind that Tumulty had made the hints that inspired the reporters. "You realize that he does not love me," he wrote, "and if there is little attachment between him and the Colonel he may have hoped to get us both 'in bad.'" He thought that with the exception of Douglas, Tumulty was the only person who could possibly have had knowledge that correspondence had passed between him and House. To House he wrote that it might interest him to know the "latest phase of my disloyalty," and he therefore inclosed with his letter copies of his telegram to Carranza and his letter to Douglas.

House replied in a cordial letter expressing appreciation of Lind's confidence in him and inquiring whether or not Lind had any objection if he showed the inclosures to the president. The colonel said he wished he could find who was responsible for the story concerning Wilson, Lind, and himself.[38]

Throughout the last days of August and the first days of September, Lind never lost faith in the president's ultimate action, notwithstanding statements given to the press by "high officials" in Washington. He was certain they did not represent the president. He assured his correspondents that the president was delaying recognition for political reasons; but that, on the other hand, Cardinal Gibbons' indiscretion in coming out in open hostility to the Constitutionalist movement made any other course suicidal for the administration.[39]

On September 11 the long-awaited reply from Carranza to the Pan-American conference was published in the American papers. The "first chief" declined to enter into any conference with

[38] Lind to House, September 9, 30, 1915; House to Lind, September 14, 26, 1915.

[39] Lind to Douglas, August 23, 1915; Lind to R. H. Cole, August 26, 1915; Lind to Samuel Untermeyer, August 27, 1915. In the *Washington Post*, August 1, 1915, Cardinal Gibbons was quoted as saying that some form of intervention by the United States was the only solution to the reign of anarchy that had existed in Mexico for several years. The cardinal said that neither Carranza nor Villa would do.

Villa or with other factions, and he suggested that the plenipotentiaries recommend to their respective governments that his government be recognized. The suggestion was in accord with Lind's advice.

This favorable development brought another summons to Lind to confer with his coworkers, and on September 14 he left for Washington. He spent considerable time with Cabrera in Washington and in New York, where they started negotiations looking to a loan to the Carranza government. Upon his return to Minneapolis on September 25, Lind wrote a long letter to Arredondo giving the impressions he had gathered in New York. These were immediately forwarded to Carranza.

Lind told his Mexican correspondent that the situation was hopeful and that, despite reports to the contrary, the president was anxious for the establishment of constitutional government and peace and order in Mexico and was willing to cooperate with the Carranza government to secure it. He further stated that "a close personal friend of the president" had informed him that it was vitally important on both sides to show a spirit of conciliation and that Carranza must make a full and fair showing of his plans for the restoration and maintenance of peace and for the resumption of government under the Constitution. If this were done, he felt certain that recognition would be forthcoming.

The net result of the conversation left on my mind is that those nearest to the president, and who can speak for him if anyone can, are sincerely interested in the success of the Carranza government and are not only willing but anxious to do everything that can fairly be done under the conventions that prevail between nations to make his government a success and to insure the permanency of peace and democracy in Mexico.[40]

On October 9, 1915, after further conferences with the plenipotentiaries, Secretary Lansing announced that the conferees had found that the Carranzista party was the only one possessing

[40] Lind to Arredondo, September 25, 1915; Lind to Douglas, September 14, 27, 1915; Douglas to Lind, September 23, 27, October 1, 1915; Arredondo to Lind, September 28, 1915; Lind to Simpson, September 24, 1915.

the essentials for recognition as the *de facto* government. On October 19 formal recognition was given. Douglas wanted Lind to be in Washington when the official action was taken, "chiefly because it will be the triumph of your counsel to the administration, now nearly two years ago"; and when recognition was assured, he wired as follows: "In this hour of great victory my heart turns to you. Both countries owe you a debt that cannot be fully discharged." [41] From Arredondo came equally cordial congratulations, and Lind wired his felicitations to Arredondo with the request that they be forwarded to Carranza. [42]

Today Mexico resumes her place in the family of nations. The chapter of her disgrace is ended. The crime from which she has s:ffered has been avenged. The courage, patriotism and the perseverence of the Constitutionalist forces have redeemed her honor. I congratulate you, and through you, the chief executive and the people of Mexico. I have but one more wish, and it is also an ardent hope that the Constitutionalists will complete the work so auspiciously begun in a manner that will insure to all the people justice and liberty under the law, and the progress, enlightenment and happiness of the Mexican nation. [43]

The recognition of Carranza was a triumph for Lind, and although he could not foresee the dangerous turn of events the coming months held in store — events that threatened to undo everything he had contended for — the recognition of Carranza really paved the way for a revolution in Mexico as profound as any that has taken place in modern times. A recent student of the Mexican revolution has pointed out that the social program of the revolution owes a great deal to the exigencies of the conflict between Villa and Carranza. Carranza was no social revolutionist, he says, but it is to his credit that he accepted the constitution of 1917, which alone would give him a place in the

[41] Douglas to Lind, October 8, 9, 1915. A. E. L. Leckie to Lind, November 24, 1915: "Our friend Douglas frankly states that yours was no small part in bringing recognition of Carranza."

[42] Arredondo to Lind, October 11, 20, 1915; Lind to Arredondo, October 12, 19, 1915.

[43] Lind to Arredondo, October 19, 1915.

social history of the revolution. This writer pronounces the constitution of 1917 "one of the most significant and influential constitutional documents of the present century"; and he believes that the chief by-product of the revolution is spiritual, "a discovery by the Mexican people of their own dignity, a dignity which they were not conscious of possessing before." [44]

Naturally Lind was gratified that the man he had selected as the hope for the triumph of democracy in Mexico received the stamp of approval of the Wilson administration, but he knew Mexico well enough not to be deceived into thinking that the country's problems were solved by the formal act of any government. He knew that Carranza was confronted with a gigantic task; that the influence of Mexico City was baneful; that the financial situation was dangerous; that there was corruption in the government; that anti-foreign sentiment in Mexico was strong; that the Americans in Mexico were anti-Carranza; that the situation on the border was "loaded"; and that there were agitators, radicals as well as conservatives, who would make the path of any government thorny. "My standard of success is not at all exalted," he wrote. "Fair success is all that we can hope for." "When I look back and reflect on the vicissitudes that we have had to contend against the last year and a half, I feel that we have accomplished what to many seemed the impossible." He did not deny that the element of personal pride, or pride of opinion, entered to some extent. "I would rather enjoy it to pat John Lind on the back very quietly and say, 'Well, John, it seems that you are not so big a fool after all, as most of your American friends in Mexico thought you to be.'" After reading Wilson's annual message of December, 1915, Lind expressed to the president his deep personal and political gratification. "The paragraphs relating to Mexico give me great satisfaction," he wrote. "They convey in direct positive words assurances more comprehensive than any opinion I have ventured to express in conversations with Mexicans on that subject. I know you will pardon me

[44] Frank Tannenbaum, *Peace by Revolution* (New York, 1933), pp. 155, 161, 167, 181.

for taking some little personal pride in having it said in Mexico: 'Lind was right; he knew the president.' " [45]

It was reported at the time that Lind received a retainer for his services in behalf of Carranza, but except for traveling expenses, he never received a cent, in spite of offers of remuneration from Douglas and invitations to associate himself with a syndicate of lawyers to handle claims against Mexico.[46]

Lind was the choice of the Carranzista leaders for the post of ambassador to Mexico, but he steadfastly declined to be considered, partly because he was not politically ambitious and partly because allegations in the press that he was a Carranza partisan made it inexpedient for the Department of State to consider his name in that connection.[47] Lind's preference for the ambassadorship was Richard L. Metcalfe, who had served for a time as civil governor of the Panama Canal Zone, because he thought he was the type of man who would not become involved in interests outside his official duties, as in the case of Henry Lane Wilson and other ambassadors. He wrote letters in Metcalfe's behalf to Colonel House and to Senator Gilbert M. Hitchcock, chairman of the Senate Committee on Foreign Relations.[48] The man appointed, Henry P. Fletcher, had a long record of service under the State Department and at the time of appointment was ambassador to Chile; but the Carranza partisans thought the choice ought to have fallen on a man "with the crust off his soul." [49]

As an expression of gratitude for their services and in order to

[45] Lind to Fred Adams, October 9, 1915; Lind to Douglas, October 18, 1915; Lind to Wilson, December 8, 1915.

[46] Lind to Fred Adams, August 14, October 9, 1915; Lind to Douglas, September 30, December 17, 20, 1915; Douglas to Lind, December 17, 1915; Lind to Arredondo, November 16, 1915; W. H. Ellis to Lind, October 21, 1915; Lind's testimony, April 27, 1920, in Senate Document no. 285, 66th Congress, 2d Session, pp. 2364–65.

[47] Douglas to Lind, October 5, 1915; W. H. Ellis to Lind, October 29, 1915; Lind to Ellis, November 8, 1915; Fred Adams to Lind, November 8, 1915. There was considerable comment in the press on the subject of Lind's candidacy.

[48] Lind to Hitchcock, October 11, 1915; Hitchcock to Lind, October 12, 1915; Lind to House, October 13, 1915; Lind to Douglas, October 8, 18, 1915; Douglas to Lind, October 16, 1915; Metcalfe to Lind, October 12, 1915.

[49] J. W. Slaughter to Lind, January 20, 1916.

promote good feeling between the two peoples, Lind and a number of other Carranza sympathizers were invited by Arredondo to meet the "first chief" on the border at Piedras Negras, across the river from Eagle Pass, Texas. Lind was out hunting near Bemidji, Minnesota, when a telegram from Arredondo inviting him to the conference reached him. His delay in answering the telegram brought another informing him that Carranza wished to see him. Lind left at once and arrived at Piedras Negras on November 4, 1915. He had an extended conversation with the "first chief."

A few days earlier the American newspapers had published a report that Carranza had been made a prisoner at Torreon by his subordinate, General Alvaro Obregon; and when Lind entered the temporary headquarters and saw the two men standing by a table, he laughingly inquired which one of them was under arrest. Lind made a fine impression on Carranza, and Lind was impressed with his host. In answer to a letter from James Gray, a Washington correspondent and former mayor of Minneapolis, in which he was asked if he told Carranza how long his whiskers had delayed recognition, Lind stated that when he talked with him he forgot all about the whiskers. "I don't think I saw them. He is really a magnificent fellow. . . . It is my judgment that if he should condescend to pose for a picture between you and me, his appearance would make the whole bunch respectable. Really he is a much bigger man in every way than I expected to find." [50]

Douglas instructed Lind to discuss certain problems of reconstruction; and Carranza was especially anxious to learn whether or not the hostile attitude of the newspapers reflected the real sentiments of the American people. In a letter to Colonel House dated November 15, 1915, which the colonel sent to Wilson for his information, Lind gave an account of the interview:

I remained two days after Carranza arrived and talked with him

[50] Gray to Lind, November 11, 1915; Lind to Gray, November 13, 1915; Douglas to Lind, November 13, 1915. The telegraphic correspondence between Lind and Arredondo is in the Lind Papers.

twice — perhaps three and a half hours all together. He first thanked me, most sincerely I believe, for the interest I had shown for the welfare of the Mexican people, as he expressed it. I explained that I had only sought to further the president's well-known attitude of neighborly interest in the cause of true democracy in Mexico; that this sentiment of the president's appealed to my personal convictions and actuated my efforts. He expressed great appreciation of President Wilson's constancy of purpose and good will toward the Mexican people.

He remarked that he and his friends had never been able to fully comprehend the purpose of the taking of Vera Cruz; that this incident subjected the Constitutionalist movement to a most severe trial. He said that it had been intimated to him that Vera Cruz was taken to prevent munitions about to arrive on a German vessel from being delivered to Huerta. But he said, "Huerta got the munitions." I took the liberty to tell him that Huerta got the munitions because Mr. Bryan was deceived by promises of German officials that they should not be delivered. (I did not tell him so, but it is a fact that the German ambassador played horse with Mr. Bryan, but he was so cocksure that the ambassador's assurance was sufficient that he omitted all precaution.) . . .

He spoke regretfully of the tone of some of the correspondence of the State Department and said that it made it difficult at times for some of the men in the Mexican department to refrain from replying in the same vein in which they were addressed. He said, however, that he assumed that Mr. Lansing could not and did not have the time to read all the letters that bore his signature, so he did not regard it personal on Mr. Lansing's part, but nevertheless it made it embarrassing for him. I called his attention to the fact that of necessity most of the department letters were prepared by heads of departments or divisions who had only limited knowledge of the real situation in Mexico; that insofar as these men came in contact with Mexicans at all it was invariably with the "emigrant" class who missed no opportunity to impress on all persons in the United States that Zapata, Villa and Carranza were three of a kind and all of them plundering bandits; that such representations in connection with newspaper reports in harmony with them could not help but influence the attitude of some of the lower officials of the department and make them more or less indifferent in respect to correspondence. . . .

At the first conference General Obregon was present. The next day I met him on the American side at luncheon given to him and our army officers at that point. Major Duncan of the general staff was present. General Obregon impressed us all as a man of great character and ability. There is no question in my mind about his loyalty to Carranza and his devotion to the common cause.

General Carranza had intended to give a dinner in my honor but on account of engagements at home I could not remain, so he excused me.

Nearly all of the men surrounding Carranza are young men under forty-five. I met all of them. Perhaps half of them spoke English — some very well. I speak some Spanish so I got along very nicely with all of them. My impression of all the men was that they were intelligent, earnest and very much devoted to their chief. I came away with a distinct feeling of relief. . . . On the whole I feel very sanguine of the Mexican situation.[51]

Members of the party at Piedras Negras included John R. Silliman, special representative of the Department of State, Richard H. Cole, Lincoln Steffens, and John W. Slaughter of Philadelphia, besides many newspaper correspondents. The paragraphers seized the opportunity to exploit Lind's reputation for silence. The following are typical comments: "We take it that Carranza comprehends the deaf and dumb manual." "It was a Quaker meeting perhaps." "We should like for John to go to Egypt and arrange a silence match with the Sphinx." "He did it once, but can John Lind go to Mexico and come back without saying anything?"

Within a few weeks Lind was to learn that even a man with his reputation for silence could say too much. Before the end of the month a paragrapher wrote: "How strange it seems to see ex-Ambassador Henry Lane Wilson threatening to sue John Lind for talking indiscreetly."[52]

[51] Lind's testimony, April 27, 1920, in Senate Document no. 285, 66th Congress, 2d Session, pp. 2364–65; House to Lind, November 17, 1915; interview with Lind in newspapers, November 5 and 6, 1915, clippings in the Lind papers.
[52] Boston Globe, November 24, 1915.

It will be remembered that after Henry Lane Wilson's recall from Mexico City, shortly before Lind's appointment as President Wilson's personal representative, the former made speeches attacking the Mexican policy of the administration worthy of the most reckless diplomat. During his sojourn in Mexico, Lind was told a number of discreditable things about the former ambassador, including the allegation that he was in the pay of Huerta after his departure from the embassy.[53] After Lind's return from Mexico, Bryan requested him to analyze Wilson's dispatches to the Department of State. This analysis convinced Lind as a lawyer that upon his own evidence "a jury would be justified in finding Henry Lane Wilson guilty of aiding and abetting, if not instigating, the Huerta rebellion, and also that he is guilty as an accessory before the fact of the assassination of Madero." He also thought the agreement between Huerta and Felix Diaz drawn up under the auspices of Henry Lane Wilson was damning evidence. On October 10, 1915, Douglas informed Lind that Juan F. Urquidi was preparing a book on the subject of Madero's assassination and had collected valuable material that revealed the ambassador's part in the tragic affair.[54] Lind also believed he had uncovered the purpose of the former administration in appointing Henry Lane Wilson to the Mexican post:

Henry Lane had a brother in Seattle, ex-Senator John Wilson, whom I knew very intimately. We were colleagues in Congress. John Wilson was an associate of Ballinger, secretary of the interior under Taft. Ballinger was the general representative of the Guggenheim interests in the Northwest and in Alaska. These interests secured his appointment. Henry Lane Wilson was transferred to Mexico to further the interests of the Guggenheim syndicate in getting control of the entire smelting industry in Mexico. The op-

[53] Lind to Woodrow Wilson, January 10, 1914; Lind to Bryan, March 5, 31, 1914; d'Antin to Lind, March 17, 1915. See H. L. Wilson, *Diplomatic Episodes in Mexico, Belgium, and Chile* (New York, 1927), p. 177, with reference to d'Antin.

[54] Lind to S. J. Graham, August 7, 1916. The Henry Lane Wilson correspondence was published on May 14, 1913, as a confidential state document entitled *Disorders in Mexico* (Department of State, Division of Information, Series A, no. 95; Mexico, no. 18). A copy of the Diaz-Huerta agreement, dated February 18, 1913, is in the Lind Papers.

position of the Madero family to this (they had a smelter at Torreon) is what caused Henry Lane's intense hostility against President Madero.[55]

Lind's mind was primed with material on Henry Lane Wilson when he gave an informal talk before a small gathering in the North Methodist Church of Minneapolis on November 15, 1915. A reporter was present; and in spite of Lind's efforts to keep the address out of the papers, extracts were published in the press throughout the country on November 22. Within two days a letter came from Wilson stating that in one dispatch Lind was reported as saying at a public meeting that Wilson "knew of the plot to assassinate Madero" and in another that "Madero was murdered by Huerta with the knowledge and consent of Henry Lane Wilson." Lind was called upon to disclaim these statements if he had been misquoted or to retract them as ill considered and not susceptible of proof.

To this Lind replied that in so far as anything he had said justified the interpretation put upon it by the press, he held himself accountable and no further. He would be glad, he said, to meet informally any friend Wilson might designate and explain to him fully and frankly what he had said, the circumstances under which it had been said, and the grounds he had for stating it. To a friend he wrote that he abhorred the publicity of a trial, but saw no escape if Wilson insisted. He could not reconcile himself to making an apology in view of Wilson's admitted complicity in the conspiracy. He had Wilson's reports to the State Department, he said, but no definite information about Huerta's visit to the American embassy on the evening of February 22. D'Antin had told him that Huerta was there between eight and nine o'clock and was closeted with Wilson in the latter's private office and that he had used the embassy telephone to remove the commandant of the prison and to appoint a new one. If this was true and could be established by testimony, he thought the case was conclusive; but even without it he thought Wilson stood convicted, at least morally, on his own admissions.

[55] Lind to Douglas, March 13, 1916.

Wilson was willing to make an amicable adjustment and, after some further correspondence, furnished his attorney with a form of statement to emanate from Lind. Lind, however, refused to subscribe to this and wrote his own "apology," which was made public in the press on January 23, 1916:

I have the honor to acknowledge the receipt of your letter.

In the course of the address to which you refer, I commented on the events which led up to and culminated in the death of President Madero. What I said was stated in good faith in the course of that discussion and in the full belief of the accuracy of my information. Press reports of my utterances detached from the other language of my remarks are misleading and susceptible of misinterpretation. I was not responsible for their publication, assume no such responsibility, and disavow them.

Although the statement was not entirely satisfactory to Wilson, he accepted it. Lind did not deny having made the statements quoted and he did not disavow them. He merely disavowed the press reports of his utterances and declined to assume responsibility for them. The disavowal extended only to the press reports and not to the speech. While the matter was pending, Lind admitted to friends that in the course of his remarks he made statements that probably justified the published reports, and he said that he could stand suit if Wilson could.[56] At one stage he even threatened to discontinue negotiations for a settlement.

The Lind-Wilson incident had a sequel in the investigation of Mexican affairs conducted by a Senate committee in 1919-20, of which the later notorious Albert B. Fall was chairman. In 1916 *Harper's Weekly* published a series of articles entitled "Huerta and the Two Wilsons" from the pen of Robert H. Murray, correspondent of the *New York World* in Mexico City and a confidant of Lind's. Murray quoted from Henry Lane Wilson's dispatches to the State Department to show his participation in

[56] The correspondence is in the Lind Papers: Wilson to Lind, November 24, December 6, 13, 1915; Lind to Wilson, December 3, 8, 11, 1915; Charles B. Elliott to Lind, December 9, 11, 1915; Lind to Elliott, December 9, 1915; Robert H. Murray to Lind, November 23, 1915; Lind to Murray, December 2, 16, 1915; Lind to Douglas, December 17, 1915.

the Huerta treason.[57] Wilson brought suit against Norman Hapgood, the editor of the weekly, who confessed judgment. At the Senate committee hearing Lind was asked whether or not he had brought similar charges against Wilson, to which he replied: "No, but what has this got to do with this inquiry?" He declined to discuss Wilson's official acts or to pass judgment upon anything he might have said or done. Asked if he did not disavow a statement under threat of a lawsuit, he replied: "I did not disavow the statement that I made, but I disavowed making the statement as reported." [58]

[57] *Harper's Weekly*, March 25 to April, 1916. Murray to Lind, February 10, 1916; Lind to Douglas, February 25, 1916.

[58] Senate Document no. 285, 66th Congress, 2d Session, April 27, 1920, pp. 2356–57. On April 24, 1920, Wilson wrote to Lind threatening suit if he did not disavow his comment on Wilson's speech delivered before the Civic and Commerce Association of Minneapolis as reported in the *Minneapolis News* of March 16, 1920. Lind was reported as having said that Wilson was an apologist for Huerta's revolution and was cognizant of all that Huerta did and proposed to do. Lind replied to Wilson that he had made no statement other than to give out Wilson's own version of what happened with reference to Huerta's solicited advice on the disposition that should be made of Madero. Lind quoted Wilson's letter to Bryan of March 12, 1913: "I did not think it expedient to assume the responsibility of advising him, but answered that he must do what was best for the people of Mexico." Wilson to Lind, April 24, 1920; Lind to Wilson, May 5, 1920. For a continuation of the published charges against Wilson see the *Living Age*, April 10, 1926, and letters to Lind from Victor S. Clark, editor of the *Living Age*, May 18, 22, 1926. For Wilson's own version of the Madero assassination see Wilson, *Diplo natic Episodes*, pp. 185 ff., and his testimony before the Senate committee, Senate Document no. 285, 66th Congress, 2d Session, pp. 2278 ff.

XVIII

THE AFTERMATH OF RECOGNITION

THE RECOGNITION of Carranza did not put an end to the nightmare of the Wilson administration. The events of the first weeks of 1916 threatened to undo everything that had been accomplished by the recognition of the *de facto* government, and the two countries came to the brink of war. As Lind's influence with both Wilson and Carranza had undoubtedly contributed to the recognition of Carranza, so his influence counted no less in keeping the two countries at peace.

The approaching presidential election greatly complicated an already difficult situation. The Mexican problem, loaded with so many possibilities, also had its attractions for the Republicans as an issue that might contribute to the healing of the schism in the party that had given Woodrow Wilson the largest electoral vote in history up to that time. The press teemed with dispatches and editorials breathing hostility to Mexico, and Henry Lane Wilson started the year with an interview in which he paid his compliments to the policy of the administration, alleging that the recognition of Carranza was dictated by political expediency and was a victory for the South American republics and not for the United States. "Perhaps," he said, "if the Carranza government can preserve itself until after the fall elections the Democratic administration can congratulate itself on having settled things in Mexico, but there is little in it for real congratulation." He stigmatized Carranza as arrogant, bombastic, conceited, and lacking the mental equipment to meet a situation that would tax the ingenuity of the greatest man.[1]

Within a few days events on the Mexican border appeared to bear out the predictions of the former ambassador; and for

[1] *New York Sun*, January 2, 1916.

months the tense relations between the two countries supplied an abundance of ammunition for the assailants of Wilson's policy. On January 10 eighteen American mining men were killed by Villa bandits near Santa Ysabel, Chihuahua, and the American government immediately demanded of Carranza that he punish the perpetrators of the crime. This precipitated a violent attack on the administration in Congress, and several senators and representatives demanded intervention. These assaults continued, and public opinion grew increasingly impatient. In the middle of February, Elihu Root, former secretary of state, flayed the foreign policy of the administration in a "ripping" speech before the New York Republican convention; and Wilson's refusal to furnish certain documents pertaining to Mexico in response to a Senate resolution brought sharp criticism from Senator Fall, an ardent interventionist.

On March 9 Villa and his bandits crossed the border and raided Columbus, New Mexico, killing civilians and soldiers. Wilson immediately ordered General John J. Pershing to pursue the bandits across the border and to capture Villa dead or alive. The order was issued before Carranza's consent was asked. Carranza asked permission of the American government to send his troops over into American territory in order to pursue the bandits, a request that was granted but not without expressions of ill feeling in the American press. Carranza had to frame his policy with reference to public opinion in Mexico, just as Wilson had to consider his constituency, and he was very cautious in committing himself to demands from the United States.

On April 12 Carranza demanded the withdrawal of American troops because the trail was no longer "hot," a demand that was refused. Throughout the winter and spring glaring headlines played up skirmishes and raids, until at last, on June 16, Carranza notified General Pershing that any movement of American troops east, west, or south would be met with bullets. The reply of the American government to this was an order from the War Department mobilizing the militia on the border and a stiff note from the State Department accusing Carranza of bad faith and warning him that if American troops were attacked, the United States would not be responsible for the consequences.

On June 22 the papers reported a battle between American troops and Carranza forces near Carrizal. The Americans were reported as having been led into an ambush. This event called forth another attack from the Republicans in Congress on the "weak" policy of the administration. In this crisis Wilson, on June 25, sent a circular to the Latin American governments stating that the United States had no intention of intervening, and to Carranza he addressed a note demanding the release of American prisoners and an early statement of his intentions. Carranza's reply was anxiously awaited while troop trains from all sections of the country were speeding to the border. Carranza's reply was preceded by the release of the prisoners, and on July 5, in a conciliatory note, he suggested friendly negotiations.

The upshot of the long train of events was the appointment by the respective governments of representatives to a joint commission, which held its first meeting at New London, Connecticut, on September 6. A protocol was signed on November 26, providing for the eventual withdrawal of American troops and for an arrangement by which the forces of both countries should patrol the border. With this background we shall have a better understanding of the part Lind played in Mexican affairs.

Prior to Carranza's recognition the problem of his advisers was to get him to be practical in his politics from an American standpoint, and the problem was even greater during the tense months that followed.[2] At the close of the year 1915 it appeared that the problem pressing for immediate solution was financial. Lind wrote to Douglas that they could render financial service to the Mexicans by showing them how to profit by American mistakes and successes. A depreciated currency, he wrote, was not always an evil to a country because it tended to raise prices and wages in the domestic sphere; the chief difficulty with a paper basis was in connection with foreign exchange.[3] This letter was submitted

[2] Lind to Simpson, October 5, 1915.
[3] Lind to Douglas, December 20, 1915.

to Cabrera, who was in Washington. After a conference between Douglas and Cabrera, Lind was requested to come to Washington; but an injury caused by a fall delayed his arrival until January 15.[4]

During his month's stay in the capital he transacted professional business and attended occasional conferences with Douglas and his associates. The tide was running strongly against Carranza, and organized propaganda was getting in its work both in Congress and in the administration. Lind asked Arredondo to furnish him with information that he might use to counteract the inspired propaganda in the press and the activity of a certain element of Mexicans who had taken refuge in the United States.[5] After his return to Minneapolis, he gave out a public statement that Villa's raid was undoubtedly inspired and financed by interests on this side of the border.[6]

Lind was disappointed that Secretary Lansing had seen fit to furnish so few documents pertaining to Mexican affairs in response to the Senate resolution. He thought the secretary was determined to shield and defend the "old Republican highbinders at all hazards."[7] He seems to have desired to have his reports from Vera Cruz made public. He also told Cabrera that he had not made use of his opportunities to inform the American people of the aims of the Constitutionalist party and suggested that the Chautauqua platform offered a good channel for this purpose.[8] He requested Douglas to send him a clipping of a speech by Father O'Reilly in New York in which he took the leaders of the Catholic church to task for their attitude toward Mexico. He thought he might have a talk with Archbishop Ireland of St. Paul, in which event a copy of the speech would be useful.[9]

At the time of the excitement over the Columbus raid in March,

[4] Douglas to Lind, December 24, 1915, January 3, 1916.
[5] Arredondo to Lind, January 20, 1916.
[6] *New York Herald*, March 11, 1916.
[7] Lind to Douglas, February 23, 1916.
[8] Cabrera to Lind, March 20, 1916.
[9] Lind to Douglas, February 25, 1916. In the Lind Papers there is an undated clipping of Father F. M. O'Reilly's speech, which was delivered at a banquet of the La Salle Institute in Troy, New York.

Lind did not believe the order to send troops in pursuit of the bandits should be regarded as an invasion of Mexico. He believed it was tolerated by international law.[10] He thought it fortunate that both countries had "discreet, patriotic, and level-headed leaders."

The entire course of history shows us that where two nations so unequal in size and power as the United States and Mexico are located side by side with an artificial boundary between them, the lesser people have always been suspicious and fearful of the intentions of their more powerful neighbor. In the case of Mexico there is historical ground for such fear. On the last occasion when American troops entered Mexico's soil the Mexicans lost almost two-thirds of their territory. They would be unlike ordinary human beings if they should not fear a similar outcome at this time, especially in view of the attitude of certain interests here and the jingo press. Under such circumstances it would be weak leadership in Carranza if he had not insisted upon the full measure of his international rights.[11]

In Lind's judgment Carranza's request for permission to send his troops across the border was a dignified statement, necessitated by the situation that confronted him.[12] He advised Douglas that his clients should immediately suggest a neutral zone to be policed jointly. This proposition Douglas presented to Senator William J. Stone, chairman of the Committee on Foreign Relations, who promised to submit it to the president. Senator Willard Saulsbury of Delaware, however, thought that at the moment the situation was too tense for a consideration of the proposal, though he believed it to be a good thing generally.[13] Douglas suggested that Lind wire Carranza that the keynote of the situation was cooperation between Wilson and Carranza in the effort to capture Villa, and on March 14 he sent the following telegram:

Ninety per cent of American people approve attitude and action

[10] Lind to Douglas, March 10, 1916.
[11] Lind to A. B. Farquhar, March 15, 1916.
[12] Lind to Douglas, March 12, 1916.
[13] Lind to Douglas, March 10, 1916; Douglas to Lind, March 13, 1916.

of president. Sentiment strong against intervention. Possible complications can be prevented by hearty cooperation between the two
armies and the prompt capture of the bandit. Such outcome would
be the turning point in the Mexican situation from the American
viewpoint and would create a strong public sentiment in favor of
your government.

Carranza wired his appreciation of this message.

In March and April Douglas conferred with Carranza. He told
Lind that if conditions were opportune, he intended to suggest to
Carranza and Cabrera that they invite Lind to come to Mexico
in order that they might have the benefit of his political sagacity
on the currency. In Mexico City Douglas met many Americans
who asked to be remembered to Lind, and both Carranza and
Cabrera spoke in most cordial terms and expressed gratitude for
his friendship for the Mexican people.[14]

On May 28, when the situation was steadily growing more
tense, Douglas wrote to Lind as follows: "From time to time,
and especially when a great crisis comes, I feel greatly in need of
your presence and advice and collaboration, and I am in that fix
just now." He said he had been laboring with Carranza and Cabrera to prevent the delivery of another note demanding the
withdrawal of troops. He frankly informed his clients that they
could do nothing more damaging to their cause in the United
States than to send such a note at that time, especially on the eve
of the assembling of the Republican convention. However, as a
matter of precedent Carranza felt he ought to make the demand.
He had told Douglas in their interview in Mexico City that he
preferred to have the record straight in the shape of a protest and
an objection to the invasion of Mexican territory.[15]

On May 31 the State Department received from Arredondo a
long note signed by C. Aguilar and dated May 22, written in
recriminating style, questioning the good faith of the United
States and threatening war. Within two days Senator Fall made
a long speech savagely criticizing Wilson's policy and demand-

[14] Douglas to Lind, March 7, May 4, 18, 1916.
[15] Copies of the confidential telegrams that passed between Douglas and his
clients are in the Lind Papers.

ing the complete occupation of Mexico. Douglas expected a sharp rebuke to Carranza from Wilson and wrote to Lind that he had not "imagination enough to imagine why it was thought best to send the last note." [16]

At this stage, when war and peace hung in the balance, Lind lost faith in the possibility of averting war, and he frankly told his Mexican correspondents that he could not continue his communications with them. Luis G. Bossero of the Mexican Bureau of Information wrote to him that he had come to the United States to try to persuade the people of the justice of the Mexican revolution and of the right of the Mexicans to settle their own questions without outside interference. He had found the American press very unfair and antagonistic and deliberately hiding the real facts. He believed Lind to be a friend of Mexico; his address on "The Mexican People" revealed a keenness of observation very rare among foreigners who had written on Mexico. "Nothing but friendship and goodwill would exist between the countries if all of your politicians were as honest and patriotic as you are." [17]

Lind replied in a letter defending the American government and condemning the Mexican press for its "yellow" policy.[18] To his Mexican friend employed in the American consulate in Vera Cruz, Josephine Bonhomme, who had continued to write to him and to send newspapers and documents, he wrote about the possibility of war and declared that Carranza had made a mistake in issuing the ultimatum. Wilson did the only thing he could have done by sending troops in pursuit of Villa, he said.[19]

On June 20 the afternoon papers published Lansing's note to the Mexican government accusing Carranza of bad faith and notifying him that American troops would remain in Mexico until the American government had assurance that its citizens

[16] Douglas to Lind, June 6, 1916.

[17] Bossero to Lind, June 10, 1916. See Luis Bossero, *The Mexican Situation from Every Angle*, a lecture delivered at the Baltimore City Club on May 27, 1916.

[18] Lind to Bossero, June 14, 1916.

[19] Lind to Josephine Bonhomme, June 20, 1916; Lind to E. M. House, July 7, 1916.

would be protected. The news of the fight between American and Mexican troops at Carrizal on June 21 "broke" at the time when the proverbial straw could break the camel's back. It was at this time (June 20) that Douglas requested Lind to wire suggestions to the State Department how war might be averted.[20] Lind declined to volunteer suggestions that might be spurned, but on June 22, 1916, he wrote the following letter to Douglas:

Headlines in the morning papers make me sick at heart. It seems as though all our efforts in furtherance of peace and good-will between the two nations have been lost. I have had no correspondence with any Mexican official for some months, but I get the leading Mexican papers and have kept in touch with the situation from day to day. The Carranza note was most unfortunate. You may recall that I have told you time and again that I had no confidence in Aguilar, the Mexican secretary. I have known him since I first went to Mexico. He always riots in phrases and in my opinion lacks judgment and a level head. He is just the kind of a man to be impressed by the encampment of the Pershing forces as a menace to Mexico. The Mexican people generally are suspicious of the situation as I gather from the press. They suspect that it is another "Maximilian" plot to restore the temporal power of the church and to subject Mexico to foreign domination. They cannot, or at least do not, seem to appreciate our viewpoint. That is the Mexican situation.

The American people on the other hand feel that our good intentions have been spurned, that our rights have been violated and our national honor affronted. These conflicting views appeal to the strongest emotions in man and are the kindling that usually starts the conflagration of war. Misunderstanding is really at the bottom of the whole trouble and it makes my heart bleed to think of the consequences and how futile it is for an individual to try to stem the tide. For God's sake, Douglas, if there is anything you can do to avert the calamity spare no effort. So far as the Mexican people are concerned they have my sympathy. Their sufferings have been great and as a people they are not without merit. But our immediate anxiety is for our own nation. As to the military phase of it, I have no apprehension. As a war it will be a picnic, but its other conse-

[20] Douglas wrote that on June 19 he had received a long telegram from Cabrera urging him to do something to avert trouble.

quences will be disastrous. There will be loss of life, more by disease than bullets, and great destruction of property. In two months the Republican politicians, who are now fostering the war spirit, will condemn the war and blatantly curse the administration "for bringing it on." Such is always the fairness and good faith of partisan politics. The mass of the National Guard troops will be utilized for guard duty — irksome work for any soldier and intolerable for militiamen. In a few weeks they will be demanding active duty or a return to their homes. The administration will be bombarded by millions of letters and complaints. I know, for I was in office in this state when we had a volunteer regiment in the Philippines — the 13th Minnesota. These letters, coming in the midst of the campaign, will tend to defeat the only administration that has accomplished big results, beneficial to the whole nation, since the time of Lincoln.

It is idle to predict that this will be a popular war. As soon as the brass bands are out of hearing — in six weeks — it will be very unpopular. The mass of the people, missing brothers, sons and employes, will begin to ask themselves what is it all for and what will we gain if we win. The cynics will answer, "The contractors and Wall Street will gain." The men and women whose minds have been wrought into fever heat on the church question — and there are millions of them — will say, "Our armies are in Mexico to restore the temporal power of the pope." It will take a generation of patient and urgent statesmanship to recover from the evil effects that will follow this war.

Do not regard these views, so frankly expressed, as absurd. I feel that they are based on fact and the future will verify them. Is there not still a chance to find a solution? I am not in a position to volunteer suggestions to the administration, but you are. I know from the talk that I had with Mexican officials at Piedras Negras last fall that they would be in favor of the establishment of a neutral zone. If war is not desired by our government — and I do not believe for a moment that it is — why could not Pershing's forces be drawn northward and consolidated "for strategic reasons"? Such move, however limited, would enable Carranza to hold his people in leash and in the meantime a neutral zone for the protection of the border could be established by diplomatic action. This would afford a way out of the dilemma that would involve humiliation to neither side. From our talks in the past, I think these views are in accord with your own. If so, I beg of you to urge them upon the administration with all the power at your command.

Douglas thanked Lind for this "very strong and really remarkable letter" and told him that he had showed it to Lincoln Steffens, who was in Douglas' office "working on his own account for peace." Charles R. Crane, an intimate friend of Steffens, was also in the office, and Steffens showed the letter to him. Crane asked to be allowed to show it to Wilson and to any of the cabinet members he might wish, a request Douglas gladly complied with.[21] The sequel is found in the *Autobiography of Lincoln Steffens*, published in 1931, pages 722–40.

Steffens had been in Mexico a number of times, and, it will be remembered, he was a member of the party that met Carranza at Piedras Negras. Steffens and John W. Slaughter accompanied Carranza on his travels after that meeting. Steffens had a high opinion of Lind. He said he had never found Wilson informed on anything that he himself knew about Mexico. Of the personal representatives Wilson sent out, Lind alone got things right, Steffens observed. Steffens relates that at the time of the crisis he went in despair to Douglas' office, where he was shown a deciphered private wire from Carranza expressing sorrow and despair. War was inevitable. Douglas allowed Steffens to examine other documents, and they convinced him that Carranza was innocent of warlike intentions. The following day Steffens was given an audience by Wilson, and he quoted to him extracts from Carranza's letters. The upshot of the interview was that Wilson was convinced that Carranza did not desire war, and he told Steffens that the information had prevented war.

The story as related by Steffens makes no mention of Charles R. Crane nor of Lind's letter. If Crane showed Lind's letter to Wilson, no record of his doing so has been found. Perhaps an extract from a letter written by Douglas to Lind on July 5, 1916, is a corrective to Steffens' version:

I have many times stated to you and sometimes written you that

[21] Douglas to Lind, June 28, 1916.

I was afraid to write a letter to anybody about Mexico for fear that by the time it would reach its destination everything I would say in it would appear ridiculous. All these observations apply with peculiar force to my last letter to you. I did not manifest to you in that letter any hope whatever of averting war. [Referring to his letter of June 28, acknowledging receipt of Lind's letter.] I could not see on that day one ray of hope, and as a matter of fact, before your letter was mailed the announcement was made at the White House that the president was disposed to go more than half way in meeting Carranza, to adjust the border troubles. The clouds, from that day, began to break and then when I succeeded in getting Carranza unconditionally to release the prisoners at Chihuahua, the black clouds began to blow away and today it looks as if we are nearer permanent peace and a clearer understanding between the two countries than we have been since the Columbus expedition. I have received this morning a telegram from Cabrera in which he says: "Note sent yesterday by Carranza through Arredondo states plainly and completely what you wish." And within the last hour I have received copy of the note which was this morning delivered to Lansing. . . . I think you will agree with me that it is the most pacific conciliatory note that has ever been sent out from the head-quarters of the Constitutionalists. It does not leave a word to be added or subtracted from the standpoint of its spirit of conciliation.

This conciliatory note paved the way for an amicable settlement in line with Lind's suggestion for a neutral zone. The administration did not want mediation or arbitration, but preferred direct negotiations with the Carranza government. Douglas wanted Lind to serve on the joint commission to adjust the differences because he was the first man who had suggested to him the idea of a neutral zone. Lind expressed himself as well satisfied with the Mexicans appointed to the joint commission. Of the American commissioners, he had a high regard for Franklin K. Lane and John R. Mott, but he knew nothing about George Gray except that he was an extreme conservative and would probably try to "lug in" financial and economic questions. Within limits, Lind thought this might be wise.[22]

[22] Lind to Douglas, September 2, 1916.

When the protocol was made public, Lind was gratified to learn that Carranza had approved it. He thought the proposal to submit claims to the Hague Tribunal or to a commission appointed under its auspices would be a dangerous experiment for Mexico; a commission composed of Americans and Mexicans would be actuated by a more just and neighborly feeling than any commission composed of Europeans.[23]

Throughout his connection with Mexican affairs, official and otherwise, Lind never lost confidence in President Wilson and was confident that he would do nothing to precipitate war unless his hand was forced by Congress or by public sentiment. Naturally, he believed the best interests of the country demanded Wilson's re-election.[24] His speeches summarized the achievements of the administration. He praised the Federal Reserve Act as the "most important constructive legislation that has been enacted since the passage of the Interstate Commerce Act"; approved of the Underwood Tariff Act; alluded to humanitarian legislation, including the Adamson Act; and indorsed the foreign policy. "It is astounding and humiliating to read the carping criticism of Mr. Hughes, and the dastardly attacks of a partisan press, on the conduct of our relations with the warring nations of Europe," he said.[25]

Even in the pre-convention campaign it was obvious that Wilson's Mexican policy would be made much of by the Republicans, and Lind was one of the targets of the Republican speakers and press. The appearance of Mrs. Edith O'Shaughnessy's book, *A Diplomat's Wife in Mexico*, was timed for the presidential campaign. Lind flatly declined to comment publicly in any way on Mrs. O'Shaughnessy's arraignment of his course in Mexico.[26] The book expressed high admiration for Huerta and his régime and was correspondingly caustic in dealing with the policy of President Wilson and his "confidential agent." It was inevitable that it should influence the political thinking of its

[23] Lind to Douglas, December 7, 1916.
[24] Lind to Douglas, June 30, 1916; Lind to Farquhar, August 7, 1916.
[25] A manuscript copy of this speech is in the Lind Papers.
[26] *Minneapolis Tribune*, June 15, 1916.

readers, in proportion, of course, as it agreed with the individual's point of view.

On July 20, 1916, Hearst's *New York American* published an accurate version of Lind's confidential communication to Bryan of November 15, 1913, in which it was stated that Mexico City must be humbled, preferably by "home talent," and that "To make a dog feel that he really is a cur he must be whipped by another dog and preferably by a cur." The inevitable headlines appeared: "Capital Stirred by Publication of Lind's Notes"; and Lind received a letter from Jesus Flores Magon, with whom he had conferred in Vera Cruz, which stated that the Havana newspapers had published some strong articles against him on the strength of the document. Douglas thought Lind ought to direct the attention of the State Department to the rumors that there were leaks in the department.[27]

Lind believed that Hughes's attacks on Wilson's Mexican policy were inspired and framed by Henry Lane Wilson. In a speech at Fort Wayne, Indiana, Hughes asserted that President Wilson had given Lind instructions when he left for Mexico to say that "Huerta will be put out if he does not get out." The *New York World* wired Lind that it would appreciate it if he would be good enough to wire at once if any such instructions were given. To this Lind replied:

Such instructions as I received relating to Mexican matters are of record in the State Department. I have no desire to compete with Henry Lane Wilson, O'Shaughnessy and Judge Hughes in exploiting our international affairs for personal or partisan ends.[28]

Undoubtedly the religious issue played a part in the campaign. The World War, the Mexican imbroglio, and certain other issues and conditions raised what at the time was called the "anti-papal panic"; and it was inevitable that Protestant and Catholic should appeal to, and should be influenced by, religious prejudice. We have already seen how disappointing the recogni-

[27] Magon to Lind, September 9, 1916; Douglas to Lind, August 1, 1916.
[28] *New York World* to Lind, September 21, 1916, and Lind's reply, September 22, 1916.

tion of Carranza was to certain Catholic prelates, and both Lind and Douglas were convinced that Catholic propaganda was making a great impression. As evidence of this Lind cited a letter written by John F. McGee of Minneapolis on November 4, 1916, which was circulated. This letter indicted the Wilson administration for failing to recognize Huerta and for recognizing Carranza. "No one has more accurately stated the net result of the almost criminal conduct of the administration in Mexico than His Eminence, Cardinal Gibbons, in interviews given by him to the public press, a copy of one of which is enclosed herewith," McGee wrote.[29]

Another line of attack was engineered by the owner of the *Los Angeles Times*, who also had considerable property holdings in the delta of the Colorado in Mexico.[30] This paper published an interview with Richard H. Cole of Pasadena, who recited the details of the drafting of the proclamation issued by Carranza preliminary to his recognition. Cole said the proclamation was framed in Washington, was edited by President Wilson, and passed through several hands. Lind was said to have spent several days on the draft, and men like Bryan, Metcalfe, Folk, and Cole were active in the Carranza campaign. When his attention was called to Cole's statement, Lind was reported as having said that he knew of no one named Cole during his Mexican work. The *Times* then printed a facsimile of a letter from Lind to Cole, dated September 2, 1915, in which he expressed dissatisfaction with the State Department and alluded to the visit of Cardinal Gibbons to the White House. The comment of the *Times* was that the letter gave a vigorous knock to the Wilson administration and to the Catholic church.[31]

[29] A photographic copy of this letter is in the Lind Papers. Lind to Douglas, October 18, 1916; Simpson to Lind, February 8, 1916; Douglas to Lind, March 7, 1916; Douglas to Cabrera, March 6, 1916; A. E. Leckie to W. S. Howard, May 27, 1916. Lind thought it significant that of the twenty-eight Democrats who refused to abide by the action of the House caucus on the Senate Philippine independence bill, eleven were connected with Tammany or with its Brooklyn annex. See *Harper's Weekly*, May 13, 1916.

[30] H. L. Scott, *Some Memories of a Soldier* (New York, 1928), p. 503.

[31] *Los Angeles Times*, October 1, 1916. There is some correspondence between Lind and Cole in the Lind Papers. As a part of the Republican cam-

The re-election of Wilson was most gratifying to Lind and bore out his prophecy that the West would vote overwhelmingly for him.[32] He had hopes that Mexico would in time set her house in order. The withdrawal of the last American soldier from Mexico on February 5, 1917, the presentation by Ambassador Fletcher of his credentials to Carranza on March 3, 1917, and the election of the "first chief" as president eight days later augured well for the future.

The publication of the Zimmerman note, which, with comments, occupied the entire first page of certain American newspapers on March 1, 1917, did not seriously disturb Lind. The so-called "German plot" consisted of a note from Alfred Zimmerman, German foreign minister, to Count von Bernstorff, German ambassador to the United States, instructing him to inform the president of Mexico that, as soon as it was certain that there would be war between Germany and the United States, Germany would propose an alliance with Mexico and financial support in a campaign to reconquer New Mexico, Texas, and Arizona. The Associated Press dispatch linked the names of Rafael Zubaran and Luis Cabrera, friends of Lind, with the alleged conspiracy.

Lind made no public comment on the Zimmerman note at the time, but in April, 1917, after war had been declared, he gave an interview in Washington in which he said that the American government had nothing serious to fear from the Germans in Mexico and need have no fear whatever that the Mexican government would assist Germany. "Carranza is too sensible a man to cooperate with the Germans against the United States," he said. "What possible advantage could come to him or Mexico by such a course? Certainly Germany is not a promising prospect just now for any nation to tie to." [33]

In line with his efforts to foster a friendly feeling between the

paign, the *New York Sun* on August 4, 1916, began a series of articles based on the reports of Henry Lane Wilson, purporting to "lay bare" the true story of Mexico's ruin and the part of the Wilson administration in it.
[32] Douglas to Lind, October 31, November 9, 1916.
[33] *Washington Post*, April 15, 1917.

United States and Mexico, Lind proposed recruiting a regiment of one thousand Mexicans for service in France. Lind knew the success of the project depended upon handling the negotiations discreetly, and he thought it better to have the proposal come from prominent Mexicans close to Carranza, though he doubted whether it would be wise to approach Carranza directly. In August, 1917, while in Washington he called to pay his respects to the Mexican ambassador, Ignacio Bonillas, and in a roundabout way sounded him out on the proposition. The ambassador seemed to think favorably of it.

Before corresponding with persons who might be interested, Lind outlined the tentative proposal in a letter to Colonel House, dated July 7, 1917.

It has been my conviction ever since I learned to know and to appreciate the many good, and I might say strong, qualities of the Mexican people that it is of the utmost importance to us as a nation, as well as to them, that there should be a better acquaintance between the peoples and relations of mutual confidence established. As the weaker one of two neighbors, and they realize fully our power and superiority, it was only natural that they should feel somewhat apprehensive of the use that may be made of our power in the future. The patience of the president and his general attitude toward the Mexican people during their late unpleasantness, has overcome the old suspicion and prejudice in a great measure. There is a much better feeling, but as yet it can hardly be said that it is one based on mutual acquaintance and respect. I believe that the situation is now ripe for affirmative work looking to the cultivation of more neighborly relations — not mere cash relations as in the past, but a community of interest in the spiritual realm. The Mexicans are idealists. They have a vivid imagination — or I might say more accurately — fancy. They will sacrifice more for an ideal, or for a mere fancy for that matter, than any other people that I have come in contact with. Our people too are idealists in a great degree and it has been my observation that strangers can be brought together more quickly by a common ideal, or even a common fancy, than in any other manner. In the present situation it seems to me that if the two peoples could be united in a common idealistic enterprise — such as the defense of France — and suffer common dangers and share in common glory on the battlefield, it would appeal to the imagination of both populations as nothing else could. It would blot out the misgivings and doubts on the part of the Mexicans and do much to unite in a spirit of good neighborhood and neighborly cooperation for the future.

The administration may not think it wise to exercise any pressure on the Mexican government to alter its attitude toward the European war so long as it remains strictly neutral. As to that, I have no opinion. It seems to me, however, in view of the strong popular sentiment in Mexico in favor of the Allies, that it might be entirely feasible and not improper for private citizens of the two nations to work out a plan by which the Mexicans who are so disposed could share with us the risk and the glory of succoring France and civilization. Suppose the Mexicans should form a brigade or two of volunteers on American soil under Mexican officers, or better still, under mixed Mexican, French and American officers; there are many Americans, and some very capable men of Mexican descent in Texas and in New Mexico, who would undoubtedly be proud to join these commands. . . . It seems to me that we could well afford to equip, transport and finance such a body of men on the western front.

Colonel House replied that for some weeks he had been trying to do just what Lind suggested and stated that if the project was a visionary one, he had to plead guilty with Lind. Other correspondents thought well of the project, but for some reason or other it never materialized.

During the remainder of his life, Lind's interest in Mexico never flagged. He wrote to William Bayard Hale that he became so intensely interested in the Mexican people during his stay that he had been unable to withdraw himself from the country. Mrs. Lind, he wrote, insisted that he was still living in Mexico. To another correspondent he wrote that while his work in Mexico brought neither profit nor glory, he found it intensely interesting — on the whole more so than any other period of his life. After his return to the United States he studied Spanish under a tutor and within a short time acquired a fair reading knowledge. The Spanish language gave him the key to a new field of psychological study. Friends in Mexico sent him Mexican newspapers, and the editor of the *Mexican Review*, at the request of Ambassador Bonillas, sent him copies of Mexican papers received at his office.[34]

The succession of events during the next few years was discouraging. On May 18, 1920, Carranza was killed in a mountain shack in the state of Puebla, a fugitive from the armies of General Obregon and General Adolfo de la Huerta, and for several years the relations between the United States and Mexico were strained. In 1920, after the Carranza government had fallen, Lind was summoned to testify before the Senate committee investigating Mexican affairs.[35] The investigation was inspired by Albert B. Fall of New Mexico, who was chairman of the subcommittee that conducted the hearings. Francis J. Kearful, an attorney and counselor at law in Mexico City, assisted in examining the witnesses. Lind had met him in Mexico and learned that he was an associate of William F. Buckley, a representative of independent oil companies in Mexico.[36]

To judge by his testimony, Lind did not take the investigation seriously and was fully aware that it was instituted for the purpose of discrediting the Wilson administration on the eve of the presidential campaign. Fall's connection with it was an indication of its purpose. It is evident that the questions Kearful addressed to Lind were designed to make him seem hostile to the Catholic church and to trap him into another controversy with Henry Lane Wilson. Lind declined to discuss the former ambassador and to comment on certain other matters. He stated that his conversations with President Wilson and Secretary Bryan on the eve of his departure for Mexico were confidential so far as he was concerned, and that he did not propose to discuss what he had reported to the State Department. If further light was needed, he offered to cooperate with the committee in making his reports public.

[34] Lind to Hale, February 16, 1917; Lind to Farquhar, August 6, 1917; G. F. Weeks to Lind, August 17, 1917.

[35] Senate Document no. 285, 66th Congress, 2d Session.

[36] Senate Document no. 285, 66th Congress, 2d Session, pp. 2360, 3304.

Addressing himself to the existing situation in Mexico, he said it behooved the United States to be patient and not to judge Mexicans by the same standards by which England, France, or Canada was judged. He did not think Mexico could be helped by intervention or by warlike action on the part of the United States. The occupation of Mexico by American troops at any time, he said, would be as disastrous to the United States as it would be to Mexico.

There is little in Lind's correspondence to reveal his opinion of the Mexican policy of the Harding and Coolidge administrations; but the notes that came from the State Department under Charles E. Hughes and Frank B. Kellogg breathe a spirit so entirely foreign to those Wilson directed Bryan and Lansing to send that Lind's disapproval may be assumed.

On January 30, 1929, in sending New Year's greetings to Rafael Zubaran and his friends, Lind wrote that many things had happened to Mexico and to the world since they had met. Many of his dearest Mexican friends had passed to the unknown, he said. He remembered with pleasure the many things in which they had labored jointly, and though it might have been forgotten, their labor was not wholly lost to the two countries. He stated that he was in his seventy-fifth year and took little active part in politics, but that he had done his utmost to bring about the defeat of Alfred E. Smith, whose election might have undone the work that Zubaran and his associates, and later Calles, had done so well.

XIX

WAR AND POLITICS

AFTER Lind left the Republican party in 1896, the only administration that claimed his whole-hearted support was that of Woodrow Wilson. The appointment of Bryan to the state portfolio was a guarantee that the president was in sympathy with the progressive wing of the Democratic party; and the appointment most unexpectedly brought Lind into close relations with the president. Though Wilson did not respond favorably to all his recommendations from Vera Cruz and was tardy in accepting others, Lind never lost faith in his integrity and ability; nor did he lose his admiration for the character and leadership of Bryan, except in the matter of the Scopes evolution trial in Tennessee, shortly before the Commoner's death, when he thought Bryan had "made a fool of himself."

On the important measures of the administration Lind was generally in agreement with the president, but he did not approve of Wilson's recommendation that Congress repeal the provision in the Panama Canal Act exempting vessels engaged in coastwise shipping from tolls. From Vera Cruz, on March 2, 1914, he wrote to Secretary Lane that he did not share the belief that the exemption violated the treaty with Great Britain. In any event, the modification proposed by the president would not appeal to the people on the Pacific Coast, not would it, he thought, be popular in the East if the press and sentiment were less under the control of the railways. Lind's solution was the passage of a supplementary act providing that vessels of any American country or possession whose territory extended continuously from the Atlantic to the Pacific, carrying cargo from one port to another of such country or possession, should be exempt from paying tolls under the same limitations as vessels of the United States engaged in coastwise trade. By placing American countries situated as the United States on a parity, even the Hague Tribunal could not find fault, for it was fundamental law, he argued, that parity of conditions was satisfied by parity of treatment. In his judgment, this solution would be just and in conformity with the treaty with Great Britain, in view of the fact that the construction of the canal had been prompted by domestic considerations more than anything else.[1]

Lind believed that the administration had made a wonderful record in securing the enactment of the Underwood Tariff and the Federal Reserve acts, especially the latter. Anything that would prevent money from being piled up in Wall Street, he said, would have a wholesome effect; it would eliminate undue speculation and bring the price of stocks down to an investment basis. No country could prosper if all its cash reserves were devoted to stock speculation, he said. In a personal letter to Bryan he advocated the location of the Federal Reserve Bank in Minneapolis; and at the Pass Christian conference, Norman Lind was present as an emissary of the Minneapolis Chamber of Commerce to bring this location to the attention of the president and his aide, Admiral Grayson.[2]

Wilson's efforts to prevent the United States from entering the World War were heartily applauded by Lind. In an address on "Peace and War" delivered in the Swedish Mission Church in Duluth in 1916, he said the American people ought to be grateful to Providence that Wilson was president, for if Roosevelt had been elected the country would by then have been at war with Germany. He did not fix the responsibility for the war on any one nation or government, but he thought the European war spirit not unlike the struggle in Wall Street. "The instrumentalities may differ," he said, "but the end is much the same." At the same time, he thought, it would be unfortunate if the

[1] In a letter to Guy D. Goff of the United States Shipping Board, January 21, 1921, Lind made the same recommendation. At that time Lind and his son Norman were interested in the Lind Navigation Company.

[2] The correspondence is in the Lind Papers. See especially Lind to Bryan, December 7, 1913, and Lind to Norman Lind, December 25, 1913.

Germany dominated by the Junker bureaucracy should triumph.[3]

With the entrance of the United States into the war in April, 1917, Lind, like his fellow citizens and in accordance with his oft-expressed conviction that it was the duty of all citizens to support the government in the prosecution of war, was willing to "do his bit" to serve the country in whatever capacity he might be called upon to fill.

In the first year of the war he addressed a loyalty meeting of Minnesotans at which Samuel Gompers, president of the American Federation of Labor, was present. After paying a compliment to Gompers, with whom he had worked in securing the automatic coupler legislation, and praising the loyal spirit of labor in Minnesota, he said:

The world is at war, and we who but a few years ago were derided by the militarists of all nations as a people too indolent and too cowardly to fight are also at war. Why is it that a people who withstood the dragooning of the press, the appeals of partisanship, who remained indifferent to the arguments and pleas of the exploiters of a nation, who refused to make war on our weaker neighbor to the south, though we had many grievances against Mexico that justified war from an international point of view, are now in arms, by the almost unanimous voice of the nation, against the most powerful war machine that autocracy ever produced? We refrained from making war on Mexico because the national conscience was not clear that force was justifiable. But now we have freely accepted the challenge of the most powerful government on earth, and for no purpose of profit to ourselves. In the one case we would have incurred comparatively little risk and possible gain; in the other it is all risk and no gain. This apparent inconsistency in our action appears to me like intuition — an evidence of that instinct which pervades all life in danger, that guides the birds in the air, the beasts of the field; that guides democracy, that guides all peoples to their own preservation when they can act untrammeled.[4]

[3] Lind to William Bayard Hale, February 16, 1916; C. A. Smith to Lind, March 9, 1918.
[4] The manuscript of this address is in the Lind Papers.

On January 24, 1918, Lind was appointed commissioner of conciliation in the Department of Labor; and on September 24 he was appointed umpire on the National War Labor Board. These duties required him to spend considerable time in Washington, but he found them more agreeable than his service as a member of the Minnesota Commission of Public Safety, established by the legislature within a few days after the declaration of war. The commission consisted of the governor, the attorney-general, and five citizens appointed by the governor.[5] Lind was appointed by Governor Burnquist. Of this body the judicious historian, William W. Folwell, has this to say: "If a hostile army had been landed at Duluth and was about to march on the capital of the state, a more liberal dictatorship could hardly have been conceded to the commission." It appears therefore that the "war hysteria" seized upon Minnesota early in the war.

The situation in Minnesota was peculiar to the state. The Nonpartisan League, which represented a revolt against the domination of the government by what its members conceived to be the reactionary and plutocratic Republican party, and which had made great inroads on that party in North Dakota, was threatening to dethrone the G. O. P. in Minnesota. At the beginning of the war the people of the state were lukewarm and many of them actually opposed to the war. There were certain elements in the foreign-born population — and in the native-born as well — that had difficulty in reconciling themselves to a war waged beyond the seas. But it is equally true that a body vested with the dictatorial powers of the Minnesota Commission of Public Safety was a dangerous instrument.

War furnishes excellent opportunities to individuals of a certain type to pay off old scores by bringing charges of disloyalty against past and present enemies. Moreover, the loyalty issue could be used with devastating effect against a party claiming the

[5] The activity of the Minnesota Commission of Public Safety is discussed in Folwell, *A History of Minnesota*, 3:556–75, and in Franklin F. Holbrook and Livia Appel, *Minnesota in the War with Germany* (2 vols., St. Paul, 1928, 1932).

allegiance of individuals like the elder Lindbergh, for example, who had attacked the abuses of big business and who, before the entrance of the United States into the war, had charged that there was a conspiracy of the money power to have the government step in to protect its interests. It is also true that in Minnesota, as well as in North Dakota, the Nonpartisan League attracted to its program men and women of socialistic convictions and tendencies.[6]

For a time Lind was much interested in the work of the Commission of Public Safety. One of his first assignments was to maintain peace on the Iron Range. After spending some time in the northern part of the state he reported that the situation was favorable and that there was no likelihood that there would be serious trouble during the remainder of the war. He found the mine owners willing to cooperate with the laborers.[7] However, as the war spirit increased, fanned as it was by high-powered propaganda and by the bitter attacks of the Twin City papers on the Nonpartisan League, the Commission of Public Safety was called upon to deal with every conceivable kind of disloyalty and alleged disloyalty. The dominating personality on the commission was Judge John F. McGee of Minneapolis, who at the very beginning of the war launched a public attack on the German and Swedish elements in Minnesota. He also declared that "A Nonpartisan League lecturer is a traitor every time. In other words, no matter what he says or does, a League worker is a traitor."[8] McGee, however, was not the only citizen who believed that what the state needed was a few "necktie parties."

Thomas Van Lear, the Socialist mayor of Minneapolis, who gave the city one of the cleanest and best administrations in its

[6] Since the hectic days of 1917–20, Minnesota has elected two Farmer-Labor United States senators, several congressmen, and a governor, and the people of the state, as well as the historian, can view the scene calmly and in perspective understand that if adherents of the Nonpartisan League were sinners, they were also grievously sinned against. If the reader desires to relive the acrimony of the past, he can do no better than to refer to the files of the Twin City dailies and the *Nonpartisan Leader*.

[7] Lind to Colonel House, July 7, 1917.

[8] Lynn and Dora B. Haines, *The Lindberghs* (New York, 1931), pp. 281–82.

history, was under fire throughout the war. With other Social-
ists Van Lear had opposed the entrance of the United States into
the war and had been instrumental in calling a peace meeting
while the war resolution was pending in Congress. Although he
was quite willing to take part in Liberty Loan parades and other
war-time activities, he was on occasion refused participation because his enemies deemed it politically inexpedient to permit him
to show his patriotism. At a meeting of the Commission of Public Safety McGee proposed to oust Van Lear and his chief of
police, but Lind blocked his plan because the procedure would
have been in violation of law and might have provoked serious
disorder. Thereupon McGee became exceedingly angry. We
shall allow Lind to relate what followed in a communication to
Dr. Folwell, dated November 19, 1924: "He called me everything vile you can think of before the committee — with the
governor in the chair. The latter sat silent and I walked out. I did
not return to any meeting. The governor begged me to come
back. I told him that I could not and would not with McGee on
the board." [9]

What is perhaps a just appraisal of the Commission of Public
Safety is given in a letter written to Lind by Ambrose Tighe,
counsel for the commission, shortly after the McGee-Lind incident. The fundamental weakness, according to Mr. Tighe, was
its departure from the principle of constitutional government.
The ruthlessness of the procedure, he said, showed how dangerous it was to vest even good men with arbitrary power. "If we
are going to have a reign of the proletariat after the war," he
continued, "I sometimes think the Commission is setting a bad
example for our future rulers. I am flattered to think that you
think I may have some influence in inducing sanity and discre-

[9] This letter is in the Folwell Papers in the Minnesota Historical Society.
In a letter from Governor Burnquist, dated January 9, 1918, replying to Lind's
letter of resignation, the governor said "that if there is any way in which you
can continue your work on the Commission I would consider it a great favor."
It is perhaps pertinent to note that on November 5, 1918, Van Lear was defeated for re-election by fewer than fifteen hundred votes, in spite of the
loyalty issue played up by the newspapers and his opponents. For McGee's
attitude toward President Wilson's Mexican policy see page 324.

tion, but I cannot see that anything I can do will count for much, now that I haven't the benefit of your cooperation."[10] Lind had written Tighe of his hopes for the early ending of the war, in which case "our local warriors would shortly have no one to fight except organized labor."

McGee carried his fight against the organized farmers and organized labor to the attorney-general's office in Washington. Lind warned Attorney-General Gregory that McGee was bitter and unreasoning; the latter replied that, though he had never met McGee personally, he felt that while in Washington he had done the people of Minnesota a great injustice.[11] With his letter to the assistant attorney-general, Lind inclosed a photographic copy of a letter written by McGee on November 4, 1916, in which he attacked Wilson's foreign policy and stated that it was absurd to give the president credit for keeping the country out of war because not one of the countries wanted war with the United States.[12] In defending in court a man on trial for alleged seditious activities by advocating the election of Charles A. Lindbergh for governor, Lind contrasted "erring Lindbergh brethren" with the "true gospel of McGeeism."[13]

In a letter to an old friend of New Ulm days, who was in trouble with officers of the law, Lind stated what he conceived to be his duty in the crisis: "As you know, I have no sympathy with the war spirit, as such, and I have always consistently fought imperialism — economic as well as military — and shall continue to do so. In the present situation, however, I find myself in absolute accord with President Wilson and I feel that there can be no world fit to live in until the Prussian military machine is destroyed, either from within or from without."[14]

Although Lind was entirely out of sympathy with the type of patriot who wrapped himself in the flag and cried, "Behold how patriotic I am!" he participated in sane efforts to inculcate a

[10] Letter dated February 13, 1918.
[11] Thomas W. Gregory to Lind, May 3, 1918.
[12] S. J. Graham to Lind, August 23, 1918.
[13] Lind's memorandum, State of Minnesota v. Eric Olson, 1919.
[14] Lind to Steinhauser, February 18, 1918.

healthy spirit of loyalty and did not hesitate to rebuke either sham patriotism or outright disloyalty. On May 3, 1918, President Wilson requested Lind to lend his efforts toward raising a fund for the Organization of Patriotic Americans of German Origin, to which Lind responded by taking the matter up with prominent Germans of the state.[15] And on September 6, 1918, he suggested to President Wilson that a certain number of people be sent to Finland to conduct propaganda favorable to the American cause. Secretary Lansing, however, advised against accepting the suggestion on account of the complicated situation in that country.[16]

At the time of the Luxburg affair Lind was deeply grieved that Sweden was made to appear a partisan of Germany. With characteristic straightforwardness, in a public address given at Stillwater in September, 1917, he said he was astonished to see that the "government of Sweden had permitted itself to become the lackey of the kaiser." "As a citizen of Swedish blood I should deplore trouble between our nation and Sweden, but you men in this audience of Swedish blood and descent must remember that we are not of the Swedish household. Whatever kindly feelings we may have toward the people of Sweden, we say to them that unless they choose to have a government in harmony with the aspirations of the free peoples of the earth they must suffer the consequences of the actions of their rulers."[17] He later wrote to the director of the Scandinavian Bureau of the Committee of Public Information suggesting that propaganda be pushed in Sweden.[18]

The political campaign of 1918 was waged when the war hysteria in Minnesota was at its height. Newspapers were publishing casualty lists, and citizens were reading daily reports of the arriving "Yanks" in France and of the retreating "Huns." This is the recollection of one of the biographers of Charles A. Lindbergh:

[15] Frederick E. Weyerhaeuser to Lind, August 19, 1918.
[16] Wilson to Lind, October 5, 1918.
[17] *Princeton Union*, September 13, 1917.
[18] Edwin Björkman to Lind, February 3, March 17, 1918.

That 1918 campaign will be remembered as long as anyone lives that took any part in it, either as an onlooker or participant. It will go down in the history of the state as one period in which Minnesota forgot the meaning of democracy and turned loose the Cossack-minded to "ride" down all those who had a different point of view. The things that happened in 1918, as one looks back upon them now, seem like a bad dream, and in no way belong to the life of a sane, law-abiding people.[19]

As election day drew near, President Wilson issued an appeal to "my fellow countrymen" to cast a vote of confidence in his policies by electing a Democratic majority in Congress. The Republicans, he said, had been pro-war but anti-administration. The Republicans attacked the president's appeal as a repudiation of his "politics is adjourned" statement made some months earlier. "The people's voice, not Wilson's, is paramount in peace," said Theodore Roosevelt. Simultaneously the Republicans in the Senate were criticizing the president's peace terms. Before election day, November 5, Austria-Hungary had accepted the harsh terms of the armistice, and the ramparts of the Hohenzollern empire were crumbling.

In Minnesota Charles A. Lindbergh filed for governor as a Republican with the indorsement of the Nonpartisan League in opposition to Governor Burnquist, but he was defeated. Throughout the campaign Nonpartisan meetings were broken up by mobs, speakers were escorted out of town by self-appointed patriots, the home of Henrik Shipstead was painted yellow, and a reign of terror was launched against those who did not express approval of Republican or Democratic candidates, notwithstanding the fact that in New Mexico Wilson had indorsed the Socialist candidate for the United States Senate who was running in opposition to Senator Albert B. Fall.

So bitter was the feeling against Lindbergh, the man who had inspired the investigation of the "money trust," that he thought it the part of wisdom to resign from the War Industries Board,

[19] Lynn and Dora B. Haines, *The Lindberghs*, p. 279.

to which he had been appointed by Bernard M. Baruch. Certain individuals had announced that they would not serve on Liberty Loan committees if Lindbergh were permitted to serve the government. In a letter to Baruch on September 10, 1918, Lindbergh stated that it was less important that he should have the honor of serving his country in a responsible position than that the 151,000 voters whose votes had been cast for him in the primaries, as well as those whose votes had been cast for him but not counted, should have all possible confidence in the war program. He declared his supporters were for the government from a sense of loyal duty and grave necessity, in marked contrast to those who had threatened to cease work for the Liberty Loan if Lindbergh's appointment to the War Industries Board were ratified.[20]

In featuring the loyalty issue the Republicans, in addition to charging the adherents of the Nonpartisan League with disloyalty, capitalized what at the time was thought to be the immense popularity of Wilson by insinuating that the president desired the re-election of Senator Nelson and Governor Burnquist. The Republican *Minneapolis Journal* said editorially: "For these reasons it is safe to reject all Socialist candidates and all Townley Nonpartisan candidates, for the essential disloyalty of these allied organizations is established beyond all question."[21]

At the opening of the primary campaign Lind was in Washington engaged in work the secretary of labor had assigned to him. He received a letter from a Minneapolis attorney informing him that there was a concerted movement "on the part of certain special interests to re-elect Senator Nelson without opposition" and suggesting that Lind file for the Senate. Lind replied that he had retired from all political activity on his own behalf and could conceive of no situation that would justify him in modifying that decision. He agreed with his correspondent, however, that the progressive elements in the state ought to have "a trustworthy organ in the upper house of Congress" be-

[20] A copy of this letter is in the Lind Papers.
[21] *Minneapolis Journal*, November 2, 1918.

cause of the many important matters, including the railway question, that would come up for solution.[22]

In spite of the fact that the Minnesota State Democratic Committee indorsed Nelson for re-election and prominent Democrats like B. F. Nelson, Fred B. Lynch, T. D. O'Brien, R. T. O'Connor, and D. W. Lawler announced their support of the Republican candidate, Lind gave out a statement in support of W. G. Calderwood, the candidate of the Prohibition party, who had the indorsement of President Wilson.[23] He stated that it was just as necessary to elect men who would support Wilson's domestic policies as men who would support him in foreign affairs. "Nelson and his friends first tried to deceive the people of this state by claiming that the president desired his election and it was claimed that a letter to that effect had been written," he said. "This was falsehood pure and simple. . . . Now Senator Nelson says he became a candidate at the instance of many *prominent* people of the state. Maybe he did. The administration hopes that the people of the state will elect Mr. Calderwood, who will voice the just interests of all the people of the state if elected." The statement also made an appeal for the election of Democrats to the House of Representatives.

Lind's opposition to a coalition of conservative Republicans and Democrats to prevent the election of liberals cloaked by the loyalty appeal aroused the ire of the Republican press. The following extract from an editorial in the *Minneapolis Tribune* of October 29, 1918, is typical:

Nonpartisanism, socialism, political prohibition, and John Lind democracy have struck hands in Minnesota at the command of the Big Boss in Washington in support of W. G. Calderwood for the Senate. . . . What a composite of class politics, sedition, and intrigue. . . . This combination will also gather to itself all the pro-

[22] Frank H. Castner to Lind, March 4, 1918; Lind to Castner, March 7, 1918. On August 21, 1918, A. Karlsson, an officer in the Brotherhood of Locomotive Engineers and Firemen, wrote to Lind that organized labor would do all in its power to elect Lind governor. "As a class," he wrote, "we appreciate what you have done for us in the past and we are confident that we will receive just treatment from you in the future."

[23] *Minneapolis Journal*, November 4, 1918.

German, Bolsheviki, I. W. W., and uncatalogued flotsam and jetsam of the state. As shown by the telegram from Democratic headquarters in Washington, the guiding spirit of this conspiracy to round up all the political corruptionists and misfits is that chief of the tribe, John Lind. With political aspirations unrealized, he takes command of all the forces he can muster against the object of his long-cherished envy and leads the fight against a man who stands in such high esteem, even with Mr. Lind's own party of latest affiliation.

Lind's expression of independence and courage was buried under a barrage of propaganda that frightened good people into voting against candidates who in reality were as hostile against the war profiteers as they were against the military foes of their country. Minnesota was "saved for loyalty" by the election of Senator Nelson, Governor Burnquist, and Republicans to Congress.

Several years later, when "Lindy," after his famous "solo flight," returned to Minnesota as the lion of the hour to receive the attention and plaudits of men and women who had branded his father a "shadow Hun" and "traitor," Lind wrote to the mayor of St. Paul inclosing a letter to the famous aviator. Lind expressed regret that so fine a young man should be surrounded by people who had no real appreciation of his antecedents, or what they stood for. The mayor replied that he had no doubt it would give "Lindy" joy to receive a letter from one who had loved his father.[24]

After the campaign of 1918 party labels meant even less to Lind than they had before. Except in 1920, he never again voted the Democratic ticket in a presidential election; and in state politics he supported liberal Republicans as cordially as liberals in

[24] L. C. Hodgson to Lind, August 17, 1927. In an article in *Svenska Amerikanska Posten*, Nils F. Brown alluded to the fact that Senator Shipstead knew whereof he spoke when in a congratulatory telegram to Lindbergh he stated that he was a worthy son of a brave father. The author of the article stated that the elder Lindbergh never compromised with the great patriots McGee, Kellogg, Nelson, and Burnquist, and that it seemed strange in latter days to hear words of praise for his son from Secretary of State Kellogg. Clipping in the Lind Papers.

other parties. In 1922 he advocated the election of Mrs. Anna Dickie Oleson, the Democratic candidate, to the Senate, and in 1923 and 1928, respectively, Magnus Johnson and Henrik Shipstead, candidates of the Farmer-Labor party; and in the 1923 Republican primary he voted for Lindbergh for the Senate in preference to Governor Jacob A. O. Preus.[25] In congratulating Governor Theodore Christianson, a Republican, on his address at a banquet in honor of William H. Eustis, Lind wrote that it gave him genuine pleasure to find that a younger man at the head of the state voiced his views so bravely on the problems before the country. He struck a note of pessimism that sounds strangely prophetic when he expressed doubt whether or not those problems could be solved by the voluntary action of capital, though he hoped time and reflection would work out a partial solution that would head off disaster.[26]

On October 19, 1926, he wrote to Frank A. Day that he was about to explain the political situation to the people. "I am not going out under the auspices of any political party," he said, "nor will I entangle my conscience by pinning any party label on it. . . . If a man's home is burning and we see it, do we stop the owner to ask him his political party, or announce our own?"[27]

Lind's indorsement of La Follette and Wheeler, the candidates of the Progressive party in 1924, was not only consistent with his political philosophy but entirely in keeping with the situation peculiar to that campaign. In Minnesota the Farmer-Labor party was the only expression of revolt against the conservative major parties, and the course of Senator Shipstead had brought several cordial letters from Lind. La Follette's criticism of the Supreme Court was directly in line with what Lind had written the editor of the *Lexington* (Kentucky) *Herald* con-

[25] W. G. McAdoo to Lind, July 20, 1922; Lind to Mrs. Anna Dickie Oleson, September 8, 1922; Lind to Mrs. Jacob Scherer, June 14, 1923; Henrik Shipstead to the author, May 13, 1933.
[26] Lind to Christianson, October 9, 1925.
[27] This letter was published in the *Martin County Sentinel* of October 26, 1926.

gratulating him on the publication of an editorial in which the
Supreme Court was condemned for its decision declaring un-
constitutional a law protecting children engaged in employment.
Lind believed it more important to curb the court in its disposition to apply antiquated legalistic precedents to the solution of
the problems of modern industrial life than it was to amend the
Constitution.[28]

The Wisconsin senator's opposition to intervention in Mexico and his denunciation of the efforts of the "interests" to provoke war after the Villa raids won the gratitude of Lind; and
his opposition to the entrance of the United States into the
League of Nations was no obstacle to Lind's support. Former
President Taft had in 1915 appointed Lind chairman for Minnesota of the League to Enforce Peace; and in 1919, when President Wilson made his speaking tour in behalf of the ratification
of the League covenant, Lind was an ardent supporter. He
thought the war had "swept from the international boards the
whole brood of emperors and kings who in the past have exercised any political power" and had removed forever one of the
most potent factors for international disturbance. "The world
has now, in a measure, in the words of our great president, 'been
made fit for democracy' and it is incumbent on us and on the
nations who pretend to democracy to make democracy fit for
the world," he said.[29]

In 1923, however, he was disillusioned. "When it [the treaty]
was formulated at Versailles, I assumed that the several allied
governments had profited by the lessons of the World War and
that they were in the frame of mind to live and let live — to live
in peace, and further a Christian civilization in spirit as well as
in name," he wrote. "But the attitude of the allied nations since
the war has opened my eyes and modified my views very materially. I dread the possibility of our people having to be bound
by the vote of the 'Council' as now constituted. . . . It was

[28] Desha Breckenridge to Lind, April 17, 1923; Lind to Mrs. Clara Ueland,
April 20, 1923.
[29] Manuscript of an undated address delivered at the "Taft meeting" in Minneapolis.

probably fortunate that we did not join the League at the time we had an opportunity. Our government at the present time does not seem to me to be guided by a spirit very different from that of the rest of the Allies. Its attitude toward Mexico and the rest of the Latin American countries does not indicate a very broad Christian spirit." [30]

The disastrous Democratic national convention of 1924, which nominated John W. Davis, coupled with the decrepit condition of the Democratic party in Minnesota, left a man of Lind's sturdy independence no alternative but to seek some other vehicle of political expression. The unspeakable corruption of the Harding administration and the colorless administration of his successor warranted the prediction of a prominent Democratic United States senator, Pat Harrison, that if the Democrats nominated a good, progressive candidate who would appeal to the Middle West and Far West, they ought to win "hands down." [31] But the prolonged fight between the McAdoo and Smith forces not only split the party hopelessly but resulted in the nomination of a candidate who made no appeal to the western farmer who had barely eked out his sustenance during four years of depression.

Lind saw no prospect for the Davis-Bryan ticket to poll any substantial vote in Minnesota. "The great majority of the liberal, sincere Democrats, as I judge the situation, will vote for La Follette, not because they want La Follette elected, but because they are averse to see this state in the Republican column committed to Coolidge and what he stands for," he said.

The more sincere element of the Democratic party cooperated, in a large measure, with the Farmer Movement, and the result has been that what is left of the Democratic organization in this state (with few exceptions) consists largely of the old ward-heeler element who had continuously been dominated by the brewery and liquor interests. This element has been in control of the party, on the whole, for some years. Their ambition seems to have been, in

[30] Lind to Alfred Lucking, May 21, 1923.
[31] Pat Harrison to Lind, May 13, 1924.

most instances, to act as handmaidens for the dominating and selfish interests of the Republican party. . . .

The vote cast for the [Democratic] ticket will be made up largely of disgruntled business men, both in the Republican party as well as among the Democrats, and the small contingent of old Democrats who will vote the ticket from force of habit. . . .

The Republican newspapers are actively advising all Democrats to vote for Davis and Bryan to save the nation and to preserve our institutions.[32]

The election returns fully substantiated Lind's diagnosis of the political situation in Minnesota. Coolidge polled 420,759 votes; La Follette, 339,192; Davis, 55,913. The Democratic showing in the vote for governor was even worse. Theodore Christianson, Republican, polled 406,692 votes; Floyd B. Olson, Farmer-Labor, 366,029; Carlos Avery, Democrat, 49,353. After the triumphant election of Coolidge, Lind breathed the prayer that men like Borah, with the help of Democrats and liberals in the Senate, would keep the ship of state safe.

It is superfluous to state that an administration so supine and ineffective as that of Coolidge made no appeal to a man like John Lind. In a letter to a Washington correspondent expressing appreciation for his comment on Coolidge's "I do not choose to run" statement, Lind wrote: "I believe our president could step into a restaurant like old Harvey's, where he would be a stranger, take a seat, receive a bill of fare, a glass of water, and be served a piece of pie without having uttered a word." [33] Apropos of Coolidge's veto of the Muscle Shoals bill, he commented: "He wants his political millionaire friends to have the property. It will not do to operate it by a company organized by an act of Congress for that purpose. It would demonstrate that electric energy could be produced profitably at one-fourth

[32] Lind to J. A. Edgerton, September 9, 1924. In a letter to Lind, September 12, 1924, Fred B. Lynch stated that he had advised his friends that if the Democratic party in Minnesota was not to go off the map, it must go radical. "The conservative Democrats," he said, "have left the party and for years have voted with the Republicans."

[33] Lind to George F. Authier, November 23, 1927.

the cost that power companies charge." [34] He did not think the "present speculative millionaire government" could last very long.

The political prospect in 1928 as the time approached for the meeting of the Democratic national convention at Houston, was not encouraging to Lind, the relentless foe of machine politics. He hoped and prayed that the convention would not be a "Tammany circus." He could not rejoice over the possibility of having a Tammany man in the White House. From the time of his first election to Congress in 1886, it was his opinion "that if we are ever to hope for a fuller and better life for all classes of our people, socially and economically, the spirit will have to come from the valley of the Mississippi and its tributaries, from the Canadian border to the Gulf." [35]

Like many other Democrats, Lind admired Senator James A. Reed for his fight against corruption, though it was hard for them to forgive his lack of loyalty to the Wilson administration.[36] In any event, Lind preferred him to Alfred E. Smith and stated frankly that he would not vote for Smith if he were nominated. He was not enthusiastic about Herbert Hoover, but there were some things in his record that recommended him. He had declared himself in favor of the St. Lawrence waterway, one of Lind's pet projects, and he had not declared himself unqualifiedly opposed to prohibition — he had at least called it "a noble experiment." Moreover, he had the support of Senator Borah. Lind's presence on the platform in the Minneapolis Auditorium at a Hoover meeting addressed by the Idaho senator on October 1, 1928, was a compliment to the speaker and a public gesture that would be understood by Republicans as well as Democrats.

On September 17, 1928, he made public the following statement:

I shall not vote for Tammany! I served with Tammany representatives in Congress for years and know it well enough to know that it is devoid of principle.

[34] Lind to Norman Lind, May 8, 1928.
[35] Lind to P. H. Callahan, June 26, 1929.
[36] Josephus Daniels to Lind, December 17, 1927.

The Tammany organization has been a millstone on the neck of the Democratic party as long as I can remember. If the party once gets rid of the Tammany influence, I am confident that we shall see a union of the liberal elements from Mexico and the Gulf of Mexico to Canada. It may not come in my time, but I have always worked for it.

We've had ideas from east of the Allegheny Mountains in control of our legislative and executive departments of the federal government for eight years, and I'm sorry to say that, in my opinion, the record is not creditable. I do not wish eastern domination to continue.

We've had one of the largest distillers of whiskey in the position of administrator of our prohibition laws. But if Smith is elected, we learn in the New York press that Raskob, whose sole announced reason for supporting Smith is that the latter is wet, will be our secretary of the treasury. I cannot for the life of me see any prospect of betterment from such a change.[37]

Lind could not forgive Smith for "kicking over" the Houston platform and substituting for it a "Tammany platform." "To my mind," he said, "there is a greater question back of it all . . . and that is whether or not the American people wish to be governed by the spirit and appetite of the great cities of New York, Chicago, Boston, and San Francisco or by the views and the best ideals of the whole American people."[38]

John Lind lived to see the debacle of 1929, but he was spared from seeing the full results of the policies and politics against which he had been a crusader throughout his life. Had he lived through the disastrous years of the Hoover administration he might have felt that events had confirmed many of his contentions, but he would have derived no satisfaction from it. The tragedy of those years was too deep to bring anything but sorrow to the crusader for political righteousness.

[37] Manuscript in the Lind Papers.
[38] Lind to H. A. Johnson, October 22, 1928.

XX

CITIZEN OF MINNESOTA

AFTER Lind retired from the office of governor in January, 1901, he transferred his residence and his law office from New Ulm to Minneapolis; and except for his service in Congress, his sojourn in Mexico, and his activity during the World War, he devoted his time to the practice of law. From 1901 to 1914 he was a member of the firm of Lind and Ueland and Lind, Ueland, and Jerome; and after his return from Mexico he practiced law on his own hook. His legal practice, which was extensive, took him on frequent trips to Washington and to the Pacific Coast. After 1907 the Linds lived at 1775 Colfax Avenue South, within walking distance of the Lind office in the New York Life Building; and the tall, stately figure of the former governor was a familiar sight on the streets of Minneapolis. He took an active part in civic and community affairs, and though he found much enjoyment in his visits to California and Florida, he never lost his attachment for his beloved Minnesota and Minneapolis.

One opportunity for service that brought the governor much satisfaction was his work as member and president of the Board of Regents of the University of Minnesota. He was privileged to witness the growth of this institution from a shaky academy to a position of leadership among western state universities. It was always a great satisfaction to browse in the library and to confer and consult with members of the faculties about his hobbies and investigations. After his return from Mexico he urged upon President George E. Vincent the cultivation of Spanish as a means of establishing cultural and commercial relations with the countries of Latin America.[1]

[1] George E. Vincent to Lind, June 14, 1914.

When Lind was appointed to the Board of Regents by Governor Johnson in 1908, the long incumbency of President Cyrus Northrop was drawing to a close, and in 1911 Dr. George E. Vincent became head of the University. As president of the Board of Regents Lind was active through correspondence and personal interviews in selecting Northrop's successor; and although Vincent was not his first choice, it was a great satisfaction to him that a man of his vision and ability was chosen. During Vincent's administration not only were men of outstanding ability added to the staff but an extensive building program was inaugurated on the enlarged campus. Lind received the cordial thanks of the architect, Cass Gilbert, for his support of the plans that had been made.

In 1923, some years after the close of his service on the University Board of Regents, Lind established the "Lind Fund for the Aid of Deserving Crippled Students." The initial endowment was made up of the pension moneys accruing to Lind on account of his military service in the Spanish-American War, and in 1926 this was supplemented by other securities.[2] William H. Eustis, Lind's defeated opponent in the gubernatorial campaign of 1898, wrote Lind as follows:

What you so kindly commend in principle is only in accord with what you have not only done, but are still doing in altruistic service in aiding worthy students whose thirst for knowledge is beyond their financial means.

Today vividly reminds us how the years come and go like the weaver's shuttle; and if we would do aught of human service worthy of the brief life the fates allot, one must be up and doing.

Lind's five years of service on the Board of Regents was brought to a close by Governor Eberhart in January, 1914, while he was in Vera Cruz. It was given out from the governor's office that Lind would not be reappointed because "advices from Washington" were to the effect that his work in Mexico would be rewarded by appointment to almost any post in the diplo-

[2] The papers and correspondence pertaining to this fund are in the Lind Papers.

matic service he might desire. The comment in the press, however, was hostile to Governor Eberhart, who was accused of
playing politics and of withholding his real reason for not re-
appointing the former governor. The Republican *Minneapolis
Journal* said that the "strongest personal reason for desiring
Lind's reappointment is that he is qualified above many and a
leader among the state's citizens." [3]

Lind refrained from making a statement to the press because
he had no desire to provoke a public controversy. [4] From President Vincent, who strongly urged Lind's reappointment, came
the following letter:

Your high ideals of what a university should be, your recognition of research and publication, your faith in academic freedom,
were all most favorable factors in the administration of the institution. I appreciated always the support which you gave me personally, and I shall not fail to take advantage of your offer of continued
interest, counsel, and aid. [5]

Among the humanitarian reforms that had engaged Lind's
attention when a congressman was the cause of the Indians. He
had grown up in the southwestern part of the state where he
had occasion to see their helplessness in competition with the
early settlers and particularly with the lumbermen. When he
entered Congress he shared the belief of most people that educational advantages would solve the Indian problem, but years
of observation convinced him that this was only one of a number of aids to a more useful life. In a long letter to the commissioner of Indian affairs, written in the last year of his life, he
wrote as follows:

In later years I became thoroughly satisfied from observation and
study that mere book learning will not "civilize" or solve the Indian
problem. Industry, work of a kind that appeals to the Indian, with
the rudiments of book learning, is the only, or at least the best and
most promising means of their civilization. I know the Chippewa

[3] The correspondence and newspaper clippings are in the Lind Papers. See
the Twin City papers for January 20, 1914.
[4] Lind to W. M. Jerome, January 25, 1914.
[5] Vincent to Lind, January 20, 1914.

Indians the best of any, and what I am about to say applies more particularly to them. They are good natured, fairly reliable, shiftless, but not lazy if they can have the kind of work that appeals to them. In woodcraft, fishing, hunting, or building or extinguishing a fire in the woods, they are superior to the white man. They are good loggers and as a rule when we had logs to cut and drive they could beat the white lumberjacks in driving a raft of logs in the streams, but that work has disappeared. They have no ponies, are not good cattle raisers and worse farmers.[6]

During the World War, when Lind was a member of the Minnesota Commission of Public Safety, in order to conserve and increase the food supply, he was instrumental in having that body adopt a resolution authorizing fishing with nets in the Red Lakes; and the Indians were supplied with nets and made large sums by catching fish. He also persuaded the legislature to appropriate money for establishing and maintaining a fish hatchery to stock the lakes. The Booth Packing Company instituted court action to prohibit the state from engaging in commercial fishing; but through an arrangement with the Indian commissioner an Indian corporation was formed for the purpose of catching and selling fish, which netted the Indians a substantial income.

Another source of revenue for the reservation was made possible through Lind's efforts. Despite the greed of the lumber interests, Lind succeeded in saving some pine timber in that region and persuaded the government to make an appropriation for the erection and operation of a lumber mill at Redby. Indians were employed in the mill, and logs were cut and brought to the mill by the red men.

In 1929 Lind suggested to the commissioner of Indian affairs that he consider the expediency of introducing sheep raising to give the Indians employment and a source of food and revenue. "The Indians . . . like animals," he wrote, "and in my judgment there is no animal that young people and people of limited means and simple attainments like better than the sheep and the

[6] Letter dated December 2, 1929.

lamb." The project appealed to the agent of the reservation, and on a trip to Wyoming Lind was told by sheep raisers that, to judge from his description of the land, it would be feasible to maintain a considerable number of sheep on the reservation. Lind told the commissioner that he would gladly go to Washington to explain the project to a congressional committee. The commissioner, whom Lind pronounced one of the best men who had filled the office, wrote that Lind presented the proposition in so favorable a light that it would be taken up at once; and he gave assurance that letters of that kind were never too long.[7]

Lind was familiar with the region and was interested in the Minnesota, Red Lake, and Manitoba Railroad, which had been built by Charles A. Smith, the lumber king, and of which Lind was president. He wrote to Commissioner Charles H. Burke that his reason for taking active part in this venture was his familiarity with the splendid white pine of the reservation, and he hoped that after the erection of a sawmill the railroad would have traffic and the Indians would have the kind of work familiar to them.[8]

Lind's benevolent interest in the Indians was equaled by his intense interest in the preservation of wild life and the conservation of the natural resources and beauty of the state. During his second term in Congress he defeated a bill to permit the sale of white pine on the reservation, because the fruit of the bill, as he said, would be some profit to the lumbermen, broken heads among the Indians, and four thousand paupers for the government and the state to feed. After Lind retired from Congress a bill to permit the sale of the lands in severalty was passed, and the result justified his fears. In 1924 he wrote Senator Shipstead that he hoped the members of the Minnesota congressional delegation would bear in mind that the proposal to sell the remaining white pine on the reservation would be a calamity to the state.[9] Instead of cutting timber, Lind obtained through the

[7] Letter dated December 14, 1929. Subsequent correspondence with the officials was very favorable.
[8] Lind to Burke, July 7, 1927.
[9] Lind to Shipstead, May 4, 1924.

division of horticulture of the University of Minnesota nursery stock for trial at Redby.[10] From Ernest C. Oberholtzer, president of the Quetico-Superior Council, which was affiliated with the Izaak Walton League, Lind received cordial thanks for his "splendid support" of the program for a great international forest among the border lakes.[11]

No Minnesota governor ever penned a more idyllic state paper than Lind's Arbor and Bird Day Proclamation of 1899. It inspired a journalist to write an editorial on "Our Poet Governor." "Minnesota has never had a poet governor before," he wrote. "We have one now in Governor Lind, whose Arbor and Bird Day Proclamation, issued yesterday, reveals the fact that he has breathed the atmosphere of that 'golden clime' where poets are said to be born. . . . Why should a governor always use the cold and formal language of the rigid proclamation style? . . . Our governor has a great reservoir of nature-love within his soul. It gushes out like April showers from April skies, full of glints of sunshine." [12] The proclamation reads as follows:

Genial sunshine and gentle showers are calling forth the slumbering bud and the vernal green. The robin is here to greet and to serve us. The thrush and the oriole will shortly join him, and they will come again and again to gladden our people with their song so long as there are trees to nest in and hearts to cheer. Providence did not intend that any portion of this fair state of ours should become or remain a treeless waste, mute to Nature's cheeriest songs. We have hill and dale, upland and meadow, myriads of lakes, streams and purling brooks, all set in a garniture of trees and flowers that stands unrivaled on the continent. Let us preserve and enhance our beautiful inheritance.

Greed and ignorance have conspired to partially denude our forests and our woodland, but an intelligent, home-loving people have already done much to clothe our prairies and beautify our homes with Nature's shelter. To the end that this good work may be con-

[10] W. H. Alderman to Lind, October 18, 1927.
[11] Oberholtzer to Lind, December 23, 1929.
[12] *Minneapolis Journal*, April 21, 1899.

tinued and taken up with renewed vigor, by young and old, in a
spirit of rivalry as well as patriotic unity, I have, pursuant to custom and law, appointed Monday, the first day of May, Arbor and
Bird Day.

Lind's letters, too, reveal his love for flowers, plants, animals,
and nature. In the spring of 1896, when politicians were thinking of little else but the approaching political campaign, Lind
wrote a letter to Norman, who was studying in Munich, in
which he said:

Our lawn is green and the tulips are coming up. The Scilla Siber-
ica are beginning to peep through and the Roman hyacinths — next
to the walk — are ready to bloom — you remember those delicate
blue flowers at the end of the tulips. I got some imported Dutch
tulips last year and I think that they are going to be fine. The
budded roses that I took care of are coming finely. The Easter
flowers have been out a long time. Yesterday afternoon Jenny and
Winifred took a walk to the woods and picked a whole basketful
of flowers.[13]

And thirty years later he wrote:

I spent last week up at Wasson Lake and discovered a fine creek,
full of springs that will make an excellent trout stream, and I have
already made arrangements for fingerslips to plant next June. You
have no idea how beautiful the surroundings of the lake are. The
deer are as plentiful as sheep in the mountains. No shooting this
year. In 28 we will have an open season and if I continue as good on
my feet as I am now I want you and John to join me and spend a
few days with Ole Reien and lay up our winter's meat.[14]

From Alameda, California, Lind wrote to his sister, Mrs.
Jacob Scherer, that on an automobile trip he had seen thousands of acres of peas in bloom and also acres of horse beans.
He recalled that his mother had planted these beans in Sweden,
picked them before they were ripe, and mashed them with new
potatoes. "I remember just how they tasted," he wrote.[15]

[13] Lind to Norman Lind, April 17, 1896.
[14] Lind to Norman Lind, November 9, 1927.
[15] Lind to Mrs. Scherer, March 11, 1928.

NORMAN

JENNY

WINIFRED

JOHN, JR.

THE SONS AND DAUGHTERS OF JOHN LIND

When the crown prince and crown princess of Sweden visited Minnesota in the summer of 1926, Mr. and Mrs. Lind rode with them from Vasa to St. Paul. Mrs. Lind and the princess talked of flowers and gardening, and His Royal Highness and the governor discussed politics, ethnology, archeology, geology, and horticulture. After their return to Sweden, Lind wrote the crown prince reminding him of their conversation and inclosing a memorandum explaining how nursery stock was transplanted in this country. He discoursed on the varieties of fruit trees that flourished in Minnesota and suggested varieties suitable for cultivation in Sweden, specimens of which were duly sent through the cooperation of the State Horticultural Experiment Station. Shortly before Lind's death, Gustaf Lindquist of St. Paul, who had just returned from Sweden, brought him a message from the crown prince that the trees had been planted and were flourishing.[16]

If Lind loved to visit his farm, to tramp around under the maples, and to graft fruit trees, he loved quite as much to make an excursion into the open with his gun. He often visited his parents' farm and brought his friends along to hunt. Back in the days when he was a rising lawyer in New Ulm he had hunted prairie chickens across the river; Mrs. Lind had done the driving, and Lind walked along carrying his gun. He stocked his library with books on birds and animals and studied maps and folders in search of beautiful camping grounds. He was an enthusiastic member of the Hennepin County Sportsman's Club, an organization interested in game and wild life and in the preservation of woodlands and water resources.

A year or two before his death, Lind delivered a radio address at the request of officers of the Izaak Walton League:

I came here to speak at the request of the officers of the Walton League. If any of the Waltonians listen in, I greet you. I am not a member of your league, so I shall not devote much time to fishing, primarily because I am not a good fisherman, nor am I given to fish

[16] Lind to W. C. Edgar, July 1, 1926; Lind to Crown Prince Gustaf Adolf, November 3, 1927; conversation of the author with Mr. Lindquist, March 29, 1934.

stories. I can handle a gun fairly well, but when it comes to baiting a hook with angle worms I haven't enough hands to manipulate the trick as cleverly as our late president, and our old cane poles have gone out of fashion. Besides, I do not think fishing is quite as sportsmanlike as hunting with a gun. You fishermen offer *your* victim something to eat, a tidbit, which is a delusion; the hunter nabs his victim on the wing or on the run. If a fisherman would file the barb off his hook and give his victim a fair show when it discovered the fraud, I would say he was as good a sport as the man with the gun, but bless you Waltonites, barb or no barb, I like your company and you are doing good work.

Those of you of my age or older have seen many changes in this world of ours since we came — cities have sprung up and cover the hills once verdant with wild flowers and trees that sheltered the pheasant and the coon. Our streams once full of fish and game have become polluted and unfit for the life of game or fish, but it is still the same old world and nature will again clothe the barren spots and purify and stock the streams if we but give her a chance. In our part of the state, the walnut, the maple, and the oak were slaughtered without discretion, in the mistaken view that bare hills make beautiful homes and productive fields, but our farmers did it in a spirit of home building and farming and now many of them, or their children, are making amends by planting trees for shade, shelter, and orchards.

But in the northern part of the state where the spruce and the pine soughed in the breeze, sheltered wild life, and conserved the water to supply the springs, the brooks, and the lakes, a different type of men took possession of the fair face of our state — not with the view of building homes, or to raise crops, but to make money. Without thought of the future of their fellow man, they slaughtered and burnt, leaving the hills, once lovely, bare and stony, like the desert where the golden calf was once erected and worshipped. I am not saying this in a spirit of personal envy or hostility to the memory of these men — most of them were good men, judged by present standards. They knew no better, and what they did they did lawfully, under laws enacted in their behalf. I feel rather sorry for them — they saw no values in life but logs, lumber, and profit. They had little thought of the life of our state, the generations to come after them, or that the life of man is brief. Those who love wild life, trees and flowers and the beauty and mystery of nature, as God has given her, will have something to enjoy in the world to come. The poor man whose whole soul has been devoted to making money and producing lumber will at least feel lonesome in that world, if he does not land in a section where the temperature is uncomfortable. But whatever we may think of the lumbermen whose work has been completed, we must give them credit for leaving the shores of the lakes and the hills virtually as nature shaped them, if they be bare and stony. With time, patience, and help our nature will again clothe them with verdure and beauty, for humanity's use and joy. If there should be a living lumberman who is not content with taking nature's first crop, but is determined to appropriate for his own use the very soil on which that crop grew, let us all with one voice say substantially as General Joffre, when he was defending his fatherland at the Marne, "This far you may come but no farther." [17]

Future generations will profit by Lind's interest in nature. As congressman, governor, and citizen he fought for legislation to rescue trees, plants, birds, and animals from the ravages of "civilization." As a young man he drafted and assisted in securing the passage of an early act to encourage the planting of groves in the prairie section of Minnesota; and during his last term in Congress he secured the donation to the state of some fifteen thousand acres of vacant land within the boundaries of the state forest reserves. While he was a member of the Board of Regents of the University of Minnesota, he visited eastern Canada and learned of a type of dairy cattle developed in the neighborhood of Quebec, a large-boned Jersey; the Board authorized Professor Haecker to visit Quebec to study the herds. Through the Canadian government he obtained a box of beaver, and soon the progeny of these interesting animals were spread over the state. He established the wildflower garden by the Old Capitol. And while he was governor he supported the movement, sponsored by the Minnesota Federation of Women's Clubs, to establish Chippewa National Forest.[18]

[17] The manuscript of this address is in the Lind Papers.
[18] *Minneapolis Tribune*, August 14, 1913; *St. Paul Globe*, January 22, 1899. See Folwell, *A History of Minnesota*, 4:253 ff.

When Lind became governor, the boundaries of Itasca State Park had already been established, but much of the land was privately owned. In his inaugural address Lind recommended that the park be enlarged, and the legislature appropriated money for that purpose. Governor Lind called on the elder Weyerhaeuser, who owned thousands of acres near the center of the park, explained to him that the appropriation was inadequate, and made him the proposition that he deed the lands to the state and reserve the right to remove trees over fifteen inches in diameter within four or five years. "We will get what we want," said the governor, "and you will have no taxes to pay on your logs." In due time the deed was executed, and the beautiful timber now on the land is in the possession of the state. The "Lind Saddle Trail" commemorates the governor's interest in this place of beauty.[19]

Lind never lost an opportunity to further the cause of preserving natural resources. He made frequent trips to the State Capitol to confer with officials, and his work was known and appreciated by many people throughout the country. His part in bringing about the treaty with Canada paving the way for protecting migratory birds was well known in the East, though not so well known among conservationists and sportsmen in his own state.[20]

In the early spring of 1920, in company with W. T. Cox, state forester, Lind went on an eight-day trapping expedition in Itasca State Park, and he wrote to Norman that he had "the time of my life." He thought the park "just wonderful."

The only trouble we had was at night. We had poor cotton blankets and the shack was open between the logs and poor floor but I

[19] J. V. Brower, "The Lind Saddle Trail," manuscript in the Lind Papers in the Minnesota Historical Society; Josephine V. Brower to Lind, November 18, 1927; Lind to Theodore Christianson, November 23, 1926.

[20] Frank D. Blair to Lind, January 17, 1925. John S. Pardee, *The Children's Heritage,* published by the Arrowhead Association in 1928, contains a rather scant reference to Lind's part in the development of state policies. John S. Pardee to Lind, July 21, 1928. For a number of years Lind was a member of the state forestry board.

stuck my feet in the sleeves of your old mackinaw and wrapped the skirts around my legs. Then I had that heavy white sweater, but we had plenty of bacon, beans, potatoes, onions, bread, flour, molasses, and canned goods — tea and coffee. We did punish the victuals. The fellows ate like wolves and I kept pace with them.[21]

Unlike some self-made men, Lind did not despise manual labor and enjoyed talking with men and women in all walks of life. He esteemed the man whose hands were calloused by toil as much as the man with a white collar job. When old acquaintances from Brown and Sibley counties dropped into his office, they were greeted as "Louis" or "Frank." To his nephew, Philip L. Scherer of Winthrop, he wrote that it was important for a boy to understand farm work; "besides, you never know just what life means until you have worked in the 'sweat of your brow' and until your limbs ache."

We are sometimes apt to condemn men who work with their hands and bodies every day because we think that they do not know as much as we do. Maybe they don't in the same way, but they know lots of things that we do not know and best of all they can support themselves and others besides. Lawyers and doctors and preachers may do good, they often do, but after all they live off their fellow men and so do the merchants. Really it isn't such a proud thing to be living off your fellows. I sometimes think that the man who owes no one but the earth and the showers and the sunshine anything for his living lives a more natural life and perhaps a happier one. Still it does not make so much difference what a man does if he does his work well and treats his fellow men with justice and kindness. All work that is well done is honorable work.[22]

Under John Lind's stern expression lurked a kindly interest in people. He was aware of his rather forbidding exterior and on one occasion wrote, "I am a sanguine cuss in spite of my looks." He had a vein of humor, but his humor was very dry. He enjoyed a joke as well as anybody, but like so many sons of Sweden, his laughter was not vociferous. Writing to Judge

[21] Lind to Norman Lind, April 6, 1920.
[22] Lind to Philip L. Scherer, February 5, 1913.

Douglas in January, 1916, about his misfortune in falling on the ice and fracturing his ribs he said:

The only trouble that I have experienced was when some of my friends dropped in to call and good naturedly related incidents that forced me to laugh. You have probably observed that laughter comes hard with me and when it does come, it is not wholesome to broken ribs. . . . Except for the ribs, which I have several times wished the good Lord might detach and transform into maidens, I have been and am very well.

Crippled children were always the object of sympathetic attention from the governor. In the last year of his life, while he and Mrs. Lind were sojourning at Lake Wasson, they happened into a home where a little girl was so crippled that she could not walk. They brought her to a sanitarium near Shakopee; and when they drove out to visit her some weeks later, they found a much improved and grateful girl. While Lind was recuperating from the effects of a fall in 1925, he received a letter signed by thirty members of the Minneapolis Council of the Camp Fire Girls bringing Christmas greetings and regrets that he had not kept his promise of the previous summer to return and tell them about the trees at Minnewashta, which had formerly been the Lind summer home.

If Lind had had the advantages of a college education, it is quite possible that instead of studying law he might have chosen a profession that would have permitted him to give free rein to his inquiring mind and studious habits. He had the instincts of the scholar. Much as he enjoyed the recreation that bridge and whist afforded, he found more pleasure in conversation with men and women eminent in various fields of scholarship and in books read in the quiet of his study. He was a subscriber to the guaranty fund of the Minneapolis Society of Fine Arts and a life member of the Minnesota Historical Society, whose publications he read with much interest. He was often seen and heard at the meetings of the Saturday Lunch Club; and a university professor who heard him address this club on the effect of national institutions upon character and moral standards said that he "had never seen it so effectively put." In the Saturday Lunch Club he found fellowship with others interested in contemporary problems from a liberal point of view. His friendship with such liberals as Louis F. Post, Raymond Robins, Lincoln Steffens, and Sinclair Lewis was highly valued.

Although Lind did not, as have so many immigrants from Sweden, spurn all association with Swedish individuals and activities, he did not affiliate with the Swedish-Americans as a group, and he worked neither through a church nor a lodge to further his political ambitions. He enjoyed the company, food, and an occasional drink as a member of the Odin Club, and he accepted membership on the board of trustees of the American Institute of Swedish Art, Literature, and Science, which was founded in 1929, but anything tinged with racial, nationalistic, or religious clannishness repelled him. In 1928, when there was talk of establishing a Scandinavian museum at the University of Minnesota, the former governor wrote to President Lotus D. Coffman that the people who desired a Scandinavian museum could build and endow it, but a museum connected with the University should be interested in all nationalities that had contributed to the upbuilding of the state.[23]

Lind was interested in the progress of Gustavus Adolphus College, where he had been a student while it was still located in Carver County and was known as St. Ansgar's Academy; and in 1903 he spoke on the floor of the Swedish Lutheran Minnesota Conference in favor of moving the institution from St. Peter to the Twin Cities.

In 1913 the king of Sweden made him a commander of the Royal Order of Vasa, but such artificial recognition made no impression on the commoner. At the banquet when the royal insignia was formally presented, Lind, to the consternation of the guests who were enamored by the glamour of the star, turned to Mrs. Lind and said: "Here, Mother, this thing looks better on you."

As the shadows lengthened and time for leisure increased,

[23] Lind to Coffman, February 9, 1928.

Lind interested himself in the early history of Scandinavia. On meeting Nathan Söderblom, archbishop of Uppsala, on the occasion of his visit to the United States in 1923, Lind found in the liberal, versatile, and ecumenical prelate a man after his own heart. In his address at a mass meeting in the Minneapolis Armory the archbishop sounded a new note in Swedish-America by rejoicing over the elevation to the United States Senate of a Swedish peasant in the person of Magnus Johnson, who did not display on the lapel of his coat a Republican campaign button. Before departing from New York, the archbishop penned a note to "The Right Honorable Ex-Governor John Lind" saying he was happy to have made his acquaintance and to have had the interesting conversation with him about "our common old friend, Adam of Bremen." To this the churchman received the following reply:

Your visit and your herculean labors to revive and further among our people that true Christian spirit of faith, hope, and charity, which the peoples of the world seem to have lost since the World War and which we now need more than anything else if the civilization we had begun is to be saved, gave us more joy and comfort than I can express.[24]

Two years later the archbishop received a letter from the former governor in which he stated that during the war he could not help but admire the sensible attitude of the Swedish people as a whole — even if individuals of the official class lost their heads and exposed the nation to embarrassment. His visit to Sweden in 1912 and his later observations, he told the archbishop, had convinced him that Sweden's most promising outlet for trade and industry was Russia. Although he did not agree with the principle of the Russian government, he had to recognize that it had restored the land to the people, and he believed the Scandinavian countries and Russia should join in a compact of peace and good will, with guarantees of arbitration.[25]

[24] Nathan Söderblom to Lind, December 6, 1923; Lind to Söderblom, December 19, 1923.
[25] Lind to Söderblom, December 9, 1925; Söderblom to Lind, January 21, 1926.

The origin of the people of Sweden was another question mark in Lind's mind, and he read Ulfilas' Bible, Jordanes' history, Tacitus, and ancient Danish laws and corresponded with Professor Gerard De Geer, a distinguished Swedish geologist, to throw light on the problem.

You must pardon these mental vagaries, bearing in mind that I have long since passed the Biblical allowance of years, and that I naturally like to think about the olden times. One thing I know, and that is: That before the last Ice Age, the climate on the Minnesota River in this state was mild enough to permit the growth of Magnolia Alternans, Andromeda Parlorii, Salix Proteaefolia, several varieties of Populus, Perseus, and Fiscus. I found beautiful impressions of the leaves of all these trees in a sandstone formation on the Minnesota River. I cannot say to what period this sandstone belonged, but it was above the Cretaceous and below the moraines of the last Ice Age.[26]

Another topic of investigation that claimed Lind's attention during the evening of life was the origin and development of the jury system. On his visit to Sweden he had the good fortune to obtain a book printed in the first years of the seventeenth century containing the laws of Sweden promulgated by the union king and the laws of Östergötland and Upland. With the aid of a lexicon he was able to translate these old provincial laws. To a Stockholm correspondent he wrote that he believed them to be the most complete codes of non-Roman laws in Europe and to give a good conception of the social and economic conditions of his ancestors.[27]

He also found time to correspond with Dr. Will Mayo with reference to complexion and the cephalic index, which, taken in connection with genetic and social environment, he had found a good "marker" for intellect and will power. This hobby he sent to Dr. Mayo "duly saddled in black and white," stating that if he had remained on the Board of Regents, he would have

[26] Lind to De Geer, May 31, 1927; De Geer to Lind, September 7, 1924.
[27] Lind to G. Fahlcrantz, November 10, 1925; Fahlcrantz to Lind, November 12, 1927.

had investigations along this line "moving by this time." "I was too busy with the planning and acquiring of the physical equipment, grounds, buildings, etc., when I was on the Board to take up many things that I had in view for the future, when the University was equipped physically and supported by a public sentiment, such as you have now." [28]

Lind's legal practice and his interest in the Pacific Timber Company and the Lind Navigation Company necessitated frequent trips to California and the Pacific Northwest. He enjoyed traveling, and in later years he spent the winter in California or Florida. His letter written in the Carribean Sea to his family telling about his trip in company with Fred Johnson of New Ulm through the Panama Canal to Portland, Oregon, in 1922, suggests the exuberance of a college boy relating to his sister experiences on a football trip. "A more successful pair of loafers never enjoyed a free ride," he wrote. "We are so contented and happy that if we could only sing we would drown the noise of the waves as they break against the port side and spray the ship." [29]

Throughout the many years of his activity as a lawyer Lind found opportunities to make investments in farms, mines, railroads, steamship companies, and lumber, but he harbored no ambition to become wealthy. It was only in the last year of his life that he could write to Norman that for the first time in fifty years he was out of debt, with "a little cash in the bank and enough income to maintain me in comfort and decency during the balance of my days." During this half century he missed very few days at his office, in court, in Congress, or in the governor's chair on account of ill health. In his seventy-fifth year, during a period when Mrs. Lind was absent from home, he wrote to his son: "I am rather enjoying the quietude at the house. Get breakfast on my way down town, oatmeal and cream and toast and coffee. Lunch at club and have dinner at club and read a while and get up to the house about 9 P. M.

[28] Lind to Dr. Mayo, September 21, 1925.
[29] Letter dated July 1, 1922.

Whistle and holler and say the Lord's prayer in bed as loud as any Methodist." [30]

At the beginning of the year 1930 Lind was still making visits to his office in the New York Life Building. He had thought of abandoning his office, but Mrs. Lind convinced him that he would be lost without a downtown office, even though he had retired. In February his health broke down so seriously that he was taken to the Swedish Hospital. By spring he had improved sufficiently to be able to return to his home; and though his condition was serious, he was able to read and dictate letters and was even planning a sea voyage through the Panama Canal to the Pacific Coast. He was still interested in public affairs, and the depression that followed the Wall Street debacle of October, 1929, reminded him of the hard times of the nineties. On June 11, 1930, he wrote to Norman that his speech on the silver question was the best he had ever made, and he was still convinced that there would be nothing better for the world than the restoration of bimetallism. His love for flowers had not deserted him; he had never seen Mrs. Lind's garden look better, he said. "We have had the nicest iris, gladiolas, and peonies that you ever saw and they are still in bloom, but you can imagine how I feel not having seen any of the roses or flowers except as brought in. I am beginning to be very tired and wish to receive an end of my dilemma, whatever way, although there are certain matters I would be delighted to clean up before I check out."

The last letter Norman received from his father, dated August 4, 1930, was dictated in a wheel chair on the porch of his residence. He was still interested in life and rejoiced in his son John's successful business venture in Hutchinson, Minnesota. He also commented on certain business possibilities for Norman, who was a resident of Tacoma, Washington. His serious condition, however, is attested by the fact that he confessed he had given up reading. "I am too damnably shiftless and lazy — perhaps not wholly on account of illness; it may be the natural trait cropping out in more extravagant form."

[30] Lind to Norman Lind, October 18, 1929.

As Thursday, September 18, 1930, was drawing to its close, John Lind, the "Northwestern Tribune of the People," passed into earthly silence. The newspapers of the country remembered him chiefly as the man chosen by President Wilson to be his personal representative in Mexico. "He was tall, spare, and silent, revealing the latter quality most strikingly when repeated efforts were made to learn what was his exact mission to Mexico and what his discoveries had been," commented the *New York Times*. "No man ever accepted and held a confidence more closely."

John Lind died with the secret of his Mexican mission unrevealed; but the care with which he preserved the papers and documents pertaining to it indicates that he expected and desired that the story be told without apology or equivocation.

The funeral services were held on Monday, September 22, 1930, under the trees of beautiful Lakewood Cemetery. It was a warm, clear day, such as Minneapolis can furnish in September and October. Among the friends and acquaintances who paid their last respects to the rugged crusader for political integrity and civic righteousness were Governor Christianson, former Governors Van Sant and Burnquist, justices of the Supreme Court of Minnesota, and leading lawyers of the state. Brief tributes were spoken by Dr. John E. Bushnell, pastor emeritus of the Westminster Presbyterian Church, and Dr. John W. Powell, pastor of the Lake of the Isles Community Church, both personal friends of Minnesota's distinguished adopted son.

BIBLIOGRAPHY

BIBLIOGRAPHY

MANUSCRIPTS

With few exceptions, the manuscripts used in the preparation of this biography are in the Lind Papers in the possession of Mrs. Lind. In addition to letters and copies of letters, this collection contains miscellaneous material such as pamphlets, mimeographed reports and memoranda, account books, and newspaper clippings. Some description of this material is given in the footnotes to the text. The following collections are deposited in the Minnesota Historical Society in St. Paul: The Ignatius Donnelly Papers, the William W. Folwell Papers, the Knute Nelson Papers, and the James A. Tawney Papers. Through the kindness of Mrs. Ruth Bryan Owen the author was given access to the William Jennings Bryan Papers in the Library of Congress.

NEWSPAPERS

America (New York), 1914–16.
Duluth Herald, 1900.
Fria Ordet (St. Paul), 1896.
Mankato Review, 1879, 1886–87.
Marshall Messenger, 1880–83.
Martin County Sentinel (Fairmont), 1886–90, 1896–1901.
Minneapolis Journal, 1896–1900, 1913, 1918.
Minneapolis Star, 1900.
Minneapolis Tidende, 1898.
Minneapolis Times, 1896–98.
Minneapolis Tribune, 1892, 1896, 1898, 1913–15, 1918.
Minnesota Stats Tidning (St. Paul), 1896–1901.
New York Times, 1913–16.
New Ulm Review, 1890–93, 1896–1900.
Nonpartisan Leader (St. Paul), 1918.
Penny Press (Minneapolis), 1896.
Red Wing Argus, 1868–69.
Representative (St. Paul and Minneapolis), 1896–1900.
St. Paul Dispatch, 1896–1901, 1918.
St. Paul Globe, 1887–88, 1896–1901.
St. Paul Pioneer Press, 1895–98, 1900–01.
St. Peter Herald, 1896, 1898–1901.
Svenska Amerikanska Posten (Minneapolis), 1896–1901.
Svenska Folkets Tidning (Minneapolis), 1898–1900.
Tägliche Volkszeitung (St. Paul), 1898, 1900.
Willmar Tribune, 1895–1900.
Winona Daily Republican, 1886, 1896.

GOVERNMENT PUBLICATIONS

Congressional Record, 1887–93, 1903–05, 1913–16.

Legislative Manual of the State of Minnesota. St. Paul, 1899.

Report of the Select Committee of the House of Representatives, Investigating the Methods and Management and Practices of the Bureau of Pensions, under Resolution of the 10th Day of February, 1892 (House Report no. 1868, 52d Congress, 1st Session, serial nos. 3049, 3050). 2 vols. Washington, 1892.

Disorders in Mexico. Department of State, Division of Information. Series A, no. 95; Mexico, no. 18. A confidential document published May 14, 1913, containing the Henry Lane Wilson correspondence.

Investigation of Mexican Affairs (Report of the Subcommittee on Foreign Relations of the United States Senate, Senate Document no. 285, 66th Congress, 2d Session, serial nos. 7665, 7666). 2 vols. Washington, 1920.

A SELECTED LIST OF BOOKS, PAMPHLETS, AND ARTICLES

Angles of the Mexican Situation from Mexican Viewpoints. 1914.

Baker, James H., *Lives of the Governors of Minnesota* (Minnesota Historical Collections, vol. 13). St. Paul, 1908.

Baker, Ray S., *Woodrow Wilson: Life and Letters*, vol. 4. New York, 1931.

Beals, Carleton, *Porfirio Diaz, Dictator of Mexico*. Philadelphia, 1932.

Bell, Edward I., "The Mexican Problem," *Outlook*, October 6, 13, 20, 1915.

Bonilla, Policarpo, *Wilson Doctrine: How the Speech of President Wilson at Mobile, Ala., Has Been Interpretated by the Latin American Countries.* New York, 1914.

Bonggren, Jakob, "Två svensk-amerikanska guvernörer," *Vintersol*, 1906, pp. 53–62.

Bossero, Luis, *The Mexican Situation from Every Angle.* Lecture delivered at the Baltimore City Club on May 27, 1916.

Cabrera, Luis, *The Mexican Situation from a Mexican Point of View.* Washington, 1913.

Calero, Manuel, *The Mexican Policy of Woodrow Wilson as It Appears to a Mexican.*

Callahan, James M., *American Foreign Policy in Mexican Relations.* New York, 1932.

Dabney, Charles W., "A Star of Hope for Mexico," *Outlook*, March 22, 1916.

Day, Frank A., and Knappen, Theodore M., *Life of John Albert Johnson.* Chicago, 1910.

De Fornaro, Carlo, *Carranza and Mexico.* New York, 1915.

Edgar, William C., *The Medal of Gold: A Story of Industrial Achievement.* Minneapolis, 1925.

Eustis, William Henry, "An Autobiography," *Minneapolis Journal*, December 22, 1929, to January 28, 1930.

Enriquez, I. C., *The Religious Question in Mexico: By a Mexican Catholic.* New York, 1915.

Enriquez, Rafael de Zoyas, *The Case of Mexico and the Policy of President Wilson.* New York, 1914. Memorandum by Lind: "The book appears to be a very clever apology for Huerta's treason and subsequent career of murder and assassination. On page 179 is a fair specimen of Huertista logic."

BIBLIOGRAPHY

Folwell, William W., *A History of Minnesota*. 4 vols. St. Paul, 1921–30.

Guzman, Martin Luis, *The Eagle and the Serpent*. New York, 1930. A novel translated from the Spanish dealing with the revolutionary period in Mexico.

Haines, Lynn and Dora B., *The Lindberghs*. New York, 1931.

Hall, H. P., *Observations : Being More or Less a History of Political Contests in Minnesota from 1849 to 1904*. St. Paul, 1904.

Hicks, John D., *The Populist Revolt : A History of the Farmers' Alliance and the People's Party*. Minneapolis, 1931.

——, "The People's Party in Minnesota," *Minnesota History Bulletin*, November, 1924.

——, "The Political Career of Ignatius Donnelly," *Mississippi Valley Historical Review*, June–September, 1921.

Holbrook, Franklin F., *Minnesota in the Spanish-American War and the Philippine Insurrection*. St. Paul, 1923.

Holbrook, Franklin F., and Appel, Livia, *Minnesota in the War with Germany*. 2 vols. St. Paul, 1928, 1932.

Inman, Samuel Guy, *Intervention in Mexico*. New York, 1919. A defense of Carranza.

Kelley, Francis Clement, *The Book of Red and Yellow : Being a Story of Blood and a Yellow Streak*. Chicago, 1915. A reply to Lind and Enriquez.

Lind, John, *The Mexican People*. Minneapolis, 1914. Reprinted from the *Bellman*, December 5, 12, 1914.

——, *Why Do the Farmers' Sons and Daughters Flock to the City?* Address delivered before the Blue Earth Agricultural Society on September 23, 1892.

Memorandum on the Mexican Situation Submitted to Mr. Secretary Lansing by Charles A. Douglas, Counsel for Constitutionalist Government.

Mexico : General Descriptive Data Prepared in August, 1913. A pamphlet issued by the Pan American Union and published in Washington, 1913.

Minnesota Biographies, 1655–1912 (Minnesota Historical Collections, vol. 14). St. Paul, 1912.

Murray, Robert H., "Huerta and the Two Wilsons," *Harper's Weekly*, March 25, 1916, to April 29, 1916.

Nilsson, Victor, "John Lind," *Valkyrian*, January, 1897.

Odland, Martin W., *The Life of Knute Nelson*. Minneapolis, 1926.

O'Shaughnessy, Edith, *A Diplomat's Wife in Mexico: Letters from the American Embassy at Mexico City, Covering the Dramatic Period between October 8th, 1913, and the Breaking off of Diplomatic Relations on April 23rd, 1914, Together with an Account of the Occupation of Vera Cruz*. New York, 1916.

——, *Intimate Pages of Mexican History*. New York, 1920.

Paganel, A., *What the Catholic Church Has Done to Mexico*.

Preus, Jacob A. O., "Knute Nelson," *Minnesota History Bulletin*, February, 1924.

Priestly, Herbert I., *The Mexican Nation : A History*. New York, 1923.

Pyle, Joseph G., *The Life of James J. Hill*. 2 vols. New York, 1917.

Qualey, Carlton C., "Pioneer Norwegian Settlement in Minnesota," *Minnesota History*, September, 1931.

Red Mexico : The Facts. New Haven, Connecticut, 1926. Published by the Supreme Council of the Knights of Columbus.

Report of the Minnesota Commission of Public Safety. St. Paul, 1919.
Rippy, J. Fred, *The United States and Mexico*. New York, 1926.
Scott, Hugh Lenox, *Some Memories of a Soldier*. New York, 1928.
Steffens, Lincoln, *Autobiography*. New York, 1931.
Strand, A. E., *A History of the Swedish-Americans of Minnesota*. 3 vols. Chicago, 1910.
Tannenbaum, Frank, *The Mexican Agrarian Revolution*. New York, 1929.
———, *Peace by Revolution: An Interpretation of Mexico*. New York, 1933.
"The Mexican Problem," *Outlook*, October 27, 1915. Communications from Henry Allen Tupper, Andrés Osuna, Heriberto Barron, and S. G. Inman.
Turner, John Kenneth, *Barbarous Mexico*. Chicago, 1911.
Wilson, Henry Lane, *Diplomatic Episodes in Mexico, Belgium, and Chile*. New York, 1927.

INDEX

INDEX

375

tion, 269; Lind's attitude toward, 274; and H. L. Wilson, 307

Uruguay, and Pan-American conference, 295

Vandiver, J. S., author of libelous articles against Lind, 122–27; in campaign of *1900*, 127

Van Lear, Thomas, 334

Van Sant, Samuel R., defeated for nomination in *1896*, 106; possible nominee in *1898*, 133, 142, 155; candidate for governor in *1900*, 127, 177, 183; inauguration, 186; attends Lind's funeral, 366

Vasa, 7, 16

Vasaly, Charles E., 199

Vera Cruz, Lind's residence in, 221 ff., 280; Lind suggests taking of, 255; captured by Fletcher, 264, 278, 284, 305; headquarters of Carranza, 278

Vilas, William F., 74

Villa, Pancho, Lind's attitude toward, 246, 268, 275, 285, 290, 343; and Benton incident, 257; and A. B. C. mediation, 265; relations with Carranza, 268, 276, 278, 291, 296, 299, 301; assisted by Carothers and Sommerfield, 276, 293; and Aguascalientes convention, 278, 285; favored by American army officers, 287; bandits of, attack Santa Ysabel and Columbus, 312

Vincent, George E., 348–50

Volstead, A. J., 192, 196

Von Hintze, Paul, German minister to Mexico, Lind's conversations with, 228, 243, 244

Wahlund, Gustaf, 119

Wakefield, James B., favors Lind for Congress, 29, 43; and Morrison Tariff Bill, 39

Wall Street, Lind's attitude toward, 331

Wallender, E. G., 180

Walsh, Thomas J., 75

Wanamaker, John, 77

War Industries Board, Lindbergh's resignation from, 338

Waseca County, 43

Washburn, William D., 64, relations with Knute Nelson, 90, 93, 94, 95, 97–102; relations with Lind, 93, 97–101, 109; Washburn-Nelson senatorial contest, 97–102; and return of Thirteenth Regiment, 175

Washburn-Nelson senatorial contest, 97–102; bearing on Lind's political fortunes, 100, 109, 110, 112, 114, 120

"Washburn Vengeance Committee," 112

Washington Post, 299n

Washington statue, in Mexico City, 277

Wasson Lake, 354, 360

Waters-Pierce interests, 285

Waterville debate, 115

Weaver, James B., 96, 141

Weiss, A. C., 202, 205

Werner, N. O., praises Lind's administration, 186

West, Duval, 292n

West, political discontent in, 28, 32 ff., 40, 43, 63 ff., 83; opposition to McKinley Tariff, 65, 66, 67; opposed to Taft, 199, 204

"West Hotel mistake," 177–79, 184, 203

Western insurgency of Lind, 32, 40, 43, 63, 67, 95, 102–04, 346

Weyerhaeuser, Frederick, 358

Wheat, tariff on, and Lind's position, 52

Wheeler, Burton K., 342

Wheelock, Joseph, 99

Whiskey, excise on, 53

Whitney, Charles C., 185

Wilfley, Lebbeus R., 229n

Wilkinson, Morton S., 55

Williams, John S., 196

Willmar Tribune, and Lind's candidacy in *1896*, 109, 117, 121

Wilson, Henry Lane, ambassador to Mexico, 209, 216, 276, 293, 303, 307; hostility to Madero, 211–13, 307; favors recognition of Huerta, 212, 218, 219; alleged part in assassination of Madero, 212, 307; relations with Wilson and Bryan, 213, 307; recall and resignation, 214; sues Lind, 306–10, 328; amicable settlement of suit,